BATTLE *of* BRITAIN

DAYLIGHT DEFEAT

BATTLE *of* BRITAIN

DAYLIGHT DEFEAT

18 SEPTEMBER 1940–30 SEPTEMBER 1940

DILIP SARKAR
MBE, FRHistS, FRAeS

AIR WORLD

First published in Great Britain in 2025 by
Air World
An imprint of Pen & Sword Books Limited
Yorkshire – Philadelphia

ISBN 978 1 39903 464 7

A CIP catalogue record for this book is available from the British Library.

Typeset by Mac Style
Printed in the UK by CPI Group (UK) Ltd, Croydon, CR0 4YY.

FSC www.fsc.org MIX Paper | Supporting responsible forestry FSC® C013604

The Publisher's authorised representative in the EU for product safety is Authorised Rep Compliance Ltd., Ground Floor, 71 Lower Baggot Street, Dublin D02 P593, Ireland.
www.arccompliance.com

For a complete list of Pen & Sword titles please contact

PEN & SWORD BOOKS LIMITED
47 Church Street, Barnsley, South Yorkshire, S70 2AS, England
E-mail: enquiries@pen-and-sword.co.uk
Website: www.pen-and-sword.co.uk
or
PEN AND SWORD BOOKS
1950 Lawrence Road, Havertown, PA 19083, USA
E-mail: uspen-and-sword@casematepublishers.com
Website: www.penandswordbooks.com

Contents

Author's Note and Glossary

The aviation-minded reader will notice that I have referred to German Messerschmitt fighters by the abbreviation 'Me' (not 'Bf', which is more technically correct), or simply by their numeric designation, such as '109' or '110'. This not only reads better but is authentic: during the Battle of Britain, Keith Lawrence, a New Zealander, flew Spitfires and once said to me 'To us they were just "Me's", "109s" or "110s", simple, never "Bf".'

In another attempt to preserve accuracy, I have also used the original German, wherever possible, regarding terms associated with the Luftwaffe, such as:

Abwehrkreis: Defensive ring.
Aufklärungs: Reconnaissance.
Bordfunker: Air force radio operator.
Eichenlaub: The Oak Leaves, essentially being a Bar to the *Ritterkreuz* (the Knight's Cross of the Iron Cross).
Erprobungsgruppe: Experimental group, in the case of *Erprobungsgruppe* 210, a skilled precision bombing unit.
Flieger: Pilot.
Fliegerkorps: Air corps.
Freie Jagd: Literally 'free hunting'.
Führer: Leader.
Führerhauptquartier: Adolf Hitler's command post.
Geschwader: The whole group, usually of three *Gruppen.*
Geschwaderstabstaffel Group staff flight.
Gruppe: A wing, usually of three squadrons.
Gruppen: Wings.
Gruppenadjutant: Wing adjutant.
Gruppenkeil: A wedge formation of bombers, usually made up of vics of three.
Gruppenkommandeur: Wing commander.
Jabos: Fighter bombers.
Jagdgeschwader: Fighter group, abbreviated to JG.
Jagdwaffe: The fighter force.
Jäger: Hunter, in this context a fighter pilot or aircraft.

Jagdfliegerführer: Chief of fighter aviation of the *Luftflotte* (Air Fleet).
Jafü: Abbreviation for *Jagdfliegerführer* (see above).
Kampfgeschwader/Kampfgeschwadern: Bomber group, abbreviated to KG.
Kampfgruppe: Combat format.
Kanal: English Channel.
Kanalfront: Front of the English Channel.
Kette/Ketten The basic section of three aircraft around which German bomber formations were based.
Kommandeur: Commander.
Kommando: Commando.
Kommodore: Commodore.
Lehrgeschwader: Literally a training group but actually a precision bombing unit, abbreviated to LG.
Luftflotte: Air Fleet.
Nachtjäger: Night fighter.
Nachtjägdgeschwader: Night fighter group.
Oberkannone: Literally the 'Top Gun' or leading fighter ace.
Oberkommando der Luftwaffe (OKL): German air force high command.
Oberkommando der Wehrmacht (OKW): German armed forces high command.
Reich: German Empire.
Reichsarbeitdienst: Reich Labour Service.
Reichsjägermeister: Reich hunting master.
Reichsluftfahrtministerium (RLM): The German Air Ministry.
Reichsminister: Reich minister.
Ritterkreuz: The Knight's Cross of the Iron Cross.
Rotte: A pair of fighters, comprising leader and wingman, into which the *Schwarm* broke once battle was joined.
Schwarm: A section of four fighters.
Seelöwe: Sealion, the codename for Adolf Hitler's proposed seaborne invasion of England.
Seenotdienst: Sea rescue service.
Stab: Staff.
Stabschwarm: Unit of fighters.
Staffel: Squadron.
Staffeln: Squadrons.
Staffelkapitän: Squadron leader.
Störflug: Harassing attacks, usually by lone Ju 88s.
Wehrmacht: Armed forces.
Zerstörer: Literally 'destroyer', the term used for the Me 110.
Zerstörergeschwader: Destroyer group, abbreviated to ZG.

Each *Geschwader* generally comprised three *Gruppen*, each of three *Staffeln*. Each *Gruppe* is designated by Roman numerals, i.e. III/JG 26 refers to the third *Gruppe* of Fighter Group (abbreviated 'JG') 26. *Staffeln* are identified by numbers, so 7/JG 26 is the 7th *Staffel* and belongs to III/JG 26.

Rank comparisons may also be useful:

Adjutant: Adjutant
Feldwebel: Sergeant
Gefreiter: Private 1st Class
General: General
Generalfeldmarschall: General Field Marshal
Generaloberst: Colonel General
Hauptmann: Squadron Leader
Kaleun: Abbreviation for *Kapitänleutnant* (Captain Lieutenant)
Kapitänleutnant: Captain Lieutenant
Leutnant: Pilot Officer
Major: Wing Commander
Major General: Major General
Oberfähnrich: (Highest) Officer Cadet
Oberfeldwebel: Flight Sergeant
Obergefreiter: Aircraftman 1st Class
Oberleutnant: Flight Lieutenant
Oberst: Group Captain
Reichsmarschall: Marshal of the *Reich* (German Empire)
Unteroffizier: Corporal, no aircrew equivalent in Fighter Command

RAF abbreviations:

AA: Anti-aircraft
AC1: Aircraftman 1st Class
AFC: Air Force Cross
AFS: Auxiliary Fire Service
AHB: Air Historical Branch
AOC: Air Officer Commanding
CAS: Chief of the Air Staff
CO: Commanding Officer
C-in-C Commander in Chief
DCAS: Deputy Chief Air of the Air Staff
DFC: Distinguished Flying Cross
DFM: Distinguished Flying Medal

DSO: Distinguished Service Order
E/A: Enemy Aircraft
FAA: Fleet Air Arm
HE: High Explosive
HF: High Frequency
HQ: Headquarters
LDV: Local Defence Volunteers (Home Guard)
MG: Machine Gun
MO: Medical Officer
MOI: Ministry of Information
NCO: Non-Commissioned Officer
ORB: Operations Record Book
OTU: Operational Training Unit
POW: Prisoner of War
RAAF: Royal Australian Air Force
RAF: Royal Air Force
RAFVR: Royal Air Force Volunteer Reserve
RCAF: Royal Canadian Air Force
RDF: Radio Direction Finding
RN: Royal Navy
R/T: Radio Telephone
SMO: Station Medical Officer
SSQ: Station Sick Quarters
UXB: Unexploded Bomb
VC: Victoria Cross
VHF: Very High Frequency

Also, 'Angels' refers to height measured in thousands of feet; hence 'Angles 15' means 15,000ft. A 'vector' is a compass course, measured in degrees, a 'Bandit' is a confirmed enemy aircraft whilst a 'Bogey' and an 'X-Raid' are, as yet, unidentified but potentially hostile radar plots. 'Tally Ho!' was shouted when the enemy were sighted and the leader was ordering an attack. To the Germans, hostile aircraft were 'Indians' and the German fighter pilot's victory cry was 'Horrido'.

Foreword

In this, the 6th volume of the Battle of Britain Memorial Trust's unprecedented eight-volume history of the Battle, the action takes place between 18 – 30 September 1940. Over these two weeks it became clear that Britain's careful, strategic use of severely limited resources – particularly its scarce fighter pilots – steadily, doggedly undermined Germany's aggressive daylight attempts to overwhelm British air defences and aircraft manufacturing. By month end, the Nazi onslaught proved to be not only ineffective, but counter-productive to its cause due to unsustainable losses of aircraft and crew. Thus, the enemy suffered what the book's title so aptly describes as its 'Daylight Defeat'.

Author and historian Dilip Sarkar MBE continues to let those at the front line tell a lively, compelling story, masterfully weaving together first-hand accounts from pilots, factory workers, civilians and others. This makes for vivid, often poignant reading as voices emerge from the past and immerse the reader in the middle of the action. However, this is significantly more than a first-hand account. It is also a forensic review of the day-to-day Battle that offers a perceptive view of the broader military and political context. There is ample evidence of significant, focussed research, frequently revealing new perspectives and fascinating insight.

In late 1974, I asked my great-uncle Keith, 11 Group commander during the Battle, to speak to my high school history class. While taken aback – "*But I'm not a historian!*" - he agreed. Unfortunately, it was not to be. In early 1975 he fell ill and died. He left no biography, and while much has been written about him since, it is deeply satisfying to read here the personal accounts of those at the forefront, and especially of his strategy being put into action by his "boys" – as he called them - the young fighter pilots who personally took on the enemy, too often paying with their lives; a burden he carried to his dying days.

Through this volume and others in the series the Battle of Britain Memorial Trust continues to ensure that memory of 'The Few', and of those who enabled them, is kept alive and relevant. It is a fresh, modern, immersive view of this most pivotal moment in history. It tells a story that remains as pertinent today and inspiring as ever, as it so comprehensively illustrates the importance of ordinary individuals displaying extraordinary courage in standing up to authoritarian aggression.

Stephen Park, LL.B., Auckland, New Zealand, 2024
[Great-nephew, Air Chief Marshal Sir Keith Park, GCB, KBE, MC & Bar, DFC]

Prologue

Target Supermarine

On 7 September 1940, the Germans began the round the clock bombing of London, a devastating and protracted raid – but representing yet another change of strategy.

In 1936, the German Academy for Aerial Warfare had re-issued *Principles of War* by *Major General* Claus von Clausewitz, first published in 1832, having decided that the theories within remained applicable to modern warfare. Foremost amongst these was the belief that 'one great decisive aim' should be pursued 'with force and determination', 'a maxim' which, von Clausewitz counselled, 'should take first place' and be persevered with. Moreover, von Clausewitz also emphasised the crucial importance of concentration: 'all forces which are available and destined for a strategic objective should be simultaneously applied to it'. Changing tactics whilst adhering to an agreed strategy to keep the enemy guessing (and von Clausewitz set great store in surprise) was one thing but changing the strategy, not once but several times, and failing to both concentrate resources and persevere with the plan were grave mistakes.

Then there was also the matter of Douhet…

The German aim was now to force RAF Fighter Command into the air in the defence of Britain's capital, enabling the en masse destruction of Air Chief Marshal Sir Hugh Dowding's fighters to devastate London as an administrative, economic and communications centre, and, through causing mass panic, disconnect the civilian population from the British government. This latter objective was strongly influenced by the pre-war thinking of Italian air power strategist *General* Giulio Douhet, who believed that the infliction of high casualties and damage to civilian areas would shatter the will to resist, even forcing populations to rise up against their own governments and sue for peace. That said, this was not, in fact, Douhet's primary strategy, which is often misunderstood. To be victorious in modern warfare, Douhet believed that control of the air was pre-requisite, arguing that the enemy's air force should relentlessly be attacked both in the air and on the ground, concurrently with his aircraft industry. The most successful means of destroying an enemy air force, Douhet made clear, was attacking it on the ground – not in the air. Only when aerial superiority had been gained, in fact, did Douhet advocate the bombing of civilian populations – not that this should precede or even be a component of operations seeking to achieve mastery of the air. The modern air force, Douhet opined, should be equipped with heavy bombers carrying the maximum destructive payloads possible, and that an air force must 'operate in mass' to achieve 'the greatest damage in the shortest possible time'. Clearly, then, the theories of both von Clausewitz and Douhet were being ignored by the Luftwaffe.

The terrifying effect of aerial bombing, though, had been demonstrated in the Spanish Civil War, and more recently the heavy bombing of Warsaw and Rotterdam had led to the surrender of Poland and the Netherlands – with the Danes surrendering at the very threat of it. Given his belief that Fighter Command was down to its last reserves, Luftwaffe chief *Reichsmarschall* Hermann Göring had begun this latest phase sublimely confident that through bombing London the desired outcome would soon be achieved. Adverse weather during subsequent days, however, prevented a repetition of the initial hammer blow; although the capital remained the enemy's primary target for the next ten days, Londoners proved they could 'take it' – and confounded both Douhet and Göring.

With better weather forecast, two huge successive raids on London were planned for 15 September 1940, and two raids further west, one on Portland's naval base, the other on the Spitfire-producing Supermarine factory in Southampton. According to Göring, Fighter Command was finished. Indeed, *Oberst* Nicolaus von Below, Hitler's Luftwaffe *Adjutant* since 1937, remembered the *Reichsmarschall's* claim that in three days of fighting in August 1940, 314 RAF fighters had been destroyed for the loss of just 73 German aircraft. Von Below, however, considered these claims 'difficult to substantiate'. As the Battle of Britain wore on, with no apparent weakening of Fighter Command despite Göring's ongoing claims of great successes, von Below requested the OKL view of Fighter Command's strength: 600 operational fighters and the same number in reserve – hardly an air force mustering its last handful of aircraft. These figures were presented to Hitler, who discussed them with Göring – who steadfastly refused to accept the OKL estimate. Consequently, on 15 September 1940, Luftwaffe aircrews were briefed to expect only token resistance from the last handful of Spitfires and Hurricanes – but were dismayed to be met over London first by 312 RAF fighters, then 279. The effect on Luftwaffe morale was catastrophic, firmly confirming both the failure of Luftwaffe air intelligence and Göring's delusion.

Von Below recalled that although the bombing of London

> caused substantial damage to property amongst the civilian populations of London and other cities, the objective of the bomber[s] was not achieved.

> The weather did not permit heavy raids to be made every night. The British fighter and anti-aircraft defences grew steadily stronger: sometimes the fighters were up in such numbers as to divert a formation from its target or frustrate the odd attack altogether. The fighting strength of the German groups declined little by little. Demand for replacements outstripped supply. Most effective were the 'terror raids' on London … Elsewhere in southern England the raids had little more than nuisance value, although in some there were serious civilian casualties. They had no influence on the determination of the British Government. If it had been possible to keep bombing night after night, week in week out, I suppose this might have had some effect, but we did not have the necessary strength to do it. It was found impossible to achieve a military victory by air attack alone. Hitler was the first in the German leadership to recognise that the air war against England had neither achieved its objective nor was likely to … from his observations I took it that he did not share Göring's continuing optimism about the bombing of Britain. If the fighting across the Channel was not successful and the RAF remained viable, Hitler would have to seek an alternative solution. He knew that very well.

Although previous days of fighting had seen more pilots and aircraft lost, or more sorties flown, the fact remains that the outcome of 15 September 1940 convinced Hitler that despite the boastful *Reichsmarschall* Göring's repeated assurances, in reality the Luftwaffe was unable to achieve a decisive victory over the RAF and thereby achieve the aerial supremacy necessary for Operation *Seelöwe* – the proposed seaborne invasion of Britain – to go ahead. Consequently, two days later, with time having run out owing to an unfavourable future moon, tides and weather, Hitler postponed *Seelöwe* indefinitely. If we are to understand that the Battle of Britain was fought to prevent the Germans achieving aerial superiority so that *Seelöwe* could set sail, a legitimate argument exists that the Battle of Britain actually began on 2 July 1940, when Hitler first agreed to the possibility of invading England and from which point on air operations were directly appended to that objective, and ended on 17 September 1940, when Hitler cancelled *Seelöwe*. Certainly, the air fighting continued – but this was no longer directly in support of an imminent invasion. The immediate crisis for Britain had passed and, beyond doubt, the real turning point was 15 September 1940 – forever, rightly, known and commemorated as 'Battle of Britain Day'.

This is not to say, of course, that the fear of invasion had completely evaporated because Prime Minister Winston Churchill expected such a threat to resume the following spring. According to von Below, though,

> Hitler had given up hope of a successful invasion of England in the spring of 1941. It was in the autumn of 1940 that he shrank back in the face of the imponderable – an improvised crossing of the English Channel.

What Churchill and his War Cabinet did not know was that Hitler, having been unable to achieve the required swift victory over Britain, was already turning his gaze towards Russia – the invasion of which did not involve a hazardous sea crossing and the conquest of which was always the *Führer*'s main aim. Indeed, Hitler was most reluctant to go to war with Britain, and after the Fall of France his preferred strategy against the 'Sceptered Isle' had actually been blockade, followed by operations against shipping in the Channel, which amounted to 'Air Fleet Diplomacy', intended to intimidate the British into surrendering through fear of German air power. None of this had worked and eventually Hitler had no choice but to authorise an all-out air assault in the hope of achieving the essential aerial superiority for *Seelöwe*. Now this had failed, it was time for Plan 'B' – but the forthcoming invasion of Russia, however, as evidenced in previous volumes in this series, was also part of a new strategy against Britain, not just conquering Russia in isolation. Hitler knew that Britain still had high hopes that neutral America would enter the war on the side of the Western Allies, and that Russia and Germany's flimsy alliance may end, also bringing the Soviets into the Allied camp. Germany invading and defeating Russia, however, Hitler reasoned, would fortify Japanese influence in the Far East, thereby occupying America's attentions and diverting the United States from interest or involvement in another European war. With America and Russia thereby neutralised, Germany could then concentrate on defeating Britain. These plans, though, were a way off, so the critical point is that at this time, Operation *Seelöwe* was off – the importance of which cannot be underestimated. Hitler had essentially missed the boat, quite literally, and such a unique opportunity would never again arise.

Reichsmarschall Göring, however, found it inconceivable that the Luftwaffe was not, it seemed, invincible and, despite all the setbacks and the indefinite postponement of *Seelöwe*, he still believed that his air force alone could force Britain's surrender. Unfettered now by the needs of *Seelöwe*, or the combined service politics arising, Göring decided that the way forward, whilst not neglecting attacks on London, especially by night, was to target the British aircraft industry. There can be no doubt that the great number of RAF fighters appearing over London influenced this decision, there clearly being a need to disrupt or prevent the flow of replacement aircraft and thereby reduce the numbers of defending fighters. Certainly, some of aircraft factories had already been attacked, including Supermarine, and this target selection had previously featured in the Luftwaffe's strategy – but now, heavy raids were being planned on a number of factories, foremost amongst them Supermarine. As a strategy, this made perfect sense, more so, arguably, than bombing London, but was it not too late in the day? Could Luftwaffe intelligence, already a demonstrable failure, properly inform target selection? Were sufficient assets available to deliver a hammer blow to British aircraft production? On 18 September 1940, these questions could not be answered – but of one thing there was no doubt: the significance of the Vickers Supermarine Aviation Works.

Southampton, on Britain's south coast, being just 60 miles from the enemy occupied French coast, was, therefore, vulnerable to air attack and became an obvious and frequently visited Luftwaffe target. In Hampshire, 70 miles south-west of London and 15 miles north-west of Portsmouth, Southampton is a major port, and at its northern end is Southampton Water, a deep-water estuary formed by the confluence of the rivers Test and Itchen, joined by the River Hamble to the south. In the twentieth century, the city's major industry was shipbuilding and repair, and during the First World War, Southampton became a major embarkation port for the military, in addition to receiving both the wounded and POWs from France. That Southampton was such a well-appointed port was sufficient for it to be targeted by the Luftwaffe – but there was another reason: the famous Supermarine factory was located on the River Itchen's west bank at Woolston.

The Supermarine Aviation Works had been born before the First World War, when one Noel Pemberton Billing decided to combine his passions for flying and boating by producing a flying boat. In 1913, he purchased and set up shop at an old coal wharf in Woolston, where the 'Super Marine Craft' was to be built. Owing to the outbreak of the First World War, however, this visionary flying boat was never built, Supermarine, as the company became known, instead producing warplanes. In 1916, Hubert Scott-Paine became the managing director and oversaw a re-organisation of the company. New faces appeared at the Woolston works, including a promising designer called Reginald Joseph Mitchell. At this time, the RN commissioned Supermarine to manufacture its flying boats, meaning that the business maintained an association with seaplanes well into the 1940s. Between the wars Mitchell oversaw the design and production of the company's entries for the coveted Schneider Trophy; nations competing in this spectacular and hugely popular annual air race at low level over water. In accordance with competition rules, the country winning the competition three consecutive times kept the prize – which Britain did in 1936 with Mitchell's Supermarine S.6B, which reached a speed of 357.7 mph, setting a world record. The competition had become a matter of enormous national pride and interest; the three victories making Mitchell and Supermarine famous.

Most importantly, the experience gained competing for the Schneider Trophy led directly to 'R.J.' responding to the Air Ministry's invitation for aircraft designers to submit tenders for a modern fast monoplane fighter, by designing the Spitfire. On 5 March 1936, Mitchell and his team gathered at Eastleigh Airport (now Southampton Airport), several miles north of Southampton, and watched Captain Joseph 'Mutt' Summers make the Spitfire's maiden flight. Coming off the back of the victorious Schneider Trophy racers, the Spitfire, with its beautiful elliptical wing, was a winner from the outset. True, the Hawker Hurricane had already flown, but Sydney Camm's fighter lacked both the lines and performance of Mitchell's fighter. Whereas the Hurricane resembled a Hart biplane without the top wing, relying upon tried and tested construction materials and techniques, the Spitfire was, like Germany's Me 109, an all-metal design, Mitchell uniting strength and lightness with a Rolls-Royce Merlin engine: it was a winning combination. On 3 June 1936, the Air Ministry ordered 310 Spitfires, and a further 200 in 1937. On 11 June that year, however, Mitchell died of cancer, aged just 42, never to know the contribution his fighter would make. The following year, on 4 August 1938, Supermarine test pilot Jeffrey Quill delivered the first Spitfire to an RAF fighter squadron, 19, at Duxford, replacing the squadron's existing obsolete Gloster Gauntlet biplanes; it would be just in time, as the following month Britain and France came worryingly close to war with Germany over Czechoslovakia. From that point on it was obvious that Hitler's demands extended far beyond righting the wrongs of the harsh peace agreement, Treaty of Versailles, of 1919 – and that war with Germany was inevitable. Spitfire production was stepped up, Supermarine's Woolston and adjacent Itchen works becoming hives of activity. In May 1940, a local teenager, Terry White, joined the company as a 'handy lad', finding himself 'utterly bewildered by the noise and, it appeared to me, confusion of what was a very, very busy factory', which would soon fill the crosshairs of German bombsights.

The first of many bombs fell on Southampton's Millbrook area on the night of 20 June 1940, causing casualties. The city centre was hit on 13 and 14 August 1940, six Sotonians losing their lives, and two days later, Flight Lieutenant James Brindley Nicolson DFC VC of 249 Squadron performed his 'signal act of valour' over the city, for which he received Fighter Command's sole VC of the Second World War. From then on, the tempo of enemy air activity directed at Southampton increased: on 11 September 1940, the German precision-bombing unit *Erprobungsgruppe* 210 arrived at Cherbourg-Ost airfield, tasked with destroying Supermarine.

At that time, the Vickers Supermarine Aviation Works, as the company was now known, was still the main base for Spitfire production, although the new Spitfire Mk IIA had started production at the huge Castle Bromwich

Aeroplane Factory (CBAF) in Birmingham. The CBAF was a huge facility at which the automotive industry's mass production techniques were being applied to manufacturing Spitfires, the inland location being far less vulnerable to air attack than Southampton. Indeed, Vickers Supermarine Aviation Works was too small a factory to produce Spitfires in the numbers now required, and ultimately, the majority of the 22,000 Spitfires built would come from CBAF – but things had yet to get into top gear there in September 1940. Consequently, Vickers Supermarine Aviation Works remained a vitally important location for Spitfire production – and this, at least, was well-known to the Luftwaffe.

The busy Woolston factory was located on the River Itchen's east bank, immediately north of the 'Floating Bridge', which ferried passengers across the estuary dividing Southampton in two. A few hundred yards to the north was the company's Itchen works. Both factories fronted the river, a 15ft high railway embankment rising up across the road behind the Itchen works. Beyond the railway, to the east, was the open land of Peartree Green, and built-up area of Woolston. Completed Spitfire sub-assemblies were transported by road to the company's hangars at Eastleigh Airport for final assembly and test flying, so to a degree production was dispersed. In terms of workforce protection, three surface shelters were constructed along the Itchen work's boundary but the main shelters were constructed in rows on the railway's far side, access gained via a tunnel just 10ft wide, burrowed through the embankment. While these principal shelters were adjacent and close to the Itchen works, the main workforce was located at the Woolston works, so had a fair distance to cover in a hurry in the event of a raid. What made Woolston personnel especially vulnerable was that warnings were sounded at the last possible minute, so that raids only disrupted production for the minimum length of time. Two practices indicated that it took too long for Woolston workers to reach the shelters, and indeed that the narrow tunnel created a dangerous bottleneck. For this reason, some staff resolved never to use the company shelters – which, as we will see, proved a wise decision.

On the afternoon of 11 September 1940, *Erprobungsgruppe* 210's target was not the actual Woolston or Itchen works, but Eastleigh airfield, where Spitfires were finally assembled and first flown, and where twin-engined Lockheed Hudson aircraft were also produced, by Cunliffe-Owen. The raiders successfully reached and bombed Eastleigh – but the Supermarine facility was fortunately unscathed. Instead, the Cunliffe-Owen factory was bombed, bringing Lockheed Hudson production to a standstill; over fifty people were killed. Nonetheless, Supermarine was now very much a primary target, and it was just a question of time before both the Woolston and Itchen works were attacked.

At 17.39 hrs on 15 September 1940, 'Battle of Britain Day', the sirens sounded across Southampton, as eighteen Me 110s of *Erprobungsgruppe* 210, led by *Hauptmann* Martin Lutz, used cloud cover to stealthily approach the city before diving at a shallow angle, from 7,000ft, approaching Woolston from the east. Bofors and other AA guns banged away, but nonetheless the Me 110s dropped twenty-three bombs on Woolston. Again, the Vickers Supermarine Aviation Works escaped any serious damage, just one skylight being smashed by flying debris. The adjacent residential area suffered though: terraced housing near the Spitfire factory and east of the railway line were devastated; six people were killed, nineteen seriously injured and twenty-three more were treated for minor injuries at Royal South Hampshire Hospital. In total, 34 houses were destroyed: 81 so badly damaged that they were consequently demolished, 351 were badly damaged but repairable and 755 sustained minor damage. This charmed life, however, was soon to end.

Elsewhere, of course, were other aircraft factories, Hawker, for example, producing Hurricane fighters, and Vickers-Armstrongs, building Wellington bombers, both located at Brooklands in Surrey – which had already been attacked by *Erprobungsgruppe* 210, on 4 September 1940, causing extensive damage and killing ninety people. The West Country was also home to several factories. Westland Aircraft in Yeovil, made Lysander communications aircraft and the cannon-armed Whirlwind fighter, and had been attacked in July 1940, the flight shed being hit and runway cratered, although the aircraft were spared. Recent building works, though, had left large patches of lightish coloured concrete, which, it was feared, would be highly visible from the air. In the event of an air raid warning, workers collected a corrugated sheet and laid these down over the concrete, thus concealing the potential landmark and breaking up the appearance of the ground near the hangars. Indeed, the main factory building and aerodrome were marked with a paint and sawdust mix to represent fields bounded by hedges and trees. Luftwaffe intelligence had allocated Westland the target reference GB 74 60, estimating the workforce at 3,500 and concluding that the factory had to be destroyed by 7 October 1940.

More important was the Bristol Aeroplane Company (BAC) at RAF Filton, producing aero engines in addition to the Blenheim Mk I fighter and Mk IV bomber, and the new long-range day and night fighter, the Bristol Beaufighter. Luftwaffe intelligence had sub-divided this huge site into three: the aircraft factory (GB 74 52), the aero-engine plant (GB 73 52) and the actual aerodrome (GB 10 81). What Luftwaffe intelligence did not realise, however, was that Filton also accommodated a 10 Group Fighter Command sector operations room, controlling fighters based at RAF Exeter and RAF Bibury. In Yate, South Gloucestershire and a few miles north-west of Filton, was Parnall Aircraft

Limited – Luftwaffe target GB 74 51 – which manufactured Frazer-Nash gun turrets, Luftwaffe intelligence reporting that 'the destruction of this factory would have a serious effect on bomber aircraft production'.

Elsewhere, Hampden bombers were built by Handley Page at Radlett airfield, and at nearby Hatfield airfield, de Havilland was both producing variable pitch propellers for the RAF and working on the revolutionary Mosquito prototype. At various locations around Manchester, Avro was manufacturing the Anson – and, most importantly, like Handley Page, working on a new four-engined bomber. In Coventry, Armstrong Whitworth made the Whitley bomber; like CBAF in Birmingham, being so far inland this was safe from a major daylight raid. The aforementioned factories in Southampton, Brooklands and in the West Country, however, would all be selected as daylight targets in the new phase of battle ahead.

Losses to the German bomber force by day, however, were becoming critical and were unsustainable. The new phase of fighting would see heavy attacks on aircraft factories and other targets, some successful – but also defeat of the Luftwaffe day bombers…

Daylight Defeat:
18 September 1940–30 September 1940

Wednesday, 18 September 1940

The British, of course, were unaware that on 17 September 1940, Hitler had postponed Operation *Seelöwe* indefinitely. Indeed, on the same day, Churchill had addressed the House of Commons, warning that 'at any moment a major assault may be launched upon this island' – having reached this conclusion based on the vast invasion fleet assembled in the various Channel ports, ships, the prime minister explained, that these were

> fully loaded with all the munitions needed for the invading armies and to beat us utterly. The shipping available and now assembled is sufficient to carry in one voyage nearly half a million men.

As the bombing continued that night, there was nothing indicating that the Germans were still anything but hell bent on achieving the necessary circumstances for invasion.

In her diary, Lady Diana Cooper, wife of Duff Cooper, the Minister of Information, recorded that the night of 17/18 September 1940 had been 'A terrific night of bombardment. A bomb fell in Park Lane not fifty yards away, another blew all the glass out of Berkeley Square.' Compared to their reception over England by day, the Germans were bombing by night with impunity, the raid described by Lady Cooper involving over 200 aircraft and lasting from 21.00 to 05.00 hrs. In an attempt to combat these nocturnal raiders, on 13 September 1940, the Boulton Paul Defiant turret fighters of 141 Squadron's 'B' Flight had flown south from Turnhouse to operate from RAF Biggin Hill and Gatwick as night fighters. On the night of 15 September 1940, Flying Officer John Waddingham and his air gunner, Sergeant Alfred Cumbers, claimed one He 111 destroyed and another probably so, and on the night of 17/18 September 1940, Sergeant George Laurence and his gunner, Sergeant Wilfred Chard, claimed a Ju 88 destroyed near Barking. Although the Defiant had previously been decimated by day, leading to its withdrawal from the daylight battle, it was now to make a more positive contribution to Britain's defence as a much-needed night fighter – a role for which, in fact, its designers had also anticipated.

On the wider stage, the night of 17/18 September 1940 also saw a dreadful tragedy: the sinking of the British passenger liner SS *City of Benares*, carrying children being evacuated to Canada, by *Kaleun* Heinrich Bleichrodt's *U-48*. Such overseas evacuations were organised by the Children's Overseas Reception Board and, so far, some dozen ships had left Britain, carrying children to safety. One of these, the SS *Volendam*, a Dutch liner, had been torpedoed off Ireland on 31 August 1940, all 230 children fortunately being rescued. Those aboard the SS *City of Benares*, which had left Liverpool with convoy OB213 on 13 September 1940, were not so lucky: of 407 passengers and crew, 147 were lost, including 77 of the 90 children aboard. The incident horrified Britain, although Bleichrodt always maintained that he believed his target to have been an armed merchantman, and the Nazi propaganda machine claimed that the ship had actually been requisitioned by the RN and was, therefore, a legitimate military target. This was nothing but lies and sadly the little children suffered for Bleichrodt's mistake.

So far as the air battle still being fought over Britain was concerned, regardless of Hitler's *Seelöwe* postponement, better weather on 18 September 1940 would see another increase in the fighting, the Luftwaffe flying 359 bomber and 1,024 fighter sorties.

The first indications of an impending attack appeared on RDF screens at 09.10 hrs, as the enemy assembled east of the Dover Strait. Immediately 11 Group controller scrambled eleven fighter squadrons, all of which were airborne when the enemy crossed the Kentish coast twenty minutes later, three German formations incoming between Hythe and Sandwich, whilst a fourth came in over the North Foreland. All four steered towards Rochester: target Tilbury Docks.

At 09.15 hrs, the Spitfires of 92 Squadron had scrambled from Biggin Hill with those of 72 Squadron, the former squadron leading, to patrol Gravesend at 20,000ft, and at 09.50 hrs the RAF fighters were bounced over the Maidstone/Ashford area by Me 109s. Pilot Officer Roy Mottram was shot down and crash-landed at Hollingbourne, thereafter being admitted to Orpington Hospital suffering from burns.

Pilot Officer Tony Bartley, Yellow 1, became separated from the rest of 92 Squadron when

> we ran through a squadron of Me 109s coming in the opposite direction.
>
> While looking forward the Squadron, I saw a Do 17 and three Me 109s going due West inland, approximately off Dungeness. I lost sight of the Me 109s and gave chase to the Do 17. I delivered an attack from the left

> quarter, ending in dead astern at about fifty yards, firing a burst of about nine or ten seconds.
>
> The Do 17 lurched badly and started losing height in a slow dive towards the coast with smoke pouring from the engines. At the same time I felt a violent bang behind me – my hood and mirror were shattered, and my petrol and glycol tank punctured. I decided to jump as I thought I was on fire. Having undone my straps and raised myself out of my seat, I saw a Me 109 attacking me from the left quarter. Realising that I would be at a disadvantage hanging from a parachute, and still having ammunition left, I turned into the Me 109 which, evidently not thinking I was damaged, made off at high speed. Having lost a lot of height by this time, I decided to forced-land as my engine was still running. I endeavoured to do up my harness again but failed, so I put down the undercarriage in the hope that I could make a normal landing. However, whilst app[roaching] the selected field my engine lost power and enveloped me in smoke, which completely spoilt my vision. I knocked my wheels off on a bomb crater and landed sideways, unhurt. I discovered that I had been hit by a cannon shell and many bullets, one of which had punctured the petrol tank.
>
> Witnesses saw the end of the Do 17, which burst into flames and spiraled [*sic*] down into the sea.

Bartley came down at Appledore, his Spitfire damaged but repairable. German casualty records, however, provide no clue as to the Do 17s identity, only recording two of the type being engaged on reconnaissance sorties over England and returning to base damaged by RAF fighters.

No. 72 Squadron did not fare well in this engagement, making no combat claims but losing two Spitfires: Pilot Officer John Lloyd was shot down, crash-landing at Martin Mill in Dover, seriously wounded, and Sergeant Howard Bell-Walker was so badly wounded that a long period of hospitalisation followed.

Having scrambled from RAF Hornchurch at 09.10 hrs, at 09.45 hrs Squadron Leader George Denholm and the Spitfires of his 603 Squadron met ten marauding Me 109s at 23,000ft over Maidstone; the CO reported that he

> saw two vics of five Me 109s pass at 20,000 feet, underneath us, and ordered the Squadron to attack. We dived down. The Me 109 which I picked out did one or two circles and then dived for home. I fired 1,600 rounds at ranges of about 150 yards and lost it in a layer of cloud, when he was emitting black smoke and not flying very fast.

The Me 109 was awarded as 'damaged' and represented 603 Squadron's only combat claim in this sharp clash with III/JG 53. Despite initially having the height advantage, the Spitfires came off second best. *Feldwebel* Hermann Neuhoff chalked up his tenth aerial victory when he shot down and killed Pilot Officer Peter Howes, who crashed at Kennington near Ashford, and Sergeant George Bailey's Spitfire was badly battered by cannon shells; the pilot was unhurt and returned safely to base, this being further evidence of the Spitfire's ability to absorb punishment but still keep flying – contrary to the popular myth.

Also, at 09.10 hrs, Squadron Leader Gerry Edge DFC led a flight of 253 Squadron Hurricanes off from RAF Kenley, with orders to patrol RAF West Malling at 20,000ft with Squadron Leader Henry 'Harry' Hogan DFC's Kenley-based 501 Squadron.

Pilot Officer Peter 'Hairy' Hairs reported that

> I was leading the second section (Yellow) of 501 Squadron … After orbiting for a few minutes I saw about four Me 109s on our right at about the same altitude. One of these turned in front of me. I therefore turned left onto his tail. He immediately flew off in a south-easterly direction, twisting and losing height. Eventually I got in range and fired a number of bursts until my ammunition was finished. White smoke and glycol came from the E/A, which was losing height rapidly. I last saw E/A at about 500 feet and about five miles off the French coast, with black puffs of smoke coming from it, so it is unlikely that it got home.

The 109 was claimed as a 'probable'. According to Luftwaffe records, a 2/JG 27 Me 109 E-1 landed at Guînes having suffered battle damage over the Channel, which is likely to have been the aircraft attacked by Hairs. This success was not without loss to 501 Squadron, however: Sergeant Cyril Saward was shot down and baled out unhurt over Staplehurst. No. 253 Squadron did not engage.

The Spitfires of 41 Squadron were up from Hornchurch and patrolling east Kent at very high altitude – 33,000ft – when engaged by Me 109s at 10.10 hrs.

Pilot Officer Eric 'Sawn-off' Lock:

> When ordered to patrol base with Mitor Squadron [author's note: radio call sign of 41 Squadron], we were attacked from above by many Me 109s. I had a full deflection shot at one E/A and it was seen to go down in smoke. The Squadron then broke up. We were ordered to re-form over Gravesend. I climbed up to 22,000 feet but could see no sign of the remainder … I climbed to 31,000 feet when I saw a lone Me 109. I chased it towards Kent. I got in an astern attack and fired a short burst, but could not see

> any effects. I closed in to about 100 yards this time, attacking from below. I gave it two short bursts, then it exploded and went down in flames just off Margate.

Surprisingly, considering Lock's description of the 109 exploding, it was awarded as probably destroyed. It is possible, however, that this was a machine of I/JG 77, the pilot of which, *Gefreiter* Still, was killed. Pilot Officer George 'Ben' Bennions also claimed a probable, concluding that he had been unable to 'definitely destroy the E/A because I was being attacked by a further section of five Me 109s'.

No. 41 Squadron suffered no losses in this action, which confirms the high-altitude performance of both the Me 109 E-1 and Spitfire.

According to the ORB of RAF Northolt's 1 (RCAF) Squadron,

> E/A were coming over in batches at about 20,000ft, making it difficult for us to engage. On one of these scrambles Pilot Officer [Eric] Beardmore, who became detached from the squadron and joined up with 219 Squadron, was forced to take to his parachute, landing near shore in the Thames. He sustained slight injuries. Pilot Officer [Otto John] Peterson obtained one damaged E/A and one probable.

Pilot Officer Eric Beardmore had been shot down over the Thames Estuary at 10.30 hrs and would not return to active duty until the following month. RAF North Weald's station commander, Wing Commander Victor Beamish DSO and Bar DFC AFC, was also in action over the Thames Estuary, claiming a 109 destroyed and a probable over the Isle of Sheppey.

By 10.30 hrs, or thereabouts, the enemy had retired. Strangely, the Do 17 attacked by 92 Squadron's Pilot Officer Tony Bartley was the only bomber reported by RAF pilots during this attack – but Tilbury was bombed by more than one aircraft, AA gunners there reporting a formation of He 111s. If so, these aircraft escaped interception, but the docks escaped damage, only domestic properties being hit. The raid clearly predominantly involved high flying Me 109s, which accounted for five RAF fighters, whilst 11 Group's pilots claimed not one Me 109 destroyed. It would seem, then, that the attack on Tilbury was secondary to the main objective – which was engaging and destroying RAF fighters. Going forward, such high-altitude enemy fighter sweeps would become increasingly frequent, and successful.

At midday, RDF screens again became alerted to the fact that the Germans were assembling over Calais. By 12.20 hrs, 11 Group had scrambled four pairs of squadrons in addition to a three-squadron strong wing from the Debden sector, and 12 Group's Duxford Wing was also requested to patrol northern Kent and southern Essex. RDF showed '100+' bandits sweeping up to Maidstone where what were exclusively fighters turned for Sheerness before returning to France via Dover without being intercepted. Four other formations were incoming between Dover and North Foreland, flying north to Whitstable before turning west. Nos. 46 and 249 Squadrons had left North Weald together to patrol Gravesend at 20,000ft, and these squadrons were the first to intercept.

No. 249 Squadron's Pilot Officer Albert Lewis DFC, a South African from Kimberley, reported that

> Ordered off as No 2 in Blue Section. Squadron attacked formation of He 111s, East of Rochester. Spotted Me 109s above us to stern. Attacked a yellow nose heading back, opening fire from slightly below, approaching E/A head-on. Gave short burst of about three seconds, pulling nose well up beneath E/A. It went down in a flat spiral and following it down saw it crash near a wood. This was confirmed by Pilot Officer Worral, Blue 3 of same Section. Pilot presumed to have baled out as parachute was seen in the vicinity.

Pilot Officer Robert Reid of 46 Squadron reported having attacked a formation of fifteen 'Do 215s [*sic*]' at 18,000ft, the bombers then turning south:

> [Climbing up behind the bombers] I suddenly found myself among several Me109s, which I had mistaken for Hurricanes. I got close to one and attacked from behind, slightly to starboard, allowing for deflection. The Me immediately put his nose down and I saw him burst into flames. He went straight down, East of Maidstone. I did not see him crash as I was myself hit from the rear. However, the Me was burning fiercely and must have crashed.

Reid was right: it had. The 109 of 1/JG 27, was, in fact, the same enemy fighter attacked and claimed by Lewis, which crashed in Squirrels Wood, Stockbury – yet again illustrating how a single German casualty could be multiplied many times on the balance sheet. No trace of the pilot, *Oberleutnant* R. Krafftschick, has ever been found but when the crash site was excavated by enthusiasts in the 1970s, amongst the many items recovered was the missing pilot's parachute release buckle – so it was not Krafftschick seen by Lewis descending under his 'brolly'. The excavation confirmed, however, that this Me 109 was a fighter bomber, its SC250 bomb exploding upon impact – thereby obliterating any trace of the pilot.

Of all the RAF squadrons airborne, it would only be 46 and 249 Squadrons that managed to engage the enemy bombers, which 46 Squadron described as 'Do 215s [*sic*]' and 249 Squadron He 111s.

Flight Lieutenant Robert Barton, a Canadian, commanding 249 Squadron's 'B' Flight, reported that at 12.30 hrs over Rochester,

> After carrying out an attack on He 111s in the rear section, from below, oil and puffs of smoke came from port engine, aircraft lagged behind formation as they returned to France.

This was accredited as damaged, as was another He 111 similarly claimed by Pilot Officer Thomas 'Tom' Neil DFC and Bar. No. 46 Squadron's Flight Lieutenant Alexander Rabagliati claimed a damaged 'Do 215', which was the sum total of any pain inflicted on the enemy bomber force.

No. 249 Squadron, however, had suffered a sad loss. Commanding 'A' Flight was 25-year-old Flight Lieutenant Denis Parnall, son of George Parnall who had founded Parnall Aircraft Limited. A successful fighter pilot, having scrambled with the squadron, he had been forced to return soon afterwards owing to issues with his air pressure system, which affected the gun firing mechanism. Undeterred, Parnall took-off immediately in a serviceable Hurricane but was then shot down and killed, very likely by *Leutnant* Heinz Ebeling, *Staffelkapitän* of 9/JG 26, his aircraft crashing and burning out on Furness Hill in Margretting, Essex.

No. 46 Squadron also suffered casualties – all three Hurricanes concerned falling to the guns of *Major* Adolf Galland, *Kommodore* of JG 26, who pounced on the British fighters over Chatham with his *Stabschwarm*. First to fall was Sergeant George Jeffreys, who baled out but was killed owing to parachute failure. Next was Flying Officer Peter Lefevre, who baled out with minor injuries, and finally Sergeant Charles Hurry, who also baled out but was admitted to Chatham Hospital suffering from burns.

At 12.35 hrs, 41 and 603 Squadrons scrambled together from Hornchurch with orders to patrol Maidstone at 20,000ft.

Pilot Officer George Bennions was leading the former squadron, later retorting that at 12.50 hrs, west of Gravesend, the Spitfires ran into '60 Me 109s':

> Intercepted loose formation of Me 109s, the lowest of which was 500 feet above. I ordered the Squadron into line-astern and turned into attack, but had to break away when attacked from above and behind.
>
> I climbed up to 32,000 feet and attacked a formation of five Me 109s circling in open echelon formation. I closed with No 5 and after two short

> bursts the machine exploded in front of me and everything was obscured. I pulled up and saw an aircraft firing at me from astern. I turned about after feeling a burst hit the port side of the aircraft, then attacked the 109 which was attacking me. I gave him two short bursts and saw bits flying off the starboard plane and thick black smoke pouring from what seemed to be the oil cooler under the starboard mainplane. He then half-rolled and my attention was distracted by a further formation of 109s coming towards me from the port rear quarter. I turned to starboard and attacked No 4, who immediately showed signs of being hit and half-rolled. I half-rolled after him and when he levelled out, I gave him a long burst, which caused a stream of white smoke to pour out in large quantities from a position about one yard from the fuselage on the port mainplane. I had exhausted my ammunition and the 109 was going down towards Dover, leaving a long trail of white smoke behind, so after looking at the damage to my aircraft, I decided to return to base and land.

Fortunately, Bennions, credited with one 109 destroyed, a probable and another damaged, was unhurt. No. 41 Squadron recorded no other casualties. Pilot Officer Eric Lock also claimed a 109 destroyed and a probable, and Sergeant Edward Darling claimed a 109 destroyed 5 miles inland of Dover.

At 13.00 hrs, as Flight Lieutenant Harold MacDonald was leading 603 Squadron at 24,000ft, 3 miles south-east of Kenley, travelling south, when six Me 109s were sighted at a similar height from the east:

> I ordered the Squadron into line-astern and continued climbing hard on the same course. This brought us across bows of Me 109s and slightly above. Then, turning in to [*sic*] the left, I gave attack and selected one myself. I gave him a short burst from the beam and he broke away from the other Me's [*sic*] and dived vertically. I followed him and gave chase as he pulled out. He tried not very violent evasive tactics and dived for cloud. I followed him, gradually closing in and gave several bursts at close range. The E/A caught fire at 3,000 feet – pilot tried to jump out but aircraft turned over and dived vertically into the ground before pilot could escape.

The timings of official records, as we have seen, are frequently inaccurate or contradictory, which may be the case here, because the only Me 109 pilot killed on this day was *Oberleutnant* R. Krafftschick.

Pilot Officer Bill Read, Red 3, was in 603 Squadron's leading section when 'many Me 109s' were engaged in a 'general dogfight' over Maidstone. Read found a *Schwarm* of four Me 109s travelling in line astern, slightly below his Spitfire, and he immediately

> fired at the leader from ahead and abeam, and allowed the others to fly through my burst. I followed through my attack on the rearmost one and saw his motor hesitate and his airscrew die to a tick-over. My ammunition then ran out and as I was engaged from astern by another 109, I did a diving aileron turn out of the combat. The four 109s at which I fired took no evasive action.

Flying the rearguard position in 603 Squadron was Pilot Officer James Morton, who in the combat over Maidstone attacked eight Me 109s 800ft below and to the north. Latching onto one of the 'tail machines', the German

> went into a steep dive. I followed and got in two good bursts. Some coolant came from his starboard radiator and he slowed up very quickly, causing me to overshoot and lose him in the clouds at 6,000 feet.

Without coolant, an aero engine will do but one thing: overheat and seize. Because the Me 109's engine was fuel injected it was, therefore, unaffected by gravity (unlike the Rolls-Royce Merlin), so the 109 pilot's standard attacking and evasive tactic was a high-speed dive. Ramming the throttle forward produced black smoke from the exhausts – and seeing a 109 plummeting earthwards at high speed led many an Allied fighter pilot to assume that the enemy fighter was destroyed. Often, though, this was not the case and the 109 would level out many thousands of feet below and head home, having 'played dead'. White smoke, as described here by Morton, was a different matter, and certainly that lunchtime two Me 109s forced-landed in Kent after combat with Spitfires: *Feldwebel* E. Schulz of 9/JG 27 came down at Sellindge, fatally wounded, and *Gefreiter* W. Glöckner, also of 9/JG 27, put his damaged fighter down safely on the Royal St George's Golf Links in Willow Farm, Sandwich, where he set fire to his machine before being captured unhurt. Which was hit by Read and which by Morton is impossible to say.

No. 303 (Polish) Squadron had been amongst those squadrons unable to engage the high-flying enemy but that would now change. At 12.20 hrs, twelve of the squadron's Hurricanes scrambled from Northolt with orders to operate with 229 Squadron, based at the same station:

> Squadron formated on 229 Squadron, vectored 270 degrees, climbed to 25,000 feet and patrolled South of Biggin Hill. Saw many friendly fighters

> and one Do 215, evidently on reconnaissance. Eight pilot shot at E/A, from which three crew baled out. E/A fell ten miles South of West Malling and broke to pieces. Sergeant Frantiszek shot down one Me 109 which was apparently escorting the Dornier. E/A came down on land. Two of our aircraft were damaged by machine-gun fire from friendly fighters. [ORB]

For once, this was actually a Do 215, of 4/*Aufklärungsgruppe Ob.de.L.*, to be precise, which crashed near Yalding at 13.15 hrs; one of the crew was killed, the remaining three captured.

As was the case in the morning, 253 and 501 Squadrons were scrambled from Kenley to operate together and patrol West Malling at 20,000ft. Sergeant Antoni Głowacki, a Pole, Blue 2, of 'B' Flight, reported that at 13.15 hrs over Maidstone:

> We sighted twenty bombers [author's note: and reportedly 100 fighters] approaching Maidstone at 18,000 feet and saw how they turned back towards France on boing attacked by Spitfires, which engaged the large fighter escort. AA fire was bursting among the bombers. A parachute below the bombers was attacked by two Me 109s at about 15,000 feet. I turned and attacked one of them from beam and quarter, and after my second burst he dived vertically from 15,000 feet down to a patch of cloud at 3,000 feet. The last two bursts I fired as he dived dead astern. When he reached the cloud I went round it, having pulled out of the dive just in time. I wanted on the side towards the French coast to intercept but saw no trace of him.

Głowacki, however, considered that given the 109's trajectory, it was 'most probable that it went straight in SW of Maidstone' but it did not, and may, therefore, have been the I/JG 54 machine, which crashed in the Channel, its pilot rescued by the *Seenotdienst.*

Głowacki's combat report, however, is of special interest, being a unique first-hand account by a pilot, written minutes after the event, describing Me 109 pilots machine gunning a defenceless airman on his parachute.

No. 501 Squadron's only loss in the engagement was the CO, Squadron Leader Henry Hogan, who was shot down and baled out, landing safely in Charing.

Little information is available concerning 66 Squadron's part in the lunchtime air battle, except to say that according to the ORB, Squadron Leader Rupert 'Lucky' Leigh led seven other 'Clickety-Click' Spitfires up from Gravesend, all but one returning safely at 13.20 hrs. The missing man was Sergeant Douglas Corfe, who had been shot down, crashing near Petham, and admitted to Chatham Hospital. No. 66 Squadron made no combat claims. Similarly, 222 Squadron was up from Hornchurch, patrolling the Canterbury area where 'enemy fighters were encountered, but no visible damage was reported' [ORB]. Sergeant Iain Hutchinson, however, was shot down and baled out slightly wounded, his Spitfire crashed near Challock at 13.53 hrs.

After this, all went ominously quiet for a short time. As in the morning, the Germans' bombing appeared of secondary importance and half-hearted, bombs only falling on Gillingham, west of the important naval base at Chatham. Without doubt, owing to fighter attacks and AA fire – the Thames and Medway gunners had fired 227 rounds in just 15 minutes, forcing the enemy formation to turn east – bombing had been disrupted and whatever the aim of the operation was, it failed.

Shortly before 16.00 hrs, RDF indicated another build-up of enemy aircraft over the Pas-de-Calais and significant German air activity over the Channel. At 15.55 hrs, several 11 Group squadrons were scrambled – but this was too late to intercept the first of two raids, '100+', which crossed the British coast over the North Foreland before flying due west to Gravesend, then withdrawing. At 16.10 hrs the Medway gunners opened up ineffectively at German fighters, although little damage was caused to the enemy's target: just one Admiralty oil tank was hit at Medway's Port Victoria, the resulting blaze quickly controlled.

With another heavy attack brewing, assistance was requested from 12 Group, which scrambled the five-squadron strong Duxford 'Big Wing' at 16.16 hrs. Earlier in the day, Squadron Leader Douglas R.S. Bader DSO and Bar DFC and Bar had led the wing on two patrols without meeting the enemy, and the legless commander, who had survived both leg amputations, had no intention of being left out of any action on this occasion. Despite orders to patrol Hornchurch at 20,000ft, the Big Wing patrolled from central London to Thameshaven at 24,000ft. Eleven squadrons of 11 Group were also scrambled, and at 16.45 hrs some forty German fighters swept in over Deal and headed for Maidstone. Nos. 66 and 92 Squadrons were patrolling at 20,000ft south of Maidstone and were the first defending units to intercept the enemy, which included the only eighteen serviceable Me 109s now available to II/JG 53. Amongst the Me 109 pilots was *Leutnant* Erich Bodendieck of 4/JG 53, the *Gruppe* technical officer, who was flying a new aircraft fitted with automatic pitch control. In the air, he would meet Flight Lieutenant Bob 'Oxo' Oxspring of 66 Squadron, who reported sighting the 109s north of RAF Hawkinge at 17.00 hrs:

> After coming down from 30,000 feet, Fibus Leader [author's note: Flight Lieutenant Ken Gillies, 'Fibus' being 66 Squadron's radio call sign] sighted and warned 92 Squadron of four or five Me 109s which were converging on them at the same height from the SE. [No.] 92 leader turned away,

> apparently for bombers which I did not see, and then Fibus Leader gave attack orders. E/A were climbing for thick cloud above. Nos 2 and 3 of leading Fibus Section (Blue) were rather out of position and I followed Fibus Leader after a Me 109. It was soon apparent that I could not keep pace, so I climbed after another 109 in fully fine pitch from his starboard and below. Green 2 [author's note: Pilot Officer Hubert 'Dizzy' Allen] kept with me as I maneuvered for position, so I knew my tail was guarded and concentrated on attack. After two very short bursts the Me 109, which obviously hadn't seen me, burst into flames. The pilot baled out …

Leutnant Bodendieck reckoned that his formation had been attacked by 'forty-three Spitfires, obviously under radar control'. The Me 109s were, he recalled, disadvantaged for once, being at 8,000m whilst the Spitfires were at 8,500m. The II/JG 53 *Kommandeur*, *Hauptmann* Günther Freiherr von Maltzahn, led the 109s in a steep climb for the clouds. Bodendieck, however, flying the aircraft with the automatic propeller, lagged behind:

> My aircraft plodded forward, gaining scarcely any height and even less speed. I felt totally helpless – for I couldn't escape by diving either, as the propeller would still have been set for cruising speed. I could only hope to slowly reach the clouds, knowing that the Spitfire was not as good as the 'Me' in a shallow climb. Meanwhile, Spitfires buzzed all around, using me for target practice, but they didn't come close enough until one of them dived beneath me and then pulled up, letting me fly through his burst of fire … He hit my tank, which was unprotected from below, and my aircraft caught fire. I had to get out – and I did. I let myself fall for a time before opening my parachute – for I didn't know if there were Poles amongst my attackers, who we knew were not above shooting at pilots in their parachutes.
>
> At about 8,000m I pulled the ripcord and recalled that the weather forecast had predicted upper winds of about 100 kph from the West, so I hoped that I would be blown across the Channel to land on the French side – but the wind was actually blowing parallel with the British coast, so after 30–35 minutes I came down in the Channel approximately two miles off Folkestone. Soon afterwards I was fished out of the water by the Coast Guard and taken to an artillery unit in Folkestone.
>
> They were very suspicious for I arrived wearing a white turtle-neck sweater, breeches and white knee socks, having lost my flying boots when I baled out. I had no ID on me, only a wallet with French and English (Guernsey pounds) money. The only clue that I was a military man was

the Iron Cross 1st Class, which was in my trouser pocket and only received earlier that afternoon.

Bodendieck's troublesome 109 crashed in Ash near Sandwich, the pilot seeing the war out as a POW.

Oxspring's wingman, Pilot Officer Hubert Allen, got another 109, as he recalled in *Ten Fighter Boys*, published in 1942:

> We suddenly intercepted some Me 109s over the coast and I protected Oxo's tail, while he got busy on one. It blew up after two short squirts, then we got together and went after four more. 'It's OK, pal', I called to Oxo, 'they're friendly, I think'.
>
> 'Mebbe [maybe] you're right', he replied, 'but we'll just make sure'.
>
> Then, 'Christ, they're 109s!'
>
> Up we went. I took on two, Oxo [took on] the other two. I squirted one and he went for home. Fastening onto the tail of the other I gave him a good one. His nose went down vertically. I followed. Down we screeched at 400 mph. We passed the coast, I squirted again, keeping a wary eye open for his boyfriend. Suddenly his speed dropped and I saw a stream of glycol. 'You poor blighter', I thought. Then I gave him a long one. Pieces fell off. He faltered, then hit the sea and vanished. I looked around but saw nothing, and so returned at zero feet feeling a prize shocker.

As previously explained, throughout the day only one Me 109 is known to have fallen into the sea, the unknown pilot of which (1/JG 54) being rescued by the *Seenotdienst*, so was Allen's victim *Gefreiter* Still of I/JG 77, who is listed as killed over southern England? We will never know.

Also, amongst the Me 109 pilots was *Oberleutnant* Ulrich Steinhilper of 3/JG 52, who claimed his first victory, a Spitfire, near Ashford. Years later, Steinhilper wrote,

> I really don't remember much about this first successful action at all. Other incidents are crystal clear but this first victory for me has been erased from my memory. Possibly it is a case that it was such an emotive experience that my mind had filtered it all out. For whatever reason I cannot remember any details at all.

That evening, the Germans claimed the destruction of at least six Spitfires – but only one was actually shot down: Pilot Officer John Mather of 66 Squadron, who baled out, his Spitfire crashing at Coldred, east of Ashford and inland of Dover; whether Steinhilper was responsible cannot be confirmed.

After the clash with the German fighters, Flight Lieutenant Ken Gillies was unable to reconnect with the rest of 66 Squadron but reported contact with 'a formation of He 111s [*sic*] flying North'. This was the main attack, although these were not Heinkels but Ju 88s of III/KG 77, a unit fresh to the battle, bound for Tilbury Docks – without a fighter escort. According to the log book of *Major* Adolf Galland, his JG 26 was tasked with escorting this force – but, clearly, something had gone badly wrong, because there was not a German fighter in sight. The bombers crossed the coast between Dover and the North Foreland at 17.15 hrs and headed for their target. Gillies reported that he

> climbed up into the sun and thin cloud with the object of diving onto E/A leader. When I got into position 3,000 feet above E/A formation I saw two squadrons of friendly fighters go in to attack [author's note: 41 and 92 Squadrons]. I ended the engagement and looked for enemy fighters, but there were none to be seen.
>
> I then dived on one E/A (He 111 [*sic*]) which had become separated from its formation, and carried out a stern attack. Whilst firing I saw rudder of E/A burst into flame and partially disintegrate. E/A's engines also began to emit smoke, and oil was then thrown onto my windscreen. During my approach for second attack another Spitfire, QV or QJ-B [author's note: 19 and 92 Squadrons respectively] fired at E/A.
>
> One crew baled out and shortly after E/A starboard engine caught fire. E/A then half-rolled, dived down and finally crashed in flames 34 miles bearing 140° from Eastchurch airfield.

This was a Ju 88 A-1 of 9/KG 77, which crashed at Cooling and was also attacked by and accredited to Sergeant Stanislav Plzak, a Czech, of 19 Squadron (see below); two crewmen were killed in the crash, and two others baled out and were captured.

No. 66 Squadron's Pilot Officer Crelin 'Bogle' Bodie also claimed a 'He 111' destroyed, and Pilot Officer Hugh Heron claimed a probable and a damaged bomber.

No. 92 Squadron was being led in the air by Flight Lieutenant Brian 'Kingpin' Kingcome who, according to 18-year-old Pilot Officer Geoffrey 'Boy' Wellum, 'was 92 Squadron'. After chasing von Maltzahn's Me 109s into cloud, Kingcome, 'Ganic Leader', sighted the bombers, which the Spitfires attacked from the starboard beam. Kingcome passed through the enemy formation at high speed, firing as he went, knocking pieces off a Ju 88 before attacking another, which spiralled down, damaged. Next, he found a Ju 88 streaming glycol, having already been hit by a defending fighter, which Kingcome attacked from above and watched it spin into the sea off the Isle of Sheppey. Pilot Officer Howard Hill, a 20-year-old New Zealander, attacked another Ju 88, which also crashed into the sea 7 miles east of Shoeburyness. The Spitfire pilot saw two of the enemy crew in the water and gallantly remained overhead guiding a motorboat to rescue them. No. 92 Squadron's only casualty in this interception was Flying Officer James Paterson, also a New Zealander, who was shot-up when attacking a Ju 88 and forced-landed at Debden, unhurt.

At 17.15 hrs, 41 Squadron was up from Rochford and the Hornchurch satellite went into action over the Isle of Sheppey; Pilot Officer Robert 'Bob' Beardsley DFC found two Me 109s at 15,000ft, scoring hits before watching both dive away, vertically. Pilot Officer Eric Aldous also claimed a 109 damaged, north of Dover, and Sergeant Edward Darling damaged a Ju 88 over Chatham; the squadron suffered no loss.

On this occasion, Squadron Leader Douglas Bader and the Duxford Wing would not be disappointed: AA fire bursting above cloud indicated the presence of enemy aircraft below. Leaving the Spitfires patrolling above cloud, Bader led his Hurricanes down through it – in search of action, as described by 242 (Canadian) Squadron's combat report:

> [No.] 12 Group Wing turned NW and sighted E/A flying in two formations close together about twenty – thirty E/A in each, unescorted, at 15[,000]–17,000 feet. They were approaching first bend of Thames West of Estuary, near Gravesend, and were South of Thames when attacked. Attack was launched in a dive from East to West, turning North into the enemy. Conditions were favourable to 12 Group wing which was screened from above by cloud – while E/A presented excellent target against white cloud base.
>
> Red 1, Squadron Leader [Douglas] Bader, made a quarter attack turning astern at leading three Ju 88s, hitting the left-hand one of this section. This Ju 88 turned in left-hand dive with port engine afire and disappeared down towards North bank of Estuary West of Thameshaven.

This Ju 88, of 8/KG 77, crashed off Sheerness. This machine had previously been damaged by Spitfires of 92 Squadron and also featured in the combat reports of both Pilot Officer Edward Pilch and Pilot Officer Wlodzimierz Karwowski both of 302 (Polish) Squadron.

The 242 (Canadian) Squadron report continued,

> Red 1 lost about 3,000 feet, regained control and proceeded SE and found a lone Do 17 [*sic*]. He closed to short range and fired short burst. E/A did not return fire; instead rear gunner baled out immediately, getting his parachute entangled in tailplane. The *Dornier* immediately fell in succession of steep dives and two other members of crew baled out. The E/A disappeared into vertical dive into cloud at 4[,000]–6,000 feet and Red One considers it crashed either in estuary or South of it, near Sheerness.

Again, this raider, another 8/KG 77 machine, was also attacked by various other RAF fighter pilots, including Pilot Officer Howard Hill of 92 Squadron and Flying Officer Jan Kowalski and Sergeant Edward Paterek of the Duxford Wing's 302 (Polish) Squadron, and crashed into the sea, off the River Nore. Later, Bader recounted his impression of this combat during a MOI radio broadcast:

> At one time you could see planes going down on fire all over the place, and the sky seemed full of parachutes. It was sudden death that morning, because our fighters shot them to blazes. One unfortunate German rear-gunner baled out of the Do 17 I attacked, but his parachute caught on the tail. There he was, swinging helplessly, with the aircraft swooping and diving and staggering all over the sky, being pulled about by the man hanging by his parachute from the tail. That bomber went crashing into the Thames Estuary, with the swinging gunner still there.

Although Bader's Hurricane was fitted with a cine gun camera, he inadvertently switched on the navigation lights in error, so unfortunately the combat went unrecorded. This enemy bomber was also attacked by 249 Squadron's Pilot Officer George Barclay, who incorrectly identified it as a 'He 111' and who saw his bullets

> rake the fuselage from the pilot's cockpit to the tail. Bits flew off the fuselage, an open parachute came out of the top of the fuselage and caught on to the rear gun position, and a yellow rubber boat flew out of the fuselage. The Heinkel [*sic*] then dived vertically through the clouds.

Bader's Pilot Officer William 'Willie' McKnight, a Canadian, Red 2, reported having dived on a 'Do 17 [*sic*]' from above and behind, setting the starboard engine ablaze and watching the crew bale out, this probably being the first bomber, actually a Ju 88, attacked by his leader. McKnight then joined a Spitfire attacking a Ju 88, the crew of which also baled out, their bomber crashing north of the Thames Estuary. It is likely that this was an aircraft of 9/KG 77 also attacked by 19 Squadron's Sergeant Stanislav Plzak, which crashed near Basildon.

During 242 (Canadian) Squadron's first diving attack, Pilot Officer Norman Campbell, Red 3, a Canadian, overshot before firing at a Ju 88, which he left falling out of formation with both engines alight. He then engaged another Ju 88, at close range, which had already been attacked by a Spitfire, again watching his target erupt in flame. Red 3 then attacked a third Ju 88 but his Hurricane was hit by return fire. Breaking away, Campbell turned to assist a Spitfire that was attacking a bomber nearby, engaging the enemy aircraft, which he reported seeing falling in flames. Other 242 (Canadian) Squadron pilots reported similarly hectic multiple combats.

The Hurricanes of 310 (Czech) Squadron had followed their leader, Flight Lieutenant Jerrard Jeffries into the attack, who shared a 'Do 17 [*sic*]' with Pilot Officer Vaclav 'Vic' Bergman, Pilot Officer Emil Fechtner and Sergeant Eduard Prchal (probably the 9/KG 77 Ju 88, which crashed at Cooling).

Flight Lieutenant Wilf Clouston, a New Zealander and commander of 'B' Flight, led 19 Squadron into action, setting a Ju 88's starboard engine on fire himself. The crew baled out, the Spitfire pilot watching their bomber crash behind a row of houses. This was the aircraft of *Major* Kleh, the III/KG 77 *Gruppenkommandeur*, who was killed when his Ju 88 crashed at Eastry Mill – having also been attacked by three other 19 Squadron pilots, namely Flight Lieutenant Walter 'Jack' ('Farmer') Lawson DFC, Pilot Officer Wallace 'Jock' Cunningham and Sergeant David Lloyd. Flight Sergeant Harry Steere also reported attacking a 'He 111 [*sic*]', which had already been engaged by Flying Officer Leonard 'Ace' Haines DFC, Green 1, this raider crashing on the Isle of Sheppey. Flight Sergeant George C. 'Grumpy' Unwin DFM and Bar shot down a Me 110, which both he and a 66 Squadron pilot confirmed crashed near Eastchurch. There were, however, no Me 110 losses that day, and so this was actually the same Ju 88 attacked by Steere. Pilot Officer František 'Dolly' Doležal, a Czech, reported attacking a 'Heinkel [*sic*]', which he watched 'spin into the sea', in reality this being one of four Ju 88s that crashed into the water. Plzak claimed a 'Heinkel [*sic*]', which crashed near Gillingham, this being the Ju 88 downed at Cooling. Lawson, however, forced-landed at Eastchurch airfield, having been hit in the glycol tank, but was unhurt and 19 Squadron was otherwise intact.

Above the clouds, at high altitude, 611 Squadron's Spitfires held off some Me 109s, 'without', according to the ORB, 'firing a shot'.

Back at Duxford there was jubilation. Such a successful interception of bombers without interference by escorting Me 109s was a gift. The Duxford

Wing's claims, however, to coin Air Chief Marshal Hugh Dowding's phrase, were 'more thoughtful wishing':

19 Squadron: 5 destroyed, 3 shared and 1 probable
242 (Canadian) Squadron: 12 destroyed
302 Squadron: 7 destroyed, 2 shared and 1 probable
310 (Czech) Squadron: 1 shared destroyed
611 Squadron: 0

Total: 24 destroyed, 6 shared, 2 probables and 1 damaged.

In total, the enemy lost eight Ju 88s in this engagement, the Duxford Wing having certainly had a hand in the destruction of six – a far cry from the twenty-four destroyed with which it was credited. In fact, the overclaiming ratio on this occasion was around 4:1. The wing itself had suffered just two aircraft damaged, the pilots of which safely forced-landed. Needless to say, the inevitable congratulatory signals were sent to 242 (Canadian) Squadron (but none of the Big Wing's other units) by both the Secretary of State for Air and the CAS.

From the German perspective, this operation was another failure. The weight of attack was incomparable to that of just three days earlier, and what the enemy was trying to achieve is questionable. Little damage was caused by bombing and the unescorted Ju 88s had suffered accordingly. By now, German bomber losses were mounting and the *Kampfgeschwadern* on the Channel coast were reaching a critical stage, in that it could not continue taking such losses by day for much longer. These comparatively ineffective bombing raids confirm, in fact, the enemy's inability to continue heavily attacking London by day, the objective now apparently being more focused on bringing Fighter Command to battle with large numbers of Me 109s. If the bombardment of London had failed to force Britain to seek terms, these latest half-hearted attacks were never going to do so.

Further west, the only action was had by RAF Tangmere's 213 Squadron, at 18.00 hrs, when Flight Lieutenant James Strickland, commanding 'B' Flight, damaged a Ju 88 whilst patrolling a convoy some 10 miles south of Selsey Bill.

By this time, there were two Spitfire conversion units in England, 5 OTU at Aston Down near Stroud in Gloucestershire, and 7 OTU at Hawarden in Chester. The final action of the day would not be fought by a fighter squadron but by the latter training unit. Both of these OTUs had already seen action during the Battle of Britain, Spitfires of 5 OTU having also engaged the Ju 88 brought down by ferry pilot Pilot Officer Alec Bird on 25 July 1940 and 7 OTU's pilots destroyed a He 111 on 14 August 1940, a Ju 88 on 7 September 1940.

At 19.30 hrs on 18 September 1940, a section of Spitfires scrambled from Hawarden, as Flying Officer G.F. Brotchie reported,

> I took off with my Section … Shortly after take-off, No 2 had to return to the aerodrome with engine trouble. I continued to climb to a height of 10,000 feet and spotted some AA fire over Liverpool. I then received a message from Control to say that bandits were reported over Liverpool at 8,000 feet. I turned towards Liverpool and almost immediately received a message that there was a bandit over base at 8,000 feet. I turned again, towards base, and received a further message that there were eight bandits at various heights. It was just after this message that I sighted the E/A at about 20,000 feet and some distance apart, flying South over Hoylake. No 3 broke off and chased one, while I went after the other.
>
> I chased the E/A down the coast of Wales, climbing all the time. At about 20,000 feet I gradually closed on the aircraft. At 250 yards I was sitting on its tail and on the point of opening fire when the E/A spotted me and dived steeply towards the ground. I followed, on its tail, firing about four long bursts. His rear-gunner only replied with one burst. His dive gradually got steeper and at about 4,000 feet he dived through some low cloud almost vertically. I eased out of my dive slightly and followed him down through cloud and was just in time to see him dive into the sea, off the coast of Anglesey.
>
> No flames were seen to come from the machine, so I judged the E/A to be either out of control or that the pilot had been killed, the speed at the time he entered cloud was 350 mph. As it was now dark I climbed back over the clouds and returned to the aerodrome.

No such loss, however, can be identified in Luftwaffe records.

From 21.00 hrs onwards, some 200 German bombers intruded over Britain, attacking London, Liverpool and Bristol – in direct contrast to the situation by day, the enemy suffered no nocturnal losses.

For RAF Coastal Command, it had been a typical day of the usual routine sorties – and an extraordinary one. On the evening of 15 September 1940, the British Overseas Airways Empire flying boat *Clare*, having left Poole two days before, took-off from Foynes in neutral Eire, bound for New York. Arriving the following day, the civilian pilots were bedazzled by New York's twinkling night lights:

> We had left the pitch-black cities of Britain, lit only by searchlights, bomb flashes and fires, but full of people confident of victory. We had arrived at

> a city sparkling with light, where, it seemed to us, the number of people who had any hopes in Britain's survival, though increasing, was still very small. We met little feeling that it was anything more than stubbornness, or that the fight would not soon be ended, though the news of the great victory of 15 September, so amazing that many could scarcely believe it, was flooding the city with a faint new hope.

Those very same British Overseas Airways Empire pilots had taken with them bundles of British newspapers, and on 18 September 1940 the *New York Post* headlined 'London Newspapers in Business as Usual'. On the same day, *Clare* returned from America to be escorted to safety by Coastal Command aircraft. Elsewhere, in broad daylight, a 53 Squadron Blenheim of Coastal Command's 53 Squadron bombed Le Touquet, and by night Blenheims attacked shipping at Den Helder and Beauforts unsuccessfully launched torpedos at the SS *Europa* at Wilhelmshaven. RAF Bomber Command's daylight sorties were minimal, owing to the lack of cloud cover – but by night the force would suffer its heaviest losses of the war so far when heavy raids were mounted on the invasion ports and communication centres in Germany; two Blenheims disappeared without trace, two Hampdens and two Wellingtons were lost, as were three Whitleys.

Daily Home Intelligence Report:

> Rumours of damage to London, some accurate but many exaggerated, are common in the provinces and the Northern region comments that the BBC's revelation on Saturday evening that a bomb fell on Madame Tussaud's was regarded as 'the most humorous remark on the wireless this year'; everyone had known about it for two days.
>
> The rumour that invasion was attempted a few days ago and failed with considerable loss to the Germans now reported to be causing excitement in the Midlands.
>
> Though strong demands for reprisals on German civilians are still reported, there are many who are satisfied that the wisest policy is to continue attacking invasion objectives.

London Region:

> Londoners remain outwardly calm and are putting up with difficulties extremely well, but there are still numbers of people anxious to get out. One Earl's Court Square has practically evacuated itself after bombing there; others in less fortunate positions need schemes to help them. A certain amount of panic shown in individual cases where people have had

> horrible experiences but this is often due to temporary physical reaction. There are still criticisms about Rest Centres – inadequately staffed and equipped – although some districts report gradual improvement. Re-billeting of homeless still causing difficulties and organization reported to be bad in some areas, e.g. Chelsea, St Pancras. ARP warden in East End and also social workers in East End feel Mayfair billeting does not solve the problems of homeless East Enders – they feel homesick and lonely and food prices are beyond them … Increase in unemployment reported in North London as many industries are without facilities for carrying on (water etc), even where property remains undamaged; this is causing a certain amount of anxiety and distress.

Thursday, 19 September 1940

High winds, low cloud and heavy rain over England greatly reduced enemy air activity, which was largely confined to isolated raids by solitary aircraft. On this otherwise inauspicious day, however, British intelligence intercepted and decoded a signal confirming that Hitler had postponed Operation *Seelöwe* 'indefinitely'. Consequently, this represents another date on which the Battle of Britain could arguably be legitimately considered to have concluded – because enemy air operations going forward were no longer appended to an invasion plan. Nonetheless, the air fighting continued, although the German daylight bombing campaign had clearly failed.

News of *Seelöwe*'s postponement, however, appears not to have reached Hitler's *Reichsminister* of Foreign Affairs, Joachim von Ribbentrop, who on this day arrived in Rome for a conference with the Italians. Benito Mussolini's Foreign Minister, Count Galeazzo Ciano, found the German *Reichsminister* elated owing to the military alliance imminently to be signed by Germany and Japan. Ciano commenting thus regarding the war with Britain:

> [Joachim] von Ribbentrop says that the weather has been very bad, and that the clouds even more than the RAF have prevented final success. However, the invasion will take place anyway as soon as there are a few days of fine weather. The landing is ready and possible. English territorial defence is non-existent. A single German division will suffice to bring about a complete collapse.

Hitler clearly thought otherwise.

The weather on this historic day was unsuitable for large scale raids and so the Luftwaffe reverted to sending lone aircraft on nuisance raids against targets in south-east England, Liverpool and South Wales. Indeed, seventy German bombers intruded over Britain but, again, little damage was caused. This activity, although on a reduced scale, still kept the defenders busy.

At North Weald, 249 Squadron's pilots were being scrambled in pairs, Pilot Officer Hugh John Beazley and Pilot Officer George Barclay making up Red Section, as Red 1 and 2 respectively. At 10.10 hrs, the two Hurricane pilots were at 20,000ft over 10/10ths cloud, south of the Thames Estuary, when the controller informed them of a bandit 10,000ft below. The Hurricanes immediately dived and sighted the raider, a Ju 88, above the clouds below. Both pilots attacked, noting their bullets hitting the fuselage and port engine, which streamed black smoke and glycol, then both engines erupted into flame. No evading action was taken, leading Beazley to conclude that Red Section had taken the Ju 88 'completely by surprise'. The victory was shared jointly by the two British pilots, when an aircraft was reported to have crashed into the Channel off Deal.

No. 302 (Polish) Squadron's 'B' Flight was patrolling the Mildenhall area at 11.00 hrs and sighted another Ju 88, as Flying Officer Julian Kowalski, Blue 3, reported,

> On sighting the E/A I attacked simultaneously with Blue 1, getting in a short burst of half a second at 250 yards. As the distance between myself and the Ju 88 increased I pulled the emergency boost and after another minute of flight was within 80 yards of the Ju 88. I got in five bursts of about half a second. From the Ju 88 fuel poured out and covered my aircraft. From the upper rear gun turret I encountered very strong MG fire. Seeing that my fire hadn't got much effect I got in two more bursts of half a second at about 80 yards. The aircraft caught fire after my second burst and it began to dive steeply through cloud. I followed closely but none of the crew jumped out. After gliding for about two minutes it crashed to earth about four miles NE of Brandon. I landed at Duxford at 1145 hrs having taken off at 1025 hrs. Three of my guns did not fire at all. The rest of my ammo was fired.

This Ju 88 belonged to 1/KG 77, and crashed at Culford School, Bury St Edmunds; three of the crew were killed, the fourth man being wounded and captured. Kowalski's need to use emergency boost to catch the Ju 88 is of interest: the Hawker Hurricane Mk I's maximum speed, at 15,650ft, was 324 mph, the Ju 88's 280 mph at 18,050ft. Tony Pickering, an 18-year-old sergeant pilot in 501 Squadron during the Battle of Britain, once recalled that

> I came across a lone Ju 88 somewhere over Kent, heading back to sea. I thought it would be no problem to catch up the Hun, press the button

> and that would be it. I slotted in behind and ran flat out to catch him. Suddenly he just pulled away from me, just left me standing, had at least an extra 50 mph on me, and that was the last I saw of him. The Hurricane just wasn't fast enough, we even used to bend our throttle levers in flight trying to squeeze a bit more out of the Merlin. A Spitfire would have caught that Ju 88.

At 11.05 hrs, Flying Officer Count Manfred Czernin DFC, leading Red Section of the Debden based 17 Squadron's 'A' Flight, was patrolling convoy ARENA off Orford Ness. Vectored onto a Ju 88 flying north at 14,000ft, Czernin attacked head-on, causing smoke to issue from the bomber's port engine, which 'stopped dead'. Sergeant Glyn Griffiths, Red 2, and Sergeant Leonard Bartlett, Red 3, also opened fire, resulting in the raider crashing into the sea 10 miles east of ARENA.

Like 249 Squadron, the Spitfires of 92 Squadron were also operating in pairs, Flying Officer Allan Wright and Pilot Officer Howard Hill intercepting a Ju 88 over their Biggin Hill base. The Spitfire pilots attacked the bomber, a game of cat and mouse developing as their target used cloud cover to escape. The last Wright and Hill saw of their quarry was 'flying over Dover with smoke pouring from both engines' [ORB].

The next German aircraft to come down in England, however, did so without a shot being fired. Whilst engaged on a weather reconnaissance sortie, the port engine of a 4(F)/121 Ju 88 failed, forcing the pilot to land on Oakington airfield, north of Cambridge; the crew, who delivered an otherwise intact Ju 88 to RAF air intelligence, were all captured unhurt.

To the west, the 10 Group Spitfires of 152 Squadron were also operating in pairs, Ju 88s also being active over the West Country:

> Green Section … up from [RAF] Warmwell were vectored to Ju 88 at 10,000 feet over the Channel. R/T of Green 1 (Pilot Officer Dudley Williams) was unserviceable and when he became separated from Green 2 (Sergeant Kenneth Holland) he returned to Warmwell. Green 2 saw Ju 88 ahead on the right, two miles away. The interception was due almost entirely to the excellent instructions given by the Controller. Green 2 gave chase and made alternate quarter attacks from left and right from 300–200 yards, aiming first at gunners' positions and then at each engine. E/A took slight evasive action but mainly concentrated on heading for cloud in a southerly direction. Return fire ceased after the first attack. White and black puffs of smoke began to appear after the second attack. Green 2 continued to attack and eventually the E/A, which was now at about 8,000 feet, dived

vertically towards the sea with both engines on fire. As his ammunition was now finished and his engine was missing slightly, Green 2 flew North, landing at Portsmouth aerodrome. He there checked his engine, found it to be in order, and returned to Warmwell. [ORB]

Sergeant Kenneth Holland's combat signified the last daylight action. One Ju 88 had been shot down over England whilst another had landed on a British airfield due to engine trouble, and three more were missing, presumably shot down into the sea; four Ju 88s returned to France having been shot-up by RAF fighters. Without a doubt, the Ju 88 was the Luftwaffe's best bomber, being heavily armed and fast, and such losses were a poor return against whatever damage these nuisance raids had caused. For once, Fighter Command's pilots actually under claimed: four Ju 88s were considered destroyed and one recorded as a 'probable'. For the defenders, it was a rare day indeed as no aircraft or aircrew were lost.

Throughout the day, Coastal Command's squadrons flew their usual patrols and escorted twenty-three vital convoys, and by night FAA Swordfish struck at shipping in Cherbourg harbour. The Me 109s of I/JG 53 were up protecting a German convoy off the French coast, the *Staffeln* taking it in turns to provide air cover. At 17.25 hrs, *Oberfeldwebel* Franz Kaiser of 2/JG 53 intercepted a Blenheim of RAF Detling's 53 Squadron, shooting the bomber down off Berck-sur-Mer; the three-man crew remain missing.

A lack of cloud over the Continent led to eleven 2 Group Blenheims aborting their daylight raids on the invasion ports, although one did bomb Dunkirk whilst other Blenheims reconnoitred the North Sea. By night, bad weather saw only Bomber Command's 5 Group Hampdens and 4 Group Whitleys engaged on operations: the former bombed the Dortmund-Ems Canal and shipping off the Belgian coast and mined the Gironde; the Whitleys attacked marshalling yards at Mannheim. No losses were suffered.

Daily Home Intelligence Report:

People are not so cheerful today … There is also evidence that physical tiredness is beginning to have an effect on nerves.

Last night the number of people taking shelter in underground stations greatly increased.

Rumours and exaggerated stories circulate widely in London and the provinces. The most important subjects are:

Terrors of the new magnetic mines dropped by parachute.

Invasion (in progress, repulsed, etc).

Spies (Fifth Column activities in shelters, signaling [*sic*] with torches etc, etc).
Damage and casualties in London.
Today, several people reported a 'petition for peace' sent to the Prime Minister from the East End. This may be due to the petitions which the People's Vigilance Committee groups, etc. are organizing in shelters.

Friday, 20 September 1940

A significant advantage enjoyed by the German fighter pilots was the ability to climb to combat altitude before reaching England. Pilot Officer Geoffrey Wellum of Biggin Hill's 92 Squadron remembered that

> During September and October 1940 the 109s were always active in the Biggin Hill Sector, and caused problems. I recall that they were always above us as we never seemed to be scrambled in time to get enough height. Our climb was always a desperate, full-throttle affair, but we never quite got up to them. I did manage to get a crack at two Me 109s on one patrol, but although I saw strikes I could only claim them as damaged.

The enemy's free roving and high-altitude fighter sweeps were certainly effective – but could be ignored. RDF, whilst providing essential advance warning of likely enemy numbers and direction of travel towards the British coast, was unable to identify whether approaching enemy formations comprised bombers or fighters, or both. Moreover, RDF, at the time, was only outward looking, and of no help, therefore, once the Germans had crossed the coast. It was then that the eyes and ears of the Observer Corps, and other visual sightings, became invaluable. Fighter sweeps, if identified as such, could be ignored, because these were only dangerous if engaged by RAF fighters – which was, of course, what the Germans wanted. Far better, then, for the defenders to ignore these incursions and watch the enemy waste time and fuel. This, though, now led to a sudden change in Luftwaffe tactics.

To ensure a reaction from the defenders, *Reichsmarschall* Hermann Göring ordered that one *Staffel* in every *Gruppe* would become fighter-bombers – *Jabos*. This, however, affected one third of his available fighter force, and was an unpopular decision with senior fighter leaders already lacking the resources necessary to achieve aerial superiority. For so long, auxiliary fuel tanks had been requested, to extend range, but instead bombs arrived. The tactical thinking behind this order was that if German formations included *Jabos*, the RAF would have to consider every sweep a potential threat and respond to it – sound in theory but not when resources were so limited.

Major Adolf Galland, *Kommodore* of JG 26:

> The fighter-bombers were put into action in so great a hurry that there was hardly any time to give the pilots bombing training, and most of them dropped their first bomb in a raid on London or on other targets in England. We had a total of 250 fighter-bombers. The Me 109 carried a 500lb High Explosive bomb … No great effect could be achieved with that … the fighter pilots were 'browned off' with carrying cargo and glad to get rid of their bombs anywhere.
>
> The fighter-bomber raids were carried out in the following way: each *gruppe* [*sic*] escorted its own bombers. The approach altitude was about 18,000 feet. At the start, we let the fighter-bombers fly in bomber formation, but it was soon apparent that the enemy fighters could concentrate fully on the bombers, so we distributed them in small units throughout the entire formation and thus brought them fairly safe over their target area. This type of raid had no more than nuisance value. The passive behaviour towards enemy fighters, the feeling of inferiority when we attacked, because of loss of speed, manoeuvrability and rate of climb, added to the unconvincing effect of single bombs scattered over wide areas, combined to ruin the morale of the German fighter pilot, already low because of the type of escorting that had previously had to be undertaken.

Suffice it to say that the *Jagdwaffe* was bitterly critical of the OKL over this move.

The first 'tip n' run' raid, as they widely became known, occurred this day, when twenty-two II/LG 2 fighter-bombers, protected by numerous fighters of JG 2, 3, 26, 27, 51 and 53, attacked London. The *Jabos* crossed the English coast at 25,000ft, making the intrusion appear to be a fighter sweep, then descended to 12,000ft. Not knowing of the enemy's new plan, the RAF controllers did not react at first and were surprised when bombs were suddenly dropped indiscriminately on the capital. Having dropped their bombs, the fighter-bombers returned to France, unchallenged by the defenders. Meanwhile, the escorting Me 109s still lurked over south-east England, unfettered now by escort duties and able to hunt freely.

Thirteen Spitfires of 222 and 603 Squadrons scrambled from Hornchurch at 10.55 hrs with orders to patrol base at 20,000ft. From on high, the British fighters were spotted by Galland – a deadly adversary indeed.

Sergeant Reg Johnson of 222 Squadron's 'B' Flight:

> Our Blue Section was led by Pilot Officer John Broadhurst, followed by Pilot Officer [Herbert Laurence] Laurie Whitbread, myself and one other in Green Section. We climbed to the suicidal height of 14,000 feet and stooged around in tight vic formation with only one pair of eyes available to scan the sky in front, perhaps over 200°. I do not think that we deserved to be jumped, but we certainly invited it. We were banking gently to the left, which allowed me at No 3 to look over the top of No 1, and I shouted the warning 'Bandits, 2 o'clock above – attacking!' I turned over and dived straight down. There is no way that Pilot Officer Whitbread could even have seen the enemy, formating as he was on the aircraft to his left and with three-quarters of his head and back to the attackers. When I left it was his right side facing the 109s, which were already in firing range. I can only assume that having received my warning he too rolled to his right, exposing his left side to the enemy and was hit before he could commence his dive. It was a tragedy.

According to the official report, over Rochester 222 Squadron's 'B' Flight was attacked from above by thirty Me 109s, Pilot Officer Herbert Laurence Whitbread being singled out and shot down by Galland himself. Mortally wounded, the 26-year-old Ludlovian managed to crash-land his Spitfire, skidding across Hermitage Road, Higham, the wrecked aircraft coming to rest in a stagnant pond. The pilot, however, was somehow thrown clear and found dead. Ludlow is a picturesque market town in Shropshire, and 'Laurie' was the small community's first fatal casualty of the Second World War. When writing to his bereaved parents on 3 October 1940, 222 Squadron's CO, Squadron Leader John Hill, spared them the actual details, stating that

> He was killed instantly by a bullet from an enemy aircraft when doing his bit in defence of his country. His passing is a great loss to us; he had been in the squadron since its formation and was always most popular, having a quiet and efficient disposition and charming manner.

Indeed, Johnson recalled the young officer as

> a very brave young man of the highest quality. Naturally courageous, he was always prepared to give his life for his country, but it was taken away from him due to the practice of unsatisfactory tactics.

Pilot Officer Herbert Laurence Whitbread was buried in the cemetery at Ludlow, his old master at the local grammar school, George Merchant, later wrote that afterwards

> we turned and went back and left him alone in his glory, with his name and rank on the gravestone and the proud badge of the RAF which he had carried through peril to the stars … He was the kind of boy you noticed first and remembered afterwards if you saw him talking in a group of his fellows, though he was probably saying less than any of the others. He was the kind of boy one does not forget and is glad to have known.

Of casualties, 222 Squadron's Sergeant Norman Ramsay had this to say:

> People missing or killed at that stage of the battle meant little to me. I had joined 222 [Squadron] from 610 [Squadron] at Biggin Hill after we had lost ten, yes, ten, pilots, so I was well-used to the disappearing faces. Having been shot down myself I had learned to survive, to get the experience necessary for survival.

Returning to the fighting on 20 September 1940, Pilot Officer William Assheton of 222 Squadron was also shot down; the Spitfire pilot baled out, landing in Latchington and was admitted to St Peter's Hospital, Maldon, suffering from slight burns; his aircraft crashed at West Hanningfield. Pilot Officer Eric Edsall was also shot-up but was unhurt; he returned safely to base although his Spitfire was badly damaged and careered through the perimeter fence on landing.

In response, 222 Squadron's only combat claim was made by Flight Lieutenant Eric 'Tommy' Thomas, commanding 'A' Flight:

> At 1115 hrs I was climbing to patrol with five other aircraft when at 25,000 feet a squadron of yellow-nosed Me 109s attacked us from the sun in a quarter-attack. I saw tracer shells going past Pilot Officer [Eric] Edsall and I broke away, getting on the tail of a 109. I opened fire from astern at approximately 200 yards and gave two long bursts of five seconds each. I then saw a trail of white vapour come from the enemy aircraft. I then broke away and carried out a deflection shot at two more Me 109s circling round in tight formation, but saw no result as I had to break away due to being attacked myself.

The enemy fighter was claimed as damaged in the combat, which occurred over Sittingbourne. White smoke, however, is coolant, without which the engine overheats, so it is possible that Thomas's target was a machine of 7/JG 53, which forced-landed at Boulogne, having managed to limp back across the Channel.

No. 603 Squadron made no combat claims.

At 10.40 hrs, Flight Lieutenant Ted Graham of 72 Squadron led eight Spitfires up from Biggin Hill with orders to patrol Maidstone, in company with 66 Squadron.

Pilot Officer Robert Deacon-Elliott, 72 Squadron:

> I recall this date vividly. At the last moment before scramble, Operations HQ requested two pilots of 72 Squadron to proceed to Hawkinge and escort an Anson aircraft with Army officers aboard who were spotting for shells landing on the French coast fired from big guns in the Dover/Folkestone area. Names were put into a hat and mine, together with Flying Officer Norman Robson came out. At this point [Pilot Officer Dennis] 'Dutch' Holland, a very dose friend of mine, approached me. He was worried about the hazardous nature of the mission and volunteered to take my place. Naturally I said 'No', as my name had come out of the hat.
>
> Whilst escorting the Anson at very low-level, reports from Operations warned us of enemy aircraft in the area, but at much greater heights. However, the Anson pilot decided to get back to Hawkinge quickly – yes, very quickly! We saw him push his nose down to sea level and beat it for base. He must have exceeded the Anson's speed limit because on seeing the aircraft at Hawkinge I noticed that the entire fuselage fabric was stripped to the extent that you could see through the aircraft. Mission accomplished it was back to Biggin Hill.

At 11.20 hours over Canterbury, Pilot Officer Dennis 'Dutch' Holland was shot down by a Me 109. Although badly wounded he managed to bale out and was admitted to hospital. Before he died, his last words to the doctor were 'I'm all right, old pal, "Dutchy" can take it.'

Deacon-Elliott, who would survive the war and leave the service an air vice-marshal:

> Back at Biggin Hill I learned of 'Dutch's' death, which, at the time, was attributed to a direct hit by our own guns. A ghastly thought – had I accepted his offer to take my place we may both still be here today.

At 12.10 hrs, 25,000–30,000ft over the Ashford/Canterbury area, 72 Squadron, still on patrol, met fifty Me 109s. Afterwards, Sergeant William Rolls submitted the following report:

> I was Red 2 in a section told to intercept the enemy fighters. We took off at 1040 [hrs] and after having completed a patrol by ourselves were

> instructed to rejoin the rest of the Squadron as the leading Section. We did this and met the enemy near Canterbury. We were climbing up towards one batch of Me 109s when we were warned by our rearguard of another lot diving down on us. We kept climbing into the sun and the rest of the Squadron had used evasive action to get rid of the Me 109s. I soon found myself over Ashford and unable to see any of my Squadron near me. I was flying along at 22,000 feet when I saw what appeared to be a Spitfire or Hurricane diving down to 16[,000]–18,000 feet and then climbing again. I decided to have a look at it so I got into a position so that I had the sun behind me and could see the machine clearly. As it came up in the climb I saw plainly that it was actually an Me 109 with a yellow nose and fin. I let it climb up again and waited, thinking perhaps it would dive again. It did so and then I dived out of the sun onto its tail and waited for it to start to climb before I pressed the tit to fire. I let it have about three seconds fire and the 109 did a stall turn to starboard and I followed it. I saw a large black piece break away from the side of the cockpit on the port side. I got it in my sights again as it turned and let it have another four seconds [*sic*] burst. This time I saw smoke and what appeared to be oil and water coming from underneath it. It turned to dive and as it did I let him have a final burst when the whole back of the cockpit dropped away and the rest dropped down towards cloud. This was at about 12,000 feet. I flew through the cloud and made for the aerodrome as I had only 10 gallons of petrol left. I watched the spot where the machine went in and it was near Wye, between a wood and lake so far as I could make out from my own position. I landed back with three gallons of petrol and a leaky glycol seal.

Rolls had shot down the only Me 109 to crash in England that day, a machine of 9/JG 27, which went down in Ospringe in Kent, killing the pilot, *Unteroffizier* Erich Clauser. Pilot Officer John 'Pancho' Villa, also of 72 Squadron, claimed a 109 damaged.

At 11.05 hrs, Squadron Leader Gerry Edge scrambled from Kenley with his 253 Squadron to patrol base at 10,000ft. Vectored to Maidstone, Yellow Section lost the rest of the squadron in cloud, emerging 5 miles east of Maidstone where the Hurricanes were attacked by twelve Me 109s. Red and Blue Sections were then flying at 14,000ft in vic formation and ordered to join friendly fighters above – only to be attacked from above, according to the ORB, by twenty 'He 113s [*sic*]'. The Hurricanes scattered and re-formed but were then dived upon by Spitfires, and once more became separated in cloud. During the action, two of 253 Squadron were shot down: Pilot Officer Anthony Barton crashed and was admitted to Ashford Hospital 'with slight wounds from cannon shell' [ORB], and Sergeant Robert Innes baled out safely. Sergeant Ernest Kee was also shot-up but returned safely to base, as Pilot Officer John Greenwood recalled,

> I remember being with Sergeant [Ernest] Kee and diving for our lives into cloud. As I recall he copped a little enemy fire and we landed together shortly afterwards having made no effort to locate the rest of the squadron. Kee's aircraft had a little fabric missing and a few holes. I think that I also stopped a .5 armour piercing bullet through my head armour, the core of the bullet lodging in my neck. It had only just penetrated but it was as sharp as a needle. I kept it as a souvenir for many years.

Barton and Innes had both been shot down by *Hauptmann* Johannes Seifert, *Staffelkapitän* of 3/JG 26. No. 253 Squadron inflicted no damage on the enemy in response.

No. 605 Squadron, up from RAF Croydon, was also attacked over Maidstone by 109s:

> Squadron did one patrol today and encountered only Me 109s which adopted different tactics to usual by flying alone in twos, threes or fours over a wide area which our pilots found very harassing, never knowing when they would swoop down on them. No losses, but Pilot Officer Głowacki's aircraft damaged Category II from cannon and machine-gun fire.

At 11.34 and 11.35 hours, the German *Oberkannone*, *Major* Werner Mölders, destroyed two Spitfires of 92 Squadron, up from Biggin Hill, over Dungeness: Pilot Officer Howard Hill was killed and Sergeant Peter Eyles was never seen again. These two victories were numbers 39 and 40 for Mölders and earned him the *Eichenlaub* to his *Ritterkreuz*, making him only the second Luftwaffe officer to receive this coveted decoration.

Flight Lieutenant Allan Wright, 92 Squadron:

> The squadron was split in half due to oxygen failure. The first half were surprised by Me 109s. Howard and Eyles, both of Green Section, were lost. I have a vivid picture in my mind of me leading Green Section on that day. After the split, the front two sections, led by the CO, Squadron Leader [Phillip James 'Judy'] Sanders, were left flying in a close formation of two vics in line astern. I happened to glance to my left and was amazed to see a 109 taking the place of the Spitfire that I expected to see there, a glance to the right showed another one! I immediately shouted 'BREAK!' and pulled up and around in a tight turn. The others probably reacted similarly. I

> noticed that we were immediately above a coastal town. I cannot remember what I did after the break, when flying at 200–300 mph one can, in just a few seconds, find oneself quite alone and unable to re-join the action.
>
> At that time, many squadrons, including ours, would be vectored towards our targets in a close formation of nine, comprising three vics with two weavers criss-crossing overhead and safeguarding the blind area behind the formation. Its advantage was that the 11 aircraft as a whole were very manoeuverable. The danger was that if anything happened to the weavers and they were unable to use their R/T, the rest of the Squadron would be utterly vulnerable. On this occasion, in the rush to scramble, one or more of the rear pilots could have failed to switch on their oxygen, or it may not have been working properly, so that in the confusion the first half were left unaware that no-one was guarding their tails. No oxygen at the height of Everest could put you to sleep without you even realising it. Very sad, especially about Howard Hill who had flown with our Squadron since the previous October.

No. 92 Squadron's Pilot Officer Trevor 'Wimpy' Wade, Red 2, attacked an Me 109 at 11.45 hrs, 27,000ft above Folkestone:

> Ganic Squadron was split up due to attack by Me 109s. I got on the tail of one and after a short burst the enemy aircraft dived away steeply. At about 4,000 feet it pulled out and started evasive tactics. After two–three minutes it headed south-east at 5,000 feet. I fired a number of short bursts from astern at 100–150 yards range but was unable to close any further. After doing evasive medium turns for a short period he pulled up steeply into cloud at 2,000 feet, 15 miles from the French coast after which I lost him. I had seen my ammunition going into the wings but without the desired effect.

No. 92 Squadron's CO, Squadron Leader Phillip James Sanders, also attacked an Me 109 at 11.45 hrs, firing 2,450 rounds at it:

> As Squadron Leader patrolling Dungeness I knew that there were enemy aircraft about and was weaving. At 27,000 feet, Blue Section, behind me, was attacked, so I broke quickly to the left and saw an Me 109 also turning left behind me. I gave one short burst about 120 yards from above and from the right. The enemy aircraft at once half rolled to the right and dived steeply for about 10,000 feet. He then pulled up and I got a good deflection shot at him from above and slightly behind. He half rolled again

> and dived. I fired intermittently at him on the way down and he did not pull out. I came out of the dive at 500 feet and he crashed into the sea about five miles south of Dymchurch and disappeared. I tried to re-group the Squadron and received instructions to return to base and land.

Squadron Leader Phillip James Sanders was also attacked during the combat and his Spitfire was damaged. He subsequently returned safely to Biggin Hill soaked in petrol from a ruptured fuel tank – only to burst into flames when lighting a cigarette shortly after landing. Fortunately, Sanders survived but was out of the battle from then on (hospitalised until October 1940, when he returned to operational duties it was to command the Defiant equipped 264 Squadron and participate in Britain's night-time defence).

The skirmish over, the *Jagdwaffe* retired to their French bases leaving behind just *Unteroffizier* Erich Clauser dead in the wreckage of his fighter. Fighter Command, however, had lost eight aircraft with four pilots killed and several others wounded. It was a salutary reminder of how dangerous the Me 109s could be. Nonetheless, successful though it had been, the bombing raid amounted to nothing more than a pin prick.

Coastal Command flew less sorties on this day. In addition to the twelve aircraft patrolling convoys, 217 Squadron's Ansons and six Blenheim fighters unsuccessfully attacked shipping off Brest, 53 Squadron raided Willemsoord harbour at dawn, and 59 Squadron hit the German airfields at Le Tréport, Saint-Aubin, Le Bois-Robert and Abbeville – one Blenheim was lost. In his report on the day's action, Luftwaffe intelligence officer *Hauptmann* Genst recorded that at 19.22 hrs (Continental time) a single Blenheim attacked the flak battery south of Dieppe, dropping two bombs: 'One *Unteroffizier* and three Mann dead, as well as three civilians dead and three injured'. The losses to the French civilian population through Allied bombings are usually overlooked – and yet sadly many lost their lives because of it.

At night, 59 Squadron attacked shipping off Cherbourg but results are unrecorded. Bomber Command also made a dawn sortie, three Fairey Battles attacking Cap Gris-Nez, but apart from a North Sea reconnaissance flight all other sorties were scrubbed owing to adverse weather. It would, however, be a busy night for Bomber Command, attacking invasion ports and targets in Germany; just one Wellington failed to return.

Daily Home Intelligence Report:

> In general, morale is excellent and in particular people are more cheerful today. The feeling of being in the front line stimulates many people and

puts them on their mettle in overcoming transport and shelter difficulties ... There is, however, evidence of increasing physical tiredness.

Taking shelter in underground stations continued last night. People were orderly but conditions were very insanitary. There is evidence that people do not intend to pay attention to official requests not to shelter there.

Saturday, 21 September 1940

After the events of the previous day, Fighter Command now had no choice but to react to every incoming German formation. Clearly, this would be exhausting, given the resources available and that burden, owing to the high-altitude nature of these operations, would largely fall on 11 Group's Spitfire squadrons. Again, however, the weather, documented by 501 Squadron at Kenley as a 'Thick ground haze and 6/10ths cloud at 6,000 feet', and '10/10ths cloud' in the morning by 602 Squadron at RAF Westhampnett, prevented a repetition of the previous day's attack. Instead, enemy operations were largely confined to the usual reconnaissance flights and nuisance raids by lone bombers. Once more, to spread resources and ensure that as many of these bandits could be intercepted, 11 Group's squadrons operated sections of pairs.

The first action of the day occurred at 08.30 hrs, when a lone Ju 88 attacked the important Hawker Hurricane producing factory on the south-west side of Brooklands aerodrome, which was also home to the Vickers-Armstrongs factory manufacturing Wellington bombers. Three SC250 bombs were dropped, two causing only slight damage whilst the third smashed through the factory roof and a wall at the far end, failed to explode and finally came to rest on the concrete driveway outside the erecting shed. The site had already been badly hit on 4 September 1940, when eighty-eight deaths were caused, and when this latest attack occurred, Lieutenant John Patton of the Royal Canadian Engineers was supervising the clearance of debris. As there was no bomb disposal unit at Brooklands, Patton volunteered to make the UXB safe and remove it. This was exceptionally brave because neither Patton nor his team of Home Guard volunteers had any knowledge of defusing live bombs. Realising that an explosion could severely affect the production of Hurricanes, Patton arranged a truck and cable, and when his CO, Captain D.W. Cunnington, arrived on the scene he was winching the bomb onto a make-shift sled of corrugated iron ready to tow the bomb to safety. Cunnington then drove the truck whilst Patton sat in the lorry, keeping watch on the device, which was lowered into an existing bomb crater 200 yards away, where the bomb exploded harmlessly the following day. For his incredible bravery and initiative, Patton was awarded the George Cross, and both Cunnington and Vickers-Home Guard section leader A.H. Tilyard-Burrows received George Medals.

The rest of the morning passed quietly by.

At Westhampnett, the Tangmere satellite was in action as 602 Squadron was brought to thirty-minutes readiness at 13.00 hrs, after a twenty-four-hour stand down, in anticipation that improving weather would bring action. At 14.05 hrs, Yellow Section, Pilot Officer Osgood 'Pedro' Hanbury, Pilot Officer Archibald Lyall and Sergeant James Gillies, took-off to patrol a convoy between RAF Selsey Bill and Bembridge. Further west, at RAF Middle Wallop in 10 Group, the two 238 Squadron Hurricanes comprising Yellow Section's Pilot Officer Charles Davis, Yellow 1, and Sergeant Eric Bann, Yellow 2, took-off at 14.24 hrs to patrol base. Davis then sighted a Ju 88 bombing Middle Wallop, which he attacked and 'hit the starboard engine and the E/A lost height rapidly' [ORB]. At 15.09 hrs, the same Ju 88, approached RAF Tangmere aerodrome at 2,000ft, from east-south-east. Lyall was 602 Squadron's Yellow Leader and attacked 'from head-on and slightly below', apparently stopping an engine – although it seems that Davis of 238 Squadron was already responsible for this damage. As the bomber lost height, Hanbury attacked, and the raider, of 3/LG 1, also engaged by Bofors guns, crash-landed at Old Fishbourne, Bosham, at 15.12 hrs, where the crew; it was an expensive loss for the enemy, considering that the aircraft's captain, *Oberleutnant* Karl Sodemann, was the 3/LG 1 *Staffelkapitän*.

At 14.45 hrs, Pilot Officer Peter Hairs of 501 Squadron took-off from Kenley on a solo flight to Gravesend airfield, sighting

> a Do 215 [*sic*] over the balloons at Brooklands but the AA barrage prevented him attacking it. This aircraft was later intercepted by Tangmere in a damaged condition. [ORB]

At 15.32 hrs, Green and Blue Sections of 602 Squadron's 'B' Flight scrambled from Westhampnett to patrol a convoy and base, whilst 'A' Flight were sent east, climbing to 12,000ft. Over Beachy Head, Green Section intercepted a Ju 88, which Green 1 and 3 attacked without result. Pilot Officer Lyall, Green 2, had been unable to keep up and after diving through cloud found and damaged a Do 17. 'A' Flight then attacked a Ju 88 10 miles off Brighton, all the pilots involved opening fire, damaging the machine before it disappeared into cloud. One of these may well have been the Brooklands raider seen by Hairs.

Lone German bombers were also active over South Wales and the Bristol Channel. At 16.58 hrs, the two pilots of 79 Squadron, Pilot Officer Thomas Parker, Red 1, and Pilot Officer George Peters, Red 2, were up from Pembury and sighted a Ju 88 15 miles south-west of Lundy Island. The raider was flying south-west, out to sea, Red 1 chasing the bandit for 50 miles. Again, the Hurricane pilot was unable to catch the Ju 88, and with petrol running low, Parker opened fire from long range, 600 yards, expending all his ammunition in one long continuous burst. Black smoke was seen coming from one of the bomber's engines, so it was assumed damaged, but made off west, towards Lundy, and escaped. At 19.05 hrs, the squadron's Red Section was again airborne, this time comprising three aircraft: Pilot Officer Owen Tracey, a New Zealander, Red 3, who at 19.45 hrs was over St David's Head and sighted a distant aircraft. A miscommunication led to the other two Hurricanes turning away, but Tracey gave chase, intercepting a Do 215, heading north. As Tracey passed in front of the bomber, attempting to positively identify before attacking it, the German pilot tried to turn on the Hurricane's tail, but Tracey turned inside the Ju 88, which then dived for the sea, its rear gunner opening fire from long range. Tracey attacked relentlessly, causing black smoke to pour from an engine as it dived to his right. With visibility fading and ammunition exhausted, Tracey broke away, claiming the bomber as probably destroyed.

There was action too over North Wales. At 16.30 hrs, a single Spitfire of 611 Squadron, now based at Ternhill in Shropshire, was scrambled to intercept a 'bogey' at 20,000ft over Liverpool; the enemy aircraft was a Do 215 of 2(F)/121 engaged on a reconnaissance sortie in preparation for the night's raid on that city. Pilot Officer Denis Adams:

> The Do 215 was at about 30,000 feet when I caught up with it. I climbed a couple of hundred feet higher on the starboard side before attacking. When I did so my third and fourth starboard guns fired two rounds each before jamming. Apparently the armourers believed that the lubricant they used froze at such a great height. One thing omitted from my official combat report was that I tried to get the Dornier to land at either Hooton Park or Speke airfields. From that height the pilot could have made either easily, but he seemed pretty single-minded, flying a straight course but losing height all the time. I think he was pretty lucky to find a field to land in, North Wales is pretty rugged country!

The enemy aircraft crash-landed at Trawsfyndd. *Unteroffizier* Peizer was killed, but *Leutnant* Book, and *Feldwebel* Jansen and *Feldwebel* Kühl were captured.

That evening, a larger raid also came in over Kent – although detail is scant. According to 92 Squadron,

> Enemy attacks were made with large fighter escorts. Squadron attacked and suffered one aircraft shot-up. Bombers forced to turn back. [ORB]

The squadron made no combat claims, but Pilot Officer Thomas Sherrington was hit by *Major* Adolf Galland, leading JG 26 on an escort mission, and forced-landed at RAF Manston, unhurt.

At 18.15 hrs, six Spitfires of 66 Squadron were patrolling between Gravesend and Maidstone when fifty Me 109s were sighted, flying in vics line astern with other formations above. Pilot Officer John 'Pickle' Pickering wrote of this engagement in *Ten Fighter Boys*:

> we sighted about thirty Me 109s about 5,000 feet above us, so we climbed to attack, but were attacked by thirty Me 109s from behind. I was attacked by six at once, but after being hit three times I managed to get away by going into a spin.
>
> After spinning from 25,000 feet to 5,000 feet I pulled out. All the time I expected to get a few more bullets in my machine because I did not realise Me 109s do not follow Spitfires and Hurricanes once they go into a spin or dive, and much to my surprise a Me 109 was about 400 yards ahead of me, flying South. I closed to 200 yards and opened fire. It dived and the last I saw was when it entered cloud at 2,000 feet with glycol pouring out of the radiator, but I could only claim it as damaged.

This was 66 Squadron's only combat claim in this engagement – although somewhat embellished in the morale boosting *Ten Fighter Boys*:

> When I got back to base two of the boys had not arrived back but they arrived later, each having shot down a Me 109. The total score for this fight was six 109s shot down, three probably shot down, and four damaged. Our only casualty was my machine, which was repaired within the hour.

According to Pickering's official combat report, 'The three outside guns on port wing of my machine did not fire owing to an enemy bullet damaging air pressure pipe to guns'.

There was no other daylight action.

The only RAF fighter pilot lost this day was not in combat but when 601 Squadron's Flying Officer Juliusz Topolnicki, a Pole, was killed in a flying accident when taking off from Exeter on a training flight. The Germans lost a Ju 88 and a Do 215 destroyed over England, with several more returning to France damaged. Only one Me 109 was lost, a machine of 5/LG 2, which crashed in the Channel, the pilot of which was rescued by the *Seenotdienst* and very likely shot down by 66 Squadron's Pilot Officer John Pickering (and not by the Dover barrage as stated elsewhere).

Up in 12 Group, the Duxford Wing had patrolled London uneventfully that evening – for the cameras. Flying Officer Stanley Devon was the man behind the lens, who had been a successful press photographer since 1923, and who became an Air Ministry photographer in 1939. In his memoir (see Bibliography), Devon, who had already been in France with 73 Squadron, wrote that

> This was the second battle which was too fast for me to photograph. There was no room for a photographer in a Spitfire or a Hurricane. I had a shot at it in a Blenheim. Under Wing Commander [*sic*] Bader two squadrons of Hurricanes and one of Spitfires operated from Duxford … and fought the [Fairey] battles over the Thames [Estuary] which broke up the first daylight raids on London. Douglas Bader was almost as keen on shooting pictures as on shooting-down planes. At a time when housewives were giving their pots and pans to be turned into aircraft to fight the Luftwaffe, he got a Blenheim – just for me. And he offered me the whole Wing to photograph. Our speed in the Blenheim was half that of the fighters. Twice, when the alarm went, I took off and waited for the Wing to overtake me and destroy the raiders before my lens. Twice they shot past me in formation, bristling with guns. But the Luftwaffe failed me by being late.

Afterwards, Devon took a series of photographs on the ground at Duxford of 242 (Canadian) and 310 (Czech) Squadrons, including the well-known image of the pugnacious Bader, standing with Flying Officer Eric Ball and Pilot Officer William McKnight, by his Hurricane, emblazoned with nose art of Hitler being kicked up the backside by a 242 (Canadian) Squadron flying boot. Devon then went to the nearby Duxford satellite at Manor Farm in Fowlmere, where he shot a reel of even more remarkable film of 19 Squadron's Spitfires, pilots and airmen – including the iconic image of Squadron Leader Brian J.E. Lane DFC shortly after landing, the 23-year-old's face clearly showing the strain. Indeed, this image, included in this book, is amongst the most well-known and haunting images of the Battle of Britain – and yet Devon, it seems, never realised what a powerful image he captured that day: the visit to Fowlmere is not even mentioned in his memoir, nor are any of the photographs taken at Duxford or Fowlmere included. Nonetheless, Devon did us good service that day, even if not the combat scenes desired, because these images are surely a unique photographic record of fighter squadrons during their 'Finest Hour'.

Whilst Devon snapped away at Duxford, Coastal Command was active, escorting fifteen convoys whilst eighty-seven aircraft flew anti-invasion and submarine patrols and reconnaissance sorties. A lack of cloud cover over France led to 59 Squadron aborting scheduled attacks on enemy airfields, bombing invasion barges at Dieppe instead, and 53 Squadron similarly struck at German shipping off Cap Gris-Nez. By night, shipping at Rotterdam was also attacked. Clear conditions over France by day led to just seven of eighteen 2 Group Blenheims managing to carry out attacks on invasion ports and shipping, six other aircraft sweeping the North Sea. After dark, the invasion ports of Calais and Dunkirk were successfully bombed by the Wellington force, and Blenheims similarly hit Dunkirk and Ostend. Lone Battles of 142 Squadron struck at Boulogne and the battery at Cap Gris-Nez, Hampdens bombed ships at Ostend, and the Whitley force also hit shipping at Boulogne. Neither Bomber, Coastal nor Fighter Command suffered any operational losses on this day.

Daily Home Intelligence Report:

> There is little change in morale: yesterday's cheerfulness is maintained.
>
> London Region:
>
> In London, conversation is almost exclusively about air raids; it is gossipy, not panicky, and is centered [*sic*] on personal matters. There appears to be very little relationship between 'the bomb at the corner of our street' and the war as a whole. Interest in the total aspect of war is very low, although demands for reprisals continue.
>
> South-eastern Region (Tunbridge Wells):
>
> People are much concerned about the problem of countering night bombers, and such questions as 'why can't Spitfires be fitted with searchlights?' are being asked. It is reported that people who left London on account of air raids and went hop-picking are now worried because they will have nowhere to go when the picking has finished.

Sunday, 22 September 1940

German air activity was so comparatively light that Fighter Command flew less sorties on this than any other day during the sixteen-week Battle of Britain. The weather was largely the cause of this lull, still being poor with cloud base down to 500ft in places. Just sixty lone raiders were active by day over Britain, causing little damage.

At 14.25 hrs, Flight Lieutenant Walter Lawson was leading Red Section of 19 Squadron's 'A' Flight over the 12 Group sector station of Duxford, patrolling below cloud, which was down to 500ft. At 15.30 hrs, a bandit, reportedly a

'Do 215', appeared from the clouds and dropped ten 28lb bombs on 'B' Flight's dispersal at Fowlmere – destroying a Spitfire. Red Section gave chase, Lawson managing an inconclusive burst of fire before the German disappeared back into cloud.

The only other action, surprisingly, was over 10 Group. At Middle Wallop, Red Section of 234 Squadron, comprising the experienced Sergeant Alan Harker, Red 1, and newly arrived Pilot Officer Terence Kane, Red 2, were scrambled to investigate a vapour trail over the aerodrome. Airborne, the Spitfire pilots were informed by Control of a bandit at 8,000ft. At 16.45 hrs, Red 1 sighted a Ju 88 at 25,000ft, heading west, which turned south-east upon sighting the approaching fighters. Red Section gave chase, Harker catching the bomber at 18,000ft, 50 miles south of Start Point. Attacking with a long burst from out of the sun, Harker expended his ammunition and set the raider's starboard engine ablaze. Red 2, in what was his baptism of fire, also attacked, after which the Ju 88 dived into the sea. The crew of 4(F)/121, which had been on a Channel weather recce, took to their dinghy and were all captured.

Apart from the Spitfire destroyed on the ground at Fowlmere, Fighter Command suffered no other combat losses on this day, although three 85 Squadron Hurricanes, which had withdrawn to Church Fenton, were damaged when landing from a patrol over Burnley in bad visibility (one of these Hurricanes was flown by Pilot Officer John 'Paddy' Hemingway, an Irishman from Dublin (and who, at the time of writing, is the last known survivor of The Few, aged 105).

No. 73 Squadron, based at Castle Camps, a Debden satellite, would record this as

> A thoroughly wet and somewhat miserable day; no flying whatever and even the Controller was affected in the afternoon when 'Readiness' was changed to fifteen minutes availability. Every one of the pilots, and those of 257 Squadron, crowded into the Mess and at the beginning of dusk we were getting a little tired of one another. Cards and darts were the chief sources of entertainment, but sleep was also popular. A welcome piece of news is that there is to be no night state henceforward for single-seater fighter squadrons. In the evening most of the pilots repaired to a 'local' for an hour or two, the 'Fox and Hounds' at Steeple Bumstead being very popular. [ORB]

Again, Coastal Command sorties were reduced, and those flown represented the typical round of commitments. Lack of cloud cover over France saw 2 Group abandon attacks on airfields and ports, although three Battles hit shipping at Boulogne. At night, Bomber Command once more targeted the invasion ports, although industrial targets near Dresden and at Berlin were also attacked. Once more, neither Bomber, Coastal nor Fighter Command suffered any casualties.

Monday, 23 September 1940

According to 73 Squadron, operating from the Debden satellite airfield at Castle Camps, the morning was 'pleasant' and 'sunny', 'with only a slight ground mist'. Unfortunately, though, the rest of the morning would be anything but 'pleasant' for 73 Squadron, which was detailed to fly in and lead a wing formation with the Debden sector's other squadrons, 17 and 257. The latter squadron arrived at Castle Camps from the RAF Martlesham Heath satellite in good time for an early breakfast, and at 09.20 hrs, 73 and 257 Squadrons joined 17 Squadron over Debden, and set off to patrol Chelmsford at Angels 20. This particular morning, the enemy looked to repeat the raid of 20 September 1940, and sent bomb-carrying Me 109s, with a huge fighter escort, to attack London – and the first defending squadrons to go into action would be the Debden Wing.

Patrolling Chelmsford at 20,000ft, the Debden Hurricanes were vectored to Rochford and Gravesend, also at Angels 20. Then, the controller informed them of bandits approaching from the east – and just Angels 5.

According to the 73 Squadron ORB:

> When told to intercept at that height, the leader of the Squadron was so astounded that he repeated the figure and obtained conformation. The Squadron had got down to 12,000 feet when they were ordered up again to Angels 20 in the direction of Dover.

No. 73 Squadron's frustration can only be imagined – then, the inevitable happened:

> It was while climbing back that the whole Squadron was pounced upon by fifteen Me 109s and the odd He 113 [*sic*] diving at 360 mph, compared with their climbing speed of perhaps 160 mph. To make matters worse, the escorting Squadron (17) did not follow 73 down in the first place, thus leaving us entirely unprotected. The results were bad but could have been far worse. [ORB]

Sergeant Fred Perkin was shot down and baled out, 'at Hasty Ferry, near Sittingbourne and was taken to Fyndale House, Faversham, practically uninjured' [ORB]. Sergeant Maurice Leng also baled out, his Hurricane crashing near Rodmersham, and was admitted to Chatham Hospital having been injured in a heavy landing. Pilot Officer Douglas Kinder and Pilot Officer Neville Langham-Hobart were both shot down and crashed in the sea, near *Lightship 93*. The two pilots were rescued and admitted to the Royal Navy Hospital, Chatham,

> with very severe burns and cuts. Their next-of-kin have been summoned and this seems to indicate the seriousness of their condition. [ORB]

Both men survived, although Langham-Hobart was so badly burnt that he required skin grafts to face and legs, becoming a 'Guinea Pig' at the Royal Victoria Hospital in East Grinstead.

During this lightning-fast action, only Sergeant Herbert Webster opened fire, 'more in anger than expectation'. The first of the survivors, Flying Officer James Smith, a Canadian, landed back at Castle Camps with news that 'something had gone badly wrong'. At intervals the other seven pilots returned, 'almost speechless with anger and it was obvious that each blamed the Operations Room…'. [ORB]

No. 257 Squadron had descended with 73 Squadron, the former squadron's CO, Acting Squadron Leader Robert Stanford Tuck sighting the German fighters coming down, two of which

> peeled off and diving past 257 Squadron delivered an astern attack from out of the sun on 73 Squadron. Flight Lieutenant [*sic*] Tuck ordered the Squadron to break up and himself went after the two E/A. Being unable to catch up the He 113 [*sic*] concentrated on the Me 109, firing a three-second burst from the quarter. The Me 109 made off towards the coast but gradually lost speed and height and Flight Lieutenant [*sic*] Tuck was able to deliver three more astern attacks. The Me 109 crashed into the sea 10 miles north of Cap Gris Nez. [ORB]

According to the same source, 257 Squadron's only loss in the engagement was Sergeant Donald Aslin, who baled out over Detling aerodrome and admitted to the SSQ there, suffering from burns. However, from the log book and notes of Pilot Officer Alan L. Hedges, who joined 257 Squadron on 10 September 1940 and recorded combat successes five days later, we know that he too was shot down. In his log book, Pilot Officer Hedges wrote, 'Fired twice at two 109s, no result observed. Shot down by 109. Baled out at 20,000 feet. Shot in the leg.'

Hedges later recalled,

> The aircraft was badly hit and the cockpit filled with smoke. I uncoupled oxygen, radio etc, rolled the plane and fell out. The parachute opened perfectly and I eventually floated down and landed in a ploughed field on the Isle of Sheppey, having tried to slip off height as I was blowing out to sea. During this incident one of my flying boots had disappeared from the leg that was hit by the bullet and was consequently badly bruised on

> landing. I was taken to Maidstone Hospital, remaining there for two weeks before re-joining 257 Squadron.

Yet again, this illustrates just how incomplete official records can be, although a casualty file exists confirming the Hurricane concerned to have been P2960.

In what was a fiasco for the Debden sector squadrons, six Hurricanes had been shot down: one pilot was injured upon landing, another wounded, and one rescued from the sea, badly burnt; it was a remarkable action in that no pilots were killed. No. 73 Squadron scored no success against the enemy in response, and 257 Squadron's only claim was the Me 109 destroyed by Tuck. The Hurricanes had, in fact, been ambushed by *Major* Adolf Galland of the JG 26 *Stabschwarm*, and *Oberleutnant* Walter Schneider's 6/JG 26. On this occasion, the German pilots' claims were 100 per cent accurate: Galland claimed two Hurricanes destroyed north of Rochester, Schneider one over Margate, whilst *Oberfeldwebel* Heinrich Gottlob and *Oberleutnant* Harald Grawatsch claimed one each over the Thames Estuary.

Having remained at Angels 20, 17 Squadron saw nothing of the enemy.

The Hurricanes of 605 Squadron were also up, from Croydon, and at 09.40 hrs were patrolling over Tunbridge Wells at 20,000ft, circling right-handed, when attacked from above, out of the sun, by two Me 109s. One of the assailants overshot and Pilot Officer Antoni Głowacki delivered a long burst, closing from 300 to 50 yards. Głowacki watched his target 'shudder' and drop away, whilst the other 109 pilot climbed and re-joined the rest of his formation. No. 605 Squadron suffered no loss, but the ORB commented that the 109s were at 25,000ft, the Hurricanes at 20,000ft and 'again jumped and continued complaints were made to Control'.

At 09.11 hrs, the Spitfires of 66 Squadron had taken-off from Gravesend to patrol between Maidstone and Deal, and in action over the Thames Estuary. Pilot Officer Hugh Reilley, a Canadian, reported that, at 09.55 hrs, 12 miles east of Chatham,

> The Squadron was attacked by Me 109s at 28,000 feet. We all split up immediately and this resulted in my being left alone. I was cruising at 20,000 feet when two Me 109s appeared out of cloud. I managed to get in one burst just beneath the cockpit, from behind. There then appeared more planes on the scene and I was unable to follow the hit Me 109, but he seemed to turn over on his side and plunge earthwards with black smoke trailing behind. The other 109 disappeared, and the new arrivals turned out to be friendly aircraft. In the engagement, as I attacked the

> first E/A, the second turned a left-hand circle and directed an accurate burst of machine-gun fire, but due to deflection did not hit my aircraft.

Returning to Gravesend at 10.25 hrs, Reilley claimed his first combat success: an Me 109 probably destroyed. Flight Lieutenant Ken Gillies claimed one damaged; 'Clickety-Click' suffered no loss.

The Spitfires of 92 Squadron had left Biggin Hill at 09.23 hrs to patrol Gravesend at 20,000ft with 66 and 72 Squadrons, and intercepted the enemy over Tonbridge at 09.40 hrs, as Flight Lieutenant Kingcome, 'Ganic Leader', reported,

> We had reached our height and I was patrolling North of our objective in order to intercept the raiders head-on when I received a vector of 170°. We continued on this vector for about two or three minutes when I sighted a formation of fifteen Me 109s flying in a defensive circle at the same height as ourselves and with a considerable number of more about 7,000 feet above. As I understood from my Ground Station that there were no bombers I waited until we were in range of the Me 109s when I gave the order to split up and attack. I selected one machine and gave it a short burst from dead astern. Glycol streamed out immediately. I gave it a few more bursts as it twisted and turned, and the pilot jumped out of the machine, which crashed NW of Dungeness. After the engagement the rest of the 109s turned and flew home, and the Squadron was ordered to pancake.

Kingcome had shot down *Oberfeldwebel* Gerhard Grzymalla of 8/JG 26, who was captured.

Pilot Officer John Drummond of 92 Squadron was also successful:

> I saw one Me 109 firing at a Spitfire and got on his tail and fired a short burst. Clouds of white smoke came from the exhaust. The 109 carried out evasive tactics down to 5,000 feet, I fired short bursts when I could get my sights on. At 5,000 feet he was obviously in difficulties and I flew round above and watched him forced-land just North of Chatham. It turned up on its nose in a dyke.

This was *Feldwebel* Arnold Küpper, also of 8/JG 26, who came down near the Yantlet Battery on the Isle of Grain and was captured.

Oberleutnant Gustav 'Micky' Sprick, *Staffelkapitän* of 8/JG 26, and *Gefreiter* Helmut Hornatschek of 9/JG 26 both claimed Spitfires destroyed in this action, although only one was shot down. Pilot Officer John Pattison, a New Zealander, 'managed to land aircraft with a severe thigh wound and was admitted to Preston

Hall Hospital, Maidstone' [ORB]. Pattison crash-landed near West Malling, his wounds caused by a cannon shell; he would spend eight months in various hospitals and not return to 92 Squadron until June 1941.

No. 72 Squadron had left Biggin Hill at 09.05 hrs, with orders to link up with 66 and 92 Squadrons and patrol Gravesend at 25,000ft, thereby providing top cover to the other two squadrons patrolling at 20,000ft. No. 72 Squadron failed to find 66 and 92 Squadrons, however, but contacted Me 109s over Canterbury.

Flight Lieutenant Ivor Cosby, Blue 3:

> The enemy fighters were above and dived to the attack. I then took evasive action and found myself alone. On look round I noticed a Spitfire engaging a Me 109. There was another Me 109 on the Spitfire's tail. I got on its tail and gave him a three-second burst. The Spitfire then became aware of the E/A and turned to engage him. I followed the original Me 109 and gave him a four-second burst. Petrol immediately gushed out of the port side of the fuselage and he began to lose height rapidly. Making sure that it was all clear behind I followed him down over Folkestone, gave him a final burst and he went into the sea about 400 yards from the pier.

This Me 109 of 4/JG 2 came down between Folkestone railway pier, from which countless British soldiers embarked for France during the First World War, and Copt Point at 10.00 hrs. It was also attacked by Sergeant Norman 'Sticky' Glew who claimed a share. The pilot, *Unteroffizier* Friedrich Dilthey, who was wounded in the shoulder and broke a leg, was seen to be in trouble by 2nd Lieutenant Maurice Edward Jacobs, watching from the pier, who swam out and supported the downed airman until both were rescued by a fishing boat.

Sergeant John White also went to the assistance of a Spitfire being attacked from astern by a 109. After a short burst, black smoke poured from the enemy fighter, which began a long and shallow dive. White was unable to wait and see if it crashed owing to the immediate presence of other 109s, but considered that if it did, 'it would probably come down in the sea East of Ramsgate'. The Spitfire being attacked by the first 109 was that of Pilot Officer Bernard Brown, a New Zealander, who lost control of his Spitfire and baled out, landing near Eastchurch with cannon shell splinters in one leg and an elbow; he was admitted to Minster Hospital. *Hauptmann* Karl-Heinz Greisert, *Kommandeur* of II/JG 2, and *Oberleutnant* Hans Hahn, of 4/JG 2, both claimed Spitfires destroyed.

Twelve Spitfires of 41 Squadron scrambled from Hornchurch at 09.10 hrs with orders to rendezvous with 603 Squadron over Rochford. No. 41 Squadron climbed to 30,000ft. Flight Lieutenant Harold MacDonald, leading 603 Squadron, took his Spitfires up to 32,000ft, the combined formation sweeping south, with 41 Squadron leading. At 10.15 hrs, 41 Squadron was over Dover with Me 109s heading home. Flying Officer Guy Cory, Yellow 2, dived and attacked two Me 109s beating it for France, emptying most of his ammunition into one which streamed

> very large amounts of glycol ... it was badly damaged. It dived vertically for the sea but as a stray bullet hit my aircraft, I broke away and lost sight of him ... I also saw bits fly off the tail and it is unlikely to have reached the French coast.

Sergeant Cyril Bamberger, Yellow 3, attacked the other 109, which lost height, but was forced to break away when attacked himself. Sergeant Edward Darling's oxygen was running low but nonetheless he attacked a *Rotte* of Me 109s, one of which began smoking whilst the other took violent evasive action: 'I then had to break away and in evading this bandit lost sight of my original target, last seen in a glide, making a long smoke streamer across the sky'. Pilot Officer John MacKenzie, a New Zealander, claimed a 109 probably destroyed, and Pilot Officer George Bennions claimed a 109 destroyed – previously accredited as having shot down *Unteroffizier* Karl Elbing of 7/JG 3, who baled out off Deal and was captured, it is possible that this was also the 109 attacked by Cory, given that Elbing's rudder was shot away. Apart from the 'stray bullet' hitting Cory's Spitfire, all of 41 Squadron returned to base intact.

Flight Lieutenant Harold MacDonald, 603 Squadron:

> I was leading the Squadron behind 41 [Squadron] at 32,000 feet, proceeding South from Canterbury, when I saw individual aircraft of 41 Squadron peeling off as if to attack.

This is of interest. As previously explained, the radio sets in use enabled pilots to communicate with others in their own squadron and ground control but not with other airborne squadrons. Consequently, co-ordinated attacks by any more than one squadron were largely impossible – in this case, 41 Squadron had obviously sighted the enemy first and were already executing an attack before 603 Squadron became aware of the Germans. Squadrons operating together, at the time of the Dunkirk evacuation, was more about travelling together in strength, rather than attacking as a cohesive wing, as became possible when VHF sets eventually became available, improving and extending communication between squadrons in the air.

MacDonald continued,

> I ordered Squadron into line astern and then observed about six 109s flying about separately, approximately 2,000 feet below us. I gave the order 'Squadron attack – dog-fight' and myself went to attack but failed at first to find a suitable target.
>
> I then saw about a dozen Me 109s in mid-Channel, 3,000 feet below and in open formation. I went to investigate and selected one to attack. I gave him two good bursts from dead astern at close range, during the second of which he emitted a long stream of, presumably, coolant and turned slowly over onto his back and dived vertically from 10,000 feet. I then had to discontinue the chase in order to protect my own tail.

Flight Lieutenant John Boulter, commanding 603 Squadron's 'A' Flight, dived on three pairs of Me 109s, 15 miles north of Dover, engaging the last aircraft in line:

> My second burst, from approximately 70 yards, caused an explosion at the centre-section of the Me 109, followed by a dense stream of white vapour and apparently flames. It then fell on its side and disappeared from my view in a vertical dive. I did not follow it down because I was able to engage the next Me 109.

The Me 109 of 3/JG 54 exploded over Barham; the pilot, *Oberfeldwebel* Helmut Knippscheer, baled out, alighting in the sea off Dover but was sadly picked up dead.

No.603 Squadron suffered no losses in this action.

At 09.30 hrs, 303 (Polish) Squadron scrambled from Northolt to patrol base and lead 1 (RCAF) and 229 Squadrons as a wing:

> Vectored South of Biggin Hill and then towards [the Thames] Estuary. Saw about twenty streamers approaching from South. Squadron at 22,000 feet, then saw about twenty Me 109s at 30,000–25,000 feet, circling the [Thames] Estuary. Wing circled slowly and E/A made no attempt to attack. Then about twelve Me 109s came behind from some other formation, apparently trying to break up the Wing. Red Section attacked and E/A fled southwards. Flight Lieutenant [Johnny] Kent caught up one Me 109 diving for France and shot it down in the sea, fifteen miles from the French coast. The pilot baled out at 4,000 feet. On returning, Flight Lieutenant Kent saw probably a Potez flying low towards England. E/A turned and Flight Lieutenant Kent saw De Wilde [author's note: incendiary ammunition] hitting E/A but his own engine began laboring, and he returned to base. Sergeant [Eugeniusz] Szaposznikow also overtook one Me 109 and shot

> it down in flames near French coast. Enemy fighters made no attempt to fight Hurricanes and showed no aptitude for evasion. Potez painted mottled dark grey with black crosses. No return fire noticed. Evasive tactics slow turns over sea. [ORB]

No. 303 (Polish) Squadron suffered no casualties and had clearly engaged the Me 109s when the latter were on the limit of their fuel endurance and needed to get home – fast. For III/JG 53, in fact, the escort mission had gone awry from the outset with the *Jabos* arrived late at the rendezvous, meaning precious fuel was wasted. Bad weather led to many of the *Gruppe*'s aircraft returning to land at various airfields in the Pas-de-Calais, and the *Gruppe*'s *Adjutant*, *Oberleutnant* Walter Radlick, landed his fighter wheels-up on the French coast, out of fuel. Me 109s down on French beaches after long flights to and from London were already a common sight.

No. 1 (RCAF) Squadron, flying with 29 and 303 (Polish) Squadrons, sighted the Me 109s high above but were unable to reach them. No. 229 Squadron saw nothing of the enemy – but Pilot Officer Peter Allcock, who was weaving behind the Hurricanes, was ambushed and shot down, baling out over Hoo and landed in Westcliff-on-Sea; he was admitted to Southend Hospital with a gashed calf and burns.

Whatever bombs were dropped appeared random, and the enemy failed to reach London. This time, the Germans substantially overclaimed, *Jafü* 2's fighters claiming twenty-one Hurricanes and Spitfires destroyed, ten by JG 26 alone. Fighter Command, however, actually suffered eight fighters destroyed and six pilots wounded. Nine Me 109s were destroyed, three more returning to France badly damaged; two German pilots were killed and four were captured. If the objective was to destroy Fighter Command in great numbers, this was a poor return indeed.

To the west, at 10.10 hrs, Pilot Officer Geoffrey Baynham and Pilot Officer Terence Kane took-off from Middle Wallop to orbit base at Angels 15. At 11.40 hrs, Baynham returned – alone. It appears that the Spitfires went looking for trouble and found it: Kane was shot down, baling out at 6,000ft, after, he claimed, destroying a 109, and was captured. No. 152 Squadron, based at Warmwell, also had a pilot missing: Pilot Officer Walter Beaumont failed to return from a routine patrol and simply disappeared. No. 7/JG 2 shared the destruction of a Spitfire north of Fécamp, which may have been one of these missing 10 Group pilots.

At 12.20 hrs, Flying Officer Henry Baker, Pilot Officer John MacKenzie and Sergeant Cyril Bamberger of 41 Squadron left Hornchurch to rendezvous with an Anson at Hawkinge, and escort this aircraft on a reconnaissance of Calais.

According to the 41 Squadron ORB, on this sortie one Me 109 was destroyed and another damaged, although no other details appear recorded.

Interestingly, on this day, Fighter Command flew as many sorties as it had on 15 September 1940, 'Battle of Britain Day', but the damage now being caused by daylight bombing was negligible. However, although some twenty RAF squadrons were being scrambled to intercept the German fighter and fighter bomber sweeps, only a handful of these defending units were contacting the Germans. Although RDF was providing early warning, because these single-engined formations moved so fast, the timespan was much less than when slower bombers were approaching. Moreover, because of the high altitude involved, combats were often fought above cloud – meaning that the Observer Corps was neutralised. From early September 1940 onwards, 11 Group had used lone Spitfires to spot the enemy and now, in an attempt to increase the accuracy of information available regarding incoming threats, permission was requested from the Air Ministry to form a dedicated look-out or 'Jim Crow' flight, the Spitfires of which would be equipped with VHF radio sets and, therefore, able to communicate directly with 'The Hole': Air Vice-Marshal Sir Keith Park's underground operations room at 11 Group HQ, Uxbridge. Meanwhile, whilst the Air Ministry's decision was awaited, the situation remained the same, Park being grateful for, but frustrated by, the limitations of RDF.

During the day, nearly 100 aircraft of Coastal Command carried out the usual patrols and convoy protection sorties. Two 22 Squadron Beaufort torpedo bombers successfully attacked a German convoy off the Dutch island of Schiermonnikoog, and three 53 Squadron Blenheims were ordered 'to attack one large ship escorted by E-boats 15 miles south of Dungeness' [ORB]. Once more, though, 2 Group's Blenheims were forced to abandon proposed attacks owing to a lack of cloud cover over the Continent. That night, however, Bomber Command mounted its greatest raid to date on Berlin, a raid lasting 3 hours, hitting 18 separate targets and mounted by 112 Wellingtons, Whitleys and Hampdens, whilst 88 other aircraft successfully bombed the invasion ports. One 83 Squadron Hampden on the Berlin raid was hit by flak and crashed in Germany, and a 311 Squadron Whitley also fell victim to flak, ditching in the North Sea: four days later two survivors were rescued by the RN, but one man died within hours; the rest of the crew remain missing.

Daily Home Intelligence Report:

> There is anger and indignation about the torpedoing of the child evacuee ship. The effect has been to increase the demands for 'reprisals on German civilians'... This is the first piece of news for a fortnight which has deflected people's interests from air raids.

People in London are cheerful but continue to enquire when there will be protection against night bombing.

London Region:

Social Workers visiting hop fields at weekend suggests that East Enders might be allowed to stay in hop field hutments rather than return to devastated areas.

Tuesday, 24 September 1940

On 24 September 1940, the Duxford Wing patrolled twice over the Thames Estuary without meeting the enemy. On the second patrol, the 19 Squadron ORB states that the wing 'Ran into No 11 Group wing. Almost a party.' Squadron Leader Raymond Myles Duke-Woolley DFC was leading the Kenley-based Hurricanes of 253 Squadron:

> Very often in those days, liaison between groups was not water-tight and one occasionally never knew before take-off that the 12 Group 'Balbo' would be in the area. The incident I remember … I was leading 253 [Squadron] on a standing patrol over Canterbury. Normally these patrols were at 15,000ft but I seized the opportunity for practice, and was at 28,000ft in our new formation. Huns were reported to be approaching the area, but no more precise information was given regarding height, direction or numbers. We accordingly increased height to 31,000ft, and seeing nothing to the East or South I gazed North, almost immediately seeing a black mass bearing down from the direction of London, and so handsomely below us. I recognised the aircraft soon after as the 12 Group 'Balbo' but they looked so determined that I felt they must be after some specific raid: I therefore felt that they might lead us to something interesting, and turned in behind them as a sort of voluntary top cover.

So, here we have the Duxford Wing patrolling over east Kent, not the Thames Estuary, as it should have been. The presence of the '12 Group wing' was a surprise to 253 Squadron, which was at its allotted patrol location, with a significant height advantage. Fortunately, Duke-Woolley identified the rogue formation as friendly – otherwise this could have ended in a tragedy comparable to the so-called 'Battle of Barking Creek', in which 74 Squadron mistook Hurricanes of 56 Squadron for enemy fighters, shooting two of them down. Imagine how easily this kind of confusion could have been avoided if only airborne squadrons could communicate with each other. Moreover, the Duxford Wing was being controlled by the Duxford sector controller in 12 Group; the 11 Group sector controllers were unable to personally speak to the 12 Group squadrons operating in their air spaces. Testimony from Duxford Ops 'B' controller Flight Lieutenant Henry 'Teddy' Morten has already indicated that frequently not even Duxford knew where the wing was. This is incomprehensible. Moreover, having climbed over twice as high as instructed, and not reported that fact to the sector controller, 253 Squadron was at the altitude Me 109s frequently operated at – so it would not have been surprising if the Duxford Wing assumed that the Hurricanes were enemy fighters. This had all the makings of a shambles.

Squadron Leader Myles Duke-Woolley:

> Feeling friendly disposed myself towards them, I turned in behind them, I never thought that they would mistake me for a German formation, but I forgot to realise that our formation was still unpublished, that Hurricanes just did not operate at 30,000ft, and that the 109 did look rather like a Hurricane. The 'Balbo', of course, did mistake us and thought they were about to be bounced – so they orbited. I thought they were orbiting to intercept my raid, and so orbited too. When the 'Balbo' straightened out to climb and 'engage' me, I naturally followed suit. They, equally naturally, had no intention of climbing up on a straight course to be bounced. Thus, for some minutes, there was complete stale-mate, until the 'Balbo' started to get short of fuel and retired in good order to the South.
>
> About a fortnight later I read a letter from 11 Group analysing in caustic terms the operation of the 'Balbo'. I remember that about eight of its trips were mentioned, the main point stressed being the comparatively short effective time on patrol. With some horror I saw one trip described under 'Remarks' in roughly these words: 'Six squadrons attempted to patrol for fifteen minutes in Canterbury area, but mistook an 11 Group squadron already on patrol for German aircraft and returned in disorder to their bases.' The story got around the Station and was received with huge delight by the ground-crew as well as aircrew. I remember feeling myself that my innocuous patrol could link me with the 11 Group report, and that if any fur was flying I was possibly going to be in the middle somewhere: the role of 'evidence' in a head-on collision between two AOCs seemed to me about as profitable as an advertisement I recalled for Cadbury's chocolate entitled 'Talking of Sandwiches' and depicting two burly giants simultaneously barging a weedy individual from opposite directions!

On at least one occasion to date, Air Vice-Marshal Keith Park had inquired as to whether the Duxford Wing was in position, as requested, above the Hornchurch-North Weald line – only to be told that the 12 Group formation was, in fact, over Kent. From the testimony of Air Vice-Marshal Christopher Brand DFC's 10 Group pilots, it is clear that they proceeded to their allocated patrol lines, as requested and dictated by 11 Group, remaining there until vectored towards the action. The 11 Group AOC had every right to expect that 12 Group's fighters would do likewise – and not wander off on unauthorised fighter sweeps over the 11 Group area. Astonishingly, it would not be Air Vice-Marshal Trafford Leigh-Mallory DSO and Bar who was scrutinised by the Air Ministry – but Air Vice-Marshal Keith Park.

On 24 September 1940, Air Vice-Marshal Sholto Douglas DFC, the DCAS, informed Air Vice-Marshal Robert Saundby DFC, ACAS (Tactics), that a number of criticisms had been received regarding Park's tactics. Saundby tasked Group Captain H.G. Crowe, the Deputy Director of Air Tactics, to investigate the allegations and report back. When Saundby subsequently forwarded Crowe's report to the DCAS, he advised Douglas to read both Park and Leigh-Mallory's responses on wing patrols, dated 17 September 1940; the 'Big Wing' had just gained another powerful ally at the Air Ministry.

Park's report included reference to wing formations:

> Had 11 Group delayed in engaging the enemy until its squadrons had been assembled in wings of four or five squadrons, there would have been no opposition to the first wave of bomber formations, who would have had time to escape without interception. With the available force massed into a few wings of four or five squadrons, a proportion of the second wave would have been intercepted and severely punished. The third wave of enemy bombers would, however, have had unopposed approach to the vital points of London, as the 11 Group squadrons would have been on the ground rearming and refuelling. After six months' experience of intensive fighting, I have no hesitation in saying that we would have lost the Battle of London in September if 11 Group had adopted as standard the use of wings of four or five squadrons as has been advocated in certain quarters since that critical battle was won.

Park continued regarding the high-altitude German fighter incursions:

> The great increase in the number of enemy fighters employed and the beginning of the autumn cloud conditions, above which the enemy fighters flew at great altitudes, increased the difficulties in obtaining accurate

information. The Observer Corps found it impossible to distinguish between enemy bombers and enemy fighters. In an attempt to overcome this difficulty and to improve detailed information generally, special fighter reconnaissance patrols were introduced to patrol at high altitudes and report by R/T details of enemy formations coming in.

During this phase and particularly the latter part of it, RDF warning deteriorated considerably. This, coupled with the increasing altitudes at which the enemy fighter patrols approached, made the problem of intercepting from the ground more and more difficult. Our fighters operating from coastal aerodromes were frequently meeting enemy fighters above them, particularly when our own fighters were on the climb preparatory to being detailed to intercept raids. For this reason squadrons were being withdrawn from the forward coastal aerodromes in Kent to bases farther back, from, which they were better able to climb sufficiently high before intercepting.

A series of Day Patrol Lines were introduced on 21 September between London and the Kentish coast, behind which squadrons attained their height, and assembled in pairs or wings of three squadrons. Whenever inland tracks of raids became confused, our squadrons were detailed to patrol lines and kept informed of the approach of enemy raids as far as practicable. After assembling on back patrol lines the squadrons were moved on to forward patrol lines.

Park's paragraph on the 'Method of Employing our Squadrons' makes illuminating reading:

The general plan adopted was to engage the high fighter screen with pairs of Spitfire squadrons from Hornchurch and Biggin Hill, half-way between London and the coast, and so enable Hurricane squadrons from London sectors to attack bomber formations and their close escort before they reached the line of fighter aerodromes East and South of London. The remaining squadrons from London sectors that could not be despatched in time to intercept the first wave of the attack by climbing in pairs formed a third and inner screen by patrolling along the line of aerodromes East and South of London. The fighter squadrons from Debden, Tangmere and sometimes Northolt were employed in wings of three or in pairs to form a screen south-east of London to intercept the third wave of attack coming inland, also to mop up retreating formations of the earlier waves. The Spitfire squadrons were redisposed so as to concentrate three squadrons at Hornchurch and Biggin Hill. The primary role of these squadrons was to

> engage and drive back the enemy high fighter screen, and so protect the Hurricane squadrons, whose task was to attack close escorts and then the bomber formations, all of which flew at a much lower altitude.

From the foregoing it is clear that Park was not averse to the use of multi-squadron formations if the circumstances demanded such a response. Park's tactics, therefore, were entirely flexible, ranging from using pairs of aircraft to wings of three squadrons, depending on the enemy's operations. The supporters of the 'Big Wing', however, were seduced by the 12 Group formation's impressive combat claims – which we now know were on occasions, frankly, absurdly exaggerated. This led them to believe that the employment of mass fighter formations was sound in both defence and offence – completely inflexible thinking that would ultimately have negative and far-reaching consequences, as we will in due course see.

So far as the day's fighting was concerned, all action was over the 11 Group area, from the Thames Estuary to Southampton in the west. With improved morning weather, two large raids were launched by *Luftflotte* 2, the first a raid on Tilbury, the second directed at London. The first raid, mounted by Do 17s and Ju 88s, once more had a vast fighter escort, including Me 109s from JGs 2, 26, 53 and 54, and included *Jabos* of I(J)/LG 2. Little damage was caused but at 09.00 hrs the venerable old TS *Cornwall* (training ship) was sunk in the Thames Estuary, a vessel, surprisingly, harking back to the Age of Fighting Sail: a seventy-two-gun frigate, originally HMS *Wellesley*, laid down in 1815, the year of the Battle of Waterloo, the ship had been donated to the School Ship Society as a training and reform school ship for boys. Re-named *Cornwall* and moored off Purfleet in 1868, before moving to Denton, downstream of Gravesend in 1928, the ship was destroyed by German bombs on 24 September 1940 and broken up; her proud figurehead can still be seen today, just inside Chatham dockyard's main gate.

Squadron Leader Robert Lister was serving with 92 Squadron as a supernumerary and at 08.10 hrs he led the squadron from Biggin Hill, with orders to patrol Swanley Junction, south of Dartford, at 20,000ft with 66 and 72 Squadrons. The Spitfires climbed north, gaining height, then turned south. Sergeant Norman Glew of the latter squadron subsequently reported that at 08.45 hrs, 72 Squadron met '100+' bandits of 'All' types flying north-west over the Thames Estuary at 19,000ft:

> We formed line astern and attacked a mixed force of fighters and bombers. I selected a Ju 88 and approached within range of 250 yards, firing a burst of five seconds into his starboard engine from astern and underneath. The

> engine emitted thick smoke and burst into flames. The Ju 88 fell away to starboard and was attacked by more Spitfires. I left them to it and climbed back to meet the 109s, firing a short burst at one before breaking away to return home.

The Ju 88 was credited as probably destroyed. Sergeant Maurice Lee damaged a Do 17, as did an unidentified 72 Squadron pilot. Flight Sergeant Jack Steere, the elder brother of 19 Squadron's Flight Sergeant Harry Steere, who was weaving behind 72 Squadron, claimed a Me 109 probable before his Spitfire was hit and damaged, although he returned safely to Biggin Hill.

Sergeant Ronald Fokes, Yellow 1, leading the last section of 92 Squadron, also attacked a Ju 88,

> which was flying lower than the rest of the formation. I did a beam attack, turning into astern, firing all the time. Large lumps came off the E/A and it turned on its side and commenced to dive. Me 109s then attacked me with cannon and machine-gun fire and I had to break off without observing the result of my attack.

This bomber was also credited as a probable. Flight Lieutenant Brian Kingcome claimed a Ju 88 damaged and a Me 109 probable, and Pilot Officer John Drummond a Ju 88 and a 109 damaged, and a 109 probable. These claims were not without loss, however: Squadron Leader Robert Lister was shot-up and his Spitfire seriously damaged; wounded in the wrist and legs he only narrowly survived a crash-landing back at base and was admitted to Farnborough Hospital. Sergeant Walter Ellis was also hit, crash-landing his damaged Spitfire on Higham Marshes, fortunately unhurt. Sadly, at 09.00 hrs, Pilot Officer John Bryson, however, 'a much-liked Canadian was shot down and crashed at North Weald. He had last been seen diving into a large formation of Me 109s' [ORB]. Bryson was killed.

In this action, Spitfires were claimed destroyed by *Unteroffizier* Fritz Schweser of 78/JG 54, *Oberleutnant* Anton Mader and *Gefreiter* Kaspar Amhausend of 1/JG 2, *Hauptmann* Günther Freiherr von Maltzahn of *Stab* II/JG 53, and two by *Oberleutnant* Herbert Ihlefeld of 1(J)/LG 2. No Me 109s or bombers were lost but a 2/KG 76 Do 17 forced-landed in France owing to combat damage, as did three Ju 88s of II/KG 77.

The Debden Hurricane Wing was also up, but 73 Squadron, it seems, was understandably still smarting from the previous day's fiasco:

> A fine, sunny, morning with 257 arriving at 0820 hrs. When refueling [*sic*] the order came for both squadrons to meet 17 Squadron at Debden and patrol Gravesend, Angels 20, 73 Squadron leading. This was later altered by the Controller to 257 Squadron leading, but too late to inform our leader who with his Squadron was in course of taking-off. Only eight aircraft of 73 Squadron could be put into the air and as only three of 257 could get away owing to having insufficient time for refueling [*sic*], these made a section and flew as part of 73 Squadron. Over Southend, Ju 88s were seen with fighter escorts, but by the time sufficient height had been gained E/A were well out to sea. Again, 17 Squadron left the Wing although they were escorting us and should have stayed with us for the purposes of protection. All our aircraft returned safely. [ORB]

No. 17 Squadron, however, had problems of its own:

> The Squadron took-off at 0830 hrs and joined 73 Squadron over base. Thirty bombers were sighted over the Thames Estuary, approaching London with masses of fighters above them. [No.] 17 Squadron, acting as rearguard, was attacked by the fighters, and in the dogfight that followed Flying Officer [Harold] Bird-Wilson [DFC and Bar] was shot down and baled out. Flying Officer [Count Manfred] Czernin, Pilot Officer Stevens and Sergeant [Glyn] Griffiths circled over him until they saw him picked up safely by a boat off Chatham. Later it was reported that Flying Officer Bird-Wilson had been taken to the Royal Naval Hospital, Chatham, suffering from burns about the legs and face, but he is not on the danger list. Pilot Officer [Denis] Wissler's aircraft was hit by cannon shell and he was slightly wounded in the arm. His aircraft crashed on landing at Debden, and Pilot Officer Wissler was taken to Saffron Walden Hospital. He is not seriously hurt. Ten aircraft landed safely at Debden at 0930 hrs, Flying Officer [Count Manfred] Czernin having probably destroyed one Me 109 over the sea off Foreness [Point], and Pilot Officer [Geoffrey Edward] Pittman having damaged another. [ORB]

No. 17 Squadron had been jumped by *Major* Adolf Galland's *Stabschwarm*, the *Kommodore* scoring his fortieth aerial victory whilst *Unteroffizier* Hugo Dahmer of 6/JG 26 recorded his eight. For Galland, this success earned the *Eichenlaub*, the coveted Oak Leaves to the *Ritterkreuz*; this exceptional fighter pilot and leader later recalled,

> Our group was in the best of spirits, for the JG 26 *Schlageter* had already made a name for itself in the Battle of Britain and no difference was made

> between my own successes and the group's. I was the third member of all the armed forces – after [*Generaloberst* Eduard] Dietl and [*Major* Werner] Mölders – to receive the Oak Leaves [*Eichenlaub* to his *Ritterkreuz*] ... Apart from the Grand Cross, which was reserved solely for the *Reichsmarschall*, this was the highest military award in those days. It did not worry me that I was grounded at the same time; things would be arranged, somehow. I had been ordered to Berlin for the investiture.
>
> Hitler received me in the new *Reich* Chancellery. It was the second time I sat opposite him. On the first occasion, after my return from Spain with the *Kondor* Legion, our meeting had been in the form of a collective reception, but now I was alone with him. Our conversation was a lengthy one. I expressed admiration for our enemy across the water. I was embittered by several insidious and false representations and commentaries by the press and on the radio, which had referred to the RAF in a condescending and presumptuous tone. Although I was expecting contradiction or anger from Hitler when I gave him a different picture, he did not interrupt me, nor did he try to change the subject, but nodded repeatedly and said that my description confirmed his beliefs.

From Galland's account of this meeting, we get a great understanding of why Hitler's was so uncharacteristically indecisive and hesitant over his strategy concerning Britain earlier during the battle:

> He too had the greatest respect for the Anglo-Saxon race. It had made it all the more difficult for him, he said, to decide on waging this life-and-death struggle which could only end with the destruction of one or the other. He called it a world historical tragedy and said that it had been impossible to avoid this war, despite all his sincere and desperate attempts. If we won the war, a vacuum would be created by the destruction of Great Britain, which it would be impossible to fill.
>
> In most convincing terms, Hitler expressed not only his sympathy for the English race, but also his admiration for the class of political and industrial leaders which down the ages had developed on a much broader basis than anything that so far existed in Germany. In their political development, favoured by different circumstances, the English were a hundred years ahead of us. All the virtues an eminent race had developed over long periods became manifest during critical phases of history, as that which England was going through then. He regretted that he had not managed to bring the English and German people's together, despite a promising start.
>
> I must admit that I was highly impressed by the *Führer*'s words at the time. He had managed to take the wind out of my sails. I no longer felt bitter.

From Berlin, Galland flew to *Reichsmarschall* Hermann Göring's East Prussian hunting estate, the *Reichsjägerhof* in the Rominterheide, and there he met his friend *Oberst* Werner Mölders, *Kommodore* of JG 51 and the 'Father of Modern Air Fighting'. Three days before, Mölders had scored his fortieth victory and was first received by Hitler, then delayed by Göring's summons – much to his annoyance given his desire to return and continue the fight. Friends but still rivals, Galland and Mölders now had an equal number of victories, and Galland wrote, '[I felt obliged to defend] the title as the most successful fighter pilot in the world'. Having received a promise from Göring that Galland would be delayed for the same length of time he was, Mölders wished Galland luck with the hunt and hastened back to the Pas-de-Calais.

Galland's previous meeting with Göring, on 7 September 1940, when the Luftwaffe chief had berated and blamed the *Jagdwaffe* for the failure to date, had not gone well but now all seemed forgotten:

> [*Reichsmarschall* Hermann] Göring came out the house to meet me, wearing a green suede hunting jacket over a silk blouse with long, puffed, sleeves, high hunting boots, and in his belt a hunting knife in the shape of an old Germanic sword. He was in the best of humour … his worries about the Luftwaffe in the Battle of Britain seemed to be spirited away.

In the adjacent forest, stags could be heard rutting – and Göring invited Galland to hunt one of his personal *Reichsjägermeister* stags. Arguably, Göring may have been better advised to be in France, directing the ongoing aerial assault on Britain.

Safely back on dry land, Flying Officer Harold Bird Wilson – possibly Galland's historic fortieth victim doubtless reflected upon his lucky escape. Of fear, the air vice-marshal, as he later became, had this to say:

> Yes, I was afraid. It came out at night mostly, when I was asleep. I had terrible nightmares. It seemed as though I was flying half the night although I was still in my bed. I think anybody who says he wasn't afraid is a bloody liar – unless he was a chap like Sailor Malan [Squadron Leader Adolph 'Sailor' Malan], a superb pilot, an excellent leader and a man of great mental stature. But people had to put a shield around themselves. Externally, some were hale, hearty, debonaire. They showed a couldn't-care-less attitude. But I'm convinced they got down on their prayer mats many, many times. When they were by themselves or before they went to sleep, I believe they had a quick conversation with the Almighty.

Returning to the fighting on 24 September 1940, between 11.00 and 11.20 hrs, 66 Squadron was scrambled from Gravesend to patrol the Thames Estuary. Me 109s were still milling about, Pilot Officer Crelin Bodie, Red 2, reporting that the Spitfires engaged thirty Me 109s over Chatham at 11.45 hrs, at 17,000ft:

> Saw lots of Me 109s, ordered to break up and engage. I steamed after about twelve or fifteen of them, firing about four short bursts at about four of the rearmost. One broke away and I, following, gave him several more bursts from stern and quarter. He seemed to be in difficulties, and was performing queer and ineffective manoeuvres to lose me. Eventually he appeared to flick into a spin (it may have been an aileron turn) and at the same time white smoke came back from his engine (possibly glycol). I overshot him, and after turning, lost him. Last seen going down towards Tenterden, making for Dungeness. Yellow nosed, normal camouflage. All the 109s fled on being attacked, none making any show of a fight and were easy to catch.

Bodie was awarded a probable, as was Sergeant Charles Cook. Pilot Officer Hugh Reilley damaged a 109, and Pilot Officer George Pickering set one on fire over the south-east coast, which was not seen to crash but credited as destroyed. The Spitfires suffered no loss in the skirmish, and it seems all the 109s returned home.

The next attack aimed at London came in at lunchtime, a large force of Do 17s escorted by the usual Me 109s. Owing to bad weather, however, the bombers turned about and returned to France with their bombs aboard. No. 41 Squadron was up and clashed over Dover with 2 and 3/JG 52, the Me 109 pilots claiming destruction of seven Spitfires. Just two, though, were actually shot down: Sergeant John McAdam baled out over the Channel and was rescued from the sea unhurt, and Sergeant Edward Darling crash-landed near Dover, also unhurt. The Hornchurch Spitfire pilots made no combat claims. No. 92 Squadron was also up patrolling Dover and clashed inconclusively with I/JG 53; neither side filed claims nor suffered losses.

All was then quiet until 16.20 hrs, when Green Section of 74 Squadron's 'B' Flight, based at the 12 Group aerodrome of Kirton-in-Lindsey, intercepted a lone Do 17 bomber over the North Sea, 10 miles south-east of Sherringham on the Norfolk coast. Pilot Officer Walter Franklin, Green 1, Pilot Officer Edward 'Wally' Churches, a New Zealander, Green 2, and Pilot Officer Roger Boulding, Green 3, all fired at and damaged their target but eventually the raider disappeared into thick mist. It is likely, however, that this was the

1/KG 3 machine, which crashed in Antwerp owing to combat damage, three of the crew being wounded.

By late afternoon the weather had turned wet and cloudy. At 17.00 hrs, Pilot Officer Ian Muirhead and Pilot Officer Witold Głowacki, a Pole, were up from Croydon and patrolling Beachy Head when they intercepted a Do 215. Chasing the bomber in and out of cloud, destroying it between them, the enemy aircraft reportedly crashing into the Channel 5 miles south-west of Cap Gris-Nez.

According to the ORB, however,

> As they emerged from cloud by the French coast, they were pounced upon by Me 109s which forced Pilot Officer [Ian] Muirhead to do some hedge-hopping over France to twenty-one miles inland to shake it off – Pilot Officer [Witold] Głowacki was not seen again.

Muirhead returned safely to Croydon, but Głowacki was shot down and crashed in France. Photographs taken by the Germans show him with a bandaged head by his wrecked Hurricane but he died later in the day. The circumstances have never satisfactorily been explained, some sources suggesting the cause of death being a severe reaction to an anti-tetanus injection, which seems unlikely, whilst others opine that the Gestapo was responsible; we will never know what happened, but it is a fact that Witold Głowacki is buried in Guînes. The Germans claimed two Hurricanes destroyed, *Unteroffizier* Adolf Benzinger of 3/JG 51 chalking up his first victory over the Channel and *Oberleutnant* Michael Sonner, of the same unit, his fourth aerial victory over Boulogne, who actually got Głowacki is impossible to say.

To the west, there had also been action, when *Erprobungsgruppe* 210 resumed its brief to destroy the Supermarine factory at Woolston. At 13.00 hrs, the precision bombing unit took-off from Cherbourg-Ost, local defence organisations subsequently recording how, at 13.35 hrs, thirty-seven bombers, escorted by fighters, dived from 20,000ft, attacking the Supermarine factory, the gas works across the River Itchen and the electricity power station next to Southampton's main railway station. Inexplicably, no 'Red Warning' was given, the sirens only sounding five minutes after the first bombs exploded.

For 'Supermariners' the drill was for the factory siren, signalling immediate evacuation to the shelters, to sound several minutes after the town's warning. On this occasion, before this happened, heavy AA fire opened up. Cyril Russell, an 18-year-old working in K-Shop, remembered that by the time he had exited the building and reached the nearby road, the noise of gunfire was 'terrific'. Looking up, to his left, young Russell saw the raiders 'with bombs already leaving their racks'. With no time to reach the shelters, which in any case he had previously vowed never to use on account of the distance involved, Russell flattened himself into the ground. Exploding bombs made the ground 'tremble and kick'. Then the gunfire stopped. Despite the lightning-fast raid, which caught Fighter Command on the hop, the all-important factory was virtually untouched. At the northern end of the road, close to the Itchen works, Russell could see 'a lot of activity', towards which he made haste, joining

> people ... with bags marked with red crosses, and metal stretchers ... soon people, running, walking and stumbling, came towards us from the opposite way. Some looked dirty, others limped, and almost all had that strained, shocked look in their eyes.

Soon the 'cause of their distress' was all too 'apparent': 'The whole bomb load had dropped short, and straddled the railway embankment', which was untouched, 'but had hit the shelters, the road, and the people making for them.' Russell's account provides a graphic description:

> It was obvious there were a lot of casualties; some poor souls had been blown up onto the railway embankment and lay like bundles of old clothing. Others had been blown into the embankment lower down, and were buried, or partly buried, by the earth thrown up from the craters. Here and there a limb protruded, or perhaps just the colour of an overall or jersey could be seen, and it was to these that the survivors who had collected their wits, and we luckier ones from the Woolston factory, turned our attention, tearing away the earth with our hands, lifting them out, trying artificial respiration, calling for stretchers, and, of course inevitably having to leave some lying there when we realised they were beyond our help.

Amongst those killed when the shelter was hit were two teenage 'Supermariners'.

One of four children, with dark curly hair and bespectacled, Douglas Cruikshank was a 14-year-old 'workshop assistant', better known as a 'handy lad', of 6 Osterley Road, at the far end of Peartree Green in Woolston. Cruikshank's father, Ronald, was a Supermarine engineer at the Woolston works, but, unlike his son, was at home when the raid occurred. As smoke billowed across the common immediately after the raid, Ronald Cruikshank dashed out onto Peartree Green, where some of his children had been playing – relieved to find his daughter Jean safe and well, after sending her home Ronald Cruikshank hastened towards the main scene of destruction, hoping to find Douglas. That he did – but not alive. Jean Cruikshank did not see her father again until the following morning – overnight his hair had turned white.

That morning, there was also a shock in store for Cyril Russell, when his foreman, Bill Heaver, told him that a particular young girl, Margaret 'Peggy' Moon, had been killed:

> He knew that a few weeks previously I had quite a crush on her, and we had gone to the Grand Theatre together. She was a secretary, and known to the lads as 'the girl in green' because of the green outfit she wore, with a little fur hat. Her name was 'Peggy' Moon, from Canada Road, and a lovelier girl one could not wish to know. Now she was dead, and how grateful I am that I was not the one who found her.

The 'girl in green' was 19 years old and, like poor Douglas Cruikshank, was buried in Southampton's St Mary's Extra Cemetery.

The use of HE bombs on this raid dictated more damage than usual to life and property. In total, 42 people were killed; 65 suffered serious injuries, 109 less serious. Again, the Supermarine factory itself escaped, with only minor damage to the main building's east corner. In nearby Woolston, the railway bridge was destroyed, and collateral damage on both sides of the River Itchen was substantial: 18 homes were completely destroyed, 53 required demolition to finish the job and 238 more sustained minor damage. UXBs were numerous, causing chaos and dictating evacuation of the factory.

Having made good their escape, *Erprobungsgruppe* 210's crews beat it back to France, rearming and refuelling – and returned to Southampton. At 16.24 hrs, sixteen enemy bombers approached on the same course as the previous raiders. This time, 25 tons of HE bombs exploded in the area around the Supermarine factory, including Peartree Green and Radstock Road – but, yet again, the Spitfire-producing factory escaped damage. How long, though, could this apparently charmed life last?

At 16.20 hrs, 10 Group had scrambled the Spitfires of 609 Squadron from Warmwell to patrol Swanage. En route, Squadron Leader 'Uncle' George Darley, Red 1, 'Sorbo Leader', was informed by Middle Wallop Control that incoming bandits had turned north-east, towards Southampton at 20,000ft. Darley saw AA fire bursting over the port and, according to the squadron's Intelligence Combat Report,

> saw two loose enemy formations of ten Do 17s [*sic*] at 14,000 feet, and a rear formation of twelve–fifteen Me 110s at 17,000 feet, about three miles behind. He ordered 609 Squadron to attack [the] first Dornier formation by sections, from quarter diving from 18,000 feet down sun.

Darley, however, was mistaken there were no Do 17s, these were all Me 110s, being the fighter bombers of *Erprobungsgruppe* 210 escorted by *Zerstörers* provided by elements of KG 76, heading for the Supermarine factory.

According to 609 Squadron's report, the German formation was 'completely broken up'. Darley inconclusively engaged a 'Do 17 [*sic*]' and a Me 110, and Sergeant Alan Feary, Red 2, and Pilot Officer Michael Staples, Red 3,

> both sent Dorniers [*sic*] into the sea off the south coast of the Isle of Wight. Yellow Leader (Flying Officer John Dundas) having damaged, if not destroyed, a Dornier [*sic*] had an exhilarating dogfight with a Me 110 in which he found he could equally hold his climb and turn inside him. He gave him a long burst at short range after he had straightened out and sent him spinning into the sea. Having attacked the same Dornier [*sic*] as Red 2, he selected and damaged another.

Pilot Officer Keith 'Skeets' Ogilvie, a Canadian, claimed a damaged 'Do 17 [*sic*]', Pilot Officer John Curchin, Green 1, claimed a Me 109 destroyed, which 'went into the sea about 15 miles south of the Isle of Wight' and Pilot Officer Rogers Freeman Garland 'Mick' Miller, Yellow 3, claimed a 'Do 17 [*sic*]' damaged.

In their subsequent reports, both Squadron Leader George Darley and Flying Officer John Dundas commented positively on 'the accuracy of our AA fire and state it was very helpful in locating E/A'. There is, however, a discrepancy in the records as to who was responsible for the destruction and damage caused to the German aircraft involved. Acknowledging that the 'Do 17s' reported by 609 Squadron were actually Me 110s, the Spitfire pilots claimed two twin-engined machines destroyed, a probable and two damaged. Two Me 110s of III/ZG 76 went into the sea and two of 4/JG 76 returned to base damaged – all, according to German records, victims of AA fire. Moreover, *Erprobungsgruppe* 210 reported the loss of a 1 *Staffel* Me 110, which also went into the sea, apparently shot down by fighters: the pilot, *Leutnant* Ulrich Freiherr von der Horst and his *Bordfunker*, *Obergefreiter* Franz Ollers, were never seen again. Clearly, these were the aircraft engaged by and destroyed by 609 Squadron, which suffered no loss in the engagement, although *Leutnant* Karl Roos of 5/JG 53 claimed a Spitfire destroyed south of the Isle of Wight.

Earlier that day, 602 Squadron at Westhampnett had patrolled as a wing with Tangmere's Hurricane squadrons, 213 and 607, over Kent without meeting the enemy. In the afternoon, 602 Squadron 'escorted', according to the ORB, the Hurricanes of 607 Squadron (a very interesting use of language) on a patrol of Portsmouth, the friendly formation being fired upon by 'Naval AA guns [Squadron 602 ORB]'. Although unrecorded in loss returns, 602 Squadron noted that 607 Squadron suffered 'several aircraft damaged'. Later, Red Section of 602 Squadron took-off on patrol at 15.30 hrs, inconclusively engaging a Ju 88, the squadron's other three sections scrambling at 16.10 hrs to patrol Southampton. The Spitfires arrived over the city at 20,000ft, but by then the attackers were being engaged south of the Isle of Wight by 609 Squadron. At 16.25 hrs, 607 Squadron scrambled from Tangmere to patrol Southampton and the Isle of Wight but could only report 'E/A seen escaping in distance, followed by AA fire. No interception.'

At 17.25 hrs, Pilot Officer Archibald Lyall led Red Section of 602 Squadron, up again from Westhampnett to patrol Swanage, at 17.40 hrs intercepted a lone Me 110 orbiting the area at 20,000ft. Lyall attacked from abeam, stopping the starboard engine, and Sergeant James Gillies, Red 3, also opened fire, noting pale blue then black smoke emitting from the intruder. After breaking away, the Spitfires lost sight of their target, which was claimed as 'damaged'.

So ended the day fighting on 24 September 1940.

Eighty-four Coastal Command aircraft had flown the usual round of patrols and escorted twenty-one convoys; an Anson attacked E-boats in the Channel but other operations were scrubbed owing to bad weather. At night, FAA Swordfish sowed mines off Brest whilst Ansons attacked the port, and Blenheims hit shipping at Cherbourg. E-boats were also attacked off Dover by 2 Group Blenheims, one of which was destroyed by *Feldwebel* Eberhard von Boremski of 9/JG 3. By night, Bomber Command hit the invasion ports and industrial targets in Berlin, although bad weather over Germany compromised the latter raid. A 301 (Polish) Squadron Battle failed to return from attacking the invasion ports and a 107 Squadron Blenheim came down in France; both crews were killed. Two Hampdens of Hemswell's 61 Squadron collided on take-off. One crewman being killed and three airmen were killed when a 58 Squadron Whitley, bound for Berlin, crashed shortly after take-off from Linton-on-Ouse.

Daily Home Intelligence Reports:

> In London people remain determined but cheerfulness varies. People are anxiously considering night life in shelters under winter conditions.
>
> Rumours and exaggerated stories continue: in particular there are stories of poisonous substances dropped from enemy planes and of 'secret weapons' with which we shall eventually stop night bombing.
>
> Except in certain areas invasion talk has receded into the background.

Wales (Cardiff) Region:

> Rumours of invasion persist.

Wednesday, 25 September 1940

Throughout the night of 24/25 September 1940, the weather improved, and dawn saw comparable conditions to days on which major attacks on London had been launched. Surprisingly, however, all was quiet over the Thames Estuary and approaches, and what little action there was over Kent and Sussex concerned lone nuisance raiders or reconnaissance aircraft. Unlike recent days, there was respite for *Luftflotte* 2's Me 109 pilots, and those from *Luftflotte* 3 that had moved into the Pas-de-Calais for the daylight assault on London returned to their bases in Normandy and Brittany – the significance of which was not lost on those monitoring British RDF screens. Moreover, RAF reconnaissance flights now noted that the barges congregated at the various invasion ports were beginning to disperse. Putting both factors together, it was clear that the immediate threat of invasion had passed.

The first of 11 Group's squadrons to see action on this day was Northolt's 229 Squadron. At 10.15 hrs,

> Pilot Officer [Vernon] Bright and [Pilot Officer John] Dewar were sent up on interception patrol. Pilot Officer Bright encountered a twin-engined E/A in the vicinity, but though he fired some 800 rounds the range was too great and owing to excessive oil temperature he was forced to break off the engagement. Pilot Officer Dewar was vectored to Enfield at 25,000 feet when a Me 110 crossed his bows at 29,000 feet, some five miles distant. He gave chase at full throttle and opened fire at 250 yards range over Tunbridge Wells, catching the E/A by surprise. There was a tumbling fight and Pilot Officer Dewar finally shot the E/A down North of Bexhill, after closing to thirty yards range, and saw it crash into a wood. It was fairly certain that the Me 110 rear-gunner was killed in the first attack. [ORB]

The Me 110 had been on a photographic reconnaissance sortie to London, the 7(F)/LG 2 machine crashing near Hastings; *Oberleutnant* E. Weyergang was killed either in the combat or crash, but *Feldwebel* G. Nelson was thrown clear upon impact – mortally wounded, he was captured but died later the same day.

At 11.10 hrs, the Spitfires of 602 Squadron took-off from Westhampnett with orders to patrol base with Tangmere's 213 Squadron Hurricanes. In due course, 602 Squadron's Yellow Section was ordered to intercept a bogey, whilst the remaining fighters landed. At midday, the Spitfires were over Brighton and sighted a Me 110 flying west over Shoreham at 10,000ft. All three pilots, namely Pilot Officer Archibald Lyall, Pilot Officer Osgood Hanbury and Sergeant James Gillies, attacked, last seeing, reported Lyall, the enemy reconnaissance machine 'flying at 140 mph at sea-level with both propellers going very slowly'; it was claimed as damaged.

From Northolt, 1 (RCAF) Squadron's Flying Officer Otto John Peterson, an American volunteer, and Flying Officer Blair Dalzell 'Dal' Russell, a Canadian, were scrambled to intercept a single snooper, at 14.50 hrs sighting and engaging a lone Do 215 off Worthing, which the Observer Corps reported had crashed into the sea; no apparent casualty, however, can be identified from Luftwaffe records.

At 14.55 hrs, 213 Squadron's Red Section, up from Tangmere, intercepted another Do 215, 2 miles north-west of Arundel, when patrolling at 10,000ft. The bandit was sighted 5,000ft below. Flight Lieutenant John 'Jackie' Sing, Red 1, and Pilot Officer Harold Atkinson, Red 2, both fired at and damaged the bomber, which was last seen to dive over Brighton and head south-east, back to France.

It was further west, over the 10 Group area, that the main attack was made – signalling the start of a concerted assault on the West Country's aircraft factories.

Luftwaffe intelligence now focused on the BAC at Filton, Bristol – the largest aircraft manufacturing plant in the world at this time, covering nearly 25 hectares – wrongly believing that the site produced engines for Hurricanes and Spitfires. The Germans sub-divided into three separate targets: GB 74 52 being the BAC, producing Blenheims, Beauforts and the new Beaufighter, GB 73 52 was the Bristol aero engine works, manufacturing the Taurus, Perseus and Hercules engines and GB 10 81, being the actual Filton aerodrome, servicing both the BAC and RAF (although no fighters were based here at this time). Filton was also important to Fighter Command for a reason that the Luftwaffe was unaware: the site also accommodated the 10 Group sector operations room controlling the fighters based at Bibury and Exeter.

The forthcoming attack was planned by the OKL Operations Staff at their forward HQ located at Laboissière-Le Déluge near Beauvais and shared with *Generalfeldmarschall* Hugo Sperrle's *Luftflotte* 3 HQ at Saint-Cloud, near Paris, by teleprinter on the evening of 24 September 1940. The raid's confirmed intention was a major attack on GB 73 52 – the BAC aero engine plant – which Luftwaffe planes wrongly believed was producing engines for Spitfires and Hurricanes. The attack was to be carried out by *Fliegerkorps* V and specifically the *Stab* and all three *Gruppen* of KG 55 *Greif*, fifty-eight He 111s in total, escorted by *Jafü* 3 fighter units: close escort by fifty-two Me 110s of ZG 26 *Horst Wessel*, whilst fifty-one Me 109s of I and II/JG 2 *Richthofen* and II/JG 53 *Pik As* would escort the raid to the Dorset coast, then return to their bases around Cherbourg and on Guernsey to refuel, and if necessary re-arm, before meeting the He 111s and Me 110s over the English coast on their return flight. Collectively, this was a substantial force, and the largest deployed against a target so far inland, outside the south-east. Diversionary raids were also ordered: eleven Me 110 fighter bombers of *Erprobungsgruppe* 210 were to hit Portland at low level, to the west and east flanks, Ju 88s of KG 51 were to attack Plymouth and those of KG 54 would bomb Portsmouth.

At 11.10 hrs, the Bristol raid was 30 miles north of Cherbourg and advancing across the Channel towards Portland when identified by RDF and designated 'Raid 22'. Why the warning came so late is unknown, but this gave the Germans a certain advantage – and their intended target, being so out of kilter with the pattern to date, would be a complete surprise to Air Vice-Marshal Christopher Brand's 10 Group. Spitfire pilots Flight Lieutenant Derek 'Bottle' Boitel-Gill, Red 1, and Pilot Officer Richard Innes, Red 2, of 152 Squadron, based at Warmwell, were already patrolling at this time. The remainder of the 'Hyderabad' Squadron scrambled at 11.15 hrs. Pilot Officer Graham 'Cocky' Cox, Yellow 1, led off Pilot Officer Fred Holmes, Yellow 2, Sergeant Ralph Wolton, White 1, and Pilot Officer Roger Hall, White 2. At the same time, 609 Squadron's Spitfires also scrambled from Middle Wallop to patrol Portland at 15,000ft. At 11.20 hrs, 601 Squadron left Exeter, with identical orders. The Germans crossed the Dorset coast, west of Portland, at 11.24 hrs, and were engaged by AA defences, which were later reported by the Germans as 'light'. A minute later, 238 Squadron was sent up from Middle Wallop to patrol 10 miles south of Yeovil at 15,000ft. As the Germans flew over Warmwell airfield, just inland of Weymouth, Squadron Leader Peter Devitt, Blue 1, commanding 152 Squadron there, scrambled with Sergeant Kenneth Holland, Blue 2, Pilot Officer Dudley Williams, Green 1, and Sergeant John Christie, Green 2. Black Section – Pilot Officer Eric 'Boy' Marrs, Black 1, and Pilot Officer Ian Norman Bayles, an Australian, Black 2 – then followed. Red Section was unable to locate the rest of 152 Squadron, and the various sections failed to form up together once airborne, so these pairs operated independently.

As the main German formation proceeded inland, *Erprobungsgruppe* 210 executed the diversionary attack on Portland's naval oil depot, fracturing the base's main water supply, damaging telephone communications, blocking the main road onto the 'island' and destroying fifteen houses. Afterwards, the Me 110s turned about and high-tailed it back over the Channel, all returning safely to Cherbourg-Ost.

Now that all but the eleven Me 110s of *Erprobungsgruppe* 210 had passed over Portland and continued inland, 10 Group controller suspected Westland Aircraft at Yeovil to be the target. With 238 Squadron already heading in that direction, 601 Squadron was diverted from Portland to also patrol there. No. 56 Squadron at Boscombe Down was also brought to immediate readiness – with the defence of Westland Aircraft at Yeovil in mind – but was not scrambled because the enemy bypassed that target and continued inland. Once Yeovil lay behind the enemy, now advancing towards the Bristol Channel, it became clear that Bristol was the target. Although Filton aerodrome accommodated a sector operations room, no fighters had been based there since June 1940, Bristol being covered by those based at Pembury, Bibury and Exeter. Therefore, No RAF fighters now existed between the Germans and their target. Consequently, 152, 238, 601 and 609 Squadrons began a frantic stern chase in the forlorn hope of intercepting the raiders before they bombed.

Flight Lieutenant Derek Boitel-Gill and Pilot Officer Richard Innes of 152 Squadron's Red Section were patrolling over The Needles at 25,000ft when first vectored to Portland, then Warmwell, and lost each other in the process. Boitel-Gill, however, sighted the enemy formation and shadowed it, 10,000ft above, 'reporting on its progress and hoping to join a friendly squadron'. Between Portland and Yeovil, Innes – the first of the defending pilots to engage – attacked the 'foremost formation of Ju 88s [*sic*]'. Both Yellow and White Sections

> climbed until they were in front and above the bomber formation. When West of Yeovil they delivered a frontal attack on the right-hand formation of enemy bombers without any noticeable effect. Again, they became separated. Yellow 1 delivered another head-on attack on a larger formation of enemy bombers when West of Bristol but as his machine was hit, he returned to Warmwell.

At 11.31 hrs, the sirens sounded in Bristol and the city's barrage balloons were deployed, and the men of 76th Heavy AA battery stood to and awaited events. By 11.38 hrs Raid 22 was over Weston-super-Mare and at which time three sections of 79 Squadron were scrambled from Pembury with orders to patrol 5 miles south of Cardiff, as a precautionary measure. Over Weston-super-Mare, the KG 55 commander and formation leader, *Major* Friedrich Kless, changed course, turning right towards Bristol. For some unexplained reason the Me 110s continued towards Cardiff, and so when they also turned and followed the bombers, the escorts were separated from their charges by 5 miles.

South of Bristol, Pilot Officer Eric Marrs made two head-on attacks on 'Ju 88s [*sic*]' without result. In a letter to his father, Marrs acknowledged that 'They were good, those Jerry bombers, they stuck like glue', and officially reported 'suffering heavy return fire'. After breaking away, Marrs reported seeing a parachute, this undoubtedly being one of the five-man crew of He 111 G1+DN of 5/KG 55, which was hit by AA fire, who abandoned their machine, which crashed near Portbury at 11.50 hrs.

Marrs, a 19-year-old Cranwellian, was then engaged by the Me 110 escorts, and when 'Things became a bit hot' the Spitfire pilot executed three flick rolls and span away, pulling out below the trouble. Marrs then climbed to attack the bombers out of the sun, finding a He 111 straggler – this being the aircraft of *Oberleutnant* Hans Bröcker, *Staffelkapitän* of 7/KG 55, which had been damaged in a previous interception and already streaming glycol from the starboard engine. A Me 110 came to the bomber's assistance, but Marrs had a long burst at the *Zerstörer*, which also streamed glycol from its starboard motor:

> Suddenly there was an almighty bang and I broke away quickly. I looked around, glanced at my engine and oil tanks and positioned myself for another attack, this time going for the port engine. I just began to fire when my ammunition petered out. I broke away and dived below cloud, throttled back, heaved a deep sigh and looked around to see where I was. I steered South, came to the aerodrome and landed. I had a look at my machine and counted eleven bullet holes in it. The one that made a bang in the cockpit had come along from the rear, nipped in the right-hand side of the fuselage and smashed the socket into which the R/T is plugged.

Marrs, fortunately, was unhurt.

Shortly after taking-off from Middle Wallop to patrol Portland, Squadron Leader George Darley, 609 Squadron, was ordered to patrol Swanage at 15,000ft instead, and was then informed that the raiders were over Yeovil at 16,000ft, heading north-north-west, about 10 miles from his current position.

Darley reported,

> Chased and caught them South of Bristol: three large formations of Do 17 [*sic*] and He 111 in arrow formation, each single formation a tightly packed arrowhead. Each formation had approx. sixty. Thirty Me 110s above, at 21,000 feet, three miles behind, fairly loose line astern … Attacked from beam, down sun from 21,000 feet on starboard formation by sections. Gave burst of four-seconds from 400–50 yards. No result seen as I passed under them fairly quickly. Dived straight under formation and climbed up for second attack from port but bombers were then turning to starboard and South and were being engaged by AA.

Indeed, the KG 55 crews would later report 'heavy flak over Bristol', and, bizarrely, 'a radial-engined fighter with wedge-shaped surfaces but not as fast as a 110'.

Darley continued,

> I was engaged by three Me 110s, turned around on their tail and gave a burst of three-seconds at 250 yards at one Me 110 on the turn, allowing deflection. Was attacked from [the] rear and broke away. Attacked another Me 110 from starboard quarter and gave three-second burst at 200 yards and saw no return fire. Got dead-astern and about 100 yards behind but had run out of ammunition. Very annoying. Returned to base.
>
> Bombers kept very tight formation. Heavy cross-fire. Me 110s did not seem very keen to engage. As bombers retreated Me 110s formed into defensive circle above them. Flew in elongated circles, i.e. long run to the South, fairly tight left-hand turn and then another turn to the South. AA fire not accurate for position, height good, but well behind.

The 609 Squadron diarist commented that 'The city's AA fire, though well meant, was more than disturbing our pilots, none of which, however, were hurt' [ORB].

Pilot Officer Rogers Freeman Garland Miller, Red 5:

> Five. [*sic*] Bandits [*sic*] were sighted over Yeovil and turned west, towards Bristol. My Section carried out a beam attack in echelon to break up E/A formation. I fired two second bursts at 400–50 yards. Me 110s above started to dive on us, but promptly climbed rapidly again before in range. I saw no return fire from E/A. I climbed up again, positioning myself in the sun. I carried out a beam attack on [the] main formation (five seconds, 300–150 yards). Me 110s diving down opened fire at long-range but broke away before coming close. I broke away and climbed.

Sergeant John Hughes-Rees, Red 3, in Squadron Leader George Darley's section, attacked a 'Do 215 [*sic*]', which was in

> close formation with fighters above (Me 110s). I fired a two-second burst (no result). I dived, climbed left, then saw two E/A separated from the main group. I attacked from the starboard quarter. E/A went into a vertical dive, hitting the water near Portishead Point.

In his combat report, Hughes-Rees specifically, although incorrectly, identifies the bombers as 'Do 215s', and correctly reports Me 110s. His claim was for a 'Do 215' destroyed, so presumably this was a He 111. No aircraft of any type, however, crashed into the Bristol Channel off Portishead Point, so Hughes-Rees must have been mistaken – more likely he had also attacked the He 111, which crashed slightly inland near Portbury. After the action, Red 3's Spitfire developed engine trouble, oil pressure dropping to 25lb, 'and engine boiling'; the pilot made a wheels-up landing half a mile south of the famous Glastonbury Tor landmark in Somerset.

The Hurricanes of 601 Squadron, having scrambled from Exeter at 11.20 hrs, with orders to patrol Portland Bill, were also now pursuing the Germans over the West Country, who were first sighted west of Yeovil, flying north-west. Red Section, however, was unable to overhaul the enemy and were vectored to Weston-super-Mare, watching the enemy formations turn east, towards their target.

Richard Newbury was a junior clerk at the BAC, working in the Wing Assembly Inspection Department:

> As we reached our shelter just before mid-day, even before the usual card school could get underway, there was a distant drone of aircraft engines that grew louder until it was so deafening as to vibrate the concrete shelter.

Now, KG 55 was on its bombing run, and *Major* Friedrich Kless closed up his formations tighter still to concentrate bombing. At 11.48 hrs, from 15,000ft, the He 111s dropped 350 bombs, a 'carpet' of which the Filton factory formed the centre.

Richard Newbury remembered the bombing vividly:

> there were thuds as bombs hit the ground and exploded causing a raging wind to sweep through the shelter. The situation lasted for several minutes but eventually it came to an end and there was utter confusion in the shelter. The air was full of dust and most of us were picking ourselves up off the shelter floor.

Lyndon McFarlane was a BAC apprentice:

> On hearing the immediate danger warning we entered our shelters and did not have long to wait. Our shelter warden was looking out and called 'There's dozens of the buggers!' As he came in and closed the door, immediately all hell broke loose, the door blew in and we were rocked by continuous bombardment that seemed to last for hours.

Richard Newbury:

> There was some delay before the All-Clear sounded and we were able to exit the shelter. As I emerged I could not believe the scene before me: the

> Flight Sheds in total disarray, bomb craters in the concrete apron in front of the sheds and damaged aircraft on the apron.
>
> An even grimmer sight across the roadway that divided our shelter from a row of shelters over the other side of the roadway leading from the Main Assembly Hall at Filton down to the Flight Sheds at the Rodney Works area: several bombs had dropped on and around these shelters and one shelter in particular had been directly hit. There were many rescue personnel operating all over the site, trying to rescue and treat people where possible.

Luck had been on the Germans' side: a bank of cloud only obscured the target after the last Heinkel had bombed. The actual attack lasted less than a minute – but the resulting damage was substantial: 900 Filton dwellings were destroyed or damaged.

Phyllis Burke lived in Bridgman Grove off Filton Avenue and was returning from the horse fair, where she sheltered with her mother, 'when the big raid came over'. Afterwards, the pair headed home:

> Walking down Bridgman Grove I said to mother, 'That's our house!'
>
> She said, 'Oh no, we don't live there, we live further down the road.'
>
> But it was our house, which had gone completely. A bomb had fallen right in the middle of a row of four houses and we lived in one of the middle ones, number 40 or 42. The house was completely gone, it was only a hole and we lost everything. My grandmother was in the shelter and they had to dig her out.

The main railway line between Filton Junction and Patchway was blocked and other lines also damaged; water mains, gas and electricity supplies, and telephone communications were disrupted – the latter being an unknown bonus for the enemy. Filton sector's operations room was now out of contact with 10 Group operations room at Box. Indeed, most of the HE bombs and all 24 oil bombs had hit the intended target – 168 bombs falling on the factory site. Extensive damage was caused to the Rodney works, the main aircraft assembly plant was seriously damaged – one building concerned with engine production was destroyed by fire and another lost its roof. Eighty new aircraft were destroyed and twenty-four damaged, and in the adjacent works' car parks various vehicles were damaged or destroyed. Tragically, six shelters had been hit at the flight shed and east engine works, contributing greatly to the overall death toll of BAC workers: ninety-six people were killed or died of injuries later, many losing their lives in the shelters. Included in the BAC death toll were thirteen volunteers of 13th Gloucestershire (City of Bristol) Battalion of the Home Guard, killed marching between the Rodney works and Patchway, and Roy Colston of the works ARP Squadron (who died the following day). At the Rodney works, four more employees were killed, and one fatality each at barrage balloon site 35/6th and 39th Searchlight Regiment, RAF 'Dazzle Defence' site at Bailey's Court Farm. Beyond the BAC site, 58 civilians were killed, 154 seriously injured and 118 slightly less so. The presence of many UXBs, which had failed to detonate due to a technical issue with their fuses, hampered rescue efforts; seven of twenty ambulances sent to the scene were damaged by these delayed explosions, which also caused nine fatalities amongst emergency and medical personnel.

After what was, from the enemy perspective, a successful attack, *Major* Friedrich Kless and his men now had to withdraw; although 10 Group had failed to prevent KG 55 bombing Filton, four defending squadrons barred the raiders' way back to France.

Squadron Leader Harold 'Harry' Fenton and the Hurricanes of 238 Squadron had made haste to Bristol but arrived when the Heinkels were already over their target. At first, Fenton ordered the squadron into line astern and climbed, with attacking the Me 110s from astern in mind but then decided to engage the bombers from a beam. Fenton, Red Leader, hit the port engine of a He 111, which began smoking, but he broke away believing escorting fighters were coming down. Fenton then pursued the retreating enemy, hoping to effect another attack but was unable to catch up and abandoned the chase over Bournemouth at 23,000ft, owing to a lack of oxygen. After inconclusively attacking a He 111, Pilot Officer Vernon Simmonds, Red 2, also chased after the bombers, reporting having attacked a He 111 4 miles out to sea, which he watched crash into the water 12 miles off the Dorset coast; no He 111s went into the sea, however, although a Me 110 of III/ZG 26 did, the crew of which were rescued by the *Seenotdienst*. Pilot Officer David Harrison, Red 3, also delivered an ineffective initial attack before following the enemy south but then realised that his Hurricane had been damaged by return fire, so landed in Frome.

Sergeant Gordon Batt, Yellow 1, fired three bursts at a He 111, watching his bullets penetrating the machine but without any other apparent effect. Similarly, Sergeant Jiří Kučera, a Czech, Yellow 2, inconclusively fired at a He 111 before breaking away when attacked himself by three Me 110s. Sergeant Fred Sibley, Yellow 3, fired two short bursts at the rearmost bombers but was also hit by return fire, writing-off his Hurricane in a forced-landing at RAF Charmy Down, near Bath; the pilot was unhurt.

Leading Blue Section, Flying Officer John Urwin-Mann, a Canadian, shot 'bits' off a He 111, which remained in formation, until, after further attacks,

> [the bomber] broke away and dived steeply. Followed and saw it turn on its back, out of control, and fired another 2-second burst from 250 yards. E/A dived straight down and hit the ground, exploding.

This aircraft belonged to 6/KG 55's *Staffelkapitän*, *Hauptmann* Helmut Brandt, and was also attacked by Pilot Officer Władyslaw Różycki, a Pole, Blue 2, Pilot Officer Ian Norman Bayles, Green 3, Sergeant Ronald Little and Sergeant Kenneth Holland of 152 Squadron, which was also now engaging the withdrawing Germans; four of the crew were killed when the aircraft crashed at Woolverton, but Brandt, who was wounded, baled out and was captured. Holland, however, was hit by return fire in the engagement and killed when his Spitfire also crashed at Woolverton.

The demise of Brandt's Heinkel had also been witnessed by Pilot Officer Noël le Chevalier 'Aga' Agazarian, Blue 2, of 609 Squadron, who, upon seeing the crew baling out and noting that 'three Spitfires were looking after it', climbed back up to find more action.

Over Bath, Squadron Leader Peter Devitt, Blue 1, of 152 Squadron, leading for Spitfires of 'B' Flight, met the raiders making for the coast. Attacking (but also misidentifying the enemy as 'Ju 88s'), Devitt closed to just 20 yards but was unable to observe results as he was temporarily blinded by petrol splashing over him from his fuel tank, positioned between the pilot's instrument panel and engine, after his fighter was damaged by return fire. Dropping out of the fight, Devitt landed safely in Skew Bridge, several miles west of Bath. Pilot Officer Dudley Williams, Green 1, was more successful, shooting down a Me 110 of 8/ZG 26, also attacked by Pilot Officer Howard Mayers, an Australian, Red 1, of 601 Squadron, which crashed at Well Bottom near Boyton in Wiltshire; the pilot, a ten-victory ace, *Feldwebel* Walter Scherer, survived and was captured, but his *Bordfunker*, *Gefreiter* Heinz Schumacher was killed. No. 601 Squadron's Pilot Officer Aylmer Aldwinckle, Red 3, claimed a 110 damaged in the Frome area, which he last saw streaming black and white smoke from the fuselage.

Having first shadowed the Germans, 152 Squadron's Flight Lieutenant Derek Boitel-Gill, Red 1, eventually attacked the withdrawing He 111s (although misidentified as 'Ju 88s') as they approached Bournemouth, and Pilot Officer Richard Innes, Red 2, again engaged the bombers over Shaftsbury and Bournemouth; all Red Section's attacks were inconclusive.

No. 609 Squadron's Pilot Officer Noël Agazarian (who, coincidentally, was flying Spitfire R6915, now preserved by and can be seen at the Imperial War Museum, London), engaged several Heinkels between Bristol and the Dorset coast and then saw a lone bomber 2,000ft below the main formation. Although short of ammunition, 'Aga' attacked, firing a short burst before breaking away beneath his target:

> I then climbed for another attack and noticed that he was being joined by two more He 111s. I attacked again and followed the attack through onto the leaders of the two E/A coming up behind. I got into position for a third attack and noticed another Spitfire attacking [author's note: Pilot Officer Rogers Freeman Garland Miller, Red 5, of 609 Squadron]. I waited, then attacked, but after a very short burst my ammunition ran out. They were diving fast and I followed one of them down. He went right down in a steep dive, pulled out at about thirty feet and went across Poole Harbour, where he machine-gunned a flying boat. The other Spitfire was still with me. As I turned back I saw one of the other He 111 going into a steep dive – two people baled out and it crashed into a house just East of Poole Harbour. He went up in flames and with him the house and neighbouring trees.

Pilot Officer Rogers Freeman Garland Miller:

> I then saw three E/A in straggly formation 3[,000]–4,000 feet below the main formation. I carried out a beam attack on the middle one, firing round to astern (rest of ammunition, 300–100 yards). Blue 2 (Pilot Officer [Noël le Chevalier] Agazarian) also fired at this machine, which crashed west of Bournemouth. Three of the crew baled out. It looked like a He 111. One He 111 flew low over the port, machine-gunning, but I had run out of ammunition, so pancaked.

The Heinkel destroyed by Agazarian and Miller was also attacked by the Hurricane of Flying Officer John Urwin-Mann of 238 Squadron. This raider was an He 111-P (2803), G1+LR, of 7/KG 55, flown by the unit's *Staffelkapitän*, *Oberleutnant* Hans Bröcker, who remained at the controls and was killed when his bomber crashed on a clifftop house, 'Chatsworth', in Westminster Road, Branksome Park, Poole. *Oberleutnant* Heinz Scholz baled out but was found dead; *Unteroffizier* Josef Hanft also baled out, but expired before being recovered from Poole harbour; *Unteroffizier* Günter Weidner was killed due to parachute failure but *Unteroffizier* Kurt Schraps landed safely in the sea off Branksome Chine and was captured unhurt.

Flying Officer Jerzy Jankiewicz, a Pole, Red 2, of 601 Squadron, reported having attacked a Me 110, silencing the rear gunner before breaking away upon being engaged himself, the Police apparently confirming having 'located' the enemy aircraft intercepted by him at 'Branksome Chine' [ORB] – but if that is so, it was not a 'Me 110' but Bröcker's He 111.

Pilot Officer John Wigglesworth, Green 3, 238 Squadron's 'Tail End Charlie', was weaving to and from behind the squadron; he first engaged five Me 110s without apparent result and experiencing a flat reflector gunsight battery. He then attacked a He 111, pieces of which were shot away, smoke poured from both engines and the undercarriage dropped. Having expended his ammunition, Green 3 followed down the stricken enemy machine of 1/KG 55, which forced-landed at Westfield Farm in Studland, west of Swanage, the RAF pilot watching as three of the crew climbed out of the wreck and 'pulled out the other two': two of the crew were unhurt, two wounded but one man was dead. This He 111 was also attacked by Pilot Officer John 'Johnny' Curchin of 609 Squadron, his squadron claiming a total of five bombers destroyed, two damaged and a probable, and a Me 110 destroyed and one each probably destroyed and damaged. Offset against this 'very good bag' [ORB] was Sergeant John Hughes-Rees forced-landing at Glastonbury and Pilot Officer Keith Ogilvie being hit by return fire and landing back at base with a burst tyre.

Eventually, it was all over. The attack, penetrating so far inland in broad daylight, had caught the defences out. Considering the damage caused to BAC in Filton, it was certainly successful, for which endeavour *Major* Friedrich Kless was decorated with the *Ritterkreuz*. To the great credit of all involved, though, electrical power was restored to the factory sites in just five hours, a feat applauded by Lord Beaverbrook, who visited the bomb damaged site personally. Production of the new Beaufighter, however, was brought to a standstill for a fortnight but picked up slowly thereafter – and this was a much needed new night fighter. The raid had no impact whatsoever, though, on the production and supply of Hurricanes and Spitfires – and that, so far as the day battle was concerned, was the primary objective.

Richard Newbury:

> Although it had been difficult to take in all that had happened that morning, the works got back to work with a further air raid warning in the afternoon. I resumed my duties until finishing at 1700 hrs.

Interestingly, the Germans believed they had been attacked exclusively by 'Spitfires', reporting '20–25' of the type intercepting them over Portland. As we know, Hurricanes were also involved, this illustrating what Group Captain Peter Townsend later described as 'Spitfire Snobbery': because of the Spitfire's superior performance, more kudos was attached to scoring successes against the type, and if units came off second best against Mitchell's fighter it was considered more understandable. Be that as it may, the number of RAF fighters involved again confirmed that this was far from a defeated air force on its last knees – it was, in fact, one able to meet the enemy in strength wherever they attacked, be that in the north, the south-east or south-west. On this occasion (although the defenders substantially overclaimed), the raiders lost four He 111s destroyed (one to AA fire and three to fighter attacks), and two Me 110s had also been destroyed; one He 111 crash-landed back in France with combat damage, as did two Me 110s. Ten enemy airmen had been killed, seven wounded and twelve were taken as POWs. Against these losses, 10 Group had suffered five fighters damaged, two destroyed and one pilot killed.

Squadron Leader George Darley, commanding 609 Squadron, though, was critical of how some pilots had fought the battle:

> Saw one formation of Hurricanes attacking one E/A formation but regret to say that I saw many other friendly aircraft attacking stragglers, who were obviously in difficulty well below the main formation. For example, three Hurricanes were attacking one disabled E/A but there were plenty of fat targets higher up.

As converse as it was bizarre, however, the OKW war diary commented that there had been 'No significant fighter-versus-fighter battles in the past eight days. The English fighters are apparently pausing to catch their breath.'

At RAF Hendon, 504 Squadron was frustrated at the lack of bomb proof facilities, flight crews spending nights sheltering under nearby railway arches because sleep was impossible in the airfield's wooden huts. On the night of 24/25 September 1940, the squadron diarist recorded that

> a landmine demolished Collingdale Station on the underground with many casualties. Bombs and incendiaries set fire to and gutted the premises of Franco Signs adjoining the Station. The aerodrome is sprinkled with incendiary bombs but the Station is not damaged. Late in the evening news is received that the Squadron is to move to Filton, near Bristol. [ORB]

This move was, of course, a precaution against another similar attack – which subsequent events would prove a wise decision.

So far as the ongoing day fighting was concerned on 25 September 1940, the Me 109s had not engaged during the morning's Filton raid. At lunchtime, however, in the wake of KG 55's withdrawal, I/JG 2 swept over Portland. Having already been in action, Flight Lieutenant Derek Boitel-Gill led six Spitfires of 152 Squadron's 'A' Flight up from Warmwell at 13.00 hrs to patrol the airfield at 15,000ft; informed of the presence of enemy aircraft over Portland, the flight proceeded there

> in search formation. Red 1 on looking round saw Me 109 sitting on the tail of Yellow 2 (Sergeant William Silver). E/A fired at Yellow 2 and burst of smoke was seen to come from his aircraft. E/A broke away and dived steeply to the South. Red 1 peeled off and dived after him, coming within range at 10,000 feet. Red 1 gave short burst from astern and black smoke appeared from machine which carried on in a steep dive through the cloud. Red 1 broke off to search for the other Me 109s. [Fighter Command Form 'F']

Silver's Spitfire crashed into the sea, killing the pilot. Both JG 2's *Gruppenkommandeur*, *Hauptmann* Helmut Wick, and *Feldwebel* Wilhelm Hermes, aces both, claimed Spitfires destroyed in this combat (although only Silver was actually lost).

The next attack also fell on the 10 Group area. At 16.17 hrs, Flight Lieutenant Michael Robinson, Red 1, had led three 601 Squadron Hurricanes of Red Sections and three of Blue Sections up from Exeter to patrol base at 15,000ft. After five minutes the fighters were vectored to Plymouth to intercept a large raid approaching from the south-east, and when west of Plymouth the enemy was sighted flying directly towards the port: twelve Ju 88s (misidentified in the Form 'F' as 'Do 215s') escorted by a dozen Me 110s. Plymouth harbour, however, was bombed just before the Hurricanes intercepted at 16.40 hrs, although little damage was caused: an oil pipe was fractured, and a crane, a jetty and a carriage shed all suffered minor damage:

> [As the raiders turned about] Red 1 attacked a Me 110 which dived down, both engines smoking. Red 3 (Flying Officer [Howard] Mayers) damaged a Do 215 [*sic*] and saw pieces falling off it. Blue 1 (Pilot Officer [Thomas] Grier) attacked a Ju 88 and brought it down in[to] the sea about twenty miles South of Plymouth. The E/A landed gently but sank at once. No crew seen to get out [author's note: no apparent matching casualty appears in Luftwaffe records]. Blue 3 (Sergeant McCann) followed a Ju 88 North and after firing two short bursts black smoke came out of both engines. Blue 3 broke away and did not observe the E/A to hit the sea. On his return to base he developed engine trouble but he managed to land safely. All pilots landed safely by 1720 hrs. [Form 'F']

So ended the day fighting on one which confirmed the enemy's primary focus was now disrupting the British aircraft industry.

At North Weald, 249 Squadron celebrated the award of two DFCs that evening, to Pilot Officer James Meaker and Pilot Officer Thomas Neil. The former, the squadron diarist wrote,

> has invariably shown calm yet extremely resolute intention of destroying the enemy, he has flown on innumerable operational flights, and can always be relied upon', and remarked of [Pilot Officer Thomas] Neil that 'He has always shown great keenness to fight and invariably keeps up his attacks to the last possible moment. He flies with great dash'. [ORB]

For Coastal Command, it had been a busy day: no less than ninety-six aircraft flew the usual patrols and escorted twenty-two essential convoys, attacking Brest by day and night. Whilst returning from one of these raids, a 59 Squadron Blenheim crashed into Chichester harbour, killing two crewmen whilst the remaining two were rescued. Bomber Command's daylight sorties comprised sweeps of the North Sea, seeking German shipping, a Blenheim crashing upon return and crashing, killing the crew. By night – as the enemy continued pounding London – Blenheims and Battles attacked the invasion ports, the longer-range Wellington, Hampden and Whitley force striking mainly at industrial and naval targets in Germany. Remarkably, a 99 Squadron Wellington crashed soon after taking off from Newmarket, bound for Calais but although the bombs aboard exploded, miraculously the crew apparently suffered no serious injury.

Daily Home Intelligence Reports:

> Northern Ireland (Belfast):
>
> It is generally thought that the RAF is inflicting more damage on Germany than is being received by London and south-east England. The possibility of invasion is still discussed ... The Belfast deputation which has been studying ARP organization is full of praise for the fortitude of Londoners in air raids.
>
> London:
>
> The need for keeping track of people who have evacuated or changed address continues. Citizens' Advice Bureau have many enquiries from men of the services home on leave who are unable to trace relatives; from Poplar a case is reported of nearly 1,000 people departing in charabancs from the West End to the country, and not even husbands knew where their wives were going.

Thursday, 26 September 1940

Following the previous day's successful Filton raid, *Major* Friedrich Kless was tasked with a major attack on the Vickers Supermarine factory at Woolston – which the precision bombing unit *Erprobungsgruppe* 210 had thus far failed to destroy. Indeed, considering the raids mounted against the all-important Spitfire producing factory, it did appear as though the works had a charmed life. Certainly, there had been damage caused, not least to adjacent Woolston, and loss of life caused to the Supermarine workforce when the Peartree Green shelter was hit two days before – but Spitfire production was unaffected.

Hauptmann Genst of *Luftflotte Kommando* 3, *Gruppe* 1c, reported that this latest assault on Supermarine involved 18 He 111s from I/KG 55, carrying 80 SC250 bombs, and 19 from II/KG 55 with 132 SC250 and 6 SC250 oil bombs. Ten He 111s from III/KG 55 were to make a diversionary raid on Portland. *Erprobungsgruppe* 210 was to hit the Woolston factory at low level with thirteen Me 110s, and fighter escort was to be provided by *Jafü* 3: forty-eight Me 110s from ZG 26, thirty-eight Me 109s from JG 2 and just six from JG 53.

The day began with no hint of what was to come, enemy incursions involving reconnaissance flights and nuisance attacks by lone raiders. That morning such a *Störflug* was mounted against the Skinningrove Iron Company Limited in North Yorkshire, all three bombs dropped hitting the target and causing such damage as to reduce the production of pig iron by a third.

Much further south, at 10.00 hrs, Squadron Leader Gerry Edge DFC, commanding 253 Squadron, took-off in company with Flight Lieutenant Raymond Myles Duke-Woolley, and Pilot Officer Tadeusz Nowak and Pilot Officer Włodzimierz Samoliński, both Poles, on an 'Interception Patrol' [ORB]. An hour later, the Hurricanes were hit by Me 109s off Dungeness: Edge was fired upon at close range from astern, his fighter bursting into flames; at 23,000ft Edge baled out, alighting in the Channel 9 miles off Dungeness and was fortunate to be rescued by a passing fisherman. Admitted to Willesborough Hospital suffering from burns, Edge was out of the battle from then on. Samoliński, however, simply disappeared and is assumed to have crashed into the sea. No. 253 Squadron made no combat claims, but *Feldwebel* Walter Meudtner of 3/JG 51 was apparently shot down into the Channel off Dungeness and remains missing. This action aside, the Me 109s of *Jafü* 2 remained on the ground.

Flight Lieutenant Raymond Myles Duke-Woolley commented that

> The Squadron was commanded by [Squadron Leader] Gerry Edge, and Kenley and Croydon worked closely together as a wing. [Nos.] 253 and 501 [Squadrons] at Kenley, and 605 [Squadron] at Croydon. Gerry had

> been a flight commander in 605 [Squadron] – he was an auxiliary – and was undoubtedly one of the unrecognized fighter wizards of the war. He pioneered the head-on attack early in September 1940, [and] took over 253 [Squadron] after it had suffered heavy losses during its first week.

With Edge now hospitalised, Duke-Woolley found himself acting CO of 253 Squadron.

During the afternoon, solo raiders penetrated inland to Coventry, damaging three large workshops, the machine shop and other buildings of the Standard Motor Company – aircraft production was unaffected but the manufacture of armoured cars was disrupted. Much of south-east England was covered in 10/10ths cloud at 6,000ft, making interception difficult. At 15.40 hrs, 249 Squadron's Red Section, comprising Flying Officer Hugh John Beazley, Pilot Officer Percival 'Percy' Burton, a South African, and Sergeant George Palliser,

> severely damaged a Do 215 near Gravesend but could not finish it off as it kept taking cover in the cloud. This aircraft was eventually lost over the English coast with white smoke and glycol streaming from starboard motor. [ORB]

At 16.30 hrs, 92 Squadron's Pilot Officer Allan Wright was leading Green Section on patrol over Tenterden, the Spitfire pilots inconclusively engaging three Dorniers, which also used cloud cover to their advantage. Although the Observer Corps reported that an aircraft had exploded on the ground at the same time of Wright's attack, there was no such casualty, so this may have been a bomb.

At Northolt, there was excitement when that afternoon King George VI visited the station, inspecting the pilots of 229 and 303 (Polish) Squadrons. Squadron Leader Ronald G. 'Boozy' Kellett, commanding the latter Polish squadron recalled,

> The record of 303 [(Polish) Squadron] was by now well-known and often mentioned by the BBC on the morning news. We often received messages of congratulations from the War Office. In addition, one had almost daily conversations with Air Vice-Marshal [Keith] Park, who was at all times polite and considerate, inviting criticism of his controllers and himself, and listened to any suggestion regarding tactics. Our greatest honour, though, was a visit by the King, George VI. I was only told on the morning of His Majesty's visit, and the Squadron was duly paraded by the aircraft, pilots and groundcrew ready for action. It seemed a somewhat strange task to

> present pilots and NCOs who knew no English to the Monarch, but it went well. I remember introducing Sergeant [Stanisław] Sobek to the King with the words 'A fine armourer, Sir.' The King shook his hand and replied that he was glad he was a good armourer.
>
> After the inspection was finished, I particularly asked the Adjutant to see that the King signed the Squadron's history book, which had been kept up to date by the Poles. Just before he signed the Squadron's book I was asked the date, and confessed I couldn't remember. I asked [Pilot Officer D.A.] Upton, who said that it was 25 September 1940, so I said 'The twenty-fifth, Sir'. His Majesty replied 'Funny, when I got up this morning it was the twenty-sixth, but anything can happen in war!' I gave the signal for caps off and the cry for 'God save the King'. Certainly, a loyal shout resulted, but I never knew what it meant!
>
> 'Battle Alert' was sounded and we were off to fight a raid coming in over Portsmouth.

The first indication of an impending heavy raid came at 16.02 hrs, when RDF provided early warning of '50+' approaching the Isle of Wight, 40 miles south of The Needles. At 16.10 hrs another plot was recorded: '20+' and one more 16.10 hrs of '35+'. All three were steering courses to pass just west of the Isle of Wight, towards Southampton or Portsmouth, making it impossible for Fighter Command to predict the enemy's intended target. At the first indication of the raid, 10 Group immediately scrambled the Spitfires of 152 Squadron from Warmwell and 609 Squadron from Middle Wallop to patrol their bases at 20,000ft, and there await further orders when the enemy's intentions became clearer. No. 11 Group sent up the Spitfires of 602 Squadron from Westhampnett to link up with 607 Squadron's Hurricanes, which scrambled from nearby Tangmere, as did those of 213 Squadron a few minutes later, at 16.10 hrs – all with orders to patrol base at 10,000ft. These deployments gave the controllers options, with 152 and 609 Squadrons positioned to protect Portland, and the other squadrons able to rapidly move to defend either Southampton or Portsmouth, which 152 and 609 Squadrons were also within swift reach of. As a further precaution, in case the Brooklands' aircraft factories were threatened, 229 and 303 (Polish) Squadrons scrambled from Northolt with orders to patrol Guildford at 12,000ft.

By 16.15 hrs, the Germans were just south-west of The Needles, the extreme western point of the Isle of Wight. No. 238 Squadron was then scrambled from Middle Wallop to relieve 609 Squadron, which was sent south-east to cover Bournemouth at 20,000ft. The Tangmere sector squadrons, 213, 602 and 607, were ordered to patrol as a wing over Portsmouth but actually operated independently, and at this point the Northolt Wing of 229 and 303 (Polish) Squadrons were also forward to Portsmouth; 152 Squadron remained orbiting Warmwell, just inland of Weymouth.

Squadron Leader George Darley and his 609 Squadron were the first defending pilots to sight the enemy

> at 18,000 feet about five miles South of the Needles. Reported to base. E/A turned NE and made for Southampton … Turned to intercept but saw Me 109s coming for us. Me 109s were yellow from airscrew to cockpit and silver fuselage from cockpit to rudder. Passed over our heads and turned to attack us from rear. Ordered Squadron to turn and protect themselves but attack bombers if possible. 'A' Flight acting as above guard looked after Me 109s and allowed most of 'B' Flight to attack bombers. Could not keep rigid formation so attacked independently. Attacked rear of bomber formation from port quarter, gave 4-second burst from 300–100 feet at Do 215 [*sic*], saw tracer hitting E/A but could not stay owing to heavy return fire. Flew into AA fire, so climbed …

The Me 109 escorts were from JG 2 and 53 German fighters being claimed as destroyed by Flying Officer John Dundas and Pilot Officer Noël le Chevalier Agazarian (although no relevant Luftwaffe losses can be found).

Having been ordered to Southampton, Squadron Leader Harold Fenton and 238 Squadron were south of Tangmere and also sighted the enemy, at 16.25 hrs, flying north over the Isle of Wight. Fenton, Red Leader, 'gave tally ho, ordered sections line astern and climbed to intercept [Form 'F']'. No. 238 Squadron attacked what were elements of the Me 110 escorts. Years later, Air Commodore Harold Fenton, as he became, recalled what happened next:

> The raid was pretty much over the target when we appeared on the scene, so I ordered the squadron to open fire as we approached, even though we were still climbing. There was then a melee on the way down and I found myself doing a head-on on a Me 110 right on top of my home at Hamble. We were firing simultaneously – I stuck it a little longer than he did but his cannon had knocked great lumps out of my Hurricane, which had oil coming out everywhere! The engine was barely responding and I managed to glide down to a dead stick landing at Lee-on-[the-]Solent – there to be met by my oldest friend and recent neighbor [*sic*], [Commander] Jack Keene-Miller, then serving in the FAA.

Fortunately, Fenton was unhurt.

Meanwhile, 238 Squadron's Pilot Officer Vernon Simmonds, Pilot Officer John Urwin-Mann, Pilot Officer John Wigglesworth and Sergeant Jiří Kučera all claimed Me 110s destroyed – but only two were: one machine, of 1/ZG 26, had its port engine stopped by AA fire before being shot down by Urwin-Mann and making a high speed crash-landing at Newport on the Isle of Wight – both crewmen were captured; Wigglesworth hit a 7/ZG 26 *Zerstörer*, which dived vertically and impacted at Freshwater on the island, killing both crew members.

Joan Tagg was a typist at the Supermarine works and recorded it in her diary as having been a

> Peaceful morning – managed catch up on my pile of invoices. Working late again so will stay on to tea. Just before tea a plane went over and was fired upon – probably a reconnaissance aircraft as no bombs were dropped.

What Tagg had heard, however, was The Solent gunners opening up on the approaching raid, although Squadron Leader George Darley considered this a barrage 'in quantity but not quality'.

'Dinks' Diaper was a riveter at the Supermarine factory and recalled,

> There was hardly any time between when the air raid siren sounded and the bombs started falling. I came running out of the factory's F-Shop onto Hazel Road. Then up Sea Road under the railway arch. The resident publican of the 'Red Lion' would leave the cellar doors open on the forecourt and I dived down into it for shelter.

Joan Tagg:

> We went across the road to the canteen for our tea and I was just raising the cup to my lips when the 'immediate danger' hooter blasted out. With one accord we all rose and rapidly made our way to the exit – like ants from an anthill. We had no intention of trying to reach the shelters, so a few friends, with some executive staff, found ourselves in a basement room under the high office block. Others, I heard later, headed for large drain pipes and some sheltered beneath the canteen. All was quiet for a while and we hoped it was a false alarm.

This, though, was no 'false alarm'.

The attack on the Spitfire factory was opened by *Erprobungsgruppe* 210's Me 110 fighter bombers, which made two low-level diving attacks. The two

Gruppen of KG 55 then made their bombing runs unopposed, as at Filton the previous day, attacking in two waves from 14,000–16,000ft.

Flieger Robert Götz was an 18-year-old air gunner in one of the Heinkels. He recalled,

> The bombs drop out and disappear in a row in the slight mist ... huge, systematically laid out industrial installations from which the smoke mushrooms up over the whole area ... Clouds of smoke are throwing a veil over the picture, and above these clouds there are many barrage balloons, sticking up undisturbed like small Zeppelins ... Suddenly there was another gigantic burst of flame, with a huge column of smoke following it, from an oil or gas storage tank [author's note: the gas works and docks across the Itchen from the Supermarine factory were also hit]. Time to go, and set our course below.

Joan Tagg:

> Suddenly there was a tremendous ear-splitting roar from the AA guns and the sound of an immense number of planes – then it came – the whine and whistle of bombs swishing down over our heads. Down they came and crashed all along the building. We lay on the floor with our arms over our heads (my fingers firmly in my ears) while the ground rose up beneath us with every crash and we were thrown around. We heard the sound of glass shattering and dust and plaster covered us. Then quiet – we looked up and saw that one wall had cracked. We sat up shakily and looked at each other in horror. Suddenly, down the stairs staggered a policeman, grey in face and covered in dust. He had been caught out in the road near the factory and had lain in the gutter when the bombs fell.

Then, KG 55's second wave hit Supermarine.

Joan Tagg continued,

> We were so relieved to be alive and were thinking of leaving, when to our horror again the roar of guns and the sound of planes. We fell to the floor and once again suffered the onslaught of bombs while the building shuddered. I found myself repeating the words of a hymn: 'Faint not nor fear, his arms are near', over and over again. It seemed to go on for eternity and we heard the sound of buildings collapsing and the crackle of flames. But it did pass and we were still there.

Supermarine drawing office draughtsman Albert 'Bill' Adams, who survived the raid, was also a member of the AFS, and afterwards wrote, somewhat graphically, to his wife,

> On Thursday we had a warning about four o'clock, so went to action station on Peartree Green. Suddenly about thirty bombers came out of the clouds and dived on Woolston. We flung ourselves on the floor of the post, and were thrown about like 'peas rattling in a tin'. After the din was over I went out to look around and saw that our Itchen Works was smashed up and burning. I went up the Station and reported to George, and suggested that we went down. He gave me the 'OK' if I thought it was safe. Well, we just got to the bottom end of Peartree Green when I looked up and saw another bunch of bombers diving out of the clouds. I flung the lads out of the car and dived with them into a shelter. We just made it, for I had just got to the bottom of the steps when the first 'egg' landed. The old shelter did everything except turn upside down. The bombs were absolutely screaming down. I was thinking of you, my dear. If I was going to be hit I wanted my last thoughts to be of you. Yet somehow I didn't think that I was going to be hit, and so it proved. The nearest one was about twenty feet away, and five fell within thirty yards. There were twenty Junkers [*sic*] in that lot and did they [*sic*] come low. I felt as if I could touch them. Well we couldn't get down to the works because the road ahead was blown up. We should have been there if my lucky star had made me look up. We doubled back to go round another way and found a house afire in Peartree Avenue. Several received direct hits up there. Anyhow we stopped and put the fire out and then reported back to the Station.
>
> When I got back I found that the Woolston Works had been hit also, one bomb landing on the Drawing Office, about fifteen feet away from my board. Another bomb hit the Dope Shop and caused a fire, several others hitting the main Works. After the 'All Clear' we were just taking the wet hose off our pumps when the siren went again.

Two days before, many 'Supermariners' had been killed when the shelters on Peartree Green suffered a direct hit; options for shelter were, therefore, more limited on this occasion, some twenty workers finding refuge under a disused railway arch or tunnel, described by William Rigby, a medic in the ARP, as being 'a railway cutting and a disused tunnel situated immediately to the East of Lower Vicarage Road and Laurel Road'. Sadly, this proved no safe refuge – the location was hit by a HE bomb. Two borough workmen, Arthur Smith and James Marsh, were in a shelter nearby and upon emerging hastened to the scene. Smith sent Marsh to fetch the rest of his ten-man road gang but before they arrived with shovels, Smith had dug out three survivors by hand. Smith's subsequent nomination for a Civil Defence Gallantry Award stated that 'he worked until his hands were raw and bleeding and to the extent of absolute exhaustion'. Despite the presence of a nearby UXB, Smith's gang recovered three more survivors and one of the six killed at that location. It was a great humanitarian effort, as Mr S.G. Stanton, the borough engineer emphasised, these were 'not rescue or demolition men but members of my Highways staff and undertook this work quite voluntarily'.

The initial ARP report stated that bombs had first fallen

> on the Docks and Chapel district of St Mary's Ward, then on the Eastern shore of the River Itchen, from White's Yard to below the Supermarine main works. At least sixty HE bombs were dropped on the West side of the river and at least eighty on the East side. The UXBs found have all been 250 KG bombs, and using this as the average, thirty-five tons of bombs were used. The most important damage was to the Gas Works, Supermarine Main works, Supermarine Annex at Itchen, and two warehouses in the Old Docks, where four or five bombs were dropped. A great deal of damage was done to private property on the West side, in Chapel district, where the sixty bombs were concentrated in an area of about one sixteenth of a square mile. As is inevitable in such a concentration as this, two or three shelters were directly hit. The total casualties were forty-eight dead, fifty-one seriously injured, and forty-three slightly injured. The damage to private property on the East side of the river was not great, the majority of the bombs falling to the river side of the houses, and a number of them actually in the river mud.

Southampton air raid warden Walter Kingston recorded that in addition to the Supermarine factory, gas works and docks, bombs also fell on Peartree Avenue, Woolston, and both Balaclava Road and Marne Road in adjacent Bitterne. At least fifty people were killed, including three members of the 13th (Itchen) Battalion of the Home Guard, and forty-seven civilians. Of the latter figure, nine of these were Supermariners, six of whom died at the railway arch. At the factory, 25-year-old Stanley Dunn of Shirley had tried to shield his 14-year-old brother-in-law, Kenneth Doswell, a factory 'Handy Lad' from Millbrook – but sadly both were amongst the dead. On the west bank of the River Itchen, two houses were hit in Melbourne Street (adjacent to what is now the St Mary's football stadium): No. 43, the five Parker children were all killed, aged between

9 months and 9 years, and at No. 23, Doris Dunford, aged 35, was killed with her 4-year-old son, Michael.

The Germans considered the attack on Supermarine another great success, KG 55's history stating that the two waves of He 111s had

> laid a carpet of precision bombs in an approach over one of the main production facilities for the Spitfire at around 16.30 hrs (BST). From 4,000m rained SC250kg bombs, around seventy tons in total on the southern factory.

Joan Tagg:

> A security officer appeared at the door and said we should get as far away as possible. The All-Clear had not sounded but we left quickly to be met with the sight of the factory in ruins under a pall of dust and smoke. On the opposite side of the road the Canteen was in flames and I thought of the people who had decided to shelter under the building. We did not wait but rushed up Sea Road to the cellar of the Red Lion pub, passing houses in ruins. This shelter was full of women and children and they were singing shakily ... The women surrounded us, asking if we knew if any of the houses were down, [I] didn't like to tell them the truth. As it was still quiet, we hurried home – people on the way kept asking if we had seen their husbands, sons, etc., who worked with us – [we] could not reassure them. I met my father rushing down to look for me. He had been working at Thorney's [*sic*, author's note: the nearby Vosper Thornycroft shipyard] and had been told Supermarine was in ruins. He was so relieved. I had never seen him so shaken.

Having climbed to avoid the AA barrage, Squadron Leader George Darley of 609 Squadron attacked the rearmost bombers as they turned after bombing – but was then

> fired at from my rear, cannon shell hitting starboard wing and aileron. Broke down and right and saw Do 215 [*sic*] going down in steep dive to starboard. Unable to follow as I thought E/A still on my tail, but he had gone. In view of damage to wing returned to base.

Pilot Officer John Curchin, 609 Squadron:

> I chased the bombers and attacked them from the quarter. They split up and one made for the clouds. I got a short burst in before it reached the

> clouds and several short bursts at it in clear patches. It then flew out of the bank of clouds and I was able to get in position for a front quarter attack. I gave it 3-seconds burst from 350–50 yards. It began to lose height quickly and dived into the sea about thirty miles from the coast.

This was the sole KG 55 He 111 destroyed, a machine of 2 *Staffel*, which failed to return, the crew of which remain missing.

As was commonly the case, 609 Squadron's pilots overclaimed, two other bombers being claimed as probably destroyed and three damaged. Apart from Darley's damaged Spitfire, Pilot Officer Keith Ogilvie's aircraft was hit by return fire and shot-up, but the pilot was unhurt and returned safely to base.

No. 607 Squadron was being led by Flight Lieutenant Francis Blackadder:

> We were ordered to Southampton. Just as we reached it the Hun was diving down to bomb the Supermarine works. We came down on top of them in a head-on attack, some say right through the balloons, the Hun disappeared to the South towards Portsmouth and we were split up. Sergeant William Cunnington and I spied another large formation of bombers, which we climbed up to meet. They had fighter escort and we were only able to carry out a rather stupid quarter attack, hose-piping the formation.

No. 602 Squadron's Spitfires, also up from Tangmere, had been vectored towards Portsmouth, circling inland of Southampton at 25,000ft, with orders to engage enemy fighters. From that high vantage point, Flight Lieutenant Robert Findlay Boyd, Blue 1, who was leading, sighted the German bombers approaching Southampton from the south-west at 15,000ft. Boyd requested permission to engage but was ordered to continue searching for German fighters. Unfortunately, whilst subsequently following Boyd into the sun, the Spitfires became separated, so whilst Blue Section complied with the controller's instructions, 'other individual pilots used their discretion, mainly separated aircraft being attacked [Form 'F']'. Blue Section did then attack Me 109s, out of the sun, Boyd attacking and claiming a Me 109 as a 'probable', reporting seeing 'the pilot fall out but did not see parachute open [Form 'F']', but, again, there is no such Me 109 casualty in Luftwaffe records. Blue 1 was then himself attacked by a 109, with a red spinner, which Pilot Officer Gerald Fisher, Blue 2, took on and claimed as a probable.

Sergeant James Gillies:

> [I] Saw [the] Me 110 attacking friendly fighter which went down in flames in sea … Attacked Me 110 dead astern … E/A went down in flat left-hand spin, obviously well on fire. Claimed as destroyed. [Form 'F']

If this aircraft crashed, it could only have been one of the two down on the Isle of Wight.

After 607 Squadron had been split up, Pilot Officer Franciszek 'Franek' ('Frankie') Surma, a Pole, later reported encountering up to thirty 'Ju 88s [*sic*]' over the sea, fifteen – 20 miles off St Catherine's Point. Below the bombers were their fighter escort of Me 109s:

> I saw a bomber break away from the enemy formation and tried to overtake him. At the same moment I saw an Me 109 gliding down behind and above the Ju 88s. I followed the enemy aircraft for a considerable distance and, when several miles south of St Catherine's Point, I made two or three long bursts from 100 to 150 yards on the tail of the enemy aircraft, which immediately went into a dive and crashed into the sea.

Again, no such casualty appears in Luftwaffe records, however.

Flight Lieutenant Charles 'Chatty' Bowen was shot down by Me 110s over the Isle of Wight. He parachuted to safety and his Hurricane crashed at Calbourne, from where he made his way back to Tangmere; both *Feldwebel* Helmut Haugk of 7/ZG 26 and *Oberfähnrich* Alfred Wehmeyer of 8/ZG 26 claimed Hurricanes destroyed over the Isle of Wight.

No. 607 Squadron's Pilot Officer John Sulman claimed a 'Ju 88 [*sic*]' damaged and Sergeant Peter Burnell-Phillips reported sending a 'Do 215 [*sic*]' into the sea south of the Isle of Wight, this actually being the sole KG 55 He 111 destroyed, also claimed by 609 Squadron's Pilot Officer John Curchin and 602 Squadron's Pilot Officer Gerald Fisher, Pilot Officer William Hopkin and Sergeant Cyril Babbage. It was also attacked and seen to crash by Sergeant Józef Jeka, a Pole, of 238 Squadron.

In this hectic action, 238 Squadron unfortunately suffered an historic casualty: Sergeant Vladimar Horsky, who fell victim to a Me 110 over The Solent, and

> was the first Czech pilot to be lost from this Squadron. He had been with the Squadron for a fortnight and was the first Czech to join us. He had but little time to get to know us, and as in the case of his compatriots and of their Polish friends, diversity of language had set a hedge about him through which converse was not easy. It may be placed on record that the death and bravery of this man is the more striking when it is remembered that they must pass hours of loneliness in a strange country, even when surrounded by pilots of their Squadron.

Pilot Officer Robert Kings of 238 Squadron was also shot down, baling out, unhurt, over the Isle of Wight, and Sergeant Józef Jeka was shot-up, returning to base with a badly damaged Hurricane.

As the He 111s withdrew, flying south over the Isle of Wight with their Me 109 escorts above, they were sighted by 152 Squadron. Flight Lieutenant Derek Boitel-Gill, Red 1, put Red Section (Sergeant Ralph Walton, Red 2, and Pilot Officer Richard Innes, Red 3) into line astern, attacking the bombers

> from the beam, out of the sun, in a shallow dive, sweeping the E/A from front to rear. Other Spitfires also attacked this formation at the same time, from above and to the rear. The Section made a second attack and three Junkers 88 [*sic*] were seen to fall away from the formation with smoke belching from them. Once crashed on the Isle of Wight [author's note: one of the Me 110s] and the other two went into the sea [author's note: certainly one He 111 'went into the sea'], several miles South of the Isle of Wight. 'B' Flight were in pairs line astern and turned echelon right to attack straggler Ju 88 [*sic*] from enemy bomber formation. Blue 1 (Flight Lieutenant Fred Thomas) attacked two Ju 88s [*sic*] firing all his rounds without apparent effect. Blue 2 (Sergeant John Christie) was shot down and landed in the sea and was dead when picked up. Green 1 (Flying Officer Christopher Deanesley) was about to attack enemy bombers when he was wounded by a shot from a Me 109, which came down on his tail. He baled out and landed in the sea off Swanage and was picked up by motor launch. When Green 2 (Sergeant Albert Kearsey) went into attack bombers he also saw two Me 109s on his tail. He climbed steeply to right and was engaged by two other Me 109s, and after firing all his rounds broke off an inconclusive dogfight. Black 1 (Pilot Officer Dudley Williams) on turning towards bombers saw a yellow Me 109 coming up beneath Black 2 (Pilot Officer Eric 'Boy' Marrs). In turning down quickly Black 1 caused Black 2 to swerve and Black 1 then fired three-second burst at Me 109 which swayed violently when hit and turned downwards. Black 1 lost sight of E/A when it was going down in the bright sun. He then saw Green 1 going down by parachute and directed rescue boats to him when he reached the sea. Black 2, in swerving to avoid Black 1, lost contact with the E/A and was not involved in the combat. [ORB]

Also pursuing the enemy back to France was 213 Squadron, Sergeant Ernest Snowden of 'B' Flight reporting,

> I saw the Dorniers [*sic*] travelling SW from Southampton, preceded by about fifty Me 109s. As I was climbing up into sun Me 109s dived down on me in line astern. I turned and fired three short bursts at the last one, which went down vertically, smoking a little. More Me 109s came down on me, so I broke off and dived down into clouds. In my opinion, he could not have pulled out.

The 109 made it home, however.

The Northolt Hurricanes of 229 and 303 (Polish) Squadrons were also on the scene. Pilot Officer John Dewar, Yellow 3, of the former squadron, had followed Flight Lieutenant Robert Smith into a beam attack on the Heinkels:

> After breaking away, I saw a Me 109 with a Spitfire shooting at it from astern. The Me 109 half-rolled and came at me head-on. After giving him a 2-second burst I had to pull above him violently. I half-rolled and saw him going down in 'S' turns with a quantity of black smoke pouring from his engine. I dived vertically on him and fired a 2-second deflection burst at 300 yards. The pilot suddenly baled out and his parachute opened. His aircraft probably fell in the [*sic*] Solent.

The only Me 109 lost on this day, though, was the 3/JG 51 machine further east, off Dungeness. Was this, then, a case of 'friendly fire': did Dewar actually shoot down 152 Squadron's Flying Officer Christopher Deanesly, who did bale out over The Solent at the material time?

No. 229 Squadron's Flying Officer William Smith claimed a He 111 probably destroyed, and Sergeant Sydney Merryweather damaged a Me 110, 'but his aircraft was hit by cannon shell and he was cut and burned about the face and forced-landed at Hambledon'. [ORB]

Squadron Leader Ronald Kellett and 303 (Polish) Squadron were also on the scene:

> Formation of about fifty He 111 with Me 109 escort some distance to starboard and above were seen to be bombing along East of Southampton Water at about 16,000 feet. Enemy turned right about sharply to North of Hamble. Squadron Leader [Ronald] Kellett led Red Section against Me's but as fighter opposition did not develop, the Squadron attacked the bomber sections in echelon from three-quarters astern. Escorting Me's attacked after the first rush and Squadron broke up, mostly dog-fighting and some pursuing bombers to France. Sergeant [Marian] Belc forced-landed at Biggin Hill and Pilot Officer Januszewicz at Wyton, near Fareham, both

> unhurt. The Squadron saw nothing of 229 Squadron which was below and behind them, being themselves barely in time and not high enough to be able to wait and lead concerted attack. Just as Squadron was about to attack all heard signal 'All Apany aircraft pancake', of which no notice was taken. Pilots claim three bombers and one Me 109 shot down on England, the rest over sea or France. The following pilots scored: Sergeant Belc – 1 Me 109. Pilot Officer Grzeszezak – 1 He 111, Sergeant Frantiszek [František] – 2 He 111 destroyed. Sergeant Andruszkow 1 He 111, Flying Officer Zak 1 He 111 destroyed and 1 damaged. Flying Officer Paskiewicz 1 He 111 destroyed. Sergeant Kowalski – 1 Me 109, Flying Officer Urbanowicz 1 He 111 destroyed. Pilot Officer [Jan] Zumbach – 1 He 111 and 1 Me 109 destroyed. Flight Lieutenant Forbes 1 He 111 destroyed.
>
> Summary: Enemy casualties: 9 He 111s destroyed and 1 probable, and two damaged. 4 Me 109s destroyed. Our casualties 2 Hurricanes Cat 2 and 1 Hurricane Cat 3.

As unpalatable though some still find it despite hard evidence, it must be said that considering actual Luftwaffe losses on this day, these claims by 303 (Polish) Squadron typically have no relationship with reality – and perfectly illustrate the gulf of difference between a combat claim and actual enemy casualties. Indeed, it is impossible to understand why they were confirmed with so little, or in most cases, no supporting evidence. Nonetheless, with the enemy now back over France, the action was over.

In Southampton, it was time to count the cost.

Albert Adams:

> I didn't leave the Fire Station until early Friday morning ... I went down to the Works. The men in the shops are all now on the dole temporarily, but we went up into our office. There is hardly any roof, no windows & only half a wall on the river end. All our stuff was blown all over the place and was covered by about four inches of plaster and broken glass. My drawing board had a hole in it where a piece of bomb case had gone right through it & there were several smaller pieces imbedded in it. Another piece had gone right through my big set square.

Supermariner Cyril Russell: 'despite what looked like massive damage, only seven bombs hit Woolston Works, and one hit Itchen (Works).'

KG 55, however, was certain that the raid had been devastating:

destroyed around twenty-five Spitfires; production had to be interrupted. For about three weeks to delivery rate to the RAF was significantly reduced. A heavy blow, and for KG 55 the most successful daytime attack on England.

Hauptmann Genst's action report noted that I/KG 55 had scored four or five direct hits on the factory, and II/KG 55 recorded one hit on the larger factory building, six hits 'in the South part of the large hall and on smaller halls. Two large explosions were observed, and fires.' The ten-aircraft diversionary attack by III/KG 55 on Portland, however, failed because the target was covered in cloud, so the raiders returned to France with their bombloads intact.

Cyril Russell:

> The damage was, by comparison with effort, minimal. About three Spitfires nearing completion were destroyed and only twenty or so damaged – but over half of these were repairable. Most of this damage was caused by the one bomb on the Itchen Works, which also spelt 'finis' to Mitchell's bomber – the fuselages we had made at Woolston were in the Itchen Works, and now one was peppered with holes, and the other suffered the indignity of being wrapped round one of the steel girders that supported the roof.

The official AHB narrative, however, accredits more success to the Germans, who

> had struck almost as severe blow at the British aircraft industry as on the previous day at Filton. The northern part of the Supermarine works was extensively damaged; two workshops received direct hits and production was completely stopped … At Southampton Docks a warehouse filled with grain was totally destroyed. The gasworks on Marine Parade was also damaged; one gasholder was set on fire and burned until the following morning; and gas supply was not normal for a few days. This made the third attack that the Germans had launched in strength against the aircraft industry since 23 August [1940].

Arguably, however, the Woolston raid was more successful that the Filton attack – because this brought Spitfire production at Supermarine to a standstill. It also emphasised the inescapable fact that Supermarine was far too vulnerable to continue operating as a major Spitfire production centre. Lord Beaverbrook himself, responsible for the Ministry for Aircraft Production (MAP), visited the site soon after the raid and shut it down. Instead, production was dispersed to the most unlikely places throughout Southampton, Winchester and even as far afield as Salisbury, where workers toiled to produce Spitfires under railway arches, in garages, and many more locations besides – an inspirational story in itself of dedication and ingenuity. Incredibly, machine-tools, lathes and all-important wing-jigs survived the raid to be salvaged and used elsewhere in the dispersed production process

Joan Tagg:

> This was the end of our time at the Supermarine Works. Days later we were back at work at 'Deepdene', a large house in Midanbury Lane. Other departments of the factory were dispersed to various buildings throughout the County and continued building Spitfires – but with less disruption.

During August 1940, 149 Spitfires had been built at Woolston and, to the great credit of the workforce, 139 were built in October 1940. However, the attack had come too late in the Battle of Britain to have any effect on its eventual outcome. By this time, Lord Nuffield had opened the new Castle Bromwich Aeroplane Factory (CBAF) in Birmingham, where the mass production methods of the automotive industry was being applied to Spitfire production. The new Spitfire MK IIAs were already rolling off the line, there but production was not yet at full capacity. Eventually, CBAF would take over as the main Spitfire manufacturing centre, and clearly, after the events of this day, that could not come too soon. Whereas Woolston was close enough to France to be bombed in daylight, CBAF, which was far beyond the range of escorting fighters, was not. CBAF, however, could be targeted at night, and so in due course this dispersed production, the 'Shadow Factories', would also be applied to Spitfire production there.

After the Woolston raid, the eight Fighter Command squadrons engaged claimed, notwithstanding the misidentification of the He 111s variously as Ju 88s, Do 17s and Do 215s, a total of seventeen bombers destroyed, two probables and seven damaged; no less than nine Me 109s were claimed destroyed, and three probables, along with five Me 110s destroyed, one probably destroyed and another damaged. The reality was much different: only one He 111 was lost and just one returned to France with combat damage; no Me 109s were lost and only two Me 110s were destroyed. On this occasion, those squadrons with the most inflated claims were 303 (Polish) Squadron, by a wide margin, followed by 238, 602 and 609 Squadrons. Interestingly, the Germans also overclaimed more than was usual; according to *Hauptmann* Genst, some fifty RAF fighters had intercepted the raid over the Isle of Wight and Southampton, the following combat claims being recorded:

> One Hurricane destroyed by *Erprobungsgruppe* 210.
> Two Spitfires and four Hurricanes by ZG 26.

> Eleven Spitfires and one Hurricane by JG 2.
> One Spitfire by JG 53.

Fighter Command actually lost two Spitfires destroyed and three damaged, and four Hurricanes, six damaged, a total of six fighters destroyed and nine damaged; two pilots were killed and two more wounded.

The daylight action, was not quite over.

At 17.15 hrs, 607 Squadron's Red Section, Flight Lieutenant Francis Blackadder, Sergeant William Cunnington and Sergeant Richard Spyer, all of whom had already flown several operational sorties on this day, scrambled from Tangmere to patrol Selsey Bill at 12,000ft. After various vectors, at 17.45 hrs the Hurricanes sighted a German reconnaissance machine over Southampton at 18,000ft, which was being engaged by AA fire. The section climbed, Blackadder opening fire and hitting the enemy aircraft, identified as a 'He 111 [*sic*]', and continued harassing the damaged German as the pilot dived away – ultimately reported 'by the Observer Corps to crash into the sea about five miles off the Needles'. [ORB] This, however, was actually a Me 110 of 4(F)/14, which crashed into the sea off Cowes on the Isle of Wight, killing the crew.

Having been shot-up and landed his damaged Hurricane in Lee-on-the-Solent, Squadron Leader Harold Fenton was 'entertained royally' by the RN,

> and then sent me back to Middle Wallop by car. I got there at about 2100 hrs and found that through casualties in the engagement we could only muster five serviceable aeroplanes. I decided to cut corners and rang direct to Fighter Command and spoke to Wing Commander Rich, the Chief Supply Officer, and told him my problem. He said 'Promise you have sent your signals.'
>
> I said 'Cross my heart.'
>
> He said 'I will do my best for you.'
>
> By lunchtime the next day, no less than eight Hurricanes had been delivered to us. To this day, I think this quite remarkable at the very height of the Battle.

Pilot Officer Harry Welford of 607 Squadron also had a recollection of this day:

> We had a very intrepid and garrulous fighter pilot in Jim Bazin's Flight called Charles 'Chatty' Bowen, who seemed to have continued success in combat. One of our Polish pilots, Pilot Officer Franek [Franciszek] Surma envied 'Chatty's' success and wished that he could borrow some of Bowen's luck. 'Chatty' was known to carry a toy stuffed elephant as his

> mascot, and Franek pleaded with, and cajoled 'Chatty' into lending it to him for a sortie. After much argument, and persuasion from other members of the Flight, 'Chatty' agreed to lend Franek the mascot to fly with, on a sortie that he was not flying himself. Franek was instructed to return the mascot to Bowen's Hurricane the moment he landed. Later Surma returned jubilant as he had destroyed an Me 109. As promised he gave the mascot to the flight rigger, who returned it to the cockpit of Bowen's Hurricane. 'Chatty', however, could not find the mascot on his next trip and cursed Surma for not returning it. On that sortie Bowen was shot down and it was assumed that his change of luck was due to Surma not having returned the toy elephant. The twist to the tale is that when the salvage team recovered the wreckage of Bowen's Hurricane from the Isle of Wight, they discovered the elephant in the cockpit; it was believed that the mascot had fallen from the gun sight and jammed the rudder pedals.

The facts here, however, had clearly become blurred over the years because on 26 September 1940, both Bowen and Surma were flying at the same time, when the former was shot down; nonetheless it remains a good story – and, indeed, as Welford said,

> The story about the mascot I may have got second hand from some-one writing to me in Ashford Hospital after I had been shot down. The story is certainly true to the characters of both Frankie [Franciszek Surma] and 'Chatty' [Charles Bowen], though. Before I was wounded, 'Frankie' had certainly tried to borrow the mascot. He used to call Bowen his 'lovelee boy', which infuriated 'Chatty' beyond all reason, as Bowen was a very senior pilot and Surma was junior even amongst his Polish comrades!
>
> The time that Franek and myself were in 'B' Flight together seems to have been extremely short, only six days – but the loss of life occurred so rapidly that the experiences of a lifetime could be crammed into a few days. Franek was the sort of person who immediately became popular and when we had a beer in the evening he would teach us how to say '*Nostravia*!', which means 'Good health' in Polish. He impressed me.

For Coastal Command it had been another typical round of patrols and sorties; two Beauforts of 217 Squadron successfully attacked Brest docks at dawn, and Hudsons of 220 Squadron were engaged by two He 115 seaplanes over 70 miles off Flamborough Head; one Hudson was damaged but returned safely to base. By night, Coastal aircraft hit shipping off Den Helder and mined the rivers Elbe, Jade and Weser. Poor weather, however, comprised daylight operations for 2 Group's Blenheims, although at lunchtime a bomber of 114 Squadron, reconnoitring Boulogne, was intercepted and shot down into the Channel by 7/JG 53's *Feldwebel* Hermann Schramm – the crew were all killed. By night, Bomber Command Blenheims attacked the invasion ports and shipping off Ostend, laid mines at La Pallice, targeted the Kiel naval base and shipping at Le Havre. A Hampden of 61 Squadron on the Kiel raid was hit by flak and crashed in Sweden, killing its crew, and a Hampden of 106 Squadron, returning from La Pallice ran out of fuel and crashed in Chilton Polden – two of the crew survived but sadly two died.

Daily Home Intelligence Reports:

Southern:

There is criticism of the government in a number of quarters over the lack of deep shelters suited to winter conditions. There seems to be some muddle in the public mind about the necessity for working after the sirens, and some parts of the Region, Eastleigh in particular having apparently refused to do so.

South-western:

West Cornwall complains that Nazi airmen have a free play over the district, and Exeter also alleges a lack of defence of the city.

North-western:

Reports of 'beating off' raiders do not completely offset the deep impression produced by stories of the raids which are in circulation. Merseyside still wants to know why it cannot have its share of credit for standing up to night-bombing.

South-eastern:

The King's broadcast and the announcement of the George Cross was warmly praised.

London:

The work of voluntary organisations has done much to prevent the breaking down of morale. In Croydon, it is reported that as a result of constant

> bombing, many people are wanting to leave and already many mothers and children are taking advantage of the Government's scheme ... Despite recent damage which has left many Silvertown workers homeless, their morale has improved since they have been allowed to continue working after the 'Alert'. From many districts comes praise of the work of demolition squads; there is some public comment that their numbers are small and their instruments primitive. In bombed areas of Kensington there is reported to have been much neighbourly help for raid victims ... There are complaints that workers losing their jobs as a result of their place of employment being damaged by air raids cannot claim unemployment benefit for the first nine days.

Friday, 27 September 1940

Reichsmarschall Hermann Göring's failure to fulfil his boastful assurances of achieving aerial supremacy over southern England led to 'difficult weeks' at the *Führerhauptquartier*, deep in the Black Forest, for *Oberst* Nicolaus von Below, Hitler's Luftwaffe aide. Having abandoned Operation *Seelöwe*, von Below recalled,

> [Hitler was now transfixed with] how he could overcome the Soviet Union in the shortest possible time ... he had not yet made his decision, but as the weeks went by it was obvious that the Russian question was going to be answered soon.

With the invasion of Britain now shelved, and with it the swift victory Germany required, Hitler's current preoccupation with Russia was not, though, simply because eastward territorial expansion and the destruction of communism lay at the heart of Nazi ideology – it was much more complex: a lightning-fast victory over the Soviets, the *Führer* believed, would indirectly lead to Britain's downfall. Churchill, of course, knew that the Nazi-Soviet Non-Aggression Pact signed between Germany and the Soviet Union in 1939 was but a flimsy alliance likely to hold up so long as it suited one or the other party. Britain's War Cabinet, therefore, hoped that this devil's agreement would collapse and bring the Russians into the Allied camp. The British also hoped that the United States would discontinue its foreign policy of isolationism and non-involvement in European events and enter the war against Germany. Hitler reasoned, therefore, that defeating Russia removed Britain's first hope, and because this would benefit Japanese influence and expansion in the Far East, the Americans would be too preoccupied in the Pacific to become embroiled in the European war. Consequently, Britain would be truly isolated and without hope of support from either America or Russia – providing Germany a free hand to achieve what 1940 had failed to deliver. It is important to appreciate, then, that Hitler's eastward gaze was also aimed at progressing the irrevocable defeat of Britain through indirect means.

Von Below also recalled that, on 27 September 1940,

> [Hitler] attended the Tri-Partite Pact involving Germany, Japan and Italy, and after all formalities dined with the guests in his apartment. He was keen for this Treaty to come to the world's attention, especially in the USA and USSR. He considered the Japanese forces to be the most important military factor in the Pacific. All his efforts in these autumn months of 1940 were directed towards welding a powerful and effective alliance against Britain.

The unstoppable Blitzkrieg, Germany's lightning victories, it seemed, was over, a much longer-term strategy now being developed. On this day, Count Galeazzo Ciano, wrote in his diary,

> One thing is certain: the war will be long. This does not please the Germans, who had come to believe that with the end of summer the end of the war would also come. A winter of war is hard to bear. More so since food is scarce in Berlin, and it is easy to see that the window displays of shops promise much more than is actually inside.
>
> Another thing that contributes to the depressed spirit of Berlin life is the constant recurrence of air raids. Every night the citizens spend from four to five hours in the cellar. They lack sleep, they are cold, there is promiscuity between men and women, and these things do not make for good humour … Bomb damage is slight but nervousness is great … the memory of the first war is being evoked and they are beginning to think the worst. But it is a fact that the spirit of Germany today is not that of last June or even of last August … I had two conversations with Hitler … No more invasion of England. No more blitz destruction of England. From Hitler's speech there emerges worry of a long war.

How times had changed for Germany, in just a short time: from triumph to uncertainty, bordering upon despair. For this change in fortunes there can be no doubt that the credit essentially goes to Fighter Command for holding out and continuing to confound the enemy through RDF-guided interceptions and the substantial numbers of defending fighters involved, and both Bomber

Command and Coastal Command for taking the war across the Channel. Arguably by now, despite the British official end date of 31 October 1940, the Battle of Britain proper, the contest for aerial supremacy as the prelude to a seaborne invasion, really was well and truly over.

Nonetheless, the air battle over Britain continued, and this day, 27 September 1940, would see a day of exceptionally heavy fighting, comparable to that of 15 September 1940 – with continued attacks on Britain's aircraft industry.

At 08.30 hrs, RDF screens indicated German air activity over the Dover Strait; three minutes later, bombs fell on Dover harbour. No. 11 Group controller, however, scrambled no squadrons until 08.50 hrs, at which time '50+' bandits were fast approaching Dungeness. From Tangmere, 213 and 602 Squadrons were sent to patrol Mayfield; 1 (RCAF) and 303 (Polish) Squadrons from Northolt were ordered to patrol base together; North Weald's 46 and 249 Squadrons went up to patrol Rochford at 20,000ft, and to Maidstone went Biggin Hill's 72 and 92 Squadrons to patrol together at 25,000ft, the latter squadron leading.

Just before 09.00 hrs, according to the Observer Corps, the Germans crossed in over Dungeness and headed for Tunbridge Wells at 20,000ft – this being a fighter sweep. Over the next few minutes three more raids were over southern Kent, some of these aircraft following the first formation to Kenley and South London, whilst the remainder, fighters, milled about between Maidstone and Tonbridge. Although RAF pilots subsequently reported the presence of Do 17s, the information available suggests that the bombers involved were actually Ju 88s of KG 77, bound for London, escorted by large forces of Me 109s.

At 09.00 hrs, 253 and 501 Squadrons from Kenley were scrambled to patrol Biggin Hill at 15,000ft, and five minutes later the Debden Wing, 17 and 73 Squadrons, took-off to cover Hornchurch and North Weald at 12,000ft. Assistance was requested from 12 Group via Fighter Command HQ, and so the Duxford Wing, now comprising the Hurricanes of 242 (Canadian) and 310 (Czech) Squadrons based at Duxford, and the Fowlmere Spitfires of 19 and 616 Squadrons, scrambled with orders to patrol north of the Thames. By 09.10 hrs, the Northolt Wing was flying south, to meet the advancing enemy, and North Weald's Wing was similarly heading south, to the Maidstone – Dungeness line. At 09.23 hrs, 605 Squadron scrambled from Croydon to patrol base at 15,000ft, and 66 Squadron was sent from Gravesend (at an unclear time) to patrol Biggin Hill, also at Angels 15.

At 09.15 hrs, 72 and 92 Squadrons were over Sevenoaks at 18,000ft, as Pilot Officer John Mansell-Lewis, Green 2, of the latter squadron, reported,

> We were vectored on to about twenty Do 17s in a straggly vic. We broke up and I gave one of the rear E/A a long burst. Smoke and glycol steam

> came out of the tail of the machine, and the Dornier turned into a steep dive southward, towards Sevenoaks. No fire was observed from the gunner. The attack was made from 200 to 100 yards.
>
> After breaking off the attack I chased after the bombers which were going towards London. I was then attacked by a 109 which dived from above on my right. Shortly after avoiding the 109 I felt a big bump. I returned to base and discovered half the tail was shot away and one bullet hole through the wing.
>
> Impossible to say if aircraft was hit by light cannon or ack-ack, but ack-ack bursts fairly close.
>
> One bomber was seen exploding in the air at that time and to the direction of Sevenoaks.

Mansell-Lewis was somewhat optimistically awarded a 'Do 17 destroyed [*sic*]'. That the pilot only discovered such substantial damage to his Spitfire after landing, however, is further confirmation of Mitchell's nimble fighter being able to keep flying regardless of such punishment – another fact contrary to the long-accepted narrative.

In addition to Me 109s attacking the Spitfires, very likely being from JG 54, Me 110s of 13 and 15(Z)/LG 1 were also involved; Pilot Officer John Drummond, Yellow 1, of 92 Squadron:

> We climbed and were attacked by fighters (109 and 110) at about 12,000 feet. I fired a short burst at a 109 and broke away. I saw a 110 in front at about 12,000 feet, fired a burst at it from astern. Smoke came from starboard engine and it began to lose height. It was then attacked by several Hurricanes, it landed in a ploughed field just South of Westerham.

This was a machine of 15(Z)/LG 1, the pilot of which, *Oberleutnant* Otto Weckseiser, forced-landed at Socketts Manor, Oxted, where he and his *Bordfunker*, *Gefreiter* Horst Brüggow, were both captured. Already, so many RAF fighters were in action that the Me 110s of *Hauptmann* Horst Liensberger's V(Z)/LG 1 were being overwhelmed; Weckseiser, in fact, was also attacked by Pilot Officer Keith Lofts, Pilot Officer James Meaker and Sergeant Henry Davidson of 249 Squadron, in addition to Sergeant Jan Budzinski, a Pole, of 605 Squadron. The *Gruppenkommandeur*, Liensberger, was attacked over Redhill by Pilot Officer Percival Burton, a South African, of 249 Squadron, who pursued the German south until his Hurricane collided with the Me 110, chopping off the Germans' tailplane – all three airmen involved were killed.

No. 92 Squadron claimed three bombers and a Me 110 destroyed in the engagement, with a probable 'Do 17 [*sic*]' and 'other bombers damaged'. 'Two experienced pilots' [ORB], however were killed: Flight Lieutenant James Paterson, a New Zealander, was shot down in flames by a 109 over Maidstone and seen struggling but failing to escape his burning Spitfire – he died in the resulting crash at Farningham, and Sergeant Charles Sydney was also shot down, being killed at Kingston-on-Thames. Like Pilot Officer John Mansell-Lewis, Pilot Officer Trevor Wade was more fortunate, returning to Biggin Hill safely in his shot-up Spitfire.

When the Biggin Hill squadrons first sighted the Germans approaching from the south, Sergeant John Gilders was weaving above 72 Squadron:

> I was weaving above the Squadron as they attacked and saw eight Me 109s in line-astern, trying to get behind us. I attacked one of these, the nearest, and caught him as he turned. I gave about a four-second burst and saw him turn over in an apparent half-roll, but one wing dropped off and he crashed straight down. I did not follow him. I then found the bombers and attacked head-on from above after climbing up. The one I hit was a Ju 88 and directly I attacked he turned starboard and dived with smoke coming back from his starboard engine. As he dived I gave another burst, about two-seconds, from astern. This seemed to kill the rear-gunner as he ceased firing. I followed him to about 10,000 feet over Dungeness and gave him a final burst, running out of ammunition. He was still diving with only his port engine going and burning in the fuselage. I left him about five miles out to sea at 5,000 feet and did consider it necessary to follow any further.

No. 72 Squadron's pilots claimed a Ju 88, a Me 109, a 'Do 17 [*sic*]' and '3½ Do 215s [*sic*]' [ORB]. Like 92 Squadron, though, 72 Squadron had lost two pilots over Sevenoaks to the 109s: Flying Officer Paul Davies-Cooke baled out but was found dead near Hayes Station, and Pilot Officer Ernest Males was killed when his Spitfire crashed in Shadwell docks in Stepney. Sergeant John White was also shot-up, making a safe forced-landing with a damaged header tank.

At 09.15 hrs, the Canadians of 1 (RCAF) Squadron had sighted the advancing Germans and positioned themselves to engage over Gatwick.

Pilot Officer Peter Lochnan, a Canadian, Green 2:

> doing search above the Squadron. As I went to attack a Me 109 I was hit by cannon and machine-gun fire. Half the right aileron was shot off. I started for home and saw a Ju 88 being attacked. I got in one burst and held off when the three Hurricanes attacking it fired him, and he crashed into a house.

This was a Ju 88 of 3/KG 77, which the crew abandoned and crashed into End Lodge in East Grinstead – and which also featured in the combat reports of Lochnan's CO, Squadron Leader Ernest McNab, Flying Officer De Peyster Douw Brown DFC, an American volunteer, and Pilot Officer Beverley Christmas, both also of the 'Caribou' Squadron, Pilot Officer Jan Zumbach of 303 (Polish) Squadron and Flight Lieutenant Christopher 'Bunny' Currant of 605 Squadron.

The action was not yet over for Pilot Officer Peter Lochnan, however:

> I climbed up to come home and saw a 'Jaguar' (110). Joined in attack and got in three good bursts, one a rear climbing, another a port quarter that caused smoke to pour out. Another Hurricane fired the starboard motor. We were down to about 500 feet. I fired again as he was coming towards me and going down. He turned and crashed at Gatwick aerodrome. I landed there and left my aircraft there to be repaired whilst I returned to base by a *Magister*.

This Me 110 was also claimed by Sergeant Robert Hogg of 17 Squadron, Sergeant Hector Barrow of 213 Squadron and Pilot Officer William Hopkin of 602 Squadron. Gatwick's aerial defences also opened up on the stricken German fighter, the *Staffelkapitän* of 15/(Z)LG 1, *Oberleutnant* Sigmund-Ulrich Freiherr von Gravenreuth, and his *Bordfunker*, *Feldwebel* Otto Reinhold, were both killed.

Squadron Leader McNab and Flying Officer Blair Russell also engaged a 110 of 13/(Z)LG 1 over Redhill, together with Pilot Officer Christopher Currant of 605 Squadron and both Flight Lieutenant John Sing and Flying Officer James Strickland of 213 Squadron. This fighter bomber went straight in at 'The Gale', Chelwood Gate in Ashdown Forest, killing both crewmen.

Russell also claimed a 109 destroyed, and Flying Officer Robert Norris a damaged 110, both over Kenley. The Canadians did not escape unscathed, however: like Lochnan, Flying Officer William Sprenger was also shot-up, landing unhurt at Kenley – but Pilot Officer Otto John Peterson, another American volunteer, was shot down and killed, crashing in Hever.

The war ended for *Gefreiter* H.-D. John at 09.25 hrs when his 5/JG 27 Me 109 was hit over Lewes, possibly by AA fire, forcing him to bale out and see out the duration of the war as a POW.

At 09.20 hrs, the Spitfires of 602 Squadron's Blue Section were attacked by Me 109s south-south-east of Mayfield and went into a right-hand defensive circle. Pilot Officer Patrick 'Paddy' Barthropp, Blue 3:

> I was attacked by a 109 so I went down to 8,000 feet in a spiral and shook off E/A. Then ordered to proceed to Mayfield and at 12,000 feet sighted

> many Me 109s above me. I came low again and at 8,000 feet saw two or three Hurricanes attacking a He 111 [*sic*] at 7,000 feet, going down 45° with smoke coming from starboard engine. I did two quarter astern attacks and saw starboard engine go up in flames. E/A then went down vertically into the ground, fifteen miles SSE of Mayfield, in a ploughed field. One of the crew baled out. I certainly hit this E/A but it was probably damaged before I attacked.

At Kenley, 501 Squadron had been at readiness at dawn and having scrambled with 253 Squadron, Squadron Leader Henry Hogan, commanding the former squadron, which was leading the formation, sighted the enemy 6 miles south of base at 09.20 hrs. Having identified the bombers as 'Do 17s', Hogan gave chase, but then

> twenty-five 'Jaguars' flying NW dived down below and behind the Squadron. Controller's approval had been given to attack these and this the Squadron did, without, however, being successful. They out-climbed us rapidly and I tried to re-form our Squadron to go after the original raid. As the Squadron did not, I went off on my own. I joined a Hurricane of 303 [Polish] Squadron which had attacked a damaged a 'Jaguar'. As it appeared his ammunition was finished, I gave a ten-second burst at the E/A and set its starboard engine on fire. One of the crew baled out and the machine crashed near Uckfield. The 'Jaguar' had not dropped its bombs, which appeared to explode when the machine crashed. There was a bright light burning in the wreckage which may have been either incendiary bombs or Verey cartridges.

Hogan had attacked the same Me 110 as Barthropp. The 303 (Polish) Squadron pilot, Flying Officer Witold Urbanowicz, and Pilot Officer David Leary of 17 Squadron also engaged the same 'Jaguar'. This Me 110 of 15/(Z)LG 1 crashed at Horam Manor Farm in Horam, killing the *Bordfunker*, *Unteroffizier* Hans Koch, whose pilot, *Unteroffizier* Hans Bechthold, baled out and was captured.

Sergeant Cyril Babbage, Green 2, was in the 602 Squadron formation and, like Barthropp, also spiral-dived away upon being attacked by Me 109s, pulling out at 500ft:

> Then [I] saw a Ju 88 flying South at 400 feet, at about 200 mph. I attacked this full beam, five times, and saw this E/A crash into the sea.

This Ju 88, of 2/KG 77, crashed off Lydd; two of the crew remain missing but both *Unteroffizier* G. Schmidt and *Unteroffizier* H. Sergocki were rescued from the sea and captured.

No. 602 Squadron's Pilot Officer William Hopkin also had a hand in destroying the Gatwick Me 110. The squadron's only casualties being slight damage to Babbage's Spitfire caused by return fire from the Ju 88 and Pilot Officer Douglas Gage being shot down by a 109, the Spitfire pilot safely forced-landing at Newchurch, unhurt.

Immediately before 303 (Polish) Squadron went into action, as on the previous day pilots were instructed over the R/T to 'Pancake', which was again ignored and later confirmed 'not given by controllers at this Station but was given in good English and in an authoritative manner' [ORB]. The squadron's diary continued,

> The Squadron attacked bombers from astern and were themselves attacked by enemy fighters which fled in disorder. In the meantime the bombers had wheeled and were heading South, and the Squadron went in to attack from astern. Vics of bombers maintained formation throughout, closing up when one or more shot down. Other Hurricanes came in to attack the bombers and immediately afterwards the Squadron noticed about forty Do 17s [*sic*] approaching head-on in single line-astern formation supported by Me 109s above. Upon going in to [*sic*] attack, the bombers formed a defensive circle [author's note: these were actually *Hauptmann* Horst Liensberger's Me 110s] and the enemy fighters above formed a similar circle. Only one pilot attacked and succeeded in shooting one down on land. Two other squadrons of Hurricanes came in and attacked the Do's [*sic*] and as far as is known broke them up and inflicted heavy casualties. Our fighter did not follow down the individual E/A claimed as destroyed but it is believed that almost all were shot down on land. [ORB]

The successful pilot referred to was Pilot Officer Jan Zumbach, who had contributed to the demise of the Ju 88 brought down at East Grinstead. On this occasion, however, the Poles had suffered a grievous loss: Flying Officer Ludwik Paskiewicz, who had scored the squadron's first aerial victory on 30 August 1940, failed to return from this operation, it later being confirmed that he had been shot down and killed, his Hurricane crashing in Borough Green. Sergeant Tadeusz Andruszkow was also killed, shot down in flames, his aircraft crashing in Cowden. Flying Officer Walerian Zak was also shot down, taking to his parachute over Horsham, landing unhurt, and both Flying Officer Zdzislaw

Henneberg and Pilot Officer Mirowslaw Feric both returned to Northolt with damaged Hurricanes.

His squadron, 501, having scattered after being bounced by Me 110s south of Kenley, Sergeant Victor Ekins was shot down by a Me 110, this possibly being *Gefreiter* Brendel of 15/(Z)LG 1, who claimed a 'Spitfire' south-west of London at the material time. The Hurricane pilot baled out over Godstone, landing by parachute in woods occupied by a Canadian ambulance unit and subsequently admitted to Sevenoaks Hospital suffering from burns.

No. 253 Squadron pursued the withdrawing enemy to the south, but an attack by twelve Me 109s broke up the Hurricanes. The Kenley pilots re-formed at 5,000ft and engaged Me 110s 20 miles north of Hastings.

Pilot Officer Alan Eckford, Yellow 3,

> dived vertically on to the E/A and observed his tracer entering the aircraft and the engines emitting a little white smoke. Yellow 3 then delivered a quarter attack from the port side and a third attack from astern, closing to fifty yards, and broke away just behind when E/A exploded, the wreckage falling in a field near Dallington.

This was another 15/(Z)LG 1 Me 110, the crew of which were killed. No. 253 Squadron made no other claims in this engagement and suffered just two Hurricanes damaged, both of which returned safely to base, their pilots unhurt (details unrecorded).

In addition to 605 Squadron's Flight Lieutenant Christopher Currant's contribution to destroying the East Grinstead Ju 88, Pilot Officer John Milne, a Canadian, attacked a Me 110 between Reigate and Dorking, both engines of which emitted smoke after his first attack, 'and his port engine burst into flames at 3,000 feet, just East of Dorking'. Sergeant Eric Wright, Yellow 1, attacked a Me 110 head-on, 5 miles south of Kenley:

> I delivered a three-second burst and the E/A stall-turned and spiralled earthwards. I watched for him to hit the ground, but at ground-level he levelled out and flew South. I gave chase and caught him about twenty-five miles South of base. His port engine was stopped and the airscrew fully feathered. I fired all my ammunition into his starboard engine in three bursts as he endeavoured to climb slowly. At 3,000 feet the starboard engine caught fire, and I left him at 1,000 feet, slowly descending towards the sea, flying South over Eastbourne.

This 13/(Z)LG 1 aircraft crashed into the sea; both crewmen were killed.

From Castle Camps, Pilot Officer Donald Scott DFC led 73 Squadron, with Debden's 17 Squadron bringing up the rear; the former squadron recorded,

> The combat with Me 110s took place in the Weybridge – Kenley area and was highly successful in the circumstances … The E/A were in the form of a large circle at 19,000 feet, and Pilot Officer [Donald] Scott led from above into the middle of the circle in successful attempt to break it up a little. Pilot Officer Scott fired at two E/A, each of which broke off combat but no effect on them was noticed. Pilot Officer [Aubrey] McFadden got his first blood when in company with Sergeant [Bernard Walter] Hopton and two unknown Hurricane pilots destroyed in flames a Me 110 near Croydon. Sergeant [Alfred Ernest] Marshall was shot down near Kenley but although his machine was on fire and windscreen covered with oil 300 feet from the ground, he landed successfully on Kenley aerodrome, uninjured …Sergeant [Geoffrey William] Garton destroyed a Me 110 near Redhill, seeing it break up in air and pancake in a ploughed field. Pilot Officer [Karel Jan] Vykoukal (Czech) lost his way back but returned safely after landing at Staplehurst to re-fuel. Sergeant [Robert] Plenderleith destroyed another Me 110 but although both engines were on fire he did not see it crash. Sergeant [Peter] O'Byrne probably destroyed a Do 17 [*sic*] South of Croydon, the port side fin falling off and other rear portions seen to break away in the air. Sergeant O'Byrne was compelled to land in a field at Staffhurst Wood, Limpsfield, his aircraft having been hit in the engine. Pilot Officer [C.A.] McGaw completed the good work of the day by damaging a Me 110. Sergeant [William Claude] Wills landed at Debden and came on to base later. All pilots arrived back at base uninjured. [ORB]

The rear section of 17 Squadron was attacked by Me 109s, one of which shot away the tail fin of Sergeant Leonard Bartlett's Hurricane, who landed safely back at Debden despite his rudder controls being inoperable.

The squadron diarist reported,

> The Squadron climbed up and attacked the Me 110s, and Flying Officer [Count Manfred] Czernin brought down one in flames, and got one more probable. Sergeant [George Arthur] Steward led Green Section inside the enemy circle and shot down one Me 110. Pilot Officer [David] Leary joined up with some Hurricanes of another squadron and getting behind two Me 110s destroyed one and probably destroyed the other. Two of the crew of the first one baled out. Sergeant [Robert] Hogg climbed inside the Me 110s and flying in the opposite direction shot down one which

Bob Morris, an engine fitter on 66 Squadron at Kenley and Gravesend throughout the Battle of Britain.

The essential groundcrew: 152 Squadron, Warmwell, September 1940.

Flight Lieutenant Ken Gillies, a flight commander on 66 Squadron prepares for a patrol from Gravesend – he would not survive the Battle of Britain.

All photographs Dilip Sarkar Archive unless otherwise indicated.

Spitfire pilots: Sergeants Bob Beardsley (left) and Frank 'ITMA' Usmar (right) with 'Mitch' Mitchell, a replacement posted to 41 Squadron after the Battle of Britain, at Catterick in early 1941. Beardsley and Usmar were both decorated and survived the war.

Pilot Officer Laurie Whitbread of 222 Squadron, the first Ludlovian to be killed in action during the Second World War, on 20 September 1940.

Sergeant John Gilders of 41 Squadron at Hornchurch.

Whitbread was most likely shot down and killed by *Major* Adolf Galland, Kommodore of JG 26, seen here preparing for a mission from his base at Audembert.

Hornchurch: from left, 41 Squadron's Sergeant Robert Angus, and Pilot Officers Edward 'Hawkeye' Wells, a New Zealander, and Roy Ford; Angus was reported missing over the Channel on 20 February 1941.

Major Werner Mölders, the so-called 'Father of Modern Air Fighting' and Kommodore of JG 51. The first fighter pilot ever to achieve 100 aerial victories, Mölders would be killed in a flying accident when General der Jagdflieger in 1941.

Stanley Devon's iconic photo, taken at Fowlmere on 21 September 1940, of 19 Squadron's exceptional 23-year-old commander, Squadron Leader Brian Lane DFC. At left is Flight Lieutenant Walter Lawson DFC, with Flight Sergeant George Unwin DFM; only the latter survived the war: both Lane and Lawson would be reported missing over the North Sea after the Battle of Britain.

Another of Devon's Fowlmere photos: 19 Squadron armourer Fred Roberts at work whilst Sergeant Bernard Jennings prepares for a sortie, 21 September 1940.

Devon also took this photo on 21 September 1940 of 310 (Czech) Squadron at Duxford.

Another iconic Devon photo taken at Duxford: Squadron Leader Douglas Bader DSO DFC of 242 (Canadian) Squadron, flanked by Flight Lieutenant Eric Ball and Pilot Officer William McKnight, a Canadian. The famous nose-art is on Bader's personal Hurricane.

Pilot Officer Eric Burgoyne of 19 Squadron, killed in action on 27 September 1940, considered by Churchill to be the third greatest day of the Battle of Britain.

A sad loss for the Poles of Northolt's 303 Squadron on 27 September 1940 was Flying Officer Ludwik Paskiewicz, famously responsible for the Squadron's first aerial victory on 30 August 1940 and whose grave is seen here at Northwood.

Although first 302 and then 303 Squadrons were operational during the Battle of Britain, other Polish pilots with good English served in British fighter squadrons. At left is Pilot Officer Franciszek Surma, who served in 151, 607, 46 and 257 Squadrons during the battle; he is pictured here at Tangmere whilst with 607 in September 1940, with Flight Lieutenant Charles Bowen, who is teaching the Pole to play 'pax'. Both pilots were later reported missing over the Channel.

Another dangerous foe: *Hauptmann* Johannes Seifert of JG 26; he would be killed in action fighting American bombers in 1943.

Major Friedrich Kless, *Gruppenkommandeur* of II/KG 55, who led the successful raids on Bristol Aeroplane Company at Filton on 25 September 1940, and on Supermarine at Woolston the following day. Kless survived the wear and became a *Generalmajor* in the post-war Luftwaffe.

He 111s on their way to England.

Luftwaffe target photo of Bristol Aeroplane Company (BAC) works at Filton (Historic Military Press, HMP).

The BAC site at Filton was the largest aircraft producing plant in the world in September 1940.

Within BAC, which was producing aero-engines in addition to Bristol Blenheims, Beauforts and the new Beaufighter.

168 bombs were dropped by KG 55, causing immense damage to the BAC site, domestic properties and great loss of life.

Many victims, servicemen and civilian, of the raids occurring 25 and 27 September 1940 are buried at Bristol's Greenbank Cemetery.

KG 55 He 111s under attack from Spitfires on 25 September 1940.

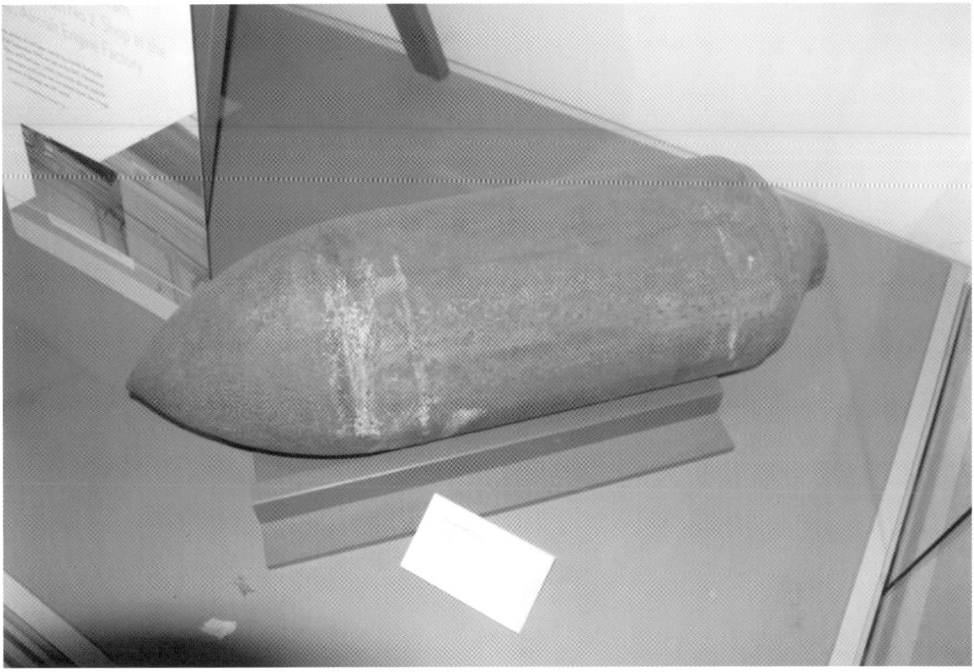

An SC250KG HE bomb dropped on Filton by KG 55 but which failed to explode – now displayed at the Bristol Aerospace Museum.

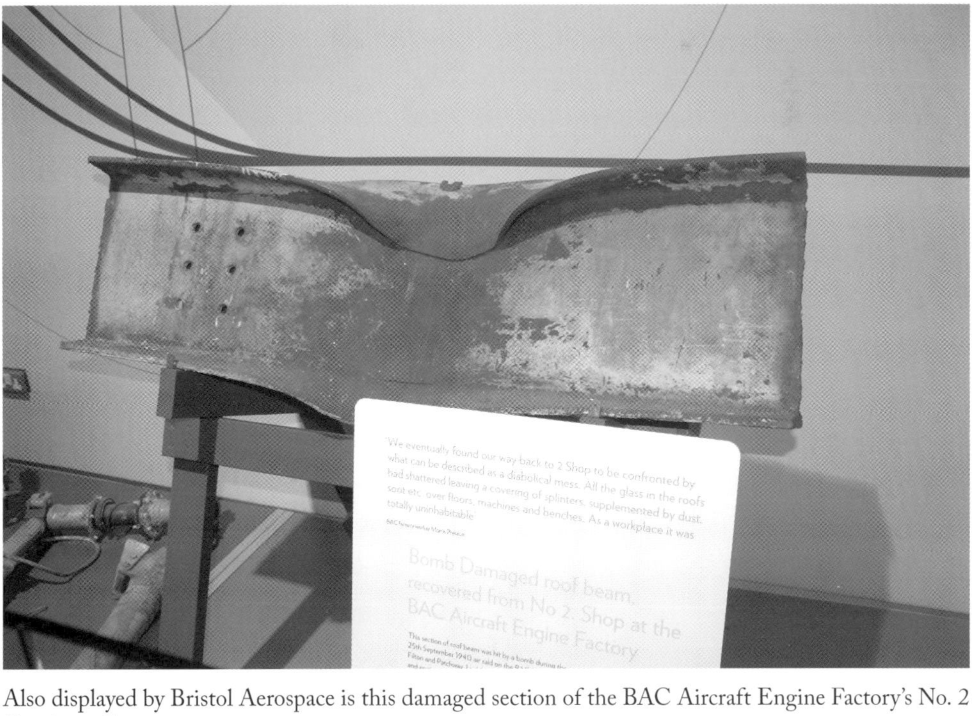

Also displayed by Bristol Aerospace is this damaged section of the BAC Aircraft Engine Factory's No. 2 Shop's roof beam.

GB 21 31 bc
N. f. D.

Woolston
Tanklager

Karte 1:100 000
Engl. Bl. 38 b

Bild Nr. 359 Z 45 Geogr. Lage 1° 23' W, 50°54' N, Höhe ü. d. M. — m Stand VIII.40.

Maßstab etwa 1: 16 500 (1 cm = 165 m)

(A) GB	10 206	Flugplatz Southampton (Woolston-Hythe)	
(B) GB	21 31	Tanklager Woolston(South.)	
		1) 6 Tanks ca. 40 m Ø	
		2) 1 Tank ca. 25 m Ø	
		3) Pumpstation	
(C) GB	45 32	Ocean Dock	
		4) 5 Lagerhallen 570x25m	(14 000qm)
(D) GB	45 33	Kaianlagen am Empress Dock	
		5) 7 Lagerhallen 1350x35m	(47 000qm)
(E) GB	45 34	Kaianlagen a.d.Südspitze	
		6) 5 Lagerhallen 850x35m	(3o 000qm)
(F) GB	45 35	Innen-und Aussendock	
		7) 3 Lagerhallen 550x35m	(19 000qm)
		8) 4 Getreidespeicher 380x35m	(13 000qm)
(G) GB	52 31	Hauptgaswerk	
(H) GB	56 32	Kühlhaus Southampton	
(I) GB	74 32	Flugzeugfabrik Southampton-Woolston Supermarine Aviation Works	
(K) GB	74 37	Flugzeugfabrik Southampton-Woolston Neue Fabrik A.V.Roe u.Co.	
(L) GB	83 31	Woolston(South.)Werft d.John I.Thornycroft u.Co.Ltd.	
(M) GB	83 36	Grosses Schwimmdock	
(N) GB	83 37	Trafalgar Trockendock	
(O) GB	83 38	Prince of Wales Trockendock	
(P) GB	83 39	4 Trockendocks im Aussendock	

Luftwaffe target map of the Supermarine factory at Woolston, Southampton (HMP).

Luftwaffe aircrews being briefed before a raid on Southampton.

The vulnerable Spitfire producing Supermarine factory at Woolston, pictured before the devastating raid of 26 September 1940.

Spitfires being built at Supermarine.

Cyril Russell, an 18-year-old working in the Woolston factory's 'K' Shop – who survived the raids of September 1940.

Supermarine draughtsman Albert 'Bill' Adams, who survived the 26 September 1940 raid, was also a member of the Auxiliary Fire Service (Dave Key).

On 24 September 1940, Supermarine was targeted by the Me 110s of Hauptmann Martin Lutz's Erprobungsgruppe 210 fighter-bomber unit. The shelter at Pear Tree Green suffered a direct hit, and it was there that most of the forty-two fatalities occurred (Dave Key).

The gutted Supermarine factory after the 26 September 1940, also led by Major Kless of II/KG 55 and for which success he received the *Ritterkreuz*.

The cover of the Luftwaffe magazine *Der Adler* in which the raid on Supermarine was trumpeted.

Auch hier liegen wieder zwei unwiderlegbare Bilddokumente vor uns, die deutsche Aufklärer aufgenommen haben. Sie zeigen ein britisches Rüstungswerk in Southampton-Woolston vor und nach dem deutschen Bombenangriff. Links ist die ganze Anlage unversehrt, wobei (1) eine Montagehalle zeigt, (2) eine Werkhalle. Bei den Hallen sind große Mate vorräte aufgestapelt. Links führt eine Eisenbahnlinie vorbei. Eine gewisse topographische Verschiedenartigkeit der beiden Aufnahmen ist darin begründet, daß das linke Bild, bei Ebbe aufgenommen, mehr Land zeigt als das rechte, das bei Flut gemacht wurde.

Das Bild rechts läßt die verheerende Wirkung des deutschen Bombenangriffs klar zutage treten. Die Werkhalle (1) ist getroffen und durch Feuer vollkommen zerstört. Im Dach der Montagehalle (2) klafft das Einschlagloch einer schweren Bombe. Sie wird im Innern das ihre getan haben. Die Hallen (5) und (6) sind gleichfalls schwer getroffen und teilweise ausgebrannt. Auch in diesem Falle wurden die Wohnhäuser links neben den Hallen (5) und (6) nicht angetastet. Interessant ist ferner, daß das große Schiff und die vielen kleinen Fahrzeuge, die auf dem linken Bilde das Wasser beleben, auf der rechten Aufnahme bis auf ein einziges Schiff verschwunden sind.

Über dem unteren Bildrand ist eine Werft zu sehen. Die Schiffe, die hier teils im Wasser, teils auf den Gleitbahnen liegen, sollen hier ausgebessert werden. Ihre

Der Adler article, showing before and after Luftwaffe reconnaissance photographs following the 26 September 1940 raid.

nn
lbions
üstung

Aufnahmen Luftwaffe PBZ (2), Werbebild (1)

große Zahl läßt eindeutige Rückschlüsse auf den Reparaturbedarf der meerbeherrschenden Flotte zu. Und damit die Ironie nicht fehle, ist auch dieses Rüstungswerk durch eine Ballonsperre „geschützt". Auf dem rechten Bilde steht rechts unten über dem Wasser eine solche Gummiblase. Die Sperre hat weder unsere Kampfflieger daran gehindert, den befohlenen Zerstörungsauftrag durchzuführen, noch unsere Aufklärer, am hellen Tage diese Aufnahme zu machen.
Wie hier, so sieht es in zahlreichen anderen kriegswichtigen Anlagen Großbritanniens aus. Nach britischen Eingeständnissen ist allein die Flugzeugproduktion durch den Ausfall vieler Werke so gestört worden, daß ein Ersatz der abgeschossenen Flugzeuge längst nicht mehr möglich ist. Wie unsere Jäger übereinstimmend berichten, versuchen die britischen Jagdflieger, jedem Kampf mit deutschen Jägern auszuweichen. Sie haben Befehl, nur noch Bomber anzugreifen. Es kommt hinzu, daß die von unseren Jägern oder von der Flak als abgeschossen gemeldeten Flugzeuge bei weitem nicht die volle Zahl der britischen Verluste darstellen. Ein erheblicher Prozentsatz ihrer Maschinen kommt aus den Luftkämpfen so beschädigt zurück, daß sie aus Mangel an Reparaturwerken für längere Zeit ausfallen.
So läßt die deutsche Luftwaffe ihre vernichtenden Schläge weiter auf die britische Rüstung niedersausen, bis zu dem Ende, dem Churchill in seinem Amoklauf unentrinnbar zustrebt.

Das Kampfflugzeug Dornier Do 215, das an den Einsätzen gegen die kriegswichtigen Ziele in England hervorragenden Anteil hat

Following the raid on BAC, 504 Squadron was moved immediately from Hendon to Filton, where its Hurricane are pictured here.

Squadron Leader John Sample, in forage cap, with some of his 504 Squadron pilots at Filton.

Pilot Officer Blair White of 504 Squadron at Filton – who hit the leading Me 110, flown by *Hauptmann* Martin Lutz, and started the rout. No. 504 Squadron's intervention prevented the bombing of Parnall Aircraft at Yate.

Hauptmann Martin Lutz was shot down and killed on 27 September 1940, crashing at Cranbourne Chase; he was the third *Gruppenkommandeur Erprobungsgruppe* 210 lost during the Battle of Britain.

Hauptmann Lutz is buried with his *Bordfunker*, *Unteroffizier* Anton Schön, at the German war cemetery on Cannock Chase.

Leutnant Joachim Koepsell and his *Bordfunker*, *Unteroffizier* Johann Schmidt, were shot down over Radstock on 27 September 1940 in this Me 110 of 3/ZG 26 by 504 Squadron's Sergeant Herbert Jones. Koepsell baled out and was captured, but Schmidt was killed due to parachute failure.

Also killed on 27 September 1940 were 3/ZG 26's *Oberfeldwebel* Hans Tiepelt and his *Bordfunker*, *Unteroffizier* Herbert Brosig, whose Me 110 exploded over Fishponds, Bristol, when shot down by 504 Squadron's Flying Officer Michael Royce. The two Germans are buried at Bristol's Greenbank Cemetery.

As the Germans retreated from Bristol on 27 September 1940, harried all the way by RAF fighters, over Weymouth 609 Squadron's Pilot Officer Rogers Miller's Spitfire collided with the 9/ZG 26 Me 110 of *Gefreiter* Georg Jackstadt during a head-on attack. Eyewitnesses saw a great 'flash in the sky'; Miller was killed, as was Jackstadt's *Bordfunker*, *Gefreiter* Emil Liedtke; the German pilot was extremely lucky to survive and become a prisoner.

Sergeant Peter Fox, a 19-year-old Hurricane pilot of 56 Squadron, shot down over Lyme Regis by a Me 110 on his first operational sortie, 30 September 1940. Fox baled out safely, slightly wounded.

Victorious pilots of 504 Squadron examining their trophies at Filton following the highly successful action of 27 September 1940.

A Luftwaffe target map showing the Yeovil area – and the Westland Aircraft factory and airfield (HMP).

In 1993, Dilip Sarkar and friends returned Peter Fox to Wooten Fitzpaine to recover the remains of his Hurricane. There Peter, on the left, met eyewitnesses to his crash and parachute descent, and became the only one of 'The Few' to own his Battle of Britain aircraft when the author arranged for the MOD to transfer legal right of ownership to Peter – although the Hurricane was in several thousand pieces!

Squadron Leader Peter Devitt, CO of 152 Squadron at Warmwell and an old boy of Sherborne School – over which he found himself fighting on 30 September 1940.

On 30 September 1940, Squadron Leader Peter Devitt of 152 Squadron was hit by a He 111's return fire but safely forced-landed his damaged Spitfire at Skew Bridge, Newton St Loe, near Bath.

On 30 September 1940, *Unteroffizier* Horst Perez of 4/JG 26 was shot down in combat with Spitfires and captured when he forced-landed on Crapham Down, East Dean, just inland of Beachy Head.

Today, *Unteroffizier* Perez's Me 109E, 'White 4', can be seen at the IWM Duxford.

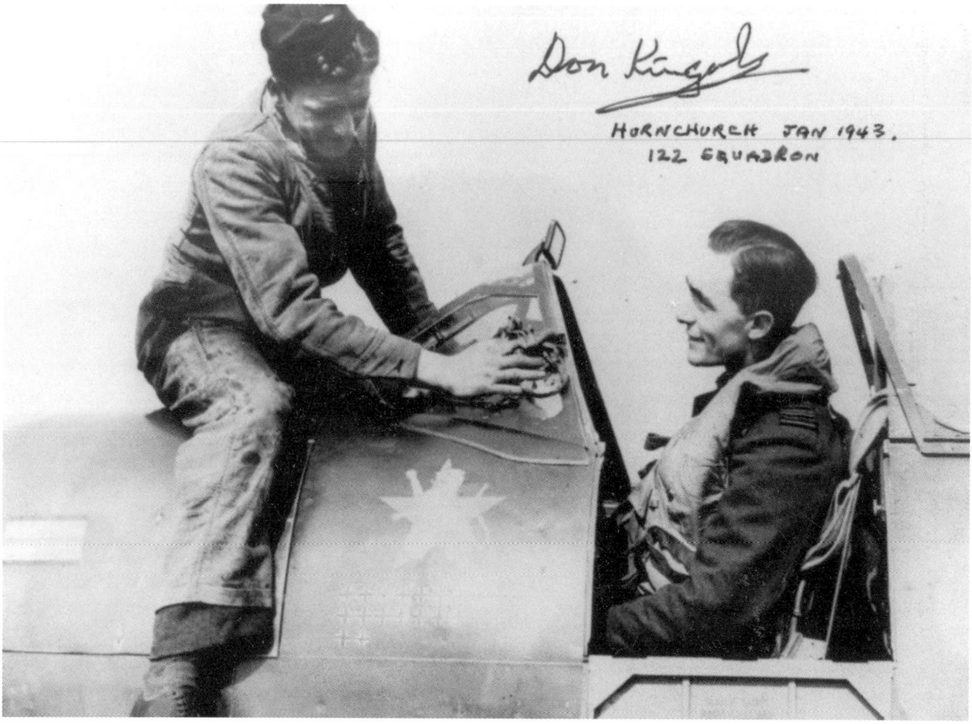

Perez was most likely shot down by either Sergeant Don Kingaby, pictured here, or more likely, Pilot Officer John Drummond, both of 92 Squadron.

Daylight defeat: Pilots of 611 Squadron pose with a trophy taken from a Do 17 shot down by Pilot Officer Denis Adams, third left, standing. By the end of September 1940, the German daylight bombing offensive had been defeated, forcing the Germans to bomb at night, which was less accurate but safer given that Britain's nocturnal defences were still in their infancy.

> finally crashed on Duxford aerodrome [*sic* – Gatwick]. Sergeant Hogg landed at Duxford [*sic*]. Other squadrons of Hurricanes and Spitfires joined in the battle, and Flying Officer Czernin followed three surviving Me 110s to the coast of France. These were believed to be the only survivors. The Squadron landed at Debden at 10.20 hrs, Sergeant Hogg returning later. The Squadron claimed five Me 110s destroyed and two Me 110s probable, our only casualty being Sergeant [Leonard] Bartlett's damaged Hurricane. [ORB]

Nos. 249 and 46 Squadron were operating together and also attacked the circle of Me 110s over Redhill, as the former reported,

> A diving attack was carried out from the sun and above. There were a number of Me 109s above the 110 formation but they showed no inclination to come down and fight. As a result of our attack on the Me 110s, eight were destroyed and five probably destroyed. [ORB]

What becomes apparent in this action is that, like the Duxford Wing, with so many 11 Group fighters involved, combat claims are wildly exaggerated, with multiple pilots claiming the same enemy aircraft destroyed. For 249 Squadron, these claims were not without loss: Pilot Officer Percival Burton was killed in the collision with *Hauptmann* Horst Liensberger's aircraft, and Pilot Officer Hugh Beazley returned to base 'with a bad bullet wound in his foot. Flight Lieutenant [Robert] Barton shot down at Gatwick, uninjured' [ORB].

Owing to fog over North Weald, with visibility down to 700 yards, 46 Squadron's pilots had taken-off singly or in pairs before forming up over base and joining up with 249. This squadron also attacked the Me 110s in the Maidstone area, Pilot Officer Allan Johnson and Sergeant Raymond Sellers participating in the demise of the Oxted Me 110 (although credited with a destroyed 110 each), and Pilot Officer William Pattullo claimed another whilst Flight Sergeant Edward Tyrer claimed a probable, and the Belgian Pilot Officer Eugene Seghers one damaged.

Flight Lieutenant Alexander Rabagliati reported,

> I attacked a mill of twenty Me 110s. I attacked one 110 from below and hit the port engine. He broke away and dived straight over the land, out to sea. I followed him down and chased him from dead astern for about ten miles out to sea, and gradually closed in to fifty yards when he turned over about fifty feet above the sea, put in his left wing and disappeared.

This was an escorting fighter of *Stab* II/ZG 76, which was also attacked by pilots of 249 Squadron and ditched in the Channel off Hastings; the pilot and *Geschwader Adjutant*, *Oberleutnant* Wilfired von Eichhorn was rescued from the water badly burnt but his *Bordfunker*, *Unteroffizier* Erich Bartmuss, was never seen again.

So far as 213 Squadron was concerned, Flight Lieutenant John Sing and Flying Officer James Strickland shared in the destruction of the Ashdown Me 110, and Sergeant Hector Barrow similarly in the Me 110 down at Gatwick. Strickland's Hurricane was shot-up by a 110 over Whitchurch, forcing the Hurricane pilot, who was unhurt, down near Redhill – but Flight Lieutenant Lionel Schwind was shot down over Gatwick and killed, his fighter crashing on Wildernesse Golf Course near Sevenoaks.

South of Biggin Hill, at 09.45 hrs and as the enemy withdrew, the Spitfires of 66 Squadron were also in action, Sergeant Claude Parsons pursuing the Me 110s to the Sussex coast, attacking repeatedly, causing the starboard engine of one to stop, 'belching black smoke and oil'. Parsons was then forced to break away when attacked by another 110, but when last he saw the German he engaged, the aircraft 'was losing height quickly and crossed the coast at Beachy Head, its altitude about 3[,000]–4,000 feet'; Parsons claimed the 110 as damaged. Sergeant Harry Cook claimed two Me 110s damaged.

Pilot Officer Stanley Baker reported,

> [seeing a 110] falling with both engines on fire with three Hurricanes still attacking. Another 110 then dived down, apparently with the intention of assisting the other 110, below me, diving in my direction. I turned onto the E/A and gave a burst of three or four seconds from 250 yards, closing to fifty yards. The port engine was on fire and the flames were heavy and appeared to be spreading along the wing. Also, one fairly large piece fell off the engine.

Owing to the presence of other enemy aircraft, Baker was unable to follow up the attack but nonetheless was credited with a 110 destroyed. When Flight Lieutenant Bob Oxspring, commanding 'B' Flight, sighted the 110s, they were 'travelling fast towards the South'.

Attacking one in company with a Hurricane, 'Oxo' watched the Me 110 'go into a spiral, almost vertical dive, and crashed somewhere ten to twelve miles SSE of Biggin Hill' – this being the Ashdown Forest 13/(Z)LG 1 machine also attacked by numerous other pilots. By 10.20 hrs, Oxspring was safely back at Gravesend, and the remainder of the squadron also landed intact.

Eventually, the Germans had been chased back to France and all was quiet again.

According to the AHB narrative,

> there is no doubt that many of the enemy bombers were forced to turn back from London, which we know was their objective. Even if the attack had been a complete success the weight of bombs dropped would have been fairly small, for no more than twenty Ju 88s and an even smaller number of Me 110 bombers were employed.

Indeed, what damage there was to London was hardly worth the enemy's substantial losses: most bombs fell in Lambeth, nine people being killed when a factory shelter in Clapham Road was hit; a sewer was fractured, the southern line between Brixton and Loughborough Junction was damaged, and in Battersea the weighbridge and Albert Yard were hit – and that was the sum total of it. In achieving this, KG 77 lost five Ju 88s destroyed by fighters, and another to AA fire which broke up over Cudham, the gunners also believed responsible for destroying the 5/JG 27 Me 109 brought down at Selmeston. It had been, however, a disastrous operation for the Me 110s of V(Z)/LG 1 – which were simply overwhelmed by the numbers of 11 Group fighters, losing eight aircraft, the dead including the *Gruppenkommandeur*, *Hauptmann* Horst Liensberger. Unable to further sustain such heavy losses, within forty-eight hours, the *Gruppe* was withdrawn to re-fit in Bavaria and morph into I/*Nachtjägdgeschwader* 3, a new night fighter unit. Indeed, this would transpire to be an especially bad day for the *Zerstörer* force – as subsequent events soon proved.

To the west, there had been action for 10 Group, at 09.20 hrs, when 152 Squadron's Pilot Officer Eric Marrs intercepted a Ju 88 of 3(F)/123 and shot the reconnaissance bomber down over Porlock Bay.

All then went ominously quiet.

Since being pulled out of 11 Group and leaving North Weald on 1 September 1940, things had so far been very quiet for 56 Squadron at its new home in 10 Group.

Pilot Officer Frederick 'Fred' W. ('Taffy') Higginson DFM:

> The main recollection I have of that period is that we were a somewhat disorganised lot. I don't know whether that is the correct word, but we had taken a beating in the preceding months at North Weald and France, and needed re-equipping and receiving new pilots.
>
> The Station Commander at Boscombe was Group Captain [Henry] Ramsbottom[-]Isherwood [DFC], who, I believe, later took a unit to

> Russia and was killed. He was a first-class chap, good rugger player and much-liked by us all. During the early part of that period I remember thinking that morale would perhaps be boosted if we had a Squadron mascot, so I went to the local town and bought a small monkey, which we named '109'. He was a great success and kept in a cage, on a lead. Anyway, the Group Captain gave a cocktail party for the Squadron and requested 109's presence. [The] 109 went down very well, until, that is, he started to undertake enthusiastic sexual self-gratification! Morals being what they were in those days we had to remove him quickly!!

No. 56 Squadron's period on inactivity was about to come to an end, as the fighting over the West Country intensified.

Emboldened, no doubt, by KG 55's successful raids on BAC in Filton and Supermarine in Southampton, *Luftflotte* 3 now turned its attention to other aircraft factories in the south-west. Today's target was Parnall Aircraft Limited at Yate, a few miles north-west of Bristol – another long-range daylight penetration. Hoping to repeat the success of 25 September 1940, when the Filton raid so confused the defenders, ten Me 110 fighter bombers of *Hauptmann* Martin Lutz's *Erprobungsgruppe* 210 were chosen for this mission. Escort to the target was to be provided by forty-two Me 110 *Zerstörers* of ZG 26, whilst even II/JG 2 Me 109s swept in front of the advancing raid to just beyond the enemy coastline. Later, twenty-nine 109s of I and II/JG 2, and seven of JG 53 were to take-off and meet the returning raiders – eighty-nine twin and single-engined fighters to protect just ten fighter bombers. What could possibly go wrong?

This was another big effort – but from the outset the operation was underpinned by poor intelligence. During the First World War, Parnall Aircraft Limited had included an aircraft repair facility, which the Germans still believed was the case in 1940: it was not. The enemy knew, though, that the factory was not manufacturing aircraft at this time: instead, it was the main production plant for twin and four-gun turrets, designed by Captain Archibald Frazer-Nash, as installed in British bombers. Considering the risks of such a deep daylight penetration, even despite the substantial fighter escort, selection of this target can only be considered surprising.

At 10.40 hrs (BST), *Hauptmann* Lutz led 1/*Erprobungsgruppe* 210 up from Cherbourg-Ost, and *Oberleutnant* Wilhelm-Richard Rössiger took-off with 2 *Staffel*. Together, the two *Staffeln* set course for Yate. The faster Me 110 fighters of ZG 26 soon caught up the fighter bombers, and the fifty-two strong formation headed for England. Ahead of the Me 110s swept the eleven Me 109s of II/JG 2, hoping to occupy any RAF fighters as the 110s raced inland. RDF soon detected two plots of '20+' north of Cherbourg, which became one raid over the central Channel area. The controller scrambling 238 Squadron at 11.01 hrs from Middle Wallop to patrol base, and at 11.05 hrs, suspecting the enemy to be heading for a target in The Solent area, 56 Squadron was scrambled from Boscombe to patrol the Isle of Wight. At 11.15 hrs, the Spitfires of 609 Squadron were sent to patrol Bournemouth at 25,000ft; four minutes later, 152 Squadron also scrambled from Warmwell (initial orders not known).

The fast-moving Germans crossed the Dorset coast over St Alban's Head, then turned north-west towards Yate. The escorting Me 110s of II and III/ZG 26, and the Me 109s of II/JG 2, then detached themselves from the advancing formation to orbit in an *Abwehrkreis* over Portland and Warmwell, there to await the raid's return. Having been scrambled so late, both 152 and 609 Squadrons were still climbing, much to their frustration, as the enemy passed high overhead, racing inland.

No. 609 Squadron recorded its dissatisfaction:

> For the second time in three days, 10 Group Control positioned the squadron so badly that they had little or no chance of catching any of the bombers over the coast. [ORB]

With The Solent now behind the enemy, as was Portland, Warmwell and Middle Wallop – all potential targets – it was clear that the raiders were heading deep inland again, possibly back to Bristol. At 11.25 hrs, therefore, the Hurricanes of 504 Squadron, freshly arrived at Filton, scrambled from there to patrol Bristol. Apart from 504 Squadron, which climbed over Bristol, the other defending squadrons were once more involved in a desperate, climbing, stern chase.

As the raid approached Frome, more escorting Me 110s broke away to orbit ready to cover the fighter bombers' retreat, the remaining thirty plus aircraft pressing on to Yate, now 20 miles to the north. So far, there was no sign of RAF fighters, and when 25,000ft over Radstock, *Hauptmann* Martin Lutz ordered the formation to commence a shallow dive towards their target. For some reason, instead of flying directly due north from Radstock to Yate, possibly to further confuse the defences or because of a navigation error, Lutz's formation flew a north-westerly course, passing over Filton. No. 504 Squadron, however, had scrambled from Filton at 11.23 hrs, with orders to patrol 'Milk "B"' (Filton) at 20,000ft, and, whilst still climbing, Flight Lieutenant Barrington Royce DFC, who was leading the squadron, was informed by the sector controller of the raid approaching from the south. At 11.45 hrs, the Hurricane pilots sighted the Me 110s 'flying NNW in loose formation at about 10,000 feet, 1,000 feet above our own aircraft which were ahead of the E/A [Form 'F']'. 'A' Flight's Pilot Officer

Murray Frisby was No. 2 of Red Section, which was weaving 1,000ft above and behind 504 Squadron, and sighted the enemy at his height, 10,000ft:

> I called the Squadron Leader and then attacked the leading E/A head-on. He was observed to dive away with white streamers from each engine, in a southerly direction.

Frisby was the first of 504 Squadron to attack and had hit Lutz's 110. Immediately the German formation broke up and individual combats ensued – within full view of excited Bristolians.

Dr Alex Moulton:

> It was a marvellous sight … it was wonderful. We're all looking at this thing; it's wonderful to see this taking place over our heads. Circle round, victory roll, some down and re-arm or re-fuel on the airfield then go up again, so this amazing sight, not a single aeroplane going in the same direction, they all split up completely, shooting off all over the sky in all different directions. I remember seeing some smoke somewhere going down, falling down, so there was the battle actually in action. The atmosphere, of course, was simply hitting back and hitting back like anything. Remember, it wasn't a night raid, it wasn't women or children, just young men in fighters.

According to the Luftwaffe after action report, as a direct result of 504 Squadron's attack, the raid on Parnall Aircraft Limited was abandoned, 'Bombs had to be dropped on the northern edge of Bristol in an emergency'. Little damage was caused, but a car was blown up at Charlton, its driver killed, and a man and two children riding a horse and trap died nearby.

The Germans now fled, harassed by AA fire and pursued by an ever-increasing number of RAF fighters; what began as a confident, deep inland penetration to a specific target had degenerated into an ignominious rout, the start of which 504 Squadron accredited to Frisby's 'single-handed' [ORB] attack.

Pilot Officer Michael Rook, younger brother of 504 Squadron's Flight Lieutenant Tony Rook, Blue 2:

> Attacked enemy with the Squadron. Started beam attack on Me 'Jaguar'. He turned towards me and the attack became head-on. Opened fire at 600 yards and passed over top of E/A, narrowly missing him. I got a 3-second burst into him and bullets were seen entering cockpit. Broke away and lost him.

> I then saw that the enemy formation had broken and was retreating, climbing fast. I climbed after them and had no difficulty in catching them. They were in ragged formation and the rear aircraft were weaving. I noticed one Jaguar underneath the main formation and climbing up to join them. I came below the enemy and formation. He was near the front of the formation and closed to about 300 yards. He then saw me and started to dive. I opened my throttle and got slightly beneath him. Pulling the nose of my aircraft slightly up, the E/A came into my sights at about 200 yards, diving across my bows. I gave him a 3-second burst, ending astern of him. Flames issued from both engines and he went down in a vertical dive, enveloped in smoke. Some oil from his engine came on my windshield. I picked up my position as South of Cerne Abbas, this was after pursuing the enemy formation South.

Pilot Officer Michael Rook had shot down *Oberfeldwebel* Hans Tiepelt and *Unteroffizier* Herbert Brosig of 2/ZG 26, their fighter breaking up at roof-top height before exploding and disintegrating in Fishponds in Bristol. Both enemy airmen, needless to say, were killed. This Me 110 was also attacked by Flying Officer Michael Royce, younger brother of Flight Lieutenant Barrington Royce, who watched the stricken fighter crash 'into the yard of a house about two miles East of Bristol where it exploded and burst into flames'.

Sergeant Herbert Jones of Green Section also went into action with 504 Squadron over Bristol, attacking a Me 110 from abeam, causing smoke to issue from its port engine. The Hurricane pilot then attacked another Me 110 head on, 'which turned over and went straight down, and crashed South of Bristol, bursting into flames'.

Jones's attack had incapacitated the *Bordfunker*, *Unteroffizier* Johann Schmidt, whom the pilot, *Leutnant* Joachim Koepsell, a 21-year-old veteran of 3/ZG 26, could see slumped and unresponsive in the rear cockpit. With his aircraft beginning to burn fiercely, Koepsell baled out, becoming a POW. The 110 crashed at Haydon Farm, Radstock; Schmidt's body was found half a mile away, near the Kilmersdon Colliery railway, his parachute unopened.

Flight Lieutenant Tony Rook, Green 1:

> I picked up the E/A and gave him a burst and crippled starboard engine, then a chase ensued and we lost height down to 4,000 feet, about ten miles North of Poole, giving him occasional bursts during the milling around. After a terrific head-on attack this machine gradually lost height, whereupon I was joined by another aircraft *US-M*, but in my opinion the

> machine was so crippled as he was flying so low and eventually crashed into a hillside.

The other RAF fighter was a Hurricane, flown by Pilot Officer Michael Maxwell, Green 2, of 56 Squadron, who had initially been forced to return to base owing to a faulty oxygen system. Rectified, the pilot immediately took-off again from Boscombe but was unable to locate his squadron. At 11.50 hrs, when at 16,000ft and 30 miles west of base, Maxwell sighted the retreating enemy 2,000ft above. Climbing, he attacked the rearmost machine:

> Fired two bursts and a piece of cowling came off. I then broke away and saw E/A losing height with black smoke emitted from port engine. Another Hurricane attacked E/A, which dived steeply, and later I attacked again after Hurricane had broken away and saw E/A (with one engine stopped) crash after endeavouring to forced-land ... Return fire from rear gun. None of the crew baled out.

This was a 2/*Erprobungsgruppe* 210 fighter bomber, the *Bordfunker* of which, *Gefreiter* Werner Zwick, had been hit and rendered unconscious. The pilot, *Feldwebel* Friedrich Ebner, was also wounded, his aircraft crashing in Iwerne Minster; both men survived.

During the pursuit, 504 Squadron's leader, Flight Lieutenant Barrington Royce, caught a Me 110 about to attack a Hurricane, which he immediately engaged from 'dead astern'. As the two aircraft turned, 'petrol appeared to be coming back from behind both engines', obscuring the Hurricane pilot's target. Having expended his ammunition, Royce returned to Filton, claiming the 110 as damaged.

After the initial charge over Bristol, Sergeant Charlton 'Wag' Haw, Green 3, chased a 110 back to the Dorset coast,

> [and for] several miles over the Channel. After a 10-second burst from below and behind, the E/A caught fire and went spinning down into the sea.

Pilot Officer Michael Stavert of 504 Squadron's 'B' Flight was also engaged with the Me 110s over Filton and during the pursuit south:

> Dived head-on at a 110 above rear end of enemy formation. [The] 110 started to fire at about 600 yards and kept firing all the time. My burst was aimed at port engine and pilot, and the engine caught fire. Black smoke followed by flames came from the port engine. At the same time another

> 110 made a front quarter attack and my machine was hit in port mainplane and tail. Cannon and machine-gun ammunition was used by E/A. After following enemy formation South saw Me below cloud but was unable to attack as a Spitfire making a front quarter attack shot it down.

Pilot Officer Blair 'Crasher' White, also of 504 Squadron, had also got in a three-second burst at *Hauptmann* Martin Lutz's leading 110 over Bristol, then pursued the Germans south at 'full boost'. East of Weymouth, White attacked a 110 from above, breaking downwards:

> When I pulled out the E/A was diving hard for the ground, turning to the left; it then went vertically up, stalled and dived straight into the ground, bursting into flames.

This was a 110 of 1/*Erprobungsgruppe* 210, which crashed at Bradle Row in Kimmeridge, killing both occupants, namely *Leutnant* Gerhard Schmidt and *Feldwebel* Gerhard Richter.

By now, 504 Squadron was spent, having surprised the Me 110s and routed them over Bristol. Sergeant Basil 'Mike' Bush found himself short of fuel after the pursuit, landing at Weston airfield, and Sergeant Charlton Haw forced-landed at Axminster. The squadron had, without doubt, done exceptionally well and had great cause for celebration. Conversely, *Erprobungsgruppe* 210 in particular had nothing to be cheerful about, having lost its third *Gruppenkommandeur* in less than two months: having first been hit by Flight Lieutenant Tony Rook over Bristol, *Hauptmann* Martin Lutz's damaged Me 110 was further damaged by various other RAF fighters, eventually crashing at Bussey's Stool Farm, on Cranborne Chase, killing Lutz and his *Bordfunker*, *Unteroffizier* Anton Schön – a significant loss indeed.

As 504 Squadron disengaged, for other 10 Group squadrons the chase was still on.

No. 238 Squadron had first patrolled base, then Salisbury, and vectored 330°, was the first of the defenders to engage the enemy, at 11.30 hrs.

Pilot Officer John Urwin-Mann, Blue 1, reported,

> When ten miles South of Bristol encountered formation of E/A stepped up – bombers in line-astern and fighters in vic at about 20,000 feet. Bombers [author's note: incorrectly recorded as 'He 111s'] and at about 15,000 feet. At same time saw friendly squadron of Spitfires [author's note: 609 Squadron] and dived to attract their attention. Then climbed and attacked Me 110 of the rear section. Fired from 200 yards … flew below,

> damaging port engine and forward part of fuselage. Engine was smoking and bits flew off. Broke away and I was attacked by three Me 110s from above and behind. Went into evasive tactics and out to sea for a bit, and shook E/A off then returned to base.

Urwin-Mann's Sergeant Józef Jeka, attacked the rearmost formation of fighter bombers, managing a short burst before being attacked himself. Returning fire, Jeka's assailant began smoking but when only 100ft above the sea, he was then attacked by two Spitfires and dived straight in.

Two Me 110s went into the 'drink', although which was shot down by Jeka, Pilot Officer David M. Crook DFC, Pilot Officer John Bisdee or Sergeant Charlton Haw, it is impossible to say. Either way, as if losing the *Gruppenkommandeur* was not bad enough, 2/*Erprobungsgruppe* 210 lost its *Staffelkapitän*, *Oberleutnant* Wilhelm-Richard Rössiger, who was shot down into the Channel and, like his *Bordfunker*, *Oberfeldwebel* Hans Marx, remains missing, and *Stab* III/ZG 26 lost its *Gruppenadjutant*, *Oberleutnant* Hans Barschal, who, with his *Bordfunker*, *Unteroffizier* Hans Kloss, also crashed into the sea and was never found.

No. 238 Squadron suffered no losses in the engagement and all pilots involved returned safely to base.

The ten Spitfires of Warmwell's 152 Squadron also sighted the retreating enemy south of Bristol, engaging the Germans near the Dorset coast:

> intercepted forty Ju 88 [*sic*] accompanied by Me 110 … heading South going very fast … Me 109 appeared above when our Squadron reached the coast and may have been a defensive patrol awaiting the return of the bombers … Red 2 (Pilot Officer Richard Innes) attacked the bombers but he broke off when gun panel on starboard wing flew off and put his aircraft out of control. When he regained control he climbed, saw a Hurricane giving short bursts at Me 109 without effect and break away. Red 2 closed on Me 109, firing bursts for about eight seconds from 300–100 yards. Black smoke came from E/A which dived straight down towards the sea.
>
> Yellow 1 (Pilot Officer Graham Cox) attacked a Me 110 in enemy formation and fired one long burst of sixteen seconds from astern and underneath at 250 yards. Large pieces flew from E/A and both engines were streaming black smoke and glycol. E/A dived down and must have been destroyed. On reaching coast Yellow 1 saw Me 109 with yellow spinners and upper engine cowlings closing from the East.
>
> Yellow 2 (Pilot Officer Ian [Norman] Bayles) attacked Me 110 and damaged one, which fell back and broke downwards in the formation. Me 109 came down behind Yellow 2 who climbed up over coast and attacked

> nine Me 109s proceeding out to sea and was hit by cannon shell on left mainplane. He also found the nose of a shell in his tyre upon landing.
>
> White 1 (Pilot Officer Fred Holmes) and White 2 (Pilot Officer Roger Hall) followed Me 110 which had already been hit and saw it crash on the ground [author's note: probably that down at Kimmeridge and shot down by 504 Squadron's Pilot Officer Blair White]. White 1 did not fire and was unsuccessful in contacting other E/A. White 2 climbed up to 15,000 feet towards the sea and chased Me 110 for ten to twelve miles, getting in short bursts, then while smoke appeared from port engine and E/A, which had been damaged, dived through mist towards the sea.
>
> Blue 1 (Flight Lieutenant Fred Thomas) attacked Me 110 which took evasive action consisting of steep turns, short dives and climbs. Attack was from 200 yards closing to 150 yards and almost all his ammunition was fired into E/A. Its port engine was throwing black smoke when Blue 1 broke away as a Me 109 was on his tail.
>
> Blue 2 (Pilot Officer Arthur Watson) attacked Ju 88 [*sic*] over Southampton from above and astern. E/A, which was smoking, went down and dived into the sea, five miles South of the Isle of Wight. He climbed up again to 15,000 feet and fired at Me 110, causing glycol to stream from starboard engine, following it down, firing intermittent bursts. When at 4,000 feet, E/A exploded and crashed West of Poole Harbour. [ORB]

This was another grievous loss to the enemy, being *Oberleutnant* Arthur Niebuhr, *Staffelkapitän* of 4/ZG 26, who as killed with his *Bordfunker*, *Unteroffizier* Klaus Thiesen, when their fighter blew up over Arne.

Pilot Officer Dudley Williams, Black 1,

> attacked a Me 110 which after attempting evasive action flew South at full speed. Black 1 continued the attack from astern. The engines of E/A were pouring out white smoke and dived steeply. Black 1 followed, giving short bursts. E/A was seen to crash on land between Weymouth and Poole Harbour, near Lulworth Cove. [ORB]

This *Zerstörer* belonged to 8/ZG 26 and forced-landed near Kimmeridge, where the pilot, *Unteroffizier* Fritz Schapp, and his *Bordfunker*, *Gefreiter* Karl Nechwatal, were both captured, wounded.

After the combat, apart from two slightly damaged Spitfires, 152 Squadron returned to Warmwell otherwise intact.

The Hurricanes of 56 Squadron were first ordered to patrol over the Isle of Wight, then vectored towards Bristol; Pilot Officer Michael Constable-Maxwell, flying solo after initially returning to base with oxygen failure, subsequently engaged and shared in the destruction of *Feldwebel* Friedrich Ebner's 2/*Erprobungsgruppe* 210 Me 110 at Iwerne Minster. According to the 56 Squadron ORB, Pilot Officer Ken Marston destroyed a Me 110 and damaged another, although no combat report appears to have survived, and Pilot Officer Frederick Higginson damaged another, these combats occurring over Bournemouth at 20,000ft; in his log book, the latter wrote, 'Attacked 110 Jaguars. Bunch of'em. Got port engine streaming glycol. Seen by F/Lt [Robert] Edwards.'

Higginson's combat report noted that 'As I broke away I was attacked by a Me 109 which had obviously been ordered to await return of bombers near coastline' – fortunately the Welsh ace escaped unscathed.

No. 56 Squadron's Pilot Officer Donald MacKenzie, a 19-year-old New Zealander, Yellow 2, pursued a 'Do [*sic*]' south,

> which appeared to be in difficulty and after his attacks the starboard engine took fire and E/A glided down towards sea. Although he did not see it crash, it appeared unlikely to reach home.

Finally, MacKenzie broke away 'twenty miles South of Portland Bill', the 110 attacked very likely being a III/ZG 26 machine, which crash-landed near Cherbourg with combat damage.

No. 56 Squadron suffered no casualties in this action – but 609 Squadron was to suffer a heart-felt loss.

Both flight commanders' R/T having failed, Pilot Officer Rogers Freeman Garland Miller, Yellow 1, an experienced fighter pilot, led the squadron into an attack on the III/ZG 26 Me 110 fighters milling around over Weymouth, south of Blandford Forum.

Pilot Officer David Crook:

> I was flying behind Mick [Pilot Officer Rogers Freeman Garland Miller] and he turned slightly left to attack a 110 which was coming towards him. But the German was as determined as Mick and refused to give way or alter course to avoid this head on attack. Their aggregate closing speed was at least 600 mph and an instant later they collided. There was a terrific explosion and a sheet of flame and black smoke seemed to hang in the air like a great ball of fire. Many little shattered fragments fluttered down and that was all. Mick was killed instantly.

Also following Miller was Pilot Officer Keith Ogilvie:

> The 110 turned out to get his cannon working on Mick [Pilot Officer Rogers Freeman Garland Miller], and they hit head on. There was a terrific explosion, a sheet of flame and a column of black smoke. I glimpsed a Spitfire wing fluttering out and the white of a parachute with something on the end. It was ghastly. Somehow, I shot straight up, half-rolled, and coming down saw a 110 float under me. I pressed the button and kept it pressed and he went straight down in a sheet of flame. The whole vicious action lasted only a few moments.

Miller, had singled out a 9/ZG 26 machine flown by *Gefreiter* Georg Jackstadt, raking the enemy fighter with machine gun bullets in his first pass. Jackstadt, however, broke formation, pursuing Miller at whom he fired several short bursts of heavier cannon fire. The nimbler Spitfire turned and attacked the German head on. Jackstadt met the challenge, both pilots giving no ground and firing continuously. At the last second, both pilots decided upon exactly the same course of action, pulling away upwards – with the disastrous result that their machines collided. Jackstadt's gunner, *Gefreiter* Emil Liedtke, screamed loudly immediately before the point of impact, upon which the 110's right wing collapsed, the aircraft catching fire and spinning away. Unable to jettison his damaged canopy, Jackstadt smashed out the Perspex panels of his burning cockpit but was unable to force his way through the small aperture. Miraculously, the German pilot suddenly found himself thrown free, due to centrifugal force – losing no time deploying his parachute and watching with horror as his aircraft, with Liedtke still aboard, smashed into the ground on the boundary of two farms at Piddletrenthide. Upon alighting by parachute, Jackstadt was rapidly taken into custody, being entertained to a glass of lemonade at Doles Ash Farm before being taken away by the local bobby. After a night in the cells, Jackstadt was treated at Dorchester Hospital, and then escorted by two armed soldiers to London by train, bound for the 'London Cage', the infamous interrogation centre housed in Kensington Palace.

During this action, Pilot Officer David Crook, Blue 3, had also attacked the orbiting Me 110s, but turned too tightly and span away; upon recovery and climbing back up, he found that

> the circle was broken up and the enemy streaming out to sea. I chased one Me 110 and soon caught him. The gunner opened fire, but I gave him a burst and am sure I killed him as there was no return fire. I then emptied my remaining ammunition into him, aiming at both engines in turn and the fuselage. Smoke poured from his port engine.

This 110 was also attacked by Flying Officer John Dundas, Red 3, who, like Crook, broke away, leaving Pilot Officer John Bisdee, Red 2, to 'finally' catch the enemy aircraft up

> about sixty miles off the coast and emptied my remaining ammunition into it from astern in two bursts. I saw the starboard motor stop after this and the E/A went down into the sea. It took me thirteen minutes at full boost to reach the English coast again.

Pilot Officer Noël le Chevalier Agazarian, Blue 2, reported that shortly after Miller had taken over the lead, 609 Squadron was 'attacked by a Hurricane squadron'. Re-forming after taking evasive action, the Spitfires climbed towards Portland, attacking the Me 110s over the coast. Agazarian attacked one, the starboard engine of which 'caught fire. The Me 110 started going down … he went into the sea about twenty-five miles South of Portland'.

It is clear that several pilots were often responsible for the destruction of the same enemy aircraft. Pilot Officer Keith Ogilvie, Yellow 3, had watched his leader collided with Jackstadt's Me 110 in 'a terrific explosion', then attacked a 110 which 'wet straight down, both engines on fire'. Ogilvie's personal combat report provides a vivid impression of the combat: 'I also saw at least three other 110s going down in flames, one hit the sea, another on land, near Portland'.

Although an understandably inflated figure, in total, 609 Squadron claimed six Me 110s destroyed, a probable and Flying Officer Terence Forshaw claimed a Me 109 destroyed over Weymouth Bay (although none of the type were actually lost).

No. 609 Squadron, however, in losing Pilot Officer Rogers Freeman Garland Miller, had suffered the defenders' only fatal casualty in what was a resounding victory against a completely routed enemy. The unfortunate Spitfire pilot was found to have fallen to earth near Dorchester. At 08.20 hrs the following morning, a telegram was sent to Mr Thomas Miller informing him of his second son's death in action:

> Regret to inform you that your son, Pilot Officer Rogers Freeman Garland Miller, is reported missing and believed to have lost his life as the result of air operations on September 27th 1940. Letter follows. Any further information received will be immediately communicated to you. Should news of him reach you from any source, please inform this department.

Having lost their eldest son, Pilot Officer John Miller, a Wellington bomber pilot with 149 Squadron, just six weeks previously, how the Millers felt is simply unimaginable.

Pilot Officer David Crook:

> I remember walking into the Mess for lunch and sitting down and suddenly recollecting that at breakfast, only a few hours before, I had sat next to Mick [Pilot Officer Rogers Freeman Garland Miller] at this very table and we had chatted together. And now, here we were at the next meal, everything was quite normal, and he was dead.
>
> That was one thing I could never get accustomed to; seeing one's friends gay and full of life as they always were, and then, a few hours later, seeing the batman start packing their kit, their shaving brush still damp from being used that morning, while the owner was lying dead in a shattered aeroplane 'somewhere in England'.

Although the Me 109s played little part in the fighting, *Hauptmann* Helmut Wick, *Kommandeur* of I/JG 2, and his wingman, *Oberleutnant* Rudolf 'Rudi' Pflanz, both claimed Spitfires destroyed east of Portland, these non-existent losses being their thirty-first and fourth victories respectively, and *Oberfeldwebel* Werner Machold of 9/JG 2 chalked up his twenty-second kill, another apparently imagined Spitfire west of Portland. *Erprobungsgruppe* 210 claimed a Hurricane destroyed, and ZG 26 four Hurricanes and two Spitfires. That the enemy so overclaimed is testimony to the hectic and confused nature of this West Country action.

From the German perspective, the Parnall raid was a complete failure, the mission having been abandoned, thanks to 504 Squadron's early intervention, which prevented the target being bombed. Later that day, Fighter Command HQ received the following signal from Lord Beaverbrook:

> The fine courage and display of the Hurricane squadron stationed at Filton undoubtedly saved this factory from serious attack this morning. All employees are heartened and encouraged by what they did. Please convey thanks and appreciation to the C-in-C Fighter Command.

This was well-deserved praise for both 504 Squadron and Air Chief Marshal Hugh Dowding's wise decision to move Squadron Leader John Sample's Hurricanes from Hendon to Filton.

In the ensuing rout following 504 Squadron's interception, *Erprobungsgruppe* 210 lost four Me 110s, with six aircrew killed, including both the *Gruppenkommandeur* and a *Staffelkapitän*, and two captured; ZG 26 suffered six Me 110s destroyed, seven airmen killed, including a *Gruppenadjutant*, and four made POWs, including another *Gruppenadjutant*. Considering that further east, during the morning's raid on London, V(Z)/LG 1 had lost eight Me 110s, the *Gruppenkommandeur* amongst the dead, it was a truly disastrous day for the *Zerstörer* force, which would soon be withdrawn from the daylight battle over England. For *Reichsmarschall* Hermann Göring, an enthusiastic supporter of the *Zerstörer* concept and the Me 110, this outcome must have been a bitter blow and another harsh reality check. The tragedy of it all, from the Luftwaffe perspective, is that the proposed attack on Parnall Aircraft Limited, so far inland and by day, considering the company's actual contribution to the British aircraft industry, as opposed to what incompetent Luftwaffe air intelligence believed, was in any case completely pointless.

In what would be one of the greatest days of fighting throughout the entire Battle of Britain, and despite the heavy enemy casualties both east and west, the action was far from over – and, in fact, concurrently with the Yate raid and West Country action, Fighter Command had also been defending London against a second raid. The morning's first attack on London was over by 10.15 hrs – but just forty-five minutes later, RDF screens came alive with indications of another raid building up over the Pas-de-Calais. It seems that the majority of enemy aircraft involved were fighters, in large numbers, escorting a small number of Do 17s: as will be seen, the bombers' intended target remains unclear.

At 11.15 hrs, the first 11 Group squadron was scrambled: 501 Squadron from Gravesend, with orders to patrol Maidstone. At 11.35 hrs, the leading German formation of up to 200 aircraft crossed in over Dover and Dungeness at very high altitude, suggesting a fighter sweep, and headed towards Maidstone. Surprisingly, it was not until that time that further defending squadrons began scrambling. At 11.35 hrs, 41 Squadron left Hornchurch, with orders to form up over base with 222 Squadron, which took-off five minutes later, and 603 Squadron, which scrambled from Rochford at 11.46 hrs, to intercept the Maidstone raiders.

At 11.40 and 11.43 hrs respectively, the Biggin Hill Spitfire squadrons, 92 and 72, scrambled to operate together and rendezvous with Gravesend's 66 Squadron over base before patrolling Maidstone at 25,000ft.

At 11.45 hrs, 605 Squadron went up from Croydon, bound for north-east Kent at 23,000ft, and at the same time both 1 (RCAF) and 229 Squadrons left Northolt to patrol the Croydon district.

Also at 11.45 hrs, 17 and 73 Squadrons left the Debden sector to patrol Hornchurch together; 257 Squadron was authorised but unable to join the formation owing to being in the process of re-fuelling.

Then, at 11.49 and 11.50 hrs respectively, the North Weald squadrons, 249 and 46, left there and Stapleford respectively to also operate as a wing and make a sweep of Canterbury to Hawkinge.

It will be appreciated, therefore, that with the exception of 501 and 605 Squadrons, Air Vice-Marshal Keith Park was continuing to meet the enemy in strength, using wings of either pairs or three squadrons operating together.

Anticipating another heavy attack, 11 Group requested, via Fighter Command HQ, assistance from 12 Group, and at 11.55 hrs the Duxford Wing scrambled with orders to patrol London.

By now, the Duxford Wing's composition had changed, however. The Spitfires of Fowlmere-based 19 Squadron, and the Duxford-based 242 (Canadian) and 310 (Czech) Squadrons were a permanent feature (and at no time were any of these squadrons rotated through 11 Group, as was normal practice) but the Poles of 302 Squadron were no longer part of the formation, and 611 Squadron was now operating one flight at Ternhill in Shropshire, protecting Liverpool, the other at Digby in Lincolnshire. Having suffered particularly heavy casualties flying from Kenley, on 3 September 1940, 616 Squadron had been withdrawn first to Coltishall, thence to Kirton-in-Lindsey, the demoralised unit's new CO, the exceptional Squadron Leader Howard 'Billy' Burton, winner of the Cranwell Sword of Honour in 1936, there to re-build the depleted squadron. Under Air Chief Marshal Hugh Dowding's Stabilising Scheme, on 7 September 1940, 616 Squadron became a 'C' unit, which is to say ineffective, but under Squadron Leader Howard Burton's dynamic leadership in short order the classification was rapidly increased to 'B' – a unit with six combat-ready pilots and available for operations if necessary. On 19 September 1940 – just over a fortnight since 616 Squadron was pulled out of the line – Burton had led no less than fourteen Spitfires to operate from Fowlmere with the Duxford Wing relieving Squadron Leader 'Sailor' Malan's 74 Squadron of that duty. From that date onwards, 616 Squadron flew from Kirton-in-Lindsey to Fowlmere on a daily basis, and had to date participated in various uneventful wing patrols. So it was now that Squadron Leader Douglas Bader led his own 242 (Canadian) Squadron and 310 (Czech) Squadron off from Duxford, with the Fowlmere Spitfires soon catching up the slower Hurricanes; Squadron Leader Brian Lane positioned his 19 Squadron above and behind the Duxford squadrons, and Burton's 616 Squadron was slightly above and behind 19 Squadron at 25,000ft. It is a common misconception that time was wasted through the Duxford Wing orbiting base and forming up but that is not the case, as Wing Commander Douglas Blackwood, then commanding 310 (Czech) Squadron, confirmed,

> There was no time wasted. [Squadron Leader Douglas] Bader took-off, set course, and everyone else followed him. There was no forming up process. Of course, Bader always had the latest aircraft, whilst others flew older machines with a lesser performance, so this left many of us flying flat out, constantly trying to catch him up. But there was no time wasted through forming up over Duxford.

As all squadrons made haste towards their allotted patrol lines, the enemy was in strength over Maidstone, the first of the defenders to engage being 603 and 501 Squadrons.

When at 18,000ft over Maidstone, 'four Me 109s', according to 603 Squadron's Form 'F',

> went across the bows. The Squadron chased them and they turned East. When in mid-Channel, two of the 109s turned about, flying back towards England.

Pilot Officer Peter Dexter DFC reported at 12.00 hrs he was mid-Channel, flying between 100 and 500ft:

> I was flying Number 2 in the Guard Section … after the Squadron had engaged the enemy, I saw one Me 109 returning to France. I turned and engaged it. Another Me 109 attacked me from the rear but a Spitfire, which I later identified as one flown by Pilot Officer [Philip 'Pip'] Cardell, came to my assistance. Pilot Officer Cardell and I chased the two aircraft towards France and shot them both down about ten miles off the French coast. One enemy pilot baled out. As we circled the pilot, five more Me 109s came towards us out of the sun.
>
> After a short engagement I could see Pilot Officer Cardell heading for home. I followed him and tried to contact him over the R/T, but he had removed his helmet, and appeared to be having difficulty with the aircraft.
>
> A quarter of a mile off Folkestone beach, at a height of 300 feet, Pilot Officer Cardell baled out. His parachute did not open. I saw him hit the water and rise to the surface almost immediately.
>
> Five minutes elapsed, and no apparent effort at rescue had been made from the shore, so called up my home base to ask them to have something done, but got no reply. I decided to 'crash-land' on the beach and organize a rescue boat myself. It took some time to get the boat launched, and we reached Pilot Officer Cardell at least 35 minutes after he hit the water. Artificial respiration was applied in the boat, and for thirty minutes after we got him to the shore, but he showed no signs of life … I phoned a report to Operations as soon as possible.

Dexter's frustration is more evident in the 603 Squadron's Form 'F', which describes how

> Pilot Officer [Peter] Dexter DFC and Pilot Officer [Philip] Cardell were together when Pilot Officer Cardell was fired at by two Me 109s. Pilot Officer Cardell baled out from 500 feet, 400 yards out to sea of Folkestone. His parachute failed to open, but he came up immediately and was floating head-up, well above the water. The machine crashed near him. Pilot Officer Dexter circled for ten minutes, calling up 'Rival' and 603 Squadron but got no reply. There were several people on the beach and he tried to attract their notice. As they showed complete apathy and no boats put out, he crashed his machine on the beach and after much waste of time, got a boat from a fisherman – but by then Pilot Officer Cardell was drowned. A naval launch arrived on the scene an hour later.

Given that Pilot Officer Philip Cardell had removed his helmet and was struggling to control his Spitfire, it is likely that his head injuries were suffered when attacked by the 109s. A doctor present, however, declared the cause of death to be drowning. Pilot Officer Peter Dexter, however, had performed an incredibly gallant act, trying to save his friend.

No. 603 Squadron suffered no other casualties in the skirmish, in which Squadron Leader George Denholm claimed a Me 109 probable, and Pilot Officer Brian McNamara one damaged.

No. 501 Squadron also went into action at 12.00 hrs, Sergeant James 'Ginger' Lacey DFM and Bar, Yellow 2, reporting eighteen Do 17s escorted by fifty Me 109s approaching Maidstone from the south at 18,000ft:

> I attacked bombers head-on but was prevented from joining combat by the fighter escort, who dived in front of the bombers. I attacked the Me 109s and a dogfight developed between five Me 109s and myself, but other Hurricanes joined in the fight, including Yellow 1, who I saw. While fighting we lost height rapidly to 7,000 feet and at that height I was able to get in a full deflection shot at close range at one of the E/A. He immediately went into a vertical dive, one of the wings came off at 500 feet and he crashed into a field near a quarry about two miles North of Maidstone and caught fire. The wing fell in the same field, about 200 yards from the rest of the aircraft. I had followed this aircraft down and when I climbed up again I could not find any E/A so returned to home base and landed. All the time I was fighting, the fight was being shelled by AA.

The 109 concerned belonged to 6/JG 27 and exploded at Hayles Farm, Eccles near Aylesford; the pilot, *Unteroffizier* J. Scheidt, was killed.

Sergeant Paul Farnes DFM of 501 Squadron claimed a damaged Do 17, but the German fighters otherwise succeeded in protecting their charges. Pilot Officer Edward Gunter, however, was shot down over Milton Regis by *Oberleutnant* Gustav Rödel of 4/JG 27, and killed owing to parachute failure, his Hurricane crashing in Teynham Court in Sittingbourne.

At 12.15 hrs, 92 Squadron was over Canterbury but was attacked by Me 109s and split up.

Sergeant Trevor Oldfield, Green 4, was weaving 1,000ft above the Spitfires:

> Owing to my being above the Squadron, I was able to turn sharply to the left and attacked a Me 109 from quarter astern. I saw pieces fly off the E/A near the wing root after I had given him a 3-second burst. I had only time to see him half-roll and dive away before I spun out. I could not see whether this aircraft crashed but about two minutes later I saw someone making a parachute descent.

The 109 was claimed as 'damaged or destroyed', and was 92 Squadron's only claim in the engagement, in which the unit suffered no losses.

Similarly, 41 Squadron was also in action at the same time, slightly to the east, over Faversham, at 24,000ft. Sergeant John Norwell succinctly reported that 'E/A dived to ground-level – attacked at close range – it burst into flames about twenty feet off ground and crashed into a field'. This was a machine of 8/JG 54, which crashed at Brenley House, Boughton near Canterbury, killing the pilot, *Oberleutnant* Anton Schön. No. 41 Squadron, though, was not unscathed: Sergeant Frank 'Itma' Usmar was shot down in flames; wounded in the right leg he baled out and managed to extinguish his burning tunic and used his radio lead to tie a tourniquet around his leg, stemming the flow of blood. Hailing from nearby West Malling, the wounded pilot's descent was watched, unknowingly, by his mother, and safely down in an orchard, hop pickers mistook Usmar for a German. Fortunately convinced otherwise, they took him to the local doctor, who arranged the pilot's admission to Preston Hall Hospital in Maidstone. Sergeant Edward Darling was also shot down, baling out wounded in the shoulder, and would join Usmar at Preston Hall Hospital.

The remaining Hornchurch squadron, 222, intercepted bombers over Maidstone at 12.20 hrs, but was also attacked by the escorting Me 109s. The skirmish ebbed south and by 12.30 hrs Pilot Officer John Broadhurst was over Dungeness:

> I chased and fired at the last aircraft of three in line astern. He dived away and I followed him down to 8,000 feet. Firing a number of short bursts on

the way down. At 8,000 feet I got a good burst at his underside, at about 250 yards. He continued to dive straight into the sea.

Sergeant Ernest Scott of 222 Squadron also engaged over Maidstone:

> I was flying in line astern when I saw what appeared to be a broken formation of twelve – fifteen He 111s [*sic*] going South. I dived on one and commenced a beam to astern attack, opening fire at 300 yards and closing into about ten yards. The E/A began to dive steeply, but I was unable to follow it down because my hood was hit by either a piece of metal from the bomber or by fire from another E/A, which I assume was a Me 109. The hood completely smashed and I was rather blinded for a few seconds by what appeared to be a flash.
>
> I commenced a steep dive with evasive action to rid myself of any following E/A. On reaching 500 feet I began to check my aircraft to see if the damage was any greater than the hood. My aircraft seemed to be in perfect condition, so I began to climb when I noticed a burning enemy wreckage. I circled it to try and confirm it as the He 111 that I had attacked, but the wreckage was spread over such a wide area that I could not be certain as to what type it was.
>
> I had circled the wreckage for a minute or so when I saw two parachutes descending. They were immediately pounced upon by farmers or the LDV.

It is likely, however, that Scott had seen the burning wreckage of the 109 destroyed by 501 Squadron's Sergeant James Lacey near Aylesford, and the two 41 Squadron pilots who had baled out; there were no bombers destroyed in this action.

No. 222 Squadron's only casualty was Sergeant Reginald Gretton, hit by a 109 and seriously wounded in the back; crash-landing at near Wennington in Rainham, Essex; a fractured spine and pelvic injuries would keep him in hospital for five months.

By 12.30 hrs, 46 Squadron was at 19,000ft, south of Maidstone.

Pilot Officer William Pattullo, Green 2:

> As three Me 109s descended on us from above and behind, I, in from Green 3 (Flight Sergeant Edward Tyrer), fell back and placed myself behind the third Me 109 and followed him, manouevring [*sic*] for position. He realised I was there but couldn't shake me off, and I finally got in a quarter attack followed by two more without success; however, after a dive I followed it and gave him a burst which smashed part of his port wing, and after that

> he pancaked in a field, in which the aircraft broke its back. The general position of the aircraft was South of Detling aerodrome.

This 109 belonged to *Stab* II/JG 52, the crash-landing taking place at Broad Street in Hollingbourne, where the pilot, *Oberleutnant* C. Treiber was captured. This was 46 Squadron's only success in this air battle, during which Pilot Officer Karel Mrázek, a Czech, was shot-up, safely forced-landing at Rochester, fortunately unhurt.

No. 46 Squadron's companions of 249 Squadron, engaged the Germans near Ashford, the squadron being led on this occasion by Pilot Officer Albert Lewis, who reported sighting a formation of Me 109s north-east of the Thames Estuary when at 15,000ft, so climbed the Hurricanes to 20,000ft – but were attacked whilst doing so. In the ensuing dogfight Lewis hit one 'in belly as he passed overhead. He crashed in a wood near Canterbury' – this being 8/JG 54's *Oberleutnant* Anton Schön, who was also attacked by 41 Squadron's Sergeant John Norwell and killed at Boughton. Lewis was then attacked by another Me 109, which he also hit and which 'went down smoking'.

Pilot Officer George Barclay, Red 1:

> I saw a dogfight going on nearby. Some Me 109s passed about 400 yards on my port side – there was no definite attack in squadron formation. I chased a 109 which dived very steeply. I had to use automatic boost to catch up the 109. I lost the 109 in haze and owing to its camouflage against the ground, but it suddenly climbed almost vertically out of the haze. I closed to about 150 yards and fired about four bursts, one almost vertically up at the 109, one almost vertically down at the E/A – two bursts from the beam. The E/A poured glycol. The cockpit roof flew off. The pilot baled out successfully. The E/A crashed (confirmed by Sergeant [George] Palliser, Red 3) on a farm SW of Ashford.

The pilot of this 109, belonging to 5/JG 52, *Feldwebel* Heinrich Hoffmann, was severely wounded by Barclay's attack and rendered unconscious. Coming to, out of control and still under fire, the German baled out and became a POW; his machine crashed at High Halden near Tenterden.

North Weald's station commander, Wing Commander Victor Beamish, was flying with 249 Squadron and claimed a Me 109 probable near Canterbury; there were no other claims and the squadron suffered no loss.

For once, 605 Squadron found itself with the height advantage, at 12.15 hrs, between Sittingbourne and Canterbury.

Flight Lieutenant Christopher Currant, Red 1, was leading the Croydon Hurricanes:

> took-off … climbed to 19,000 feet, circling Biggin Hill, Croydon and Kenley. We were ordered to climb to 20[,000]–25,000 feet to intercept a raid over Maidstone. This raid appeared to turn back under fierce AA fire before we could contact. We patrolled Canterbury at 25,000 feet and I saw AA fire over Rochester at approximately 20,000 feet. I turned towards the AA bursts and saw nine Me 109s at 18,000 feet in front and below me. I informed the Squadron of their position and dived down out of the sun on the E/A, which were passing below, going East. I attacked a Me 109 with a full beam at 250 yards with a short burst. The E/A dived and I fired from astern at 300 yards and saw bits flying off. I then had to do a quick breakaway as I saw another aircraft behind me – this proved to be a Hurricane. A general dogfight took place with the E/A going rapidly SE.

The 109 was claimed as damaged, with Pilot Officer Thomas 'Tom' Cooper-Slipper and Sergeant Eric Wright damaging others, whilst Sergeant Lawrence Sones claimed a probable. No. 605 Squadron's pilots all returned safely to base, landing between 13.10 and 13.20 hrs to re-arm and re-fuel.

At 12.30 hrs, Flight Lieutenant Gordon McGregor, Red 1, of 1 (RCAF) Squadron, was leading the Canadians and 229 Squadron on patrol at 18,000ft over Gatwick:

> After several vectors sighted twenty Me 109s about 2,000 feet above, continued irregular patrol in sections line-astern. After several minutes three 109s dived to attack leading Section. Red 2 and 3 broke off to confuse attack and 109 attacking Red 3 passed me close to port. I got two good bursts on him in a left, then in a right-turn. He spun down, issuing smoke. I could not follow owing to taking avoiding action from further 109 attack.

None of the other Northolt-based pilots engaged, and neither 1 (RCAF) or 229 Squadrons suffered any loss.

By 12.30 hrs, the Spitfires of 72 Squadron had swept down to Dungeness, between there and the South Foreland encountering

> more than forty Me 109s at 25,000ft. The E/A took flight on seeing our fighters. In the ensuing fight we damaged three Me 109s. [ORB]

Who made those claims, however, is unknown and all ten of 72 Squadron's pilots returned safely to Biggin Hill.

The Hurricanes of 17 Squadron were also in action over the Channel, having been ordered to patrol from the south coast to Chatham.

Sergeant Glyn Griffiths, Yellow 1, was the only pilot to engage:

> [I] sighted Me 109s North of Dover, Me 109s. The Squadron split up and in company with five other Hurricanes I chased two Me 109s, which were too fast for me, so I broke away and saw two more Me 109s flying about 3,000 feet below me, southwards over Dungeness. I chased the rear one and attacked from above and astern at 11,000 feet, fifteen miles South of Dungeness at about 1245 hrs. I opened fire at about 150 yards and closed to about fifty yards, giving about three secs burst. The E/A emitted a black smoke trail and dived vertically into the sea. The other Me 109 made no attempt to help his partner and went very quickly towards France. I made no attempt to chase it.

No casualties were recorded by 17 Squadron.

So far as the Duxford Wing's action was concerned, Squadron Leader Douglas Bader led the wing on patrol 'South of the Estuary'. Over the Dover-Canterbury area, the wing sighted a large gaggle of German fighters, aimlessly milling around at 18,000–20,000ft. Bader, however, had climbed the wing ever higher – and had a height advantage of 3,000ft. Attacking from up sun, this was the perfect 'bounce'.

Bader reported that, at 12.30 hrs,

> I chose an Me 109 which was passing underneath me and turned behind and above him and gave a short two second burst with the immediate result that he became enveloped in thick white smoke, turned over and dived vertically. I did not follow it down, but as it was the first 109 shot down it was seen by Pilot Officer [Denis] Crowley-Milling, Pilot Officer [Charles] Bush and Flight Lieutenant [Percival Stanley] Turner, in fact almost the whole Squadron. I also had my camera gun in action which will give further confirmation.

No one saw the 109 actually crash, however, and no likely candidate is among the enemy aircraft known to have crashed on English soil that day. Bader also fired at several more fleeing 109s, causing 'white vapour and black smoke' to issue from one. At such close range was his attack delivered that the windscreen of Bader's Hurricane was covered in oil from the damaged enemy fighter. This

109 was last seen over the Channel, 'gliding down quietly and apparently under full control with his engine dead'; many Luftwaffe fighters would crash-land on the occupied French coast that afternoon, this machine no doubt among them.

During what was now a fast cut and thrust combat, Pilot Officer Charles Bush, a New Zealander, of 242 (Canadian) Squadron, fired a long burst at an Me 109 which crashed into the sea. Pilot Officer John Latta, one of Bader's Canadians, shot another down into the Channel. Pilot Officer Michael Homer, however, became a 'flamer' over Sittingbourne and was killed. Flight Lieutenant Eric Ball, commander of 'A' Flight, was more fortunate: hit by a 109, his engine burst into flames – but the pilot made a safe forced-landing near Sandwich and was unhurt.

When 310 (Czech) Squadron's attack was delivered, Sergeant Jan Kaucký attacked an Me 109, upon which a Spitfire also dived and shot it down. Sergeant Josef Komínek claimed a 109 which 'dived vertically into the sea some five miles SW of Dover', and a Do 17 probable. Flight Lieutenant Gordon Sinclair, however, was shot down, later recalling,

> I was attacked by an Me 109. The first burst destroyed my ailerons, the second set my Hurricane on fire. Because my ailerons had been shot away I was unable to invert my aircraft and drop out, and as the machine entered a steep dive I had some difficulty in extricating myself from the cockpit and getting over the side. I landed by parachute in the branches of a fir tree near Callam [Chilham], from which some farm hands helped me down to mother earth. My Hurricane was practically burnt out before it crashed. This was the second time I had baled out during the Battle of Britain.

No. 616 Squadron was attacked by high-flying Me 109s: Pilot Officer Kenneth 'Ken' Holden claimed an Me 109 destroyed, and Sergeant Percy Copeland a probable, but the squadron's weaver, Pilot Officer Don Smith, was shot down; crash-landing near Faversham, he died of wounds the following day.

No. 19 Squadron was also hit by 109s from above: Pilot Officer Eric Burgoyne was killed, his Spitfire crashing in Coldred, just inland of Dover, at 12.30 hrs. Sergeant David 'Little Boy' Cox was also shot down, baling out over Wye:

> Upon scramble I had jumped into the nearest Spitfire, QV-L, as mine would not start. This aircraft was nearly always flown by Sergeant [Stanislav] Plzak, our 6'6' Czech who had dubbed me 'Little Boy'. To save time I buckled on his parachute, which was already in the cockpit – more of that later!
>
> We were top cover of the Duxford Wing but were attacked by a large number of Me 109s in the Dover area. After some hectic moments avoiding

being shot down, I found myself more or less on my own between Ashford and Folkestone. I then saw towards Folkestone a Hurricane being attacked by four Me 109s. Before I could give any assistance, which was my intention having got within a few hundred yards of the scrap, the Hurricane went down in a vertical dive inland [author's note: the Hurricane was probably Flight Lieutenant Gordon Sinclair's, which crashed at Godmersham, a few miles north of Wye].

The four Me 109s then turned their attentions to me. They knew their stuff as two got above me and two below. Naturally I had some hectic moments of turning this way and that as they came at me in attacks from all directions. I remember doing quite a lot of firing of my guns, but I think it was more in the hope of frightening them or raising my morale than in any real hope of shooting anything down!

All of a sudden there was a loud bang in the cockpit and for a second or two I was dazed. When I became normal again there was a lot of smoke about and my Spitfire was in a steep climb. As I lost flying speed I opened the hood, turned the aircraft over, undid my straps, and fell out, quickly pulling the ripcord of my parachute. When the canopy opened it gave me a severe jolt and several days later a lot of bruises showed on my chest and shoulders. Remember that the parachute harness was fitted for a man of 6'6' – I was lucky not to fall out of it!

As I floated down a 109 came and had a look at me and then flew off. It was then that I felt a lot of pain in my right leg and saw lots of holes in my flying boots out of which blood was oozing. Ground observers said that I took about 15 minutes to come down as I was so high up – I know that it was jolly cold up there when I came out of the aeroplane. I landed in the corner of a ploughed field near a farm. By this time I was feeling rather rough and must have looked it as the farmer handed me a bottle of whisky, from which I took a large swig. I was later taken to hospital at Walsford where a surgeon from Folkestone Hospital extracted several large pieces of cannon shell from just below my knee cap down into my ankle. I was in hospital about six weeks and off flying until December 1940.

No. 19 Squadron's CO, Squadron Leader Brian Lane, had a lucky escape – but not at the hands of the enemy. Two days previously the squadron had begun re-equipping with Mk II Spitfires, one of which the CO was flying in this combat. After firing two short bursts, Lane's Spitfire became uncontrollable and skidded away, the pilot using all his strength to recover. This was only achieved at 3,000ft, by which time Lane was considering baling out. Back at Fowlmere the aircraft was found to have a mis-shapen rudder and a wrongly adjusted trim tab which prevented one elevator functioning correctly.

Lane's wingman, Flight Sergeant George Unwin, chased an Me 109 over the Channel for ten minutes; dangerously near the French coast, a 30° deflection shot sent the enemy fighter into the Channel.

19 Squadron: 7 destroyed, 1 probable and 0 damaged
242 (Canadian) Squadron: 4 destroyed, 2 probable and 1 damaged
310 (Czech) Squadron: 1 destroyed, 0 probable and 0 damaged
616 Squadron: 1 destroyed, 1 possible and 0 damaged

Total: 13 destroyed, 3 probables, 1 'possible' and 1 damaged.

Only four Me 109s crashed in England, none of which can be attributed to the Duxford Wing; eight more went into the Channel and a further seven returned home damaged – how many of those crashing into the sea or crash-landing back in France that could be accredited to 12 Group is impossible to say. Significantly, however, the 'Bader Wing' had lost three Spitfires and three Hurricanes shot down, with three of their pilots killed, whilst the ten 11 Group squadrons engaged lost just three Spitfires, all pilots of which were safe. Nonetheless, for the third time in a day, therefore, the scales were tipped in the defenders' favour.

From the enemy perspective, and again considering the effort involved, comparatively little, was achieved by this raid. At midday, up to forty HE bombs and incendiaries fell on Maidstone, hitting the railway station, sidings and a railway bridge. That this bombing was accurate suggests that Maidstone was the intended target, and that these bombs had not been jettisoned as an emergency measure owing to strong fighter opposition preventing penetration to London. Railway communications in London were also damaged by a small number of bombers: all southeastern, as were others at Loughborough Junction and Herne Hill; lines from Victoria were blocked. That railways were targeted at both locations further suggests that Maidstone was deliberately bombed and was not a random or secondary target.

After two major raids on the south-east and another on the south-west, at 14.45 hrs RDF gave the first indications of yet another raid assembling over Calais. These two formations of '20+', however, at first made no attempt to strike out across the Dover Strait, as a result of which 11 Group controller initially reacted cautiously, scrambling 92 Squadron immediately from Biggin Hill with orders to rendezvous with Gravesend's 66 Squadron and patrol Maidstone at 20,000ft. Five minutes later, the North Weald Wing of 46 and 249 Squadrons were scrambled to patrol Hornchurch, also at Angels 20, and at 14.55 hrs up went 1 (RCAF) and 229 Squadrons from Northolt to patrol base at 15,000ft. Just after 15.00 hrs forty plus bandits were incoming over Dover and Dungeness at 19,000ft, and at 15.05 hrs another raid of similar size did likewise at 12,000ft; both enemy formations steered towards Maidstone. What seems late in the day, more defending squadrons were then scrambled between 15.10 and 15.15 hrs: 41, 222 and 603 Squadrons from Hornchurch on a 'defensive patrol', 72 Squadron from Biggin Hill to patrol the Maidstone line, whilst 303 (Polish) Squadron was sent east from Northolt, and 605 Squadron went up from Croydon to intercept the advancing enemy. The Debden Wing was sent to patrol Maidstone, and Tangmere's squadrons were held over Horsham, the enemy's intentions as yet unknown. Again, assistance was requested from 12 Group via Fighter Command HQ, and at 15.15 hrs, Squadron Leader Bader led the Duxford Wing to patrol Hornchurch. Over Maidstone, the Germans turned north-west towards Dartford, then east towards Biggin Hill – target London. Once more, the bombers were Ju 88s of KG 77, drawn from I and II *Gruppen*, supported by a large force of Me 109s, including aircraft of JGs 27, 51, 52, 53, 54 and 77.

At 15.00 hrs, Flight Lieutenant Brian Kingcome was 'Ganic Leader' and 18,000ft over Sevenoaks:

> I was driving the train of 92 and 66 Squadrons, and intercepted a formation of about fifteen Ju 88s with scores of Me 109s [author's note: first-hand and corroborated evidence contrary to many secondary sources claiming that the Ju 88s were unescorted] coming over in waves about 500 feet above.
>
> We attacked the bombers head-on. I gave a Ju 88 a 2-second burst and saw it drop back out of the formation. I climbed back and attacked another Ju 88 from ahead and this machine also dropped straight back, losing height. I then noticed another Ju 88, which turned away from the formation and headed South, and as it appeared to be undamaged I attacked it. Two more Spitfires then turned up and also attacked it, the machine crashing in flames in a wood.

This bomber – which would feature in the combat reports of several RAF pilots – belonged to 6/KG 77 and broke up over Sevenoaks, the bulk of wreckage coming down near Chiddingstone; a wounded crewman baled out and was captured but his three comrades were killed.

It is likely that Flight Lieutenant Allan Wright, Blue 1, leading 92 Squadron's third section, also attacked the same enemy aircraft:

> The Me 109s forbore to attack in force and the Squadron attacked en-masse from below, beam and head-on. I fired several bursts from below

> starboard and saw pieces come off one of the 88s. I broke away and saw an 88 break away from the formation. I followed and attacked with about four other Spitfires. In a few minutes it burst into flames and dived into the ground by the oblong lake near Gatwick and exploded.

Pilot Officer Geoffrey Wellum:

> I got in position under the bombers and fired a long burst into an 88. I then broke away and about two minutes later observed a Ju 88 leave its formation. Three other Spitfires and myself chased it. They got to the 88 before I did and I gave the 88 a short burst from long range as it dived into the ground. The crew of the 88 baled out. The aircraft crashed several miles South of Rochester.

It was the start of another rout.

No. 92 Squadron's Flying Officer John Drummond and Pilot Officer Tony Bartley also claimed Ju 88s destroyed, and Sergeant Walter Ellis and Flying Officer Thomas Sherrington shared another. Sergeant Trevor Oldfield, though, who had earlier claimed a 109 destroyed in the lunchtime engagement, was shot down and killed, his Spitfire exploding upon impact near Dartford.

Flight Lieutenant Ken Gillies, who was leading 66 Squadron, following 92 Squadron, reported sighting twelve bombers flying north-west from Maidstone:

> After evading one or two Me 109s which were coming down on us from behind, I led the Squadron into a quarter attack on the bomber formation from slightly below. I broke away and repeated the attack. Individual E/A began to break away from their formation. In company with two other friendly fighters I attacked one of these, and eventually saw E/A crash in flames [author's note: again, the Chiddingstone Ju 88].

Pilot Officer Hugh Reilley was with 'Clickety-Click' when the squadron went into line astern and attacked the bombers:

> [The] 109s peeled off on our rear section, they were a good 1,000 feet above. Two of the 109s became separated and I was in a position to attack one. I gave him a 3-second burst while climbing up just beneath his tail. He staggered but tried to climb steeply to get out of range. I then climbed and was able to get a deflection shot from just above his cockpit. My burst shattered the whole glass and killed the pilot. The 109 didn't spin but seemed to float down. I did follow him down and saw the plane hit the

> ground and burst into flames in the wooded area near Wrotham. Some Hurricanes were, as usual, on the spot where it crashed but definitely did not fire because they weren't close enough, but the 109 crashed without their assistance.

Which Me 109 this was, however, is unclear. Wrotham is to the east of Sevenoaks and mid-way between there and West Malling – and there was no Me 109 down there. Indeed, all four of the 109s down over England this afternoon were all further east, and all of their pilots were captured, two baling out, the other pair forced-landing. Nor does the location fit with any of the RAF fighters shot down that afternoon, the only conclusion, therefore, being that Reilley was mistaken regarding the location.

Reilley was the only 66 Squadron pilot to engage the 109s; Pilot Officer Hugh Heron claimed a 'Do 17 [*sic*]' probable over Dartford. Pilot Officer George Corbett, Sergeant Claude Parsons, Sergeant Dudley Forrest and Sergeant Matthew Cameron all claimed Ju 88s destroyed over the Biggin Hill area. Corbett's Spitfire, however, was hit by AA fire during his attack, the pilot crash-landing at Orpington, fortunately unhurt.

At 15.09 hrs, Flight Lieutenant Gordon McGregor was leading 1 (RCAF) Squadron, with the Hurricanes of 229 Squadron following, at 16,000ft over Biggin Hill. The bombers, wrongly identified as 'Do 215s [*sic*]' were sighted 5,000ft above and up to 15 miles ahead. McGregor led the Northolt Wing west after the enemy, the Germans then turning south, thereby enabling contact. Individual attacks ensued, during which McGregor damaged two bombers, with Flying Officer Paul Pitcher, Flying Officer Arthur 'Art' Yuile and Flying Officer Blair Russell also claiming bombers damaged in company with 229 Squadron. Pilot Officer De Peyster Douw Brown was more successful, shooting down a 3/KG 77 Ju 88, which crashed and burned out at Horsmonden; three of the crew were killed, the fourth man captured, badly wounded.

Bringing up the rear of the Northolt formation, at 15.15 hrs, the Hurricanes of 229 Squadron attacked the bombers south-east of London.

Pilot Officer Vernon Bright, Red 2:

> I went for one He 111 [*sic*] which was about 800 feet below me and a quarter of a mile behind the others. It had glycol coming from starboard engine. I gave him two to three second burst from 300 yards closing to fifty yards from astern, followed by another two-second burst. His port engine burst into flames – one man baled out and the aircraft dived steeply and crashed with an explosion in some trees by a house on the outskirts of London (Croydon?).

This was actually a Ju 88 of *Stab* II/KG 77, which would feature in various other pilot's combat reports. Abandoned by two crewmen, the aircraft crashed at Penshurst near Tonbridge; *Feldwebel* A. Adler and the pilot, *Oberleutnant* Karl Heinz Lutze were both killed, although no trace of the latter was ever found.

Bright continued,

> I returned to the main formation, and a Spitfire came down followed by a Me 109. I turned on his port beam with three-second burst from 150–100 yards. He went down on his back with brown and white smoke pouring from the engine about ten miles south-east of the first crash.

When patrolling over Hornchurch, the North Weald Wing, comprising 249 Squadron, leading 46 Squadron, sighted the Ju 88s and their Me 109 escorts flying above the Thames Estuary, towards London.

According to 249 Squadron's Form 'F',

> [the Ju 88s] were flying very fast … in vics of three line astern, with a large escort of Me 109s stepped up to 25,000 feet. No particular method of attack was adopted owing to the high-speed, the Me 109s dived to attack and there was a general melee. The enemy was engaged in a running fight out to sea. The pilots confirm that not one of the enemy bombers reached the French coast, as a lot of other Hurricanes took part in this combat.

In the ensuing action, Pilot Officer William Millington, an Australian, claimed a Ju 88 destroyed over Guildford, and shared another, over the sea, with Pilot Officer Thomas Neil – this possibly being the 5/KG 77 bomber down off Beachy Head, the crew of which were all killed.

Sergeant Henry Davidson, Green 3, fired at a straggling Ju 88 from abeam, its starboard engine bursting into flame. After further attacks bits of wing and cowling flew off. At this point the pilot of E/A or other member of the crew baled out and E/A crashed in field by road. E/A crashed approx. near Chiddingstone, near Penshurst aerodrome.

Pilot Officer George Barclay 'had to use boost to catch up the Ju 88 which he destroyed', although his Hurricane was damaged in the process, forcing the pilot down at West Malling. Pilot Officer Albert Lewis claimed a Ju 88 destroyed over the sea and two Me 109s over land, bringing his total claims on this day to six destroyed, earning him a Bar to his DFC. Sergeant John Beard claimed a 'Do 215 [*sic*]' damaged and two Me 109s shot down into the sea. Pilot Officer James Meaker

> attacked a close formation of five Ju 88s on his own and his aircraft was completely shot-up by heavy cross-fire from the cannons now fitted in the rear of these aircraft [*sic*].

Meaker baled out but was found dead at Warren Field in Brightling. He was 249 Squadron's second fatality on this day: that morning, his friend, Flying Officer Percival Burton having also been killed in action.

No. 46 followed 249 Squadron into action.

Flight Lieutenant Alexander Rabagliati reported,

> [seeing a Ju 88] very close, heading South. I turned and chased him. Caught him at 15,000 feet five miles North of Maidstone and gave a long burst of 3-seconds into E/A. Starboard engine caught fire and port engine aircrew fully feathered. Flew up alongside and saw that hood was open and crew were about to climb out. Two Hurricanes attacked after that and crew of two baled out, one parachute did not open. Flight Sergeant [Edward] Tyrer reports that three more baled out lower down. Aircraft crashed South of Maidstone.

This was the Ju 88 down at Horsmonden, also claimed by 1 (RCAF) Squadron's Pilot Officer De Peyster Douw Brown, and was 46 Squadron's only claim; the squadron suffered no loss.

After 92 Squadron's initial head-on charge, Flight Lieutenant Allan Wright also engaged the retreating enemy:

> I climbed up again and met Ju 88s returning, only about seven of them, with many Hurricanes and a few Spitfires and about thirty Me 109s in attendance. I got in four good bursts at 300–250 yards from below starboard and saw pieces coming from one of the Ju 88 and the starboard engine of another caught fire as I finished my ammunition.
>
> After a few moments I left them, only three bombers remaining travelling on the same course a little East of Horsham.

Sergeant Hugh Bowen-Morris, also of 92 Squadron, went after a Ju 88 heading south-east, firing a short burst at it before being attacked himself by two Me 109s, which flew off as the Spitfire pilot

> turned steeply towards them. I climbed up and attacked E/A from port beam with about three bursts of about 3-seconds duration, and saw smoke come from the port engine. After the next attack I noticed port engine had

> stopped and machine was losing height. These attacks were carried out in unison with another machine, LZ-M [author's note: Sergeant Claude Parsons of 66 Squadron]. I saw the E/A crash-land in a field near Sheerness.

The crew of this 3/KG 77 Ju 88 forced-landed on the Graveney Marshes near Faversham, where the crew were captured. Bowen-Morris's Spitfire, however, had been damaged by return fire in the exchange, the pilot crash-landing back at base, unhurt.

No. 66 Squadron's Flight Lieutenant Ken Gillies also joined the southerly chase:

> I climbed up again and then met several E/A returning in loose formation. I attacked one and saw his starboard engine burst into flame. Both engines of E/A then stopped, and although obviously finished, the E/A was attacked by the Hurricanes. E/A wagged wings in surrender and I then left him to attack another E/A, flying South about 2,000 feet above me. I continued the attack on this E/A until he crossed the coast. I left him at 1,000 feet. E/A's port engine was stopped and starboard one was on fire. Cockpit cover was missing and machine was badly shot about [author's note: the Graveney Marshes Ju 88]. Two Hurricanes arrived and continued to attack E/A. Having received orders not to pursue E/A across the Channel I turned back and returned to base.

Pilot Officer John Dewar and Pilot Officer Victor Ortmans, a Belgian, of 229 Squadron, evaded some Me 109s, then, according to the former,

> I pursued the He 111 [*sic*] formation to Hastings and saw Pilot Officer [Victor] Ortmans break away from one He 111 which had its starboard engine damaged. I went in from astern with six short bursts opening at 300 yards. I saw my De Wilde ammunition entering his starboard engine, and left him about ten miles from the French coast going down from 2,000 feet.

Having already contributed to the Penshurst Ju 88's demise, and damaged a 109, Pilot Officer Vernon Bright, also of 229 Squadron, caught up with three retreating bombers near the coast:

> with twelve of our fighters attacking. I picked out a Ju 88 which was attacked by nine Hurricanes and one Spitfire. He made two attacks from 150–50 yards from astern. Pieces broke off and came past me, also oil from the engine. The Hurricane and Spitfire continued attacking, then I made a final attack, and he crashed in the sea about fifteen miles out from Bexhill.

The lone Spitfire was flown by 72 Squadron's Sergeant Maurice Lee, who had also pursued the enemy south, albeit incorrectly identifying the bombers as 'He 111 [*sic*]'. Having damaged this Ju 88's engine, Lee focused on the rear gunner, who was returning fire, which then stopped. 'At this point several Hurricanes attacked the bomber'. Lee attacked again, causing a long stream of vapour to issue form the bomber, which began a shallow glide until 'In the end the bomber came down in the sea off Brighton, three of the crew escaping in their lifejackets'.

This aircraft is believed to have been that of 5/KG 77's *Staffelkapitän*, *Hauptmann* G. Zetsche, who crashed into the Channel; none of the crew were rescued.

No. 72 Squadron claimed two 'He 111 [*sic*]' and a Me 109 destroyed for no loss.

No. 229 Squadron, as did all squadrons involved, substantially overclaimed after this action: three 'He 111s [*sic*]' destroyed and three more damaged, a Ju 88 destroyed and two damaged, and a Me 109 probably destroyed. The squadron suffered a sad loss, however: Flight Lieutenant Frank Rimmer, an experienced pre-war pilot, was shot down and killed, his Hurricane exploding over Burmarsh. Pilot Officer Ronald Bary, a New Zealander, was shot-up by return fire when attacking a Ju 88, returning safely to base, and Flight Lieutenant William Smith was also caught in the bombers' defensive crossfire, writing-off his Hurricane in a crash-landing at Lingfield.

The Spitfires of 41 Squadron had played little part in the action, owing to having been broken up when attacked by Me 109s, during which Flight Lieutenant Norman Ryder was shot down and took to his parachute over East Malling, landing safely and unhurt. Sergeant Cyril Bamberger, Yellow 3, however, having lost contact with the rest of 41 Squadron,

> sighted a lone enemy fighter on a course for home. I made an attack from below and astern and the E/A started to lose height rapidly and smoke issued from the engine or cockpit. I then sighted a formation of 109s about to attack from above, so I broke off the engagement.

The 109 was claimed as damaged and was 41 Squadron's only claim.

At 15.45 hrs, Squadron Leader George Denholm was leading his 603 Squadron at 25,000ft over Maidstone:

> We were behind 222 Squadron when some Me 109s fell in behind them and we came in on their tails. They ignored 222 but turned sharply round onto the end of our formation. There were more Me 109s above us and a dogfight ensued. I fired a short burst at close range and saw my incendiary hitting the Me 109. After twisting about, three or four 109s made off to

> the south-east and dived into cloud. Several of us chased them and the cloud was so thin that we had no difficulty following them. Pilot Officer [Ronald 'Raz'] Berry and myself were soon alone with two Me 109s and we carried out a number of attacks on both of them. One went down very steeply, emitting smoke and glycol, about ten miles East of Canterbury, but I did not observe him hit the ground. The other one crashed near Eyestone Station.

Pilot Officer Ronald Berry:

> Patrolling with the Squadron as guard leader over the Maidstone area at 23,000 feet on the fringe of heavy cloud, out of which appeared several Me 109s. The Squadron went into line astern and gave chase. As I entered cloud, I felt violent slipstream and found myself on tail of a 109. I fired four short bursts after dropping slightly below. Immediately his hood and other things flew off and the pilot baled out.
>
> I then continued to chase two 109s eastwards with the CO. I gave the first a 4-seconds burst from 50 yards and in turn with CO, sent 109 down towards Estuary, emitting heavy smoke.
>
> Then pursued the other 109. Made three attacks at close range in turn with CO. The last attack shot off the hood from E/A and followed him down to ground level, where he crashed into some trees. Yellow nose and cowlings and yellow rudder.

Berry claimed one Me 109 destroyed, another destroyed jointly with Denholm and a probable.

Flying Officer Colin Pinckney was also fighting Me 109s with 603 Squadron:

> I saw thirty Me 109s flying beneath us at 25,000 feet and after being ordered in line astern, attacked a single machine at the back of the formation. After my first burst from astern, E/A took evasive action by turning in towards me, with glycol streaming from its engine. I followed him down through cloud to 2,000 feet, attacking it from the quarter astern. Last seen, the E/A was a few feet above the ground near Herne Bay, the engine ticking over.

At the bottom of Pinckney's personal combat report is a sad postscript:

> Flight Lieutenant Harold MacDonald fired at an Me 109, seen by Flying Officer [Colin] Pinckney to catch fire and crash two miles South of Gravesend.

This was a successful action for 603 Squadron, in which the enemy suffered the following casualties: 9/JG 3: *Unteroffizier* H. Struwe baled out, landing at Selling and was captured, his 109 crashing at Owen's Court Farm, Gushmore – for which Pilot Officer Berry was believed responsible.

No. 4/JG 52: *Feldwebel* F. Bogasch, who was hit by Denholm, Pinckney and Berry, crash-landed into anti-invasion obstacles, losing a wing and rudder at Saint-Nicholas-at-Wade, where the German was captured.

No. 4/JG 52: *Gefreiter* E. Bosch wounded and captured after crashing through HT cables when forced-landing near Sandwich – courtesy of Denholm and Berry.

No. 4/JG 52: shot down in flames, crashing at Petham, the pilot, *Leutnant* H. Geist, baling out and also captured.

Later, back at Hornchurch, however, 222 Squadron had a pilot missing: Sergeant Ernest Scott, who had apparently disappeared. It would seem that the Me 109s had not 'ignored' 222 Squadron, as Denholm reported, *Major* Werner Mölders, the 'Father of Modern Air Fighting' and *Kommodore* of JG 51 claimed a Spitfire destroyed over Maidstone at the material time. Scott, it is now known, was killed and crashed in Greenway Court Road, Hollingbourne (from where he was eventually recovered by the authorities in 1990 and afforded a funeral at Margate Cemetery with full military honours the following year).

There was action too for 303 (Polish) Squadron, who were sent due east from Northolt, encountering the enemy over London just as the bombers turned about for the coast, travelling very fast, at 330 mph. The Hurricanes gave chase, going flat out, but only caught up with the retreating Germans over Hastings. Indeed, only three pilots managed to engage, attacking from astern and below.

Flying Officer Witold Urbanowicz:

> [I] fired a short burst at a Ju 88 which started to smoke and lost height, and after firing a second short burst a crew of three baled out, landing in the sea just off the coast. [ORB]

This being a 5/KG 77 machine, which crashed off St Leonards-on-Sea. Urbanowicz then fired at a 'second Ju 88, and after a medium length burst it fell into the sea in flames' [ORB]. Flight Lieutenant Johnny Kent, a Canadian, was hit in the aircrew and canopy by a Ju 88's rear gunner, whom he quickly silenced with a short burst. Kent then hit the bomber's port engine, causing it to smoke:

> Two Hurricanes were in the vicinity but Flying Officer [Witold] Urbanowicz states that these Hurricanes did not fire and he saw the bomber crash into the sea. [ORB]

The same 5/KG 77 machine claimed by Pilot Officer William Millington and Pilot Officer Thomas Neil of 249 Squadron. Sergeant Eugeniusz Szaposznikow, a Pole, was attacked from above by a Me 109, which overshot, Szaposznikow pursuing the enemy fighter in the dive: 'firing two bursts at it, the enemy turned on its side and dropped into the sea' [ORB]. No. 303 (Polish) Squadron suffered no casualties, apart from Kent returning unhurt to Northolt with his damaged Hurricane.

Croydon's 605 Squadron also chased the Germans to the East Sussex coast, engaging over Hastings, the Hurricane pilots 'destroying one by themselves, assisting in the destruction of three more, and seeing the fifth one crash near Winchelsea' [ORB]. All the 'County of Warwick' Squadron pilots returned safely to base.

So ended what had been another rout, executed entirely by 11 Group's squadrons as the Duxford Wing, being north of the Thames Estuary, made no contact.

The final curtain, however, had still yet to fall on the daylight fighting: at 18.45 hrs, Red Section of Pembrey's 79 Squadron, led by the CO, Squadron Leader John Heyworth, intercepted 'ten He 111s [*sic*] out at sea off the Irish coast. The Section attacked and several E/A jettisoned their bombs in sea' [ORB]. The Hurricanes claimed one bomber destroyed, another probable, shared between Red Section, which also comprised Pilot Officer Raymond Clarke and Pilot Officer George Nelson-Edwards. In fact, these were Ju 88s of 7/LG 1, two of which were destroyed when shot down over St George's Channel, the crews of which were all killed.

As dusk fell, it was time for both sides to count the cost.

For the defenders, it was another highly successful interception, 249 Squadron's Form 'F' documenting the reason why:

> Our success in this combat seems to be due to the fact that for once the enemy were engaged by equal or superior numbers of our fighters. There were enough friendly fighters about both to keep the enemy fighters busy and to see that not one bomber escaped … most of our fighters were not molested in their attacks on the bombers.

For some time now, Air Vice-Marshal Keith Park had been meeting the enemy in strength, with either pairs or wings of three (but no more) squadrons, meeting the Germans on more equal terms – and the tactic was working. In the combats over southern England on this hard-fought day, Fighter Command lost fourteen Spitfires destroyed and eleven damaged, and twelve Hurricanes destroyed and twenty damaged – a combined total of twenty-six fighters destroyed and thirty-one damaged. Nineteen pilots were killed – the second highest number of any day throughout the sixteen-week battle – and seven more were wounded. Considering how little bombing had taken place, that on two occasions the Germans had been prevented from attacking their targets by defending fighters and the losses inflicted upon the enemy, Air Chief Marshal Hugh Dowding and his group commanders had every reason to be satisfied with the day's results.

The Luftwaffe, however, lost fifty-six aircraft destroyed and ten damaged, one which saw the defeat of the Me 110 on daylight operations over England. *Zerstörers* would not yet be withdrawn completely from the day battle – but never again would they operate in these numbers or with such audacity. It was not simply an expensive day for the enemy in terms of aircraft: amongst the dead were two *Gruppenkommandeurs*, two *Gruppenadjutant* and four *Staffelkapitäns* – highly experienced professional officers and airman the Luftwaffe could not afford to lose.

Across the Channel, *Major* Adolf Galland was still at *Reichsmarschall* Hermann Göring's East Prussian *Reichsjägerhof*, and remembered the reaction when news of the Luftwaffe casualties was received:

> They were devastating … [*Reichsmarschall* Hermann] Göring was shattered. He simply could not explain how the painful losses of bombers came about, and I assured him that, in spite of the heavy losses we were inflicting on the enemy fighters, no decisive decrease in their number or in their fighting efficiency was noticeable. At the great altitudes where aerial combats took place it was only possible in rare cases to follow the possible victim down to its final crash in order to verify the kill. Even if the German figures of enemy aircraft destroyed were perhaps over-estimated, the fact that their fighter strength obviously did not diminish could only be accounted for in this way: England, by a great concentration of energy, was making up her losses in the peaceful nine-tenths of her territory.

Clearly, the reality of the situation was at last dawning on Göring himself. Indeed, so far as Churchill was concerned, 27 September 1940 was the third greatest day in the Battle of Britain – on which '[*Reichsmarschall* Hermann] Göring gave up hope that his method of winning the war might succeed'.

Throughout the day, that stalwart service, Coastal Command, had carried out its routine duties, including escorting fourteen convoys. No. 53 Squadron's Blenheims attacked a torpedo manufacturing plant at Den Helder, but owing to adverse weather just one mine was dropped off Cuxhaven. By night, further attacks were made on Den Helder, and more mines sewn in the Weser, Elbe and Jade estuaries. The weather also led to 2 Group's Blenheims largely abandoning their reconnaissance tasks, but by night Blenheims targeted invasion ports of Ostend, Boulogne and Calais, and Hampdens attack German shipping at Lorient and Saint-Brieuc. Shipping at Ostend was also attacked by Wellingtons, which also bombed Ostend and railway facilities in Germany. There were two losses: a Hampden of 83 Squadron became lost and disorientated returning from Lorient and abandoned by the crew to crash on Lincoln's St Matthias Church – one man was killed owing to a failed parachute, the other three survived; a 214 Squadron Wellington was monitored signalling SOS at 04.33 hrs and failed to return.

Daily Home Intelligence Reports:

South-western (Bristol):

Bristol stood up magnificently to the heavy raid on Wednesday, and there is warm praise for the defence and repair squads. The release of the name of Bristol in connection with the raid has had a good effect. Rumours about the result of the raid, particularly with regard to damage and casualties, are flourishing, but not as bad as expected.

Midland (Birmingham):

Those who a few weeks ago were not in favour of bombing German towns unless they contained military objectives are now wholeheartedly in favour of reprisals for the wanton attacks on London.

London:

Reports from many districts still show the spirit of London is extremely good, even when people have suffered seriously.

Saturday, 28 September 1940

The weather remained fine with generally good visibility despite 6/10ths cloud between 1,000–3,000ft and some haze. Smarting from heavy losses, though, the OKL planned no major bombing operations on this day, which would instead feature high-flying fighter sweeps. Enjoying the advantages of height, sun and surprise, and free to roam, the Me 109 pilots were in their element and at their most lethal.

At 09.40 hrs, Flight Lieutenant Harold MacDonald led 603 Squadron from Hornchurch on a 'defensive patrol' [ORB], and at the same time Flight Lieutenant Norman Ryder took-off from the same aerodrome with 41 Squadron to 'Patrol as ordered' [ORB]. Exactly what those orders were, however, is unknown – but by 10.00 hrs, a large number of Me 109s were sweeping over Kent.

By 10.20 hrs, 603 Squadron was at north of Ashford.

Pilot Officer James Morton:

> I was rearguard to the Squadron, flying North … at 28,000 feet, when I was attacked from behind and out of the sun by two Me 109s. I gave the alarm and then observed many more Me 109s – about thirty – above and all around us, preparing to attack. The Squadron tried to form a defensive circle, but was split up before being able to do so.

The Hornchurch Spitfires had been ambushed by JG 26.

Morton continued,

> I eventually found a single 109 and engaged him at 24,000 feet. Our combat continued to ten miles out to sea off Hythe, when my ammunition gave out. When I left, the 109 was heading for the French coast at 100 feet, streaming coolant and losing speed rapidly. He appeared to be preparing to forced-land in the sea. I did not stay with him as it was very hazy and I was uncertain of my position relative to the French coast.

The Spitfire pilot had shot down *Feldwebel* Fritz Schür of 3/JG 26, who crashed in the Channel and was killed; Morton was awarded a 'probable', which was 603 Squadron's only claim in the action. The squadron, however, suffered a rather tragic casualty in the clash: Flight Lieutenant Harold MacDonald was hit by a 109, dived away and, having shaken off his assailant, headed for Hornchurch – a densely populated urban area over which his Spitfire burst into flame. MacDonald could have jumped but to avoid the inevitable civilian deaths his crashing Spitfire would undoubtedly cause, remained with the doomed machine in an attempt to still regain base. When the heat and flames engulfed the fighter, however, MacDonald did jump – but the minimum recommended height for a parachute descent is 500ft and he was only at 400ft. Inevitably, there was insufficient time for the canopy to fully open and consequently MacDonald was killed. Perhaps ironically, his Spitfire crashed onto the parade ground at Brompton Barracks without causing anyone injury.

The loss of this gallant ace and experienced flight commander, though, was not just a grievous loss to 603 Squadron; for the MacDonald family of Edinburgh, this was a double blow: on 23 August 1940, Harold's younger brother, Pilot Officer Donald MacDonald, had also been killed with 603 Squadron. Shot down off Dover by a 109 on his first combat sortie, the younger MacDonald crashed into the Channel and was never found. No. 603 was the 'City of Edinburgh' Squadron of the Auxiliary Air Force, which was based around the territorial principle, personnel being locally recruited. It was not uncommon, therefore, for family members and friends to serve together – but such losses consequently affected morale badly – 609 'West Riding' Squadron's suffering in the early stages of the Battle of Britain being a case in point, and well-documented by Pilot Officer David Crook in his memoir *Spitfire Pilot* (see Bibliography). Already, though, the composition of these auxiliary squadrons had completely changed, owing to casualties and replacements from other stables, not least volunteer reservists and foreign pilots, and soon little or no trace would remain of the original auxiliaries or their socially elite identity.

Returning to the fighting on 28 September 1940, at 10.30 hrs, 41 Squadron was also jumped by Me 109s, over Canterbury. Pilot Officer Harry Chalder baled out seriously wounded, his Spitfire exploding over Chilham; the 'Geordie' pilot was admitted to Chartham Hospital but died there of his injuries on 10 November 1940. Flying Officer John Boyle, a Canadian, was also shot down and killed, his aircraft crashing at Charing. Pilot Officer Eric Aldous was more fortunate, being just slightly wounded when crash-landing his damaged Spitfire at Pluckley. No. 41 Squadron made no combat claims in this unsuccessful action.

At 09.23 hrs, Flight Lieutenant Christopher Currant left Croydon with orders to rendezvous with Kenley's 501 Squadron and patrol Sevenoaks at Angels 20. The two squadrons having joined up, with 605 Squadron leading, the Hurricanes climbed.

Flight Lieutenant Christopher Currant reported,

> When 605 Squadron were at 22,000 feet near Tenterden, with 501 Squadron behind and below, twelve Me 109s were seen above at 26,000 feet, flying NW. These dived round and down onto the rear section of 501 Squadron.

In this ambush over Deal, two Hurricanes were shot down immediately: Pilot Officer Frederick Harrold was killed, his Hurricane crashing at Ulcombe, and Pilot Officer Everett Rogers baled out unhurt, his fighter going in at East Sutton. Flying Officer Denys Jones was also shot-up, crash-landing back at Kenley; *Oberleutnant* Gustav Sprick, *Staffelkapitän* of 8/JG 26, claimed one Hurricane destroyed at the material time. No. 501 Squadron, however, scored no successes and Currant would make the squadron's only claim:

> I turned right and dived down on the Me 109s and chased one East at 15,000 feet. I got within range over the coast between Folkestone and Dover and gave a burst at 300 yards astern and just below E/A, no deflection.

> The E/A began to dive, still going East. I watched from three miles East of Dover and saw the E/A dive into the sea ten miles SE of Dover.

This was the same 109 claimed by 603 Squadron's Pilot Officer James Morton. No. 605 Squadron suffered no loss in this skirmish.

At 09.45 hrs, Flight Lieutenant Walter Lawson, commander of 'A' Flight, led the Spitfires of 19 Squadron up from Fowlmere to join the Duxford Wing on a patrol, according to 242 (Canadian) Squadron's ORB, of 'South London'.

Pilot Officer Richard L. Jones was 19 Squadron's weaver that day:

> When patrolling the Tenterden area at 29,000 feet, the Controller informed us that as there were apparently no enemy aircraft in the vicinity we could return to 'Pancake'. I was 'Arse-End Charlie' and relaxed slightly as we dived to 20,000 feet. Suddenly, about four feet of my starboard wing just peeled off – my initial thought was that it was a poor show on a new aircraft. Then a loud bang and hole appeared above the undercarriage. I was obviously the target of an enemy fighter up-sun. Immediately, I took evasive action. Simultaneously my engine cut [out] for good and I was suddenly in a high-speed stall and spin. My radio was u/s so I was unable to inform the Squadron, which returned to base blissfully unaware that I had been shot down.
>
> I recovered from the spin at about 10,000 feet – the aircraft was not responding to the controls – I realised too that the hood was completely jammed. I subsequently crash-landed with a dead engine in one of only two suitable fields in a heavily wooded area just outside Hawkhurst in Kent. Unfortunately I did so amongst a flock of sheep and regret that several were killed. I was rescued by the Army and first taken to the Hawkhurst doctor who treated a flesh wound to my leg, then to the Mess prior to returning safely to Fowlmere. My Spitfire had a broken propeller and radiator, a few holes and some missing parts, but was otherwise relatively intact.

In his log book entry for this day, Pilot Officer Richard Jones wrote, 'Shot down and crash landed at Hawkhurst, Kent. Killed three sheep. What a bloody mess!!!' Unusually, this incident, however, went completely unrecorded in all other official records but concerned a new Spitfire Mk IIA. What we do know, however, is that at around 10.00 hrs a high-altitude German fighter sweep was made of Kent, some twenty RAF squadrons being scrambled to intercept. The Germans, therefore, had the height advantage and weavers like Jones were vulnerable to ambush. Adding to the mystery is who shot Jones down? According to German records (OKL Fighter Claims Chef für Ausz. und Dizsiplin Luftwaffen-

Personalamt L.P.(A)V OKLs), at 09.45 hrs (BST) *Hauptmann* Gerhard Schöpfel, *Kommandeur* of III/JG 26, claimed a Spitfire destroyed north of Dungeness, so the time and location fit (although unrecorded in published lists of Schöpfel's aerial victories), but at 10.07 hrs (BST) *Oberleutnant* Günther Scholz of *Stab* III/JG 54 also claimed a Spitfire destroyed – location unknown. Who, therefore, shot Jones down cannot be confirmed.

The next threat appeared on RDF screens in early afternoon.

At 13.40 hrs, 41 Squadron was over Canterbury when bounced and split up by a large force of Me 109s. Only Pilot Officer George Bennions would inflict any damage on the enemy, as the action ebbed south-west, to Newhaven in East Sussex, having noted 'several groups of 109s above 2,000 feet above on the port side':

> I allowed about twenty-five to pass and then turned into attack. I closed with one of the rear ones and after a short burst I saw bits fly off the port mainplane near the fuselage, and coolant pouring from the tail. I re-sighted and was about to fire again when I was hit by a cannon shell on the port side and had to break away. I climbed up again and sighted another formation of approximately fifteen Me 109s diving down. I turned down after the last 109 and after a short burst he slowed down and turned right to a southerly course. I fired a few more bursts from dead astern and black smoke and white streams poured back from the tail. I left him four miles South of Brighton at 4,000 feet, gliding down, because I was short of petrol and miles away from my home base.

The German had a lucky escape. Bennions's fuselage was found to be badly damaged by cannon shells upon his return to base; 41 Squadron suffered no other casualties.

The Hurricanes of 249 Squadron were up from North Weald to patrol base:

> [sighting] groups of Me 109s … well above the Squadron, but no contact made. Sergeant Beard got separated from the Squadron and destroyed a Me 109 out to sea. [ORB]

No other claims were made but Pilot Officer Albert Lewis was shot down over Faversham by *Hauptmann* Rolf Pingel, *Gruppenkommandeur* of I/JG 26, and baled out badly burnt 'but alright and taken to Faversham Cottage Hospital' [ORB].

The Spitfires of Gravesend's 66 Squadron and Biggin Hill's 72 Squadron were ordered to patrol Sevenoaks together at Angels 20, contacting the enemy fighters at 13.50 hrs, north of Hastings at 18,000ft. Flight Lieutenant John Villa, commander of 72 Squadron's 'A' Flight, was 'Tennis Leader':

> The Me 109s manoeuvered [*sic*] to attack from out of the sun. I turned the Squadron towards them and the Me 109s turned away and again endeavoured to attack out of the sun, and I turned towards them again. The Me 109s then split up and about five dived down on the Squadron. These aircraft opened fire a long way out of range and didn't appear to be firing at any particular aircraft but just generally at the Squadron. The Squadron then split and started milling around. I saw an Me 109 on the tail of a Spitfire and turned to attack it. The E/A half-rolled and dived straight for the clouds and due South. I followed E/A and caught him as he levelled out to enter clouds. I opened fire at 300 yards, tending to overshoot. I hit one of his radiators with my first burst and he then dived down into cloud. I followed through cloud and found E/A in front of me. I closed up again, dead astern, and fired all my rounds in short bursts, closing very slowly. I then broke away to starboard. E/A went into a slight right-hand turn and dived onto the sea eight miles South of Hastings.

Villa had shot down Pingel, who was rescued by the *Seenotdienst*. All of 72 Squadron returned to base intact.

Over Mayfield, 66 Squadron was bounced by Me 109s, Pilot Officer Arthur Watkinson being shot down, baling out wounded in a leg and shoulder, and Sergeant Kenneth Wright was shot-up, successfully forced-landing. Broken up, 66 Squadron scattered and made no combat claims. According to the ORB, '109s were seen but not engaged'.

Things did not go well, either, for 605 Squadron, which was also ambushed over East Sussex and made no combat claims. Flying Officer Peter Crofts, a pre-war Cranwellian, was shot down and baled out but fell to his death at Dallington. Flying Officer Ralph Hope was also shot down and took to the silk. A relative of the former British Prime Minister Neville Chamberlain and an Old Etonian, Hope recalled his experiences in a letter to his mother, written the same day:

> Saturday was not such a success from my point of view, as on our third patrol I lost my aircraft. We were at about 21,000 feet when we got involved with a squadron of Me 109s. They got me before I even saw them, which is very annoying. I first felt a kind of funny bump, and as I turned to see what was up, my controls suddenly felt funny, a lot of red sparks and black smoke appeared round my feet and a cloud of white smoke, probably glycol,

began streaming back from the engine. The aircraft began going downhill fast. I slid back the hood and began to get out, my goggles were shipped off and my helmet began to lift up in the slipstream; I realised I hadn't undone my straps so I pulled out the retaining pin and stood up, standing on anything which came in handsy (the seat, the instrument panel or the stick, I don't know, really).

The air seized hold of me and there was a wrench as my oxygen tube snapped off (I had forgotten to undo it) and I shot out into the sky. The aeroplane disappeared. It was a nice and cool feeling. I was head down, of course, but found the position quite comfortable; there was no sense of speed or feeling of falling. I had a look at the clouds below (they were about 4,000–5,000 feet) and then collected the odd bits of my helmet and had a look around. My parachute was still on my seat, both my boots were on, and I did not seem to have lost anything except my goggles, and a handkerchief and map, which must have fallen out of the pockets in my knees when I first went upside down. After a while I thought about pulling the rip cord. 'What about giving the old brolly a try out?', I thought. I seemed to have fallen a goodish way, so I pulled. The canopy streamed out, there was a hard jerk and there I was, right side up, quite comfortable and floating slowly, Oh! So slowly earthwards. I was about 9,000–10,000 feet, so I had fallen free for about 8,000 or 9,000 feet (from about 18,000 feet) and might have fallen further with advantage.

When I looked up I could see a shining white canopy above me, and little silver specks having no end of a dogfight in the clear blue above me. A Spitfire dived down past me with a high-pitched whine, but that was the only disturbance. The parachute began to swing about and it wasn't long before I felt sick, very sick, in fact, by the time I landed. It was fun going into the clouds as the sun played a sort of 'spectre of the Brocken' effect on my shadow as I approached them. When I emerged the countryside looked pleasantly open, and after drifting quite a way I thought I saw where I should land. Two farm hands had the same idea. We were all wrong as in spite of attempts on my part to avoid it, I came down in a spinney of young oak trees, pulling up short about twenty feet from the ground, hanging in my harness. I managed to get hold of a trunk, pull myself over to it, get out of the parachute harness and climb to the ground, where I remained quite still until I was found. The Army soon took charge of me, gave me a drink and some lunch, and drove me back to Croydon.

The only damage I sustained was a hefty bruise on my right shoulder from hitting the tail as I jumped, and a bruise on my leg, and a torn trouser from the somewhat unceremonious descent through the upper branches of

> the oak tree. Now I go about with my arm in a sling, feeling particularly good as I have been given a week's sick leave.

The next enemy incursion came further west by *Luftflotte* 3, a sweep of the Isle of Wight and The Solent area by some fifty Me 109s of JG 2 and Me 110s of ZG 26.

Squadron Leader Harold Fenton's 238 Squadron scrambled from Middle Wallop at 14.23 hrs to patrol Southampton at 15,000ft. East of the Isle of Wight the Hurricane pilots sighted some Me 109s, which flew off to the right, leaving twenty-five Me 110s milling around in a circle, which 238 Squadron attacked:

> Just as the attack was about to be delivered, the Squadron in sections line astern, it was attacked by fifteen Me 109s which dived from about 300 feet higher, out of the sun. These are considered to be the Me 109s which had previously sheered [*sic*] off ... The Squadron was compelled to adopt evasive tactics and was unable to carry out attack on Me 110s. The Squadron was split up and it is believed that three of our aircraft were in difficulties as Me 109s attacked from the rear.

Pilot Officer Władyslaw Różycki made 238 Squadron's only claim, a Me 110 destroyed 10 miles west of Selsey Bill (although no such loss appears in Luftwaffe records). Sergeant Eric Bann, however, was shot down by a 109 and baled out over the Isle of Wight – but fell on Brading Marshes and was killed owing to parachute failure. Sergeant Ronald Little was shot down east of the Isle of Wight and never seen again, and Pilot Officer David Harrison was similarly shot down into The Solent, his body washing ashore at Brighton some days later. After the combat, low on fuel, Pilot Officer Vernon Simmonds became lost, putting down at Andover, but crashed on take-off when his engine cut owing to petrol starvation – the pilot was unhurt.

No. 213 Squadron, ordered to patrol Selsey Bill, was attacked over the sea, Pilot Officer James Talman DFC was shot down by a Me 110's return fire, baling out and being rescued from the sea off Bembridge. Flying Officer Raymond Kellow's Hurricane was badly shot-up by a Me 110, the pilot, who was unhurt, crash-landing back at Tangmere.

No. 607 Squadron had also scrambled from Tangmere:

> The Squadron patrolled areas between Beachy Head, Selsey Bill and Bembridge for about an hour, flying at about 12,000 feet. Three to four miles off Selsey the presence of about 40 enemy aircraft at 20,000 feet was reported by the Sector Controller. The Squadron climbed to investigate,

> and in doing so were attacked by a section of Me 110s, which had detached from the main enemy formation which was flying in circles and stepped up from 20,000–25,000 feet. The Hurricanes took evasive action and, although considerably damaged by cannon and machine gun fire, all but two returned to base. 'B' Flight was unable to climb fast enough to follow. The Squadron had climbed into the sun, and so patrolled Portsmouth until ordered to land. Whilst returning to base, two rear guard aircraft of 'A' Flight attacked a Do 215 [*sic*] flying at 5,000 feet over the sea, south of Selsey Bill, but without result. They were at once attacked by two Me 109s but took successful evasive action.

Sadly, two longstanding members of 607 Squadron were missing from this engagement, namely Flight Lieutenant William Gore DFC and Flight Lieutenant Maurice Irving, neither of whom were ever seen again.

Once more, the German fighters had performed superbly, and it is likely that the formation sighted by 238 Squadron and which cleverly lured the Hurricanes into a trap were led by *Hauptmann* Helmut Wick, *Gruppenkommandeur* of I/JG 2, who claimed a Hurricane destroyed himself. Two of Wick's pilots, *Oberleutnant* Karl-Heinz Krahl and *Feldwebel* Erwin Richey, both of 3/JG 2, also claimed Hurricanes in the clash, with pilots of 8 and 9/JG 2 claiming four more. Just one claim was recorded by the Me 110s, namely by *Feldwebel* Helmut Haugk of 7/ZG 26.

The Germans suffered no losses.

The final daylight action occurred to the east at 18.00 hrs, when 605 Squadron's Sergeant Eric Wright damaged a Ju 88 bombing shipping off Beachy Head. It had been a busy day for 605 Squadron – which was critical of controlling:

> The Squadron was up in the air four times today, twice encountering Me 109s above them and each time being jumped from a superior height. Feeling is growing rather strong about being sent up against the Me 109s without bombers at an inferior height, and complaints continue to be made to Control. It is realised, however, that Group Controllers are confronted with a difficult task when twin-engined fighters are sent over with single-engined fighters, thus making it difficult for the Observer Corps to accurately report the presence of bombers amongst single-engined fighters. [ORB]

Unfortunately, unless standing patrols could be maintained at high altitude from dawn to dusk, which the resources available could not provide for, this would always be a problem, going forward, when dealing with Me 109s – which the Germans never failed to exploit to their maximum advantage. On this day, Fighter Command fared particularly badly: fourteen RAF fighters had been destroyed in combat and four damaged. Worse, nine pilots had been killed, a daily total never reached again throughout what remained of the Battle of Britain, and four more wounded, one of whom died later of his injuries. Offset against these depressing statistics, just two Me 109s had been lost, with one pilot killed, the other, a decorated *Gruppenkommandeur*, rescued from the sea by the *Seenotdienst*. This was yet another salutary reminder of how lethal the Me 109 pilots were when free to roam and enjoying the immeasurable advantages of height, sun and surprise.

Throughout the day, seventy-two Coastal Command aircraft flew the usual round of sorties and escorted twenty-two convoys. Beauforts of 22 Squadron mined the river Elbe; a 10 (RAAF) Squadron Sunderland inconclusively engaged a Do 17 90 miles from Bishop Rock, Isles of Scilly, and by night, 42 Squadron's Beauforts dropped more mines at Lorient, one of which failed to return. A 269 Squadron Hudson was also lost on a Norwegian patrol, shot down off Herdla by a JG 77 Me 109, the crew all missing. Armed reconnaissance of the invasion ports, however, was abandoned by five of 2 Group's Blenheims owing to adverse weather conditions, the remaining two aircraft attacking Ostend's barges. Bomber Command's nocturnal focus was once more the Channel ports, thirty-four Blenheims successfully attacking enemy shipping at Dunkirk, Calais and Boulogne.

Group Captain Tom Sawyer of 10 Squadron recalled one such 'barge bashing' sortie:

> These trips were quite enjoyed by all because they entailed a quick dash over the enemy coast and back without hours of stooging over blacked out enemy territory ... There was much searchlight activity with several aircraft obviously in the vicinity, and on our run in a great increase in the amount of light flak tracer which seemed to be sprayed up all over the place almost indiscriminately and in all directions in prodigious quantities. Multi-coloured strings of orange, red and even green were hosed upwards, sometimes with a sort of 'S' bend in them as the gunners swung their barrels around. White a yellow blobs of fairy lights creeping up almost lazily at first, then with gradually increasing velocity to zip past the wings at terrific speed, and some a little too close for complacency.

By this time, however, the shipping assembled on the Channel coast to transport Operation *Seelöwe* was dispersing, which the British knew from photographic reconnaissance and Enigma decrypts. From the German communications, for example, it was gleaned that by 21 September 1940, Coastal Command and Bomber Command had 'bashed' and sunk around 12.5 per cent of the 1,865 barges – enough to indicate that should an invasion ever occur, RAF bombers would be a force to be reckoned with.

On this particular night, the heavy gun battery at Cap Gris-Nez was also bombed – and III/JG 53's base at Le Touquet. There, men of the Organisation Todt labour service worked throughout the night, making good the airfield's cratered runway.

Hampdens and Wellingtons attacked transport networks and industrial targets in Germany, and bombed shipping at Le Havre, whilst the Whitley force hit power stations and gas works in Berlin, Amsterdam's Fokker aircraft factory, which could not be located because of cloud, and shipping at Wilhelmshaven and Hamburg. A Wellington of 9 Squadron crashed near Antwerp, all but one of the crew being killed, and another of the same unit crashed upon return, killing a crew member, and a 149 Squadron Wellington was lost on the Hanau raid.

Sunday, 29 September 1940

In Germany, prior to military service young men had to serve in the *Reichsarbeitdienst* labour corps; Frank Kamp received his call-up papers after his second term at college and he was ordered to report to the Stadthalle in Münster. Posted to the *Reichsarbeitdienst*, training along military lines, after the Battle of France, Kamp was sent to the Pas-de-Calais and billeted in a school at Marquise:

> Everybody was aware that Dover was just across the Channel, and it was not long before I got my first look at England. Strangely, although we were so close to England, we were unaware that the Battle of Britain was taking place, and in fact I remained ignorant of any great air battle throughout the entire time I spent on the *Kanalfront*. We were, however, fully aware of the airfield's fighters.
>
> At Marquise, our commander, Hoppner, conveyed to our unit of 120–150 men exactly what was required from us regarding our general behavior [*sic*], not least towards the civilian population. He also explained that our work would involve building and extending, in addition to maintaining, airfields for fighter aircraft. At that stage he did not actually tell us that we would be on *Major* Adolf Galland's airfield at Audembert, near Wissant.
>
> I was then selected for military training, which included rifle drill. On this very day, Luftwaffe steel helmets and rifles were produced. However, we were concerned as we had no weapons training – but were told not to

worry as we would not be issued with ammunition! Therefore, we had to mount guard without bullets! This ridiculous situation went on throughout our entire time in France, despite the fact that Dover was clearly visible! As a result, I formed the opinion that the Germans were clearly bluffing, the French shocked, and the British had no idea of the risks actually being taken by their adversary.

We worked alongside Galland's 'Schlageter' Geschwader and I often saw him either taking-off or returning from a mission. Initially, we built service roads on the airfields and later constructed hangars for the Me 109s and 110s. Their engines were test-run in these constructions. It appeared as though there were something like 700 fighters in the Pas-de-Calais.

During our activities on the various airfields, I had many opportunities to travel in the area around Boulogne, the coast, Calais and St Omer. We acquired an abandoned British lorry, and I was usually the driver's mate. On one such trip we ended up in a large quarry. I have long since forgotten our duty that day – but not what we found there. The quarry was out of bounds to the local civilian population. In it was a huge railway gun, which upon our arrival appeared poised to fire. The gun had been rolled out of its bunker and its aim was northerly, towards England. I learned that Dover was their intended target. This massive artillery piece ran on its own rails, carrying its own colossal shells and gunpowder. Everything was handled by mechanical means. When the first salvo was fired the shell could actually be seen leaving the barrel. There was an incredible recoil. It occurred to me that these shells were probably not that accurate, and so this bombardment also falls into that dreadful undertaking, quite preposterous and futile, calculated to strike fear and despondency into the civilian population.

The enormous K5 280mm railway guns had been shelling 'Hellfire Corner' since 12 August 1940, causing considerable damage. On 25 August 1940, Churchill wrote to the Admiralty, requesting 'a shoot by [HMS] *Erebus* against the German batteries at [Cap] Gris-Nez ... We ought to smash these batteries ...' HMS *Erebus* was an old First World War monitor with two 15-inch guns, and arrangements were made for the prime minister's 'shoot' to be made on the night of 28/29 September 1940 – but this was abandoned due to bad weather. It was decided to mount another attempt on the following night. Indeed, the weather was now starting to turn as autumn matured.

Since 10 September 1940, 66 Squadron had been stationed at Gravesend, the Biggin Hill satellite opposite Tilbury, on the south bank of the Thames Estuary.

AC1 Bob Morris was an engine fitter there on 'Clickety-Click':

At Gravesend we used to watch the German aircraft coming in, heading for London or elsewhere, the trails in the sky, and how relieved we were when the passed overhead and flew straight on! During that September, as we were close to the river, there would often be ground mist that lasted all day. You may have a day with absolute thick fog in which no aircraft could take-off, or no bombing could take place because the Germans could not see us. We used to get all our work done by early afternoon on such days, and then, inevitably, a football would appear from somewhere and a game would start on the edge of the aerodrome. We never used to pick a side, you just joined in with whichever side appeared to be winning and that was the direction you kicked! On one occasion we were busy playing in thick fog – you could only see about half way across the airfield – when we heard these German aircraft circling round above us, looking for something to bomb. Suddenly, right through the fog came a parachute flare which landed on our football pitch – someone kicked dirt onto it and we just kept playing. No-one ran for shelter, that was how used we had become to it all.

By this time we were finding the living conditions at Gravesend a bit trying. We had a half day off every ten days. We used to spend that half day fast asleep. We were exhausted, working such long hours, from dawn to dusk. At Gravesend there were no billets, so a restaurant about three-quarters of a mile away, called 'Laughing Waters', adjacent to a big lake, was commandeered. We were taken there in our usual mode of motorized transport – a Bedford three-tonner. The building was just a shell, nothing on the floor and all we had to sleep in was two blankets. It was a mighty cold place with just two blankets and the floor, on the edge of a lake! The only thing that had not been taken away were the rowing boats, so every morning to get warm we rowed around the lake.

Fortunately we were not in 'Laughing Waters' for very long before they moved our billet again, this time to Cobham Hall, the Earl of Darnley's estate. We slept in the servants' quarters but at least we had beds. We were quite near Cobham Village and it was strange, wherever we were the officers would find a restaurant or similar for their evening drinks, whilst we Other Ranks would find a pub. We never went to theirs and they never into ours. Our entertainment was to walk to Rochester or Strood, to the pictures, then walk back again. We also went to dances at the Co-op Hall in Gravesend.

I remember the Spitfires damaged in combat. I remember Pilot Officer [Crelin] 'Bogle' Bodie coming back with his port mainplane knocked about by a cannon shell, and I had to rip part of the aileron off for him which he proudly took as a souvenir. I always remember a Spitfire coming in making a horrible whistling noise – it had a bullet hole right through a

> propeller blade. We did not have a new propeller, however, so we smoothed out the hole and drilled corresponding holes in the other two blades – it then flew for another fortnight with that same airscrew! We had to drill the other holes as when the propellers assembled it is very finely balanced to prevent vibration.

Turning back to 29 September 1940, this would be another day of light attacks and fighter sweeps.

German daylight operations began with the usual reconnaissance flights. At 08.10 hrs, Pilot Officer Vernon Bright of 229 Squadron left Northolt on a weather test, climbing to 16,000ft over Luton when he was vectored north-west. Below, Bright sighted a Do 215 at 9,000ft, which he attacked from up sun. The bomber immediately dived for the 10/10ths layer of cloud 3,000ft below, pursued by the Hurricane:

> I stalked him just in cloud and opened fire from astern at 250 yards with another 5-second burst. Accurate tracer fire from the rear-gunner forced me to take evasive action but I renewed the attack until all my ammunition had gone. The rear-gunner ceased firing – the port engine and wing were in flames and the starboard engine was covered in brownish black smoke. E/A fell into cloud apparently out of control in Maidenhead district.

No German aircraft was found to have crashed, however, but a Ju 88 of *Stab* II/KG 76 was damaged over England and forced-landed at Calais-Marck, and a *Stab* I/LG 1 Ju 88 was seriously damaged over England and abandoned by three of its crew over France – the fourth man was killed in the resulting crash. It is likely, therefore, that one of these was the 'Do 215 [*sic*]' attacked by Bright.

The next combat was similar, over the 10 Group area, when at 13.45 hrs Pilot Officer Kenneth Dewhurst and Pilot Officer Janusz Żurakowski, a Pole, intercepted and engaged what they identified as a 'Me 110' 10 miles south of Exmouth, claiming a probable.

Low cloud and rain led to a quiet day until late afternoon, when a fighter sweep came in over the 11 Group area, including Me 109s from JGs 3, 26, 27, 51, 53 and 77, and, according to one defending squadron, a number of Me 110s.

At 17.00 hrs, the Spitfires of Squadron Leader George Denholm's 603 Squadron were patrolling north of Beachy Head; Pilot Officer Ronald Berry reported,

> I was Green Leader when the Squadron was at 30,000 feet on our patrol line. Squadron Leader sighted some aircraft below and asked me to investigate.

> I dived down at saw a vic of three 109s and tally ho'd to Squadron Leader. With others above and around, I attacked the port one of the vic of three. Bits and pieces fell out of the 109 and as I looked to port I found two 109s firing heavily at me. I took violent evasive action and climbed into the sun. I saw another lone 109 below and attacked out of the sun. It took no evasive action and fell into the cloud with black smoke pouring from it. As I overtook, I had been firing all the time till I swerved to port. E/A was not seen again.

Berry's target, however, was destroyed, *Oberleutnant* Walter Leyerer of 2/JG 77, who was killed, crashing into the sea. This was 603 Squadron's only claim and the Spitfires returned to Hornchurch without loss. Things did not, though, go as well for 253 Squadron:

> Eleven Hurricanes took-off Kenley at 1610 hrs in company with 501 Squadron, 501 Squadron leading, and were ordered to patrol Sevenoaks line at 15,000 feet to intercept Raid 2. Squadron joined up with 501 Squadron over base and climbed to 15,000 feet when told that Me 110s were approaching from SE at 14,000 feet. Some seventy Me 110s in two waves were then sighted at 17,000 feet and 20,000 feet in the vicinity of Hayward's Heath, flying in a flat vic of seven or nine aircraft. The Squadron milled and lost height to 12,000 feet but were then engaged by twelve Me 109s which dived from above, breaking up Squadron formation and a general dogfight ensued. [ORB]

No. 501 Squadron was also broken up and scattered by the attack from II/JG 3 but suffered no casualties.

No. 253 Squadron's 'Yellow 1' (identity unknown) fired at a 109, followed by Sergeant Václav Cukr, a Czech, Yellow 2, who attacked the same enemy aircraft three times, the 109 then diving vertically and disappearing into cloud, emitting thick black smoke.

Pilot Officer Richard Graves, Red 3,

> saw a Me 109 attack a Hurricane at 14,000 feet and dived towards the cloud base. Red 3 dived after E/A, delivering a three-quarter astern attack and observing his bullets entering the cockpit, after which E/A dived into cloud and Red 3 saw a red glow in could, suggesting that the E/A was on fire. Police confirm crashed Me 109 in vicinity of the engagement [author's note: there was none, in fact]. Red Section then re-formed and Red 3 attacked a second Me 109 and saw pieces breaking off E/A which

> endeavoured to join up with another Me 109. Red 3 gave chase and noticed that a Hurricane was on his tail, immediately after which he was attacked from astern and his aircraft caught fire. Red 3, who asserts that it was a Hurricane which shot him down, baled out and saw a Hurricane circling the wreckage of his aircraft. [ORB]

Graves, an unfortunate victim of so-called 'Friendly Fire' was admitted to Brockley Park Hospital suffering from burns, his Hurricane having crashed at Chailey. Indeed, such was the fog of war that Flight Lieutenant Raymond Myles Duke-Woolley, Red 1,

> who had his rudder controls shot away and his gravity tank holed, states that he was attacked by a Hurricane. A bullet retrieved from this aircraft was sent to the Armoury for inspection. [ORB]

Sergeant Alwyn Edgley, Yellow 3, was shot down by a 109, his machine crashing near Newhaven whilst the pilot landed by parachute at South Heighton; wounded in a shoulder, Edgley was admitted to Horton Hospital.

In this action, 253 Squadron had lost two Hurricanes and one damaged, according to the pilots involved two of them being attacked by Hurricanes. These were, however, the only Hurricanes hit by this fighter sweep – although the Germans claimed thirteen Hurricanes destroyed – so considering the number of enemy claims offset against the lack of RAF claims, 'Friendly Fire' seems unlikely on this occasion. As we have repeatedly seen, aircraft identification was often consistently poor on both sides; was that the case here?

The Spitfires of 66 Squadron were also hit by the 109s at 17.20 hrs, Sergeant Peter Willcocks being shot down and crash-landing, wounded – although where is unclear. *Hauptmann* Walter Oesau, *Gruppenkommandeur* of III/JG 51, claimed two Spitfires destroyed, location unknown, and *Leutnant* Günther Hess of 2/JG 53 another '5km East of Brighton'. One of these must have been Willcocks, whose was the only Spitfire either damaged or brought down on this day.

Again, the day went to the German fighter pilots who had destroyed two Hurricanes and damaged another, also shooting down a Spitfire (which was repairable) – just one Me 109 had been destroyed. Two Me 109s, though, only just returned to France – machines from 4/JG 54 and II/LG 2 forced-landing at Berck-sur-Mer out of fuel. The constant need to be ever conscious of fuel states, and the limited time for combat over England, was a perennially vexing issue for the Me 109 pilots. *Oberleutnant* Lothar Siegfried Stronk of 8/JG 53, for example, had only recently run out of fuel and ditched in the Channel; on 29 September 1940, he wrote to his friend, Gerhard von Szymonski, another pilot:

Dear Szy!

Thank you very much for your letter. I was very happy that you did not forget me. With two old Upper Silesians this would rarely happen anyway.

Now, we have switched roles in relation to our activity. You now see from your own view how miserable one feels at home. But calm down, every useful man is brought to the front again. This is especially true for the hunt. The losses are sometimes enormous. I recommend that you switch to 109! In the present war, this is maybe the last time there will be true fighter combat, true hunting.

The destroyers shoot down what they can, whenever they can get in a shot, but even more so they get shot down themselves.

We are, whenever the weather permits, used daily as escort to London. I can tell you, for the 109 a pretty criminal act, because with [*sic*] we have to watch our fuel to the last minute and drop (or not, as once with me), and secondly, the Channel is causing a great deal of trouble for the return flight. Any simple shit-cooler hit, or otherwise harmless thing in a dogfight over London and you're done – meaning an emergency-landing in England or swim in the Channel. The latter I have recently experienced, not because of a hit, but simply due to running out of fuel.

In the middle of the Channel I had to make a belly landing, which went very well despite high waves. The 109 always sinks immediately, but I was equally fast getting out. Swimming and cursing – quite funny – not! Since I had radioed in my location before the rather watery landing, a 109 came after about half an hour, so I fired red and green flares, but unfortunately this pilot also ended up paddling in the water with me.

After ten minutes, a rescue seaplane arrived, which broke two struts while landing, but still managed to get me out, up in the air again and brought me home. I have to say getting out feels much better than getting into the water. Big piece of luck I reckon. Ricki doesn't know yet and shouldn't know for now.

Otherwise, of course I am doing fine. I only have three aerial victories. I am disadvantaged by having missed the whole experience of the fighting in France. But I'm also pretty satisfied, because most rookies are shot down without having shot down anything – and shooting down enemy planes is far from easy. Well, I am sure you will experience it yourself.

Nothing else to report.

Like many other German aircrew, Stronk was fortunate that the Luftwaffe had the foresight to organise an effective air sea rescue service – in direct contrast to the poor arrangements made on the British side.

There was little further action on 29 September 1940. At 18.00 hrs, 92 Squadron's Pilot Officer Dennis Williams intercepted a Do 17 reconnaissance bomber between Maidstone and Canterbury, attacking and damaging the raider which escaped into cloud.

Away to the south-west, Spitfires of 234 Squadron were over the Cornish coast and sighted ten enemy bombers heading north but being over 20 miles off Land's End the bandits were too distant to engage. Without doubt, these were He 111s of III/KG 55 en route to Liverpool. Instead of taking the usual and direct route, however, making landfall over the Southampton area and flying north-west, hoping to avoid RAF day fighters the Heinkels flew across the English Channel, skirted around Land's End and crossed the Bristol Channel before flying north over the St George's Channel, between Pembroke coast and the Irish coast, intending to approach Liverpool after dark from seaward. At 17.51 hrs, though, eleven Hurricanes of 79 Squadron scrambled from Pembrey in South Wales to patrol Pembroke Dock at 20,000ft. Informed that nine (not ten as reported by 234 Squadron) were 20 miles off St David's Head and approaching from the south-west, the RAF pilots set off to investigate. The He 111s were soon sighted, according to the Form 'F', 'in a very tight vic formation and return fire [was] considerable'. Yellow Section attacked, Pilot Officer George Nelson-Edwards, Yellow 2, being the first to fire and claimed a probable west of Strumble Head – but his Hurricane was hit by return fire and streamed glycol. 'Nelson-Eddy' baled out and was fortunately rescued from the sea fortunately being picked up by the SS *Dartford* and taken into Milford Haven. Individual attacks then ensued, during which Pilot Officer Don 'Dimsie' Stones DFC, Blue 1, attacked

> the extreme right aircraft as the whole vic turned West and South for home. Both engines smoked after the first burst, second attack was full astern and all remaining rounds put into the enemy. Both engines smoking, wheels down and bombs dropped, the aircraft crashed into the sea. Three other Hurricanes fired at the aircraft as it lost height.

This bomber belonged to 9/KG 55, the crew of which were al killed, and crashed into the Irish Sea off St David's Head. Another 9/KG 55 He 111 crash-landed at Saint-Lô, having been damaged, all of its crew wounded, and one forced-landed near Brest. Having been turned about, the raid, and the Heinkels' ruse, was a complete failure.

Pilot Officer Henry Peters's Hurricane, however, was hit by return fire, the pilot crashing into the Irish Sea, he was never seen again. Pilot Officer Peter Mayhew pursued the retreating Germans far out to sea, but in fading light and low on fuel was forced to land in Enniscorthy in County Wexford, where he was interned by the neutral Irish authorities.

So ended the day fighting.

The comparatively poor weather reduced operations for both Coastal Command, although a 224 Squadron Hudson and a 210 Squadron Sunderland inconclusively attacked U-boats. Blenheims of 53 and 59 Squadrons respectively struck at Rotterdam and Lorient during the evening, and Beauforts mined the Weser and Jade estuaries. No. 2 Group's Blenheims uneventfully swept the North Sea, seeking enemy shipping, but reconnaissance of the invasion ports was scrubbed because of the bad weather. At night, Bomber Command Blenheims 'bashed barges' at Flushing, Ostend, Calais and Le Touquet, and the Hampden, Whitley and Wellington forces continued their assault on Germany. One Hampden disappeared without trace; *Oberleutnant* Heinrich Greise of 1(N)/JG 1 destroyed a Wellington of 37 Squadron near Osnabrück, the only surviving crewman being captured; a 75 Squadron 'Whimpy' crashed at Lynton, having run out of fuel returning from Leipzig; one man was killed.

The night of 29/30 September 1940 also saw HMS *Erebus*, assisted by the Dover tug *Lady Brassey*, positioned mid-Channel. At 02.00 hrs, the old monitor opened fire, loosing off seventeen shells towards Calais before a technical issue brought the shoot to a premature end. The exercise would not be repeated until 16 October 1940 – but inevitably a few hours later, in daylight, the Germans responded – and Dover suffered once again.

Monday, 30 September 1940

At dawn, most of England was shrouded in low-lying mist and swept by a light, generally north-easterly wind. The day was cool and the Meteorological Office predicted the further outlook to be 'Quiet and dry except in the extreme North'. Given these weather conditions action was likely – and such thoughts were uppermost in the mind of 609 Squadron's Pilot Officer David Crook when he awoke at Middle Wallop that morning:

> The weather was brilliantly clear, and when we got up we shook our heads dismally as we knew there would be a lot of trouble. As 'Mac' [author's note: Flying Officer Henry MacDonald 'Mac' Goodwin, killed in action on 14 August 1940] used to remark, 'We should have quite a job to keep the Grim Reaper at bay'.

Certainly, some aircrew on both sides would not live to see dusk on another day of heavy fighting.

Operations began with lone German reconnaissance bombers active over Britain from 06.35 hrs, probing inland as far as Farnborough. The first action of the day was fought by 151 Squadron's Red Section, up from Digby, when the three Hurricane pilots, namely Flight Lieutenant Kenneth Blair, Pilot Officer Michael Ingle-Finch and Sergeant Douglas Nicholls, intercepted and destroyed a Ju 88 90 miles off the Humber Estuary – the gunners of which first hit and damaged the Hurricanes of Blair and Nicholls. Most likely a Netherlands-based aircraft of III/KG 30, the German crew were never found despite a search by two Battles and a patrol boat. This being 151 Squadron's first aerial victory since having been withdrawn from North Weald to Digby on 1 September 1940, later in the day the squadron was visited by the 12 Group AOC, Air Vice-Marshal Trafford Leigh-Mallory, and congratulated.

At 08.35 hrs, Yellow Section of 501 Squadron scrambled from Kenley with orders to intercept a lone raider, which Sergeant James Lacey, Yellow 2, sighted at 08.50 hrs, a Ju 88 at 7,000ft, 10 miles to his north-west, over Brooklands. Having chased the bandit for 10 miles, Lacey attacked out of the sun, causing glycol to stream, from the Ju 88's starboard engine, which then stopped, but the raider was lost in broken cloud.

The first major threat appeared on RDF screens at 08.55 hrs when '12+' and '50+' were detected just east of Dungeness, the Observer Corps reporting how these forces split into a number of sub-formations, some flying over Biggin Hill and Kenley whilst others swept over Farnborough and further south. Scrambled from Kenley at 08.50 hrs to patrol Maidstone, at 09.00 hrs the Hurricanes of 501 Squadron were bounced by Me 109s (wrongly identified in the ORB as 'He 113s [*sic*]') over Tunbridge Wells, Flying Officer Nathaniel Barry, a South African, possibly being hit by *Feldwebel* Walter Matoni of 9/JG 27, who claimed his first victory; the Hurricane pilot was unhurt and safely forced-landed his damaged fighter at Pembury.

At 09.00 hrs, 1 (RCAF) and 229 Squadrons were ordered up from Northolt to patrol Biggin Hill together, but were bounced by *Major* Adolf Galland's JG 26 over Tonbridge at 09.35 hrs. The Canadian squadron took no part in the combat, the 109s attacking 229 Squadron in small groups, breaking up the Hurricanes. Flying Officer Malcolm Ravenhill was shot down in flames and killed, his Hurricane crashing at Ightham near Sevenoaks; Pilot Officer Noel Stansfeld, a Canadian, who had only joined the squadron from 242 (Canadian) Squadron the previous day, was also shot down, baling out wounded, his machine too crashing at Ightham; Pilot Officer Fred Robshaw was shot-up and wounded, crash-landing west of Ash; Sergeant Rupert Ommanney was wounded but returned his damaged Hurricane to Northolt, as did Pilot Officer Reginald du Vivier, who was unhurt. JG 26 claimed five Hurricanes destroyed in the engagement for no loss, the damage executed by *Oberleutnant* Walter Horten of Stab/JG 26, *Oberfeldwebel* Walter Meyer and *Unteroffizier* Karl Schieffer of 5/JG 26, and *Oberleutnant* Walter Schneider and *Unteroffizier* Hugo Dahmer of 6/JG 26.

Although none of the Hurricane squadrons made combat claims, *Oberleutnant* H. Betram, the *Gruppe Adjutant* of I/JG 27, was shot down and killed in combat with Hurricanes over East Grinstead, crashing near Haywards Heath, and *Unteroffizier* A. Sander of 3/JG 27 crashed in flames and was killed, also near Haywards Heath.

No. 66 Squadron's Spitfires had left Gravesend at 09.10 hrs, climbing to 20,000ft when informed of bandits approaching.

According to Sergeant Harry Cook at 10.00 hrs over Tenterden,

> Red Section was put into line-astern and we brushed with the enemy, but I did not get into range. Red Section was then separated from the main formation and we searched for E/A, finding them at 20,000 feet. The Section broke up and one Me 109 came straight for me, head-on. When he was about 250 yards away I opened fire, and almost immediately he fired, but I saw his fire going wide. He turned away at about fifty yards distance and I did a quick turn to get on his tail, but I observed him going into a spin, which continued until I lost him in the clouds. Seeing no more E/A near I went through clouds but could not see any trace of the E/A. I got a pip [author's note: homing course] from 'Rastus' [author's note: Biggin Hill control] and landed base at 1020 hrs.

The 109 was claimed as a probable and was the only RAF combat claim arising from this first engagement, during which the only bombs reported were near RAF Odiham and RAF Portslade. A further raid was then incoming at 10.05 hrs, comprising sixty aircraft in four formations, which came in over Hastings and Dungeness, penetrated to Biggin Hill before turning about and returning to France via Beachy Head. Bombs were dropped on Bexhill and Hastings at 10.30 hrs, both towns reporting significant damage to domestic property and a disruption of public services. The raid, though, was not intercepted because the majority of 11 Group's squadrons were on the ground re-fuelling after their earlier patrols. Somewhat late in the day, 609 Squadron was scrambled from Warmwell at 10.30 hrs to patrol London, 11 Group controller having called upon 10 Group for assistance, but was recalled half an hour later.

It was now that the German railway guns responded after the nocturnal HMS *Erebus* bombardment. Just before 11.00 hrs, a ranging shot fell outside Dover harbour, the next round exploding at Ladywell where the fire station was damaged, causing one casualty. Tapley's Garage, Cambridge Road, was also damaged, and a man was killed in Barwick's Yard. Another shell reduced a terraced row in Dickson Road to rubble, where there were three more casualties, and two more civilians were injured when the windows were blown out at Market Square's Westminster Bank. By 11.48 hrs the reprisal attack was over – it could have been much worse.

The next raid was launched against Hampshire and the West Country, a *Freie Jagd* by some 100 Me 109s of I and II/JG 2, II/JG 53, and Me 110s of I and II/ZG 26. At 10.45 hrs, RDF had indicated two raids of 50+ north of Cherbourg – an entirely accurate assessment of size – and by 11.00 hrs these formations were 30 miles south of Weymouth Bay.

At 11.00 hrs, 56 Squadron, which had earlier that morning flown down from Boscombe to operate at Warmwell, was scrambled to intercept the approaching raid. At the same time, 609 Squadron was also scrambled from Warmwell, as Pilot Officer David Crook later described,

> I threw this diary into a chair, the card, players dropped their hands, and everybody sprinted out of the door towards their machines. All the airmen were running hard too, and by the time I got to my Spitfire two men were already there to help me on with my parachute and then fasten it when I was in the cockpit. I put on the starter and ignition switches, turned on the R.T., gave the priming pump a couple of strokes, and pressed the starter button. The engine started immediately, and I put on my helmet and oxygen mask. Within ninety seconds of the alarm coming through we were all taxying [*sic*] out on the aerodrome. I was leading Green Section with Pilot Officers 'Novi' Nowierski and Johnny Curchin behind me, and we got to our taking-off point and turned into wind. Looked round at 'Novi' and he gave me the 'thumbs up', meaning everything okay, and Johnny did likewise. I dropped my hand, opened the throttle and we all accelerated rapidly over the aerodrome and took-off. The rest of the Squadron were either taking-off or already in the air, and we all joined up and started to climb towards Swanage, nearly fifty miles away [*sic*: Swanage is 20 miles south-west of Warmwell].

No. 504 Squadron also scrambled from Filton at 11.00 hrs, patrolling base as a precaution in case BAC was once more the enemy's target; on this occasion, Squadron Leader John Sample's men would not sight the enemy, however. Twelve minutes later, 238 Squadron was ordered up from Middle Wallop to patrol Bournemouth – although they did not meet the enemy, two Hurricanes collided and were lost; Pilot Officer Vernon Simmonds and Pilot Officer Robert Kings both baled out safely, although the latter was severely shaken as his parachute had ripped on the Hurricane's tail. Pilot Officer Richard Covington landed his Hurricane in a field adjacent to where Kings landed, and having confirmed that his friend was unhurt, returned safely to base. Sergeant Frederick Sibley, however, became lost so landed at Weston-super-Mare where he refuelled and later also returned safely to Middle Wallop.

No. 56 Squadron's Hurricanes had been ordered to climb to 22,000ft and patrol Warmwell, but when at just 16,000 feet and still climbing, the enemy was sighted approaching from the south-east and out of the sun – Me 110s at 22,000ft and Me 109s higher still. Pilot Officer Frederick Higginson was Baffin Leader and led the Hurricanes for the Me 110s in a head-on attack – as he later recorded in his log book, there were 'Dozens of'em!' At 11.25 hrs, Higginson opened fire at the leading *Zerstörer* of *Hauptmann* Ralph von Rettburg's II/ZG 26. As the two aircraft flashed by at a terrific closing speed, 'Baffin Leader' immediately delivered a six-second burst at an Me 109, but from 400 yards range his fire was ineffective. Sergeant George Smythe, Red 3, saw the Me 110 attacked by Higginson break away and head for France, its port engine streaming smoke.

Hauptmann Helmut Wick, *Gruppenkommandeur* of I/JG 2, and his *Stabschwarm* then pounced on 56 Squadron. Within seconds the German ace had added numbers 32 and 33 to his score, and *Oberleutnant* Franz Fiby, I/JG 2's *Adjutant*, scored his second success. Two of 56 Squadron were shot down: Flying Officer Ken Marston who crash-landed at East Knighton, and Sergeant Ronald Ray, who suffered a broken arm when his aircraft crashed.

Fortunately for 56 Squadron, 609 Squadron's Spitfires intervened, on this occasion led by Flight Lieutenant Frank Howell, who, upon sighting the enemy, had cleverly led his Spitfires up sun over Weymouth Bay. 'Sorbo Leader' then ordered sections line astern, attacking the Germans from above and out of the sun. Howell led 'A' Flight to attack from starboard, whilst Pilot Officer Michael Appleby, Blue 1, led 'B' Flight, consisting of his Blue Section and Pilot Officer David Crook's Green Section, off to port. Three Me 109s in line astern, and at the same height, passed Appleby's port side, travelling in the same direction. At first the Spitfire pilot thought these fighters were Hurricanes, and swung round to protect their rear, but soon realised his mistake; 'B' Flight then dived out of the sun on them. Appleby fired six two-second bursts onto the rearward Me 109, noting hits around the cockpit area and flashes from within as the enemy aircraft dived. Having followed the 109, Appleby broke off when another fighter appeared in his rear-view mirror, although fortunately this proved to be a Spitfire.

Pilot Officer Michael Appleby,

> Looked for more Me 109s or our own aircraft, but as so often happened in this kind of scrap could not see anyone else anywhere, a strange phenomenon peculiar to air fighting.

Pilot Officer David Crook was about 100 yards behind Blue Section, and after Blue 1 broke away, saw Appleby's target

> more or less break up in mid-air – some very nice shooting on Michael's part. I distinctly remember him saying on the R.T., 'That's got you, you bastard!'

In his own dive after a Me 109, Crook's speed built up to 500 mph, the sea rushing up at him. Coming out of the dive, the strain was terrific, and a black mist formed in front of his eyes. Upon levelling out, however, Crook attacked the 109 from below and astern as it too pulled out. The enemy fighter rolled over onto its back, burst into flames and dived straight into the sea off Swanage. The pilot did not get out. Crook wrote,

> A few of our Spitfires were chasing Me 109s all over the place and obviously a very nice little massacre was in progress as a few minutes later I saw another Hun go into the sea.

Crook then spotted a lone Me 109 going flat out for France, dived again and easily caught the Me 109, at which he fired a 'good burst'. The 109's cockpit canopy broke off, flashing by dangerously close to the pursuing Spitfire, and the Me 109 also plunged towards the sea. To Crook's amazement, though, at sea level the aircraft flattened out and climbed, streaming glycol and continued travelling at full speed for France:

> For the first time in this war I felt a certain pity for this German pilot and was rather reluctant to finish him off. The last few moments must have been absolute hell for him, I could almost feel his desperation as he made this last attempt to get away.

Nonetheless, Crook emptied his remaining ammunition into the enemy fighter from very close range, the 109 crashing into the sea at great speed. The chase had taken Crook to just 15 miles off Cherbourg – a very dangerous place for a lone Spitfire to be. Hastily returning to the English coast, elated at having destroyed two enemy aircraft in one sortie, Crook approached the cliffs in Weymouth Bay at 300 mph, just above the wave tops. At the last minute he pulled back on the stick, rocketing over the top 'to the very considerable amazement of some soldiers!'

Meanwhile, Flight Lieutenant Frank Howells's 'A' Flight was also engaged. Pilot Officer John Bisdee, Yellow 1, was flying in line astern on Sorbo Leader when three Me 109s attacked Yellow Section from abeam. Bisdee shouted 'Break Left!' and the Spitfires scattered. 'The Bish' then saw a lone Me 109 some 300ft below, diving south, so rolled over inverted, so as to prevent his engine from cutting, and fired all his ammunition at the enemy aircraft. Pieces of the tail unit broke off, and thick black smoke poured from the engine. Bisdee was then attacked from behind and immediately broke off, and Pilot Officer Michael Staples, Red 3, got in a quick deflection shot at a fleeting Me 109, which emitted glycol as it dived seawards.

Pilot Officer Keith Ogilvie:

> We ran into a swarm of Me 109s. I paired off with one and we commenced turning. I was pleased that the Spitfire was able to turn inside of the 109, but he suddenly flipped over and disappeared before I had fired a shot – a moral victory only!

As quickly as it had begun the fight was over, the Germans heading back to France. Thanks to 609 Squadron's timely intervention, 56 Squadron only lost two Hurricanes with both pilots safe. The RAF pilots claimed four Me 109s destroyed, and certainly *Feldwebel* Wilhelm Hermes of 2/JG 2 and *Gefreiter* Fritz Schumacher of 5/JG 2 were both missing.

At 13.00 hrs the Meteorological Office recorded various weather data at numerous locations throughout the British Isles. At Portland Bill a force 4 north-north-east wind was noted, the sky by then 'generally cloudy'. The cloud was low, and at 4,000ft recorded as 10/10ths. At the same time, cloud in the Bristol area was reported as being 8/10ths at 3,000ft. The West Country was virtually hidden, from those heights, by an almost unbroken blanket of cloud – this would later prove significant, but the next raid, at 13.00 hrs, was again directed towards London.

At 13.00 hrs, 41 and 222 Squadrons were scrambled from Hornchurch to patrol Chatham-Rochford at 30,000ft, and 603 Squadron left there alone and headed for Maidstone, also to patrol at 30,000ft. The Biggin Hill sector's Spitfire squadrons, 66, 72 and 92, scrambled at the same time, also heading for Maidstone at 30,000ft, this height in response to the high-flying Me 109s. Five minutes later, 1 (RCAF), 229 and 303 (Polish) Squadrons took-off to patrol base at 15,000ft; 253 and 501 Squadrons left Kenley to patrol Sevenoaks at 20,000 feet, and 605 Squadron went up from Croydon, also to patrol base. At 13.20 hrs,

46 and 249 Squadrons came south from North Weald to patrol Hornchurch at 20,000ft. As those two squadrons scrambled, the Germans crossed the coast.

Between Rye and Folkestone, some bandits were incoming and steered towards Kenley and Biggin Hill, from where 30+ headed west to the Thames Valley, whilst others flew in the opposite direction, towards Dartford and Chatham. The majority of enemy aircraft involved were Me 109s, those of JG 53 escorting some thirty Do 17s of KG 3 to London.

The first RAF pilot to see the enemy was 41 Squadron's Pilot Officer Henry Baker, 10 miles south-west of Dungeness:

> I was detached from Squadron as reconnaissance machine and climbed up to 25,000 feet, when I sighted a formation of twin-engined aircraft at about 15,000 feet. I reported this and a large formation of Me 109s were brought to my notice by one of their number diving past my starboard wing. There were about fifty or sixty Me 109s at about 28,000 feet in no formation at all. Five detached from main formation and attacked me. I dived, turning towards the clouds and then pulled out. There were no more signs of enemy activity, so I continued the patrol.

Flight Lieutenant Eustace 'Gus' Holden DFC, 501 Squadron:

> I was flying as Blue 1 of Blue Section of 501 Squadron when it was ordered to patrol Sevenoaks at 20,000 feet at 1315 hrs, in company with 253 Squadron. Only seven aircraft of the Squadron left the ground owing to unserviceability, and the rendezvous was not made with 253 Squadron. Large formations of E/A sighted South of Thames, flying West. Close bomber formations escorted by fighters flying all over the sky. Blue Section split up to deal with individual fighters and I struck off after a Me 109. I fired a slight deflection at 400 yards of 4-seconds, and bits started to fly off it. Losing height and dropping speed, he was obviously done for, and I gave him a further burst of 2-seconds from dead behind and black smoke belched from him. I then broke off the engagement on being myself attacked from behind.

This was 501 Squadron's only claim, timed at 13.35 hrs, very likely being a 4/JG 52 Me 109, the pilot of which, *Gefreiter* Erich Mummert, forced-landed near the perimeter fence of Detling aerodrome and was captured unhurt. No. 501 Squadron suffered no loss.

The Biggin Hill Spitfires, 66, 72 and 92 Squadrons, were climbing hard to intercept the raiders when at 17,000ft, as Flight Lieutenant Ken Gillies, leading the former squadron, reported, at 13.30 hrs,

> we encountered several Me 109s and as these attempted to carry out an attack on the rear of my Squadron, I went into a turn and attacked them instead. One Me 109, which appeared in front of me, offered a simple 'no deflection' shot and I fired a 4–5 second burst at him. Pieces of E/A flew off, and grey and white vapour streamed from him (It is confirmed by Pilot Officer Heron, 66 Squadron, that my first burst carried away E/A's hood and windscreen). E/A went into dive, and I broke off attack in case I was being attacked by other E/A. I did no see E/A crash but when last seen he was losing height at reduced speed whilst still a good way from the coast.

The 109 was claimed as a probable.

Pilot Officer Hubert Allen, Red 3, was at the rear of 'Clickety-Click':

> When we were at 24,000 feet I saw a Me 109 heading SE about one – two miles South of the Squadron. As I was some considerable distance behind the Squadron, with no specific orders, I broke formation after the 109. I caught it up very easily and gave it a 5-seconds burst at 200 yards, closing to 100 yards, obviously surprising the pilot who appeared either to lack intelligence or to be singularly inexperienced. He turned and dived about 4,000 feet and then continued on a straight course SE. Grey smoke was billowing from his glycol region by this time. I kept behind him and gave him another 5-second burst at point blank range (50 yards). He dived once more, pieces falling from him, and continued on his course, just above cloud. I came up behind and administered another 5-second burst at 100 yards, when black smoke poured out and he dived vertically through cloud. I looked over and above cloud but could see nothing of him. The final burst was administered in the region of Wittisham and Appledore. There was obviously considerable armour plating behind the pilot.

Allen's report, however, is incorrectly timed at 12.40 hrs; it should correctly be 13.30–13.40 hrs. Pilot Officer Hugh Reilley described how 66 Squadron became split up whilst engaging the 109s, and how he then made for the coast, seeking 'any returning aircraft'. Reilley found

> five bombers ... flying parallel to the coast, NE. The formation was already damaged, two Me 110s were forming a rear-guard but they were all very close together. I made a quarter attack on a 110 and saw my bullets entering his fuselage but no real damage was done. I ... made a head-on attack on the leading Do 215 and managed to smash all the glass cabin. By this time the 109s were too close for comfort so I dived down below cloud and landed at 1358 hrs. The Squadron took-off at 1258 hrs.

(Reilley's report is also incorrectly timed at 12.30 hrs.) Reilley's claim was for one damaged Me 110 and a Do 215.

No. 92 Squadron's Spitfires were also involved in this now chaotic action; at 13.45 hrs, Sergeant Kenneth Parker was over Maidstone and chased a 109 down to 6,000ft but was unable to get within range so attacked another from astern, damaging it before the enemy fighter 'disappeared into clouds and I lost it'. At the same time, Sergeant Ronald Fokes engaged a 109 between Biggin Hill and Beachy Head, firing all his ammunition, watching his target 'go down with glycol fumes … machine entered cloud about twenty miles North of Beachy Head'. For some reason, Flight Lieutenant Allan Wright had taken off with 72 Squadron, and was now 'operating with two pilots of 72 [Squadron]':

> We gained height to 11,000 feet over Redhill, a squadron of Spitfires passed overhead and then a squadron of Hurricanes passed in front at 12,000 feet. I noticed that there were many Spitfires milling around underneath, hen one of the Hurricanes suddenly dived with glycol streaming from it. A few seconds later I saw a 109 chasing a Spitfire. I shouted 'Look out!', and chased the 109.
>
> After my first burst he broke off and tried to climb away into the sun. I managed full out to keep up and fired a burst which caused much glycol to pour out. He died and I got in a burst from underneath. Black smoke poured out and I had to throttle back to keep behind him. He then took much evasive action and I lost him in the cloud at 6,000 feet, travelling South. He was then slightly East of Hayward's Heath at 1340 hrs.

Wright claimed a probable, but it is likely that he was more successful: at 13.56 hrs, *Unteroffizier* Fritz Marcks of 7/JG 54 was forced down near Pevensey having been damaged in combat, his engine overheating; the enemy pilot was captured unhurt.

Over Maidstone and south-west of Biggin Hill, 603 Squadron's Spitfires intercepted the enemy bombers and Me 109s, which were still travelling inland, heading north-west, at 13.35 hrs. A successful running battle then ensued with the German fighters, lasting twenty-five minutes. As ever, the combat reports of the pilots concerned tell the story…

Pilot Officer James Morton, Yellow Leader:

> over Maidstone when we sighted twenty to thirty Me 109s at 28,000ft and attacked in line-astern. I got on the tail of one, but was unable to fire, as the violent manoeuvres had dislodged the reflector sight bulb. I fixed this and got on to another, giving him a 2-seconds burst from 150 yards

> on his starboard quarter. He broke away an went down, but I could not see what happened as there were many E/A around.
>
> I then got on to another and gave him two good bursts. After the second one, he turned very slowly onto his back, gradually going into a vertical dive. He disappeared into cloud at 7,000 feet, still diving vertically.
>
> I then attacked a third 109, getting in two good bursts with 30° deflection. After the second one there appeared to be an explosion in the cockpit as the hood blew off and the E/A was enveloped in flames.

This 109 belonged to 6/JG 52, which crashed and burned out at Kingswood Church in Dorking, the pilot, *Gefreiter* G. Strasser, having baled out, seriously wounded.

Morton continued,

> After a minute or two I saw two aircraft below me and not being sure that the attacking one was friendly, I investigated. They proved to be a 109 being pursued by a Spitfire. The Spitfire was diving on the 109 and overshot after a short burst and broke away. I waited for him to return but he went right away, so I closed on the 109, which dived for cloud. He had some vapour coming from the fuselage. I gave it a good burst and there was a flood of coolant from the radiators. The E/A appeared very reluctant to enter cloud and we dodged about on top of the cloud layer. I got in one or two short bursts and after a bit the coolant stream became less and the E/A slowed up. It then got into a cloud and I overshot and lost it. On emerging, after about three-quarters of a minute, I observed the E/A going quite slowly on top of cloud 500 yards to starboard. I turned in, but he was immediately dived on by Pilot Officer [Ronald] Berry and went down in flames after a short burst. I returned to base shortly after this as I had fired nearly all my ammunition.

The pilot of this second 109, *Unteroffizier* W. Braatz of 9/JG 54, was killed, his aircraft crashing near Tonbridge.

Flight Lieutenant John Boulter was leading 603 Squadron's Guard Section and attacked the last aircraft in a *Schwarm* of four Me 109s flying in line astern, attempting to form a defensive circle whilst climbing. Initially firing from 'long range', Boulter slowly overtook his target, from which coolant streamed and it slowed up. The Spitfire pilot closed to 'fire an effective burst from 100–50 yards. Bits flew off the aircraft and it caught on fire, did a bunt and dived away inverted'. This combat occurred between Chatham and Rochford, Boulter having hit *Unteroffizier* Ernst Poschenrieder of 7/JG 53 – for whom things had gone awry from the start:

> While taking-off, one of my machine's wheels ran into one of the just-filled bomb craters from the previous night; the aircraft was tossed into the air but immediately came down to earth again as it had not achieved sufficient speed to remain airborne. I lost some time as a result of this and therefore lagged behind the *Gruppe*.
>
> I caught up with my *Staffel* and positioned myself next to my wingman, *Feldwebel* [Hermann] Neuhoff, when the latter advised he was having engine trouble and dived away and headed back. I radioed to ask who would now cover me. *Oberleutnant* [Heinz] Altendorf replied that I should join the first *Schwarm*, but this was 500m higher and soon in combat. Then, over the radio, I heard warning of an attacking fighter – too late, for right away a burst hit one of my radiators, and I was only able to escape from the immediate danger by executing a half-roll and dive. I saw coolant streaming out of the damaged radiator, leaving a white trail behind my machine. It was obvious to me that this would be my last flight and I began preparing for a forced-landing.
>
> As I descended I saw an English fighter climbing towards me – I had heard there were English fighters whose task it was to intercept crippled German aircraft on the way back and shoot them down. I turned towards this aircraft and fired a long burst, scoring several hits, but I could not see what came of it as once again I had to worry about survival. Then I found a small meadow on which I could land. Before I reached it, however, AA guns added to my troubles by scoring a serious hit, and to top it all off I was fired upon by machine-guns as I touched down.

Poschenrieder crashed in Strood, his 109's back being broken as it slewed across the field; the injured German pilot was captured.

Pilot Officer Ronald Berry followed Flight Lieutenant John Boulter into the attack on the 109s: 'I caught one up and after a few short bursts the port wing caught fire and it dived down in flames'. This 109 is believed to have been the 7/JG 51 machine that crashed in Leigh, killing the pilot, *Feldwebel* Kurt Hübel. Afterwards, Berry was separated from his Squadron:

> A few minutes later I saw a 109 on top of a heavy cloud bank and I dived out of the sun and gave it a 5-second burst, closing until I had to break away to avoid collision. The 109 burst into flames and dived and crashed

> near Tonbridge area. On landing I ascertained Pilot Officer Morton of 603 Squadron had previously fired at this 109.

Pilot Officer John Soden, Red 2, followed his leader to attack a *Schwarm* of 109s climbing in line astern (probably the same formation attacked by Boulter), one of which he attacked from below:

> He rolled over on his back and I spun away. He was still diving when I came out of the spin. I followed him through cloud and saw him hit the earth. He was streaming glycol.

The pilot of this 7/JG 51 Me 109, *Unteroffizier* Paul Limpert, was killed, his fighter crashing near Redhill.

Pilot Officer Robert Dewey, who had only joined 603 Squadron three days before, fired his guns in anger for the first time during this engagement, hitting a 109 over Biggin Hill area which

> broke away from the formation and dived, issuing quantities of brownish smoke, losing speed rapidly, as I had difficulty in remaining astern. It then disappeared in the clouds at about 6,000 feet and I did not see it again.

Sergeant Edward Darling also attacked a 109, west of Biggin Hill, observing the enemy aircraft

> turn over and fall into a spin that looked unintentional. Black smoke issuing from his engine as he continued downwards … I then swung round to the right and caught the next nearest in my sights and gave him a three to four second burst at close range. Observed bits of aircraft break off from either tailplane or rudder. He also turned left as I was firing. By this time I was right in amongst them, so dived away and spiraled [*sic*] downwards.

Pilot Officer Basil 'Stapme' Stapleton, a South African, also recorded a success, hitting a 109 from out of the sun which 'put his nose down vertically' and seen by Pilot Officer John Soden to 'crash vertically into the sea'.

No. 603 Squadron suffered no losses and had done exceptionally well in this action.

No. 222 Squadron, also up from Hornchurch, sighted the German bombers and fighters at 13.35 hrs 'South of the Thames'. Squadron Leader John Hill put the Spitfires into line astern and dived to attack the enemy. Pilot Officer Eric Edsall, Green 2, gave a 109 a quick burst before stalking two 109s 'flying above the main formation, away to the West'. Attacking from out of the sun, Edsall hit the second 109:

> Dense black smoke immediately appeared from the engine and started to flame. He went into a vertical dive for the ground through rather thick cloud. No 1 then turned to attack me. I gave him a short burst. The plane shuddered and reeled, my fire going right into the aircraft. I was then attacked by two more 109s and dived for the clouds and evaded them. All E/A had yellow tails and noses.

Edsall claimed one 109 destroyed and a probable. Sergeant Rainford Marland claimed two 109 probables but Sergeant Iain Hutchinson was shot-up and forced-landed, wounded, at Denham; *Oberleutnant* Johannes Steinhoff of 4/JG 52 claimed his fourth victory over Dorking at the material time, which may well have been this Spitfire.

Having left Northolt with initial orders to patrol base, 229 Squadron was then vectored to the Thames Estuary. Whilst en route, '100 Me 109s were seen some 10,000 feet above' [ORB]. The Hurricanes had been spotted by *Oberleutnant* Ulrich Steinhilper of 3/JG 52 over Ashford, who was leading a *Schwarm* of four, his wingman being *Feldwebel* Siegfried 'Sigi' Voss, the second *Rotte* comprising *Feldwebel* Karl Rüttger and *Unteroffizier* Kurt Wolf. After crossing the coast, Steinhilper's *Schwarm* had been authorised to detach from the main formation and fly a *Freie Jagd* over south-east England. Steinhilper remembered that

> having gained plenty of height, we spotted a Squadron of Hurricanes climbing below us, amongst other formations. They were flying in three vic formations in line-astern, very orthodox by our standards. I judged that they must have been somewhat inexperienced and decided to attack. Over the R/T I gave instructions that I would attack the leading formation, [*Feldwebel* Siegfried] Voss the next, [*Feldwebel* Karl] Rüttger and [Kurt] Wolf the third. I was conscious that there were many other formations of enemy aircraft in the area, but we were hungry for action and thought our height and speed would see us through unmolested.
>
> On my order, we dropped into the attack, picking up terrific speed in the dive and dropping below and behind the Hurricanes. From this position we were able to hit them from slightly below with complete surprise. I gave the order to assemble after the attack in a left turn. We were not sure exactly what happened, we think one of the others pressed his transmission button on his radio at the same time as me, but the actual effect was that the first two words of my order were cut off, leaving just the

order to assemble in the left-turn. I went on firing for a good few seconds, sweeping right through the vic formation, not realizing that the others were breaking off almost immediately. They were understandably annoyed that they hadn't been able to press home their attacks, particularly in the light of our shared feelings about the officers who apparently risked all to raise their own personal scores.

There was little time to debate what had happened there and then because some of the other enemy fighters had seen our attack and turned on us with great fury. Our small formation was broken up with Voss and me making it home and Rüttger limping in a little while later. I was witness to Wolf's fate, seeing him hit by numerous shells from a Spitfire, the aircraft beginning to burn immediately.

Unbeknown to Steinhilper and friends, however, Wolf was not dead: possibly shot down by Pilot Officer Eric Edsall of 222 Squadron or Sergeant Ronald Fokes of 92 Squadron, he baled out and was captured with leg wounds, his 109 crashing at Peasmarsh. Steinhilper claimed his fourth victory, a Spitfire, in the clash, which may have been 222 Squadron's Sergeant Iain Hutchinson because 229 Squadron suffered no loss.

The defenders' efforts, however, failed to prevent the bombers reaching London. Bombs were dropped on Staines, Walton-on-Thames and Southall, although around 100 fell on Greenford near Northolt – this being more than on any previous raid on London since 15 September 1940. Great damage was caused to civilian property, but no military objectives were hit, this suggesting that the actually intended target may have been the Brooklands aircraft factory at Weybridge, the thick coverings of cloud perhaps confusing the German bombardiers. After the bombardment, the Germans turned for home and another running battle back to France began.

Pilot Officer Victor Ortmans, a Belgian, sighted the retreating Dorniers 'out to sea' and broke away from 229 Squadron, which continued patrolling as ordered with 1 (RCAF) Squadron, and pursued the enemy:

I first attacked a Me 109 which was on the tail of a Spitfire which was going for the bombers. After a short beam attack I gave four short bursts from astern. The Me 109 gave up any attempt at evasive action or attack and went into a steep dive with black smoke pouring from its engine.

I then attacked a Do 215 [*sic*] from astern with a 4–5 second burst from 200 yards, closing to 100 yards. The rear-gunner returned my fire. Two Me 109s caused me to break away and on returning I saw the Do 215 had left the formation and was going down in a 30° dive. I went in again

> from astern, opening fire at 200 yards and closing to point blank range. The starboard engine was in flames and the port engine stopped when the rear-gunner put a burst into my tank and I was covered in oil and could not see. By this time the E/A was only about twelve feet from the sea. I made my way back to the coast and forced-landed on the beach at Lydd. The Coastguards reported that they had seen four bombers crash into the sea.

The Northolt Wing was vectored to Dungeness, but for some unknown reason the rest of 229 Squadron and 1 (RCAF) Squadron failed to engage. The Poles of 303 (Polish) Squadron, however, were flying behind and below those two squadrons, at 14,000ft, and sighted the Dorniers heading towards the coast

> in close herring bone formation of nines escorted by Me 109s above, and rearguard was in vic of three *ketten* [author's note: the basic section of three aircraft around which German bomber formations were based, see Appendix].

When the wing showed no inclination to engage, 303 (Polish) Squadron broke away, like 229 Squadron's Pilot Officer Victor Ortmans, and gave chase. Catching up, 303 (Polish) Squadron's 'A' Flight attacked the bombers from behind and above.

Flying Officer Witold Urbanowicz, Yellow 1:

> After the second attack two E/A broke away from their formation. One, smoking, fell into the sea. The other was attacked by our fighters and also fell into the sea, smoking. Over the Channel I noticed a Do 215 [*sic*] slowly making its way to France. I attacked and fired three bursts from the rear and above … without result. E/A only lost height. Then two fighters appeared above the bomber. Thinking that they were ours I joined them in order to attack the bomber together. Getting close to them I discovered that they were two Me 109s protecting the bomber together. From a distance of about 50 yards I fired a burst at one of them. Next, I fired a longer burst at the other Me, which did not smoke or burst into flames but immediately dived headlong into the sea. I again attacked the bomber from a distance of 30 yards to the rear, and fired once more without result. I continued the attack and E/A, which was now over France, made as if to land, hit the ground with its right wing and burst into flames. None of the crew got out. I noticed that the enemy bombers flew in close formation the whole of the way to France and at great speed. Me's circled over the bombers in ones and twos.

Sergeant Jerzy Radomski was also attacked the bombers with Yellow Section, being joined by a Spitfire which flew away after the bomber's left engine was stopped: 'E/A fell into the sea about fifteen miles from Dungeness'.

Sergeant Stanislaw Karubin, Red 2:

> attacked one Me from below, firing short bursts. E/A began to smoke, then burst into flames and fell earthwards towards the clouds [author's note: 10/10ths]. Next, I chased the bomber formation towards the coast but could not get within range. I saw two enemy bombers break formation and dive to earth.

Heading home, Radomski was then surprised by an explosion in his engine – having been hit by cannon fire from an unseen Me 109, possibly by *Oberleutnant* Franz Götz of 9/JG 53, who claimed a 'Spitfire' destroyed over Dungeness at the material time (all of the Germans claims were for Spitfires in this early afternoon raid). Radomski himself describes events:

> the whole aircraft began to tremble and smoke, and flames issued from the exhausts; so thick was the smoke that in the cockpit that I was unable to take any reading from the instruments. As I was over the Channel at a height of 2,500 feet I decided not to jump. I closed the throttle, turned off the petrol, and switched off the engine and side-slipped as the smoke was blinding me. I glided and side-slipped as far as the coast and landed on shingles without my undercarriage. From the moment of switching off my engine and petrol, smoke and flames continued to issue from my exhausts.

Radomski, who was unhurt, forced-landed on the beach at Lydd; 303 (Polish) Squadron recorded no other loss.

No. 41 Squadron's Pilot Officer Henry Baker, the first defending pilot to sight the enemy, was also now in action over the coast:

> At the end of my patrol, I saw one Me 109 going for home with a slight glycol leak. I attacked the 109 and it dived towards the sea. I again attacked it and it went into the sea about ten miles SW of Dungeness. Two boats turned out towards the wreck.

Other 41 Squadron pilots had also chased the Germans to the coast. Pilot Officer Peter Brown followed 'Mitor Leader', Flight Lieutenant Norman Ryder, to the attack the rear section of Dorniers off Dungeness:

> fired three bursts into No 2 of rear section – heavy black smoke from port engine, but when I broke away, the E/A was still in the enemy formation. Slight fire from top rear-gunner.

Off Hastings, Flying Officer Tony Lovell also damaged a Do 17 but was hit with cannon fire from a 109 and crash-landed his seriously damaged Spitfire back at Hornchurch. Three miles south of Dungeness, Sergeant Robert Beardsley attacked a Do 17 several times, leaving its starboard engine smoking and which was last seen 'in the uninterrupted glide ten miles from the French coast'. Years later, Beardsley recalled that after engaging that Dornier,

> I followed him down over the Channel to 5,000 feet where I spotted a Me 109 solo, going home below me. I tucked in behind and fired my remaining ammunition – when he reached about 1,000 feet he rolled onto his back and dived towards the sea. However, at this stage I was closer to France than England and on turning north again was horrified to spot six Me 109s behind me as I turned for the coast on the horizon! I managed to evade by popping in and out of small clouds at 2,000 feet but one persistent fellow chased me back to within sight of Hythe and hit me with cannon shells, one of which broke the throttle linkage, but luckily the engine continued at full power (where it had been for some time!). I had no radio or hydraulics and the engine was now smoking and clanking. I, however, was praying as hard as I ever had. At 1,000 feet I was hit again and the engine packed up.
>
> I could see Hawkinge on the cliffs and reckoned I could just about make it when a lone Hurricane of a Polish squadron flew towards me and scared the 109 pilot off. I blew down my undercarriage (no flaps) and stretched my glide and, my prayers being answered, made a good landing inside the fence! The Station Fire Engine followed. I stood on the wing root and jumped off, the Spit continuing, pursued by the Fire Engine! As I walked to the Control Tower a He 111 flew slowly over the airfield at 1,000 feet on the way home. The Bofors gunners were firing frantically some ½ mile behind, knowing nothing about deflection shooting, and I was hopping up and down, swearing heartily as he disappeared towards France!

No. 41 Squadron suffered no other casualty.

No. 92 Squadron's Pilot Officer Desmond Williams, Green 1, had climbed to Angels 15 after the Spitfires broke up following their initial attack on Me 109s over Maidstone and orbited Hawkinge. Sure enough, at 14.15 hrs Pilot Officer Dennis Williams saw the German fighters and bombers approaching, flying south on their homeward journey. 'In company with four or five other

Hurricanes and Spitfires', he engaged the Dorniers, which dived from 15,000 to 5,000ft. Williams watched 'one of the 215s [*sic*] drop out of the formation with an amount of smoke coming from its engines' but he was then attacked himself by 109s as the Germans, now mid-Channel, turned east, towards Calais. The '109 trouble' proved 'too hot' so Williams broke off and landed at Hawkinge.

Eventually, it was all over. The RAF fighters had done extremely well, although, again, it seems that German records, contrary to popular belief, are incomplete because so far as can be ascertained from the evidence available, just one Do 17 of 8/KG 3 is recorded as having failed to return from this mission, whilst four more of II and III/KG 3 crash-landed back in France with combat damage. From the RAF pilots' combat reports, however, there seems no doubt that more than one bomber went into the Channel. Nonetheless and overall, the Me 109s had succeeded in largely protecting the bombers but at a cost: of some 150 Me 109s on this mission, from eight *Gruppen*, twelve were destroyed; of these, three pilots were killed and eight were now POWs. Striking is the ease with which damaged 109s streamed glycol – coolant, without which the engine would overheat, the aircraft only going one place: down. Indeed, the underwing-mounted twin radiators were the 109's weak spot, and a damaged radiator could not be isolated by the pilot – a definite design fault. Conversely, no RAF fighters were destroyed or any pilots killed, missing or wounded – just three Spitfires and two Hurricanes damaged. The Germans, however, substantially overclaimed on this occasion, filing claims for nineteen British fighters destroyed – all Spitfires and another example of 'Spitfire Snobbery'.

There would, however, be no respite on this day of intensified fighting. In what transpired to be the Germans' last major daylight assault of the Battle of Britain, three more attacks were to be made – simultaneously – with a view to overwhelming the defences. All three threats were detected by RDF at 15.45 hrs: to the east, a similar attack to the morning's raid on the Surrey aircraft factories, involving Ju 88s of KG 77 escorted by many Me 109s, 180 aircraft in all. *Luftflotte* 3 sent eleven Ju 88's of I/KG 51 to Southampton, which was actually a feint to conceal the day's major attack: thirty-nine I and II/KG 55 He 111s, escorted by a large force of JG 2 Me 109s and ZG 26 Me 110s, were to hit Westland Aircraft at Yeovil. Having mounted their unsuccessful mission to Liverpool the previous evening, I/KG 55 was left off the battle order. Considering the resounding successes at Filton on 25 September 1940, and Southampton the following day, KG 55 was doubtless reasonably confident of success. Each of these raids will be dealt with separately – the latter in great detail.

For some reason, RDF warning of the eastern raid was short, the first two defending squadrons, 41 and 603, at Hornchurch, only scrambling as the enemy were incoming over the coast. The two Spitfire squadrons were initially ordered to Maidstone at 25,000ft but fortunately common sense prevailed: realising that such an order placed these squadrons in grave danger of being bounced by high-flying Me 109s whilst still climbing, the controller instead ordered them to climb over base before proceeding south of the Thames. By 16.15 hrs, the Germans had reached Tonbridge, and it was only then that further squadrons took-off: the Biggin Hill Wing, 66, 72 and 92 Squadrons, to patrol base at 25,000ft (although 72 Squadron was late getting off so was unable to join with the others as instructed), and the Northolt Wing, 1 (RCAF), 229 and 303 (Polish) Squadrons also went off to patrol base, at 20,000ft.

After gaining height, the Hornchurch Spitfires flew south-west, 41 Squadron encountering a large number of enemy fighters over Biggin Hill at 16.30 hrs, an unknown pilot apparently claiming a 'He 113 [*sic*]' [ORB] probably destroyed (no other details known). No. 603 Squadron was at 25,000ft above cloud over the Biggin Hill area, Flight Lieutenant John Haig, commanding 'A' Flight, reported carrying out 'a diving attack' from in front on one vic of three Me 109s but saw no result before repeating the process on another three:

> On looking round after breaking away, I saw one Me 109 diving steeply away from the formation with white glycol streaming out. I did not follow the aircraft down.

Over Farnborough, Pilot Officer Peter Dexter followed Flight Lieutenant John Boulter to attack

> a large number of Me 109s flying at about 25,000 feet. I did not fire on my first dive but on coming out at 15,000 feet found myself among about twelve Me 109s, one of whom dived down. I fired at him from the rear and saw my bullets enter his wings. The 109 rose suddenly, seemed to stall and then spun away into the clouds.

The Spitfire pilot then lost his target in 'a thick haze' and claimed a probable.

At 16.45 hrs, Group Captain Stanley Vincent AFC, the station commander at Northolt, was also in action over Farnborough:

> I was climbing over Northolt to watch the Northolt Wing in action, and saw, approximately five miles SW and West of base, streamers from very high enemy fighters. When at 20,000 feet I saw approaching from the South a formation of about eighteen He 111s [*sic*] at approx. 17,000 feet with a very large number of Me 109s on each side, above and behind, mostly about 2,000 feet above the bombers.

> I was therefore able to carry out a head-on attack on the bombers, breaking away below, and then one from vertically below and stalling away. I was unable to see any possible result owing to the Me 109s. The bombers then turned back to the South.

Group Captain Stanley Vincent continued,

> I climbed upwards towards the sun and tried to attack a Me 109 but had to leave it owing to others coming down onto me from above, but I saw three Me 109s chasing a Hurricane at right angles to me from left to right, and when the Hurricane dived away (straightening out 5,000 feet below) and the Me's turned back on their course, I was able to get in a good position on the tail of the third one. Before I opened fire I saw No 1 burst into flames and the pilot jump out in a parachute; he had obviously been shot down by No 2 who was close in astern of him.
>
> I then gave one very short burst of about one second at No 3 at about 200 yards and immediately pieces came off from the port side of his fuselage, and he burst into flames, half-rolled and the pilot jumped – He [*sic*] would come down, I estimate, to the South of Farnborough. I could not then see No 2 as my attention was diverted by the two parachutes. All 109s had light blue undersurfaces and dull blue-grey mottle top surfaces with black crosses on fuselage.

This was some achievement for a 43-year-old who had also destroyed three German aircraft during the First World War and damaged a Do 17 on 15 September 1940. The two Me 109 pilots who took to their parachutes in this action were *Hauptmann* Walter Kienzle of *Stab* JG 26, who was flying as *Major* Adolf Galland's wingman and being assed as a potential *Gruppenkommandeur*, and who was captured seriously wounded, landing at Haslemere, and *Leutnant* Hans Schmidt of 6/JG 27, who was captured unhurt, also at Haslemere.

Flight Lieutenant Gordon McGregor was leading 1 (RCAF) Squadron,

> [which was] flying lead to (Northolt) Wing with standing orders to engage fighter screen. On vector 155 at 20,000, sighted bomber formation of approx. twenty-five with fighter escort above and behind of about forty Me 109s. About half the Me 109s dove to attack. I held course through this attack, then turned and engaged a 109 which was attacking a Hurricane. Hurricane broke right and 109 turned left, where I opened fire. Towards end of full burst he streamed smoke and spun down through clouds South of Brooklands.

Pilot Officer De Peyster Douw Brown claimed a Me 109 damaged but during the combat his port aileron was hit, causing his Hurricane to nose over upon return to Northolt; the pilot was unhurt and the Canadian squadron suffered no further casualties.

At 16.50 hrs, Squadron Leader Arthur Banham led 229 Squadron into action over Woking:

> in a quarter head-on attack on the first section of bombers and then gave a long burst into one of the Ju 88s at the back. He dropped behind the formation and turned in the opposite direction with glycol streaming from the port engine. Four of five Me 109s then distracted my attention.

Pilot Officer Ronald Bary:

> followed my CO and when he broke away I attacked the Ju 88 from astern. The rear-gunner did not reply and E/A suddenly pulled up its port wing and then straightened out, steadily losing height and with white fumes pouring from his port engine. One of my cowlings came adrift and I had to retire.

The Ju 88 was claimed as damaged. Pilot Officer Lewis Way, however, was shot down by *Major* Adolf Galland and baled out unhurt, and Sergeant Claude Hodson, a Rhodesian, was shot-up and forced-landed, injuring his nose.

No. 303 (Polish) Squadron had left Northolt fifteen minutes after 1 (RCAF) and 229 Squadrons, so climbed at full boost in an attempt to catch up. 'A' and 'B' Flights became separated and neither caught up with the wing. 'A' Flight was attacked over Brooklands and broken up by Me 109s, one of which was claimed as destroyed by Flying Officer Witold Urbanowicz (unfortunately no combat report survives), but, even for the gallant Poles, the 'odds were too great' and 'cloud cover alone saved heavy casualties' [ORB]. 'B' Flight headed for the German formation, which was over Croydon and heading south-east; Sergeant Marian Belc saw a Hurricane being attacked by three Me 109s and hastened to the aid of 229 Squadron's Pilot Officer Way, who baled out – after 'seeing him safe', Belc returned to base. No. 303 (Polish) Squadron's Czech ace, Sergeant Josef František, had experienced difficulty starting his engine, so had taken off alone:

> After taking off I flew in a SE direction. Flying above the clouds I noticed a large number of planes and in that moment six Me 109s made to attack me. I looped in order to meet them, but they formed a circle and I circled

> within theirs. One E/A came out of line slightly and I fired a burst. E/A began to circle to earth. I followed and again fired from the left side. E/A burst into flames and fell to earth. I then fired at another in the circle, and saw him smoke, but falling into clouds myself I could not find them again and returned to Northolt.

In addition to the two Me 109s pilots abandoned, *Oberleutnant* Karl Fischer of 7/JG 27 was also shot down – by whom it is impossible to be certain but Boulter and Exeter of 603 Squadron, and McGregor of 1 (RCAF) are all contenders. Hit in the radiator and petrol tank, Fischer elected to forced-land near Queen Anne's Gate at Windsor Great Park, where his aircraft overturned; the pilot was captured unhurt and his aircraft was subsequently shown at various locations promoting the Spitfire Fund.

Flight Lieutenant Ken Gillies was 'Fibus Leader' and led his 66 Squadron up to 27,500ft over the Biggin Hill area and pounced on five Me 109s below at 23,000ft. Flight Lieutenant Bob Oxspring lost sight of Gillies in the sun, so 'didn't get a shot in'. 'Oxo' then saw three Spitfires, which he presumed belonged to 92 Squadron, attacking a formation of twelve bombers. Owing to his high-speed, however, the Spitfire pilot realised that he could only manage a fleeting shot at the Germans, so instead attacked escorting Me 109s to port:

> I let them fly through a fairly short burst. No 3 of the Section broke away, doing roughly a steep climb and a half-roll I came down again on this 109's tail from above. Another short burst resulted in white, then black smoke, then finally fire from underneath the fuselage at approximately the wing root. Aircraft dived away steeply towards clouds, still in flames, and disappeared.

Oxspring was most likely the man responsible for the demise of 9/JG 26's *Gefreiter* Helmut Hornatschek, who was killed, his 109 exploding, wreckage falling to earth at a variety of locations around Canterbury.

Flight Lieutenant Ken Gillies and his wingman, Pilot Officer Hugh Heron, chased two Me 109s which were heading for the south coast, attacking simultaneously over Horsham.

Flight Lieutenant Ken Gillies reported,

> On my first burst of fire, E/A shuddered violently and began to stream grey vapour. E/A then began a diving turn and I fired again. By this time the E/A was over the coast of Brighton and rapidly losing height. I then ran out of ammunition and waited only to see E/A crash in water before

> taking evasive action from another 109, which was about to dive on me from above.

This German pilot was *Gefreiter* Helmut Ziemens of 7/JG 26, who was also killed.

No. 92 Squadron had joined up with 66 Squadron as ordered.

Flight Lieutenant Allan Wright reported,

> The Biggin Hill R/T was very bad and they gave us little information. We were patrolling at 25,000 feet above 10/10ths cloud when we met about seven Me 109s. They made some dummy attacks on the Squadron so we stuck together. Then I saw about fifteen bombers at 15,000 feet, heading SSE. I called to Ganic Leader that they were there and broke away to attack.

Wright was forced to abandon his attack on the bombers when 109s interfered, so the Spitfire pilot broke away and climbed to 20,000ft, up sun:

> I came across another group of seven Me 109s behind the bombers and attacked the rearmost with a 2-second burst from starboard beam. He broke away and dived but I continued to attack with the remainder of my ammunition. Glycol streamed from his radiator and he crossed the coast, descending to sea-level. I was interested to see how long he could still fly so I followed him until he landed in the sea and sank. He had continued to fly for about seven minutes.

Wright had shot down 1/JG 52's *Leutnant* Kurt Kirchner off Newhaven, who was captured.

Wright continued,

> I at once turned for home but although I had kept a very good look-out I was surprised by two Me 109s who hit me with several cannon shots and bullets from astern. I myself was struck in the right thigh by pieces of burst cannon shot. Another had pierced my starboard wing, wheel and flap. My tail was useless but I managed to get back and landed OK, at Shoreham, after finding that Wilmington was obstructed.

Wright was admitted to Southlands Hospital in Shoreham. Two pilots of 3/JG 27, *Leutnant* Heinz Schmidt and *Oberleutnant* Gerhard Homuth, claimed Spitfires destroyed south of Eastbourne.

No. 92 Squadron's Sergeant Don Kingaby

> encountered two 109s at 8,000 feet North of Lewes and carried out a quarter attack on the leader. I gave him a 4-second burst and heavy black smoke came from his engine. The other 109 attacked me and I broke off the combat.

Kingaby claimed the 109 as damaged.

Pilot Officer John Drummond, Yellow 1, of 92 Squadron, was patrolling with the squadron at 27,000ft north-west of Brighton at 17.00 hrs. Fifty Me 109s lurked in the sky above, but the Spitfires went into line astern to attack fifteen withdrawing bombers 10,000ft below:

> On the way down I encountered two Me 109s, I fired a burst at the leader and broke away. I saw two Me 109s at 20,000 feet and attacked from the quarter and below, firing a 4-second burst at 350 yards.
>
> White smoke came from the exhausts of the 109 and he began to lose height. I was attacked by two more 109s, fired one burst and broke away downwards.

Significantly, Drummond added that 'I last saw the damaged 109 losing height in the direction of Beachy Head'. Claimed as a probable, this was actually the 4/JG 26 machine of *Unteroffizier* Horst Perez, who forced-landed his virtually intact but overheating 109 on Crapham Down, a hillside at East Dean, just inland of Beachy Head (and which can be seen today preserved at the Imperial War Museum, Duxford).

No. 72 Squadron, also of the Biggin Hill Wing, reported 'several groups of Me 109s' flying

> NNW at 23,000 feet. Squadron attacked E/A in line astern and the enemy then climbed and returned the attack in a half-hearted manner, firing from extreme range and then climbed away.

An unknown member of 72 Squadron claimed a 109 probably destroyed. Apart from 92 Squadron's Flight Lieutenant Allan Wright being shot-up, the Biggin Hill squadrons suffered no other loss.

No. 501 Squadron was also up on patrol, having left Gravesend at 16.35 hrs. Ordered to 20,000ft, Sergeant Paul Farnes remained with the squadron until 14,000ft was reached, but because his hood was jammed fully open, by that height the pilot was so cold that he decided to return to base. Descending through cloud west-south-west of Gatwick when, 8 miles north of there, Farnes sighted a lone Ju 88 flying south which was diving fast, trailing white smoke, having clearly already been damaged. Farnes gave chase and at 4,000ft over Gatwick the German tuned towards his pursuer, a head on attack ensuing:

> continuing firing till I broke away twenty yards behind his tail. I turned to make another attack but could not see him. At that moment I saw several vehicles driving across Gatwick aerodrome, and looking in the direction they were going I saw that the E/A had crash-landed on Gatwick racecourse. After the combat I landed at Gatwick Aerodrome and was informed by eye-witnesses that after my attack both engines had caught fire, emitting black smoke, and the E/A forced-landed immediately after.

This was, however, the only Ju 88 brought down during this raid, and was possibly the bomber previously damaged by 229 Squadron over Woking. Belonging to 2/KG 77 three of the crew were captured wounded at 16.45 hrs, the fourth man having been killed.

Once again, despite excellent fighter protection, the Germans failed to inflict any damage to the aircraft factories or any other military target: around seventy bombs were dropped, exploding harmlessly in a marshy area near Marlow. Air Vice-Marshal Keith Park was certainly satisfied with the result, and especially pleased with 603 Squadron's performance, which he signalled:

> Group Commander sends warm congratulations to 603 Squadron on their successful fighting without casualties to themselves, showing exceptional leadership and straight shooting.

This was high and well-deserved praise for one of the very best Spitfire squadrons in Fighter Command.

To the west, concurrent with the violent events occurring over the south-east, there was more action. The feint on Southampton was also detected at 15.45 hrs, the approach of eleven Ju 88s of I/KG 51 being picked up when 50 miles south of The Needles. Just two minutes later the Spitfires of 602 Squadron scrambled from Westhampnett to patrol Selsey Bill at 15,000ft, being diverted to patrol over the Isle of Wight. When 5 miles east of Bembridge, the Ju 88s were sighted at 13,000ft and approaching from the South. Surprisingly, the raid was unescorted. Squadron Leader Alexander 'Sandy' Johnstone, Red 1, was leading 602 Squadron and ordered individual attacks before himself attacking the rearmost Ju 88 from out of the sun. Leaving the bomber trailing black smoke from both engines, Johnstone attacked another Ju 88 without result, damaged a third, stopping the enemy's starboard engine. The German then disappeared in cloud:

> I later saw E/A come below cloud, travelling South, some distance to the southward of me. I gave chase and fired a final burst from below and astern and saw this E/A turn sharply to starboard and dive into the sea from a height of 2,000 feet.

This was 3 miles east of Bembridge.

Pilot Officer Osgood Hanbury, Red 2 and 'Villa Leader', followed his CO into the attack. Firing at a bomber in the middle of the formation, Hanbury stopped its port engine:

> He dived below clouds and I followed him, making attacks from all quarters until I had finished my ammunition. Flying in front of him I saw him turn back towards our coast and followed him until he crashed about half a mile South of Selsey Bill. No survivors. Pilot Officer [Allen] Edy confirmed seeing aircraft in water.

Sergeant Andrew McDowell, Green 1, was in the last Spitfire to attack, having first ensured that there really were no German fighters present. Picking out a straggling Ju 88, which he chased into cloud, throttling right back and flying slower than the enemy bomber, McDowell opened fire and watched 'this E/A break into pieces in mid-air and dive into the sea seven miles South of Selsey Bill'. Then,

> After watching my first E/A crash into the sea, I climbed up again and saw a second Ju 88 appear out of the clouds with one engine stopped and the propeller feathered. E/A saw me when about 500 yards off and tried to climb back into the cloud. I fired at one the motor which was still working and stopped it. E/A then stalled and dived straight into the sea.

The second Ju 88 attacked by McDowell was probably that also claimed by Squadron Leader Alexander Johnstone, this combat also having taken place 3 miles east of Bembridge.

Pilot Officer Archibald Lyall, Blue 1, attacked a Ju 88 in the rearmost *Kette*, watching his tracer ammunition 'entering the nose of the machine and starboard motor'. The bomber then descended to 500ft above the clouds and 'fall into a slow left-hand spiral and disappear into clouds out of control at about 8,000 feet'. The Spitfire pilot, considering the Ju 88 probably destroyed left it to its fate and sought fresh targets. The enemy formation, in the face of this interception by 602 Squadron, abandoned their mission to bomb Southampton and turned about for France, flying south-east. Lyall followed, catching five Ju 88s 'in a straggly formation', and attacked the last of these, scoring hits and exhausting his ammunition:

> On breaking away I observed an explosion just behind the rear-gunner and there was a cloud of black smoke. E/A fell behind formation and began losing height slowly. I followed it at a distance as long as possible and broke off when I was about forty miles South of Beachy Head. E/A was 7,000 feet when I attacked and had lost height to 3,000 feet when I left.

Lyall was credited with one probable Ju 88 and another damaged.

Sergeant Basil Whall, Blue 2, attacked the last Ju 88 but one from the formation's end and saw the port engine stop as it dived into cloud – this doubtless being the same aircraft later attacked below cloud by McDowell. Whall then attacked another bomber

> head-on and saw entire glass nose shatter. When he last saw this E/A it was still flying straight and level, as a well-trimmed aircraft will when one takes one's hands and feet off the controls, but he almost certainly wounded all of the crew, and the damage done to the E/A was so great that he thinks it was probably destroyed.

Again, this diversionary raid, apart from tying down a Spitfire squadron, achieved nothing – and that it was unescorted is astonishing. Here, though, we have irrefutable evidence that Luftwaffe loss records are incomplete, contrary to what some consider a virtual irrebuttable presumption that they are. These records are not for propaganda purposes but internal audit – but repeatedly throughout the course of this new narrative there are examples of RAF pilots definitely seeing German aircraft crash into the sea but no record of such losses existing in Luftwaffe documents. These are not cases of multiple pilots attacking and claiming the same enemy aircraft destroyed or mistaking what they were seeing – and this is one such case. In this combat, one Ju 88 was clearly shot down by Johnstone off Bembridge, one by Pilot Officer Hanbury half a mile off Selsey Bill, and another by McDowell 7 miles south of there; McDowell also claimed another destroyed, off Bembridge, although this is likely to have been the same Ju 88 claimed by Johnstone. Either way, it is clear that 602 Squadron destroyed at least three and possibly four Ju 88s, in addition to damaging others and turning the raid about. According to German loss records, however, only one Ju 88 is detailed as lost, a machine of 1/KG 51, which apparently crashed 'three miles off Beachy Head'. It is impossible, therefore, to rationally and realistically conclude anything other than the demonstrable fact that German records are wrong in this case.

From 602 Squadron's perspective, this was an entirely successful action and another example of the folly of sending unescorted bombers to attack Britain. The squadron's only casualty was Canadian Pilot Officer John Hart's Spitfire being hit by a Ju 88's fire, although he returned safely to base and was unhurt; a Spitfire was claimed destroyed by *Unteroffizier* Schlig of 1/KG 51 '15km South of Insel Wight, 3,000m'.

This action off the Isle of Wight and Selsey Bill was fought at 16.15 hrs – but a much bigger raid was now halfway over the central Channel and heading for Portland Bill. This was, in fact, the day's major raid: target Westland Aircraft, a mission allocated to KG 55, now doubt emboldened by the highly successful raids on the BAC on 25 September 1940, and the following day's devasting attack on Supermarine at Woolston.

Earlier in the day KG 55's operations officer, *Major* Dr Ernst Kiihl, had liaised with the *Wetterstelle* (Meteorological Office), and in the *Kartenstelle* (map room) had prepared an operational order for the attack Westland at Yeovil. Kiihl was an artillery officer during the First World War and had not learned to fly until he was 44. At the age of 52, a veteran of many bombing missions during the Battle of Britain, he now proposed to participate in the attack on Westland. His plan was transmitted from the *Gefechsständ* (command post) by teleprinter to the I and II *Gruppenkommandeurs*, *Major* Joachim Roeber and *Major* Friedrich Kless – the latter having received the *Ritterkreuz* for his leadership of the Supermarine raid. Four He 111s of the *Geschwaderstabstaffel* were to lead the attack, each carrying fifteen SC250 HE bombs. No. I *Gruppe* was to supply 16 bombers carrying a total of 76 SC250s and II *Gruppe*'s 23 He 111s were to be the fire raisers with 8 SC500s, 131 SC250s and 15 Flamm SC250s. In total, therefore, the formation was to carry 245 bombs. The forty-three He 111s were to assemble over Normandy, then proceed to Cherbourg and rendezvous with their fighter escort provided by *Jafü* 3: forty-seven Me 109s of JG 2, eight of JG 53 and forty Me 110s of ZG 26. The entire formation was then to steer for Portland Bill before advancing inland just over 20 miles to Yeovil.

RDF detected the approaching raid of '100+', seen as two distinct plots designated '163' and '165'. The first defending 10 Group squadron to be scrambled was 238, at 16.00 hrs, from Chilbolton, the nine Hurricanes of Blue, Green and Yellow Sections, led by Flight Lieutenant Michael Robinson, ordered to patrol the Worth Matravers Line. Robinson, Blue 1, led the Hurricanes on course, below the cloud, which he reported as being '10/10ths at 4,000', before climbing up through it. The ground controller informed Robinson that the enemy were approaching from the south-east, so the Hurricanes turned westwards and climbed. When 15–20 miles south of Portland, at 16.20 hrs, Blue 1 sighted the enemy formation 3,000ft below, at 15,000ft, heading north. No. 238 Squadron was up sun and in an ideal tactical position. Robinson led the Hurricanes into a head-on attack, himself delivering a continuous burst of fire as he dived through the leading *Kette* of Heinkels. After the initial charge, Flying Officer Bob Doe, Yellow 1 – posted from 234 Squadron only the previous day to command 238 Squadron's 'A' Flight – attacked a He 111 from 150 yards, below and behind, setting the bomber's starboard engine alight, its undercarriage dropping. Doe was then forced to break away when the fighter escort intervened. Losing his assailants, Doe then found another Heinkel, swiftly setting its port engine alight. The KG 55 pilot dived towards the thick clouds before turning back towards England when just above them. Yellow 1 gave chase, the rear enemy gunner returning fire. After emptying his remaining ammunition into the damaged Heinkel, Doe watched his target crash into the sea some 15 miles off Portland. Doe's aircraft had not escaped unscathed, however, and during the return flight to Middle Wallop his Hurricane vibrated strangely. Upon landing it was discovered that a bullet had split one of the Hurricane's three laminated wooden propeller blades.

No. 238 Squadron's Sergeant Jiří Kučera, Yellow 3, had also fired at an He 111 on the squadron's first pass, but was attacked by an Me 110 so broke away. Kučera then selected another Heinkel, which he attacked from astern, closing from 300–100 yards. Smoke poured from one engine and that bomber also plunged into the sea. There were no parachutes. Sergeant Józef Jeka, Green 3, attacked an Me 110 from the rear, but a *Schwarm* of Me 109s intervened. When Jeka broke away, the 110 was in a gentle southerly glide, pouring smoke from its starboard engine.

In this initial interception by 10 Group, 238 Squadron claimed two Me 110s and two He 111s destroyed, and a 109 probable; the squadron suffered no loss.

At 16.08 hrs, twelve Spitfires from Squadron Leader Peter Devitt's 152 Squadron had scrambled from Warmwell, followed two minutes later by six Hurricanes from Boscombe Down's 56 Squadron, led by Squadron Leader Herbert 'Pinners' Pinfold. Both squadrons arrived, over Portland and Lyme Bay respectively, at 16.30 hrs.

Pinfold, Red 1 and 'Baffin Leader', had climbed 56 Squadron slightly to the west of Portland Bill to get up sun. When at 16,000ft and flying due south, 'Pinners' sighted 'God knows how many Do 215s [*sic*] and Me 110s', the bombers being at 19,000ft with the escorting fighters 5,000ft above and behind. All the bombers appeared to open fire simultaneously on 56 Squadron, so Pinfold climbed the squadron up to 19,000 feet – but as the Hurricanes attacked the bombers from behind, the enemy fighters came down. Pinfold attacked a Heinkel but a bullet from the *Gruppenkeil's* combined firepower hit his Hurricane and glycol fumes filled the cockpit. Red 1 broke off the engagement, and later remembered,

> With the cockpit full of glycol fumes do I bale out over the sea or land on it? I then saw a small 'hole' in the cloud to the North. I throttled right back, opened the cockpit hood and glided towards it, keeping an eye on the engine temperature which was slowly going up due to loss of coolant. When over the 'hole' I was delighted to see land, and even more so to see Warmwell airfield where I executed a 'dead-stick' landing. Subsequent inspection revealed no damage to the aircraft or engine other than a few bullet holes in the fuselage and glycol tank, which was just in front of the cockpit. Lucky me!

Pilot Officer Frederick Higginson last saw Pinfold's target 'going downwards with both engines streaming black smoke'.

Sergeant Peter Robinson, Red 2, attacked a He 111 and saw smoke coming from its starboard engine as tracer suddenly whipped around him from behind. He broke right and saw another bomber heading south, streaming glycol from one engine. As Robinson approached, a Hurricane attacked the raider, which was losing height, so he attacked after the first British fighter had broken away. His ammunition exhausted, Robinson watched the other Hurricane return and attack again before the Heinkel reached the safety of nearby cloud.

Flight Lieutenant Richard Brooker was leading 'B' Flight's Green Section. As Pinfold's fighters attacked the enemy from out of the sun, the section flying in front of Green attacked some Me 110s, but Brooker successfully led his fighters to the bombers' rear. Green 1 selected a target and fired in one long burst. A large section of cowling broke away, and the Heinkel throttled right back, causing the Hurricane to overshot. The rear gunner, however, put a bullet through Brooker's petrol tank, which thankfully did not ignite.

Sergeant Peter Fox was in action with 56 Squadron for the first time:

> I was 19 years of age, had flown Hurricanes for twenty hours but just couldn't believe it when I saw the enemy, which I understood to be a 60+ raid of Heinkels and their fighter escort. I had never seen so many aircraft together before. As far as I knew, we of 56 Squadron would be attacking the bombers whilst a Spitfire squadron engaged the enemy fighters. Tally Ho! My mouth felt very dirty tasting with apprehension. We gained height going out to sea, and then curved down and round into attack the Heinkels which were going towards the English coastline. One or more of ours went

to attack the enemy leaders, and others the rear. I selected one of the latter, aimed first at one engine, pressed the gun button and sprayed across to the other. I did not see any return fire, but suddenly the Heinkel started to slow down and slowly peel off to port. I started to follow him down, still firing, when there was an explosion and I saw there was very little left of my instrument panel. I had been advised by an 'old-timer' to fly with my hood open when in action as bullets could damage it and prevent it sliding back. Luckily, I had followed this advice – otherwise my head would have been blown off as the shell hit the canopy. I broke to starboard, pulling upwards and away, with all controls seemingly working correctly.

I got over land at about 3,000 feet and was wondering whether I would make Warmwell when I saw flames coming up between my legs. I don't think I even thought of my next action, but turned the kite upside down, released my harness, and saw my feet way above me and the plane above my feet, presumably stalled. Where was the rip cord? I told myself to calm down, as I remembered a film where a German was shown dead on the ground with fingernail marks where he had clawed at his ripcord when his parachute had not opened. I also recall remembering that someone had told me that three or six, or some number, should be counted before pulling the cord. My hand went to the metal 'D' ring, all was forgotten about counting and I pulled! I had never pulled a rip cord before, never seen one pulled, never seen a parachute packed, and never had any instruction. The 'D' ring was flung into the air followed by some wire. Obviously, I'd broken it. Whether my hands moved towards the parachute strapped to my backside or not I'll never know, but my thoughts were that I had to open the pack somehow, when I felt the small tug of the pilot 'chute, followed almost immediately by the full wrench of the main parachute. I was safe! The next second, I was aware of an 'enemy' racing down to shoot me, a pilot over his homeland who, if he survived, could fight again. A flaming plane – my Hurricane – then missed me, literally by inches. The kite slowly screwed round, going into a steeper and steeper dive until almost vertical, aimed directly at the cross hedges of four fields to the NE of a wood towards which I was drifting. It hit the cross hedges spot on. A short, but noticeable pause and then a huge explosion followed by another pause before flames shot up to a great height. I'm glad that I wasn't in it!

I was safe again, although I didn't feel so as the sea looked rather close and I didn't want to end up swimming. I then recalled the film about the German parachutist which had shown how, if you pulled the parachute cords on one side or the other, the direction was slipped off accordingly. I tried, but which side, as I could not see which way I was drifting. I certainly could

> not think aerodynamically at that moment. Leave well alone, I thought. I was safe again. Blood! Trickling down my right leg. I tried to lift my leg to see, but couldn't. I'd met aircrew who had lost limbs but told me how they could still feel extremities which were no longer there. My leg had been shot off and would crumble under me when I landed. I was getting close to the ground, worried about my 'shot off leg', when I remembered the tale of a pilot being shot in the foot by the Home Guard. 'British!' I shouted at the top if my voice for the last few hundred feet. Oh Lord, I'm going straight into that wood. I grabbed the harness above my head to ease the bump of landing on my 'shot off leg' and pulled hard as my 'chute clipped a tree on the edge of the wood. I only fell over gently, when the wind pulled the 'chute sideways. I shouted 'British!' again, but as no-one came, started to roll up my parachute when a farm labourer climbed over a fence requesting confirmation that I was okay. My 'shot off leg' was not shot off. In fact it was a tiny wound about half an inch long on my knee where a small piece of shrapnel had entered, and another the same size also half an inch away where it had come out. A lady with a horse then came along and I draped my parachute over the animal, and off we went on foot until a van took me to Lyme Regis Police Station. I was entertained in a local pub to await squadron transport back to Warmwell. Someone from Air Sea-Rescue came in and I told him that I was pretty sure the Heinkel I had engaged had gone down into the 'drink'.

Although Sergeant Peter Fox was safe, his Hurricane having exploded at Wootton Fitzpaine, the air battle above was gaining in ferocity. Other 56 Squadron Hurricanes were also despatched from the fight: Pilot Officer Bryan Wicks had forced-landed at Warmwell with a damaged aircraft, and Pilot Officer Michael Constable-Maxwell crash-landed safely in a mined area on Chesil Beach, opposite the Abbotsbury Swannery. Flight Lieutenant Robert Edwards, commanding 'B' Flight, was also shot down and forced to bale out.

No. 152 Squadron's Spitfires had also attacked from the west and from the sun at the same time as 56 Squadron. To reach the enemy, 152 Squadron had flown through cloud 'on instruments' for twenty-five minutes, as later recorded in the log book of Flight Lieutenant Frederick 'Fred' M. Thomas, commanding 'B' Flight. Pilot Officer Dudley Williams sighted the enemy whilst still over the sea, heading for Lyme Regis, informing his CO, Squadron Leader Peter Devitt, who led the Spitfires into attack the bombers, after which the squadron broke up and individual dogfights ensued.

Pilot Officer Dudley Williams, Green 1, attacked a Me 110, which dived into the cloud mass below with smoke pouring from both engines. He climbed again, finding another 110, flying south-east, with one engine emitting white smoke. The Spitfire pilot finished off his ammunition, and then Pilot Officer Frederick Higginson attacked the same target. The two pilots last saw the 110 going down west of Portland, streaming smoke from both engines.

Devitt's Pilot Officer Graham 'Cocky' Cox, Red 2, fired at one of forty Me 110s during the squadron's attack and watched fascinated as 'bits flew off it'. Nine Me 109s then surrounded Cox, who managed a short burst at one of them, before half-rolling and diving away into cloud.

Sergeant Albert Kearsey, Green 2, and Sergeant Leslie Reddington, Green 3, had been weaving behind the squadron, but joined in the initial charge. Kearsey surprised a Me 110, closing to 50 yards and attacking, the *Zerstörer* flipping on to its back and diving vertically over Chesil Beach. Reddington, a family man from Coventry, was shot down and crashed into the sea, never to be seen again.

Pilot Officer Eric Marrs, Blue 3, managed to attack the Heinkels from the beam and got in a short burst before an enemy bullet smashed into armoured windscreen, shattering the glass. Another bullet from KG 55's heavy crossfire hit his petrol tank but fortunately this did not explode.

Marrs wrote,

> Crash! and the whole world seemed to be tumbling in on me. I pushed the stick forward hard and went into a vertical dive which I held until I was below cloud. I had a look around. The chief trouble was that petrol was gushing into the cockpit. My knee and leg were tingling all over as if I had pushed them into a bed of nettles. There was a bullet hole in the windscreen where a bullet, had come in and entered the dashboard, knocking away the starter button. Another shell, I think an explosive one, had knocked away one of the petrol taps in front of my joystick, spattering my leg with little splinters and sending a chunk of something through the backside of my petrol tank near the bottom. I made for home at top speed to get there before my petrol ran out. I was about fifteen miles from the aerodrome and it was a heart-rending business with all that petrol gushing over my legs and the constant danger of fire. About five miles from the [aero]drome smoke started to come from under the dashboard. I thought the whole thing might go up at any minute, so I switched off the engine. The smoke stopped. I glided down towards the 'drome and tried putting my wheels down. One came down but the other remained stuck up. I tried to get the one that was down up again. It was stuck down. There was nothing for it but to make a one-wheel landing. I switched on my engine again to make the aerodrome. It took me some way and then began to smoke again so I hastily switched it off. I was now near enough and made

> a normal approach and held off. I made a good landing, touching down lightly. The unsupported wing slowly began to drop. I was able to hold it up for some time and then down came the wing tip to the ground. I began to slew round and counteracted as much as possible with the brake on the wheel which was down. I ended up going sideways on one wheel, a tail-wheel and a wing tip. Luckily, the good tyre held out and the only damage to the aeroplane, apart from that done by the bullets, is a wing-tip which is easily replaceable.

At 16.20 hrs, eight Hurricanes of 87 Squadron were also scrambled, led by Squadron Leader Ian 'Widge' Gleed DFC. Pilot Officer Andrew McLure and Sergeant Herbert Walton of 'B' Flight were first to sight the enemy formation, which was about to cross the Dorset coast over Lyme Bay. The two Hurricanes attacked from out of the sun, but as McLure approached the bombers an Me 110 was soon on his tail. Turning steeply into a left-hand turn, the position was reversed, McLure attacking the Me 110 from 200 yards; the enemy fighter's starboard engine caught fire and it dived into the cloud some 14,000ft below. McLure again climbed up sun and executed a quarter attack on a group of bombers. Selecting one of these and firing a long burst, he noted the Heinkel 'go out of control and divert slightly', but then resume its course. A further burst of fire saw the bomber dive steeply, but ammunition exhausted and with enemy fighters closing around him, McLure broke off and headed home.

Squadron Leader Ian Gleed and Pilot Officer John Cock, an Australian, were the next of 87 Squadron to arrive, just as the enemy passed over Bridport. Whilst still climbing and at 8,000ft, just above the clouds, Cock was attacked by a Me 109 which overshot, becoming a target itself. Cock fired from astern, the 109 flipping on to its right side and disappearing into cloud. The Hurricane gave chase, but over Dorchester encountered a lone Ju 88. Having fired at the enemy aircraft immediately, from abeam, Cock swung round to attack from the rear, setting alight the starboard engine and fuselage, the Ju 88 then commencing a right-handed dive into cloud. This was Ju 88 of 1/ *Aufklärungsgruppe* 123, operating from Buc and Bordeaux, tasked with photographing the result of KG 55's impending attack. The reconnaissance aircraft later crashed into The Solent off the Isle of Wight, the crew all killed.

Gleed suddenly found himself alone amongst 'Seventy Ju 88s [*sic*]' and attacked the right-hand bomber, which broke away, spiraling down through the clouds. Lying in the bombardier's prone position within the glazed nose of his Heinkel, it appeared to 18-year-old *Flieger* Robert Götz that at first the Hurricane was trying to formate on the bombers. Momentarily stunned by the close proximity of the British fighter, Götz and the formation's other gunners opened fire. As the

Hurricane pitched into a dive, Götz's *Staffelkapitän* instructed the *Bordfunker* to broadcast their position to the *Seenotdienst*, hoping that if he went down in the sea then the British pilot could be rescued. Gleed's Hurricane had been hit several times, but fortunately no serious damage was caused and he was able to return safely to Exeter.

At 16.15 hrs, Flight Lieutenant Frank Howell had led 12 Spitfires of 609 Squadron from Middle Wallop towards the action on what the squadron diary called 'The now customary tea-time scramble'. When the Spitfires arrived, the enemy had already crossed over Lyme Bay and were heading inland, the course of the Germans' advance plotted and reported by the ever-vigilant Observer Corps.

As 609 Squadron followed the enemy from the south, having swung round and approached from a direction of Swanage, also out of the sun, a formation of fighters was sighted below and to the left of the Spitfires. Suspecting them to be Hurricanes, Howell ordered Pilot Officer David Crook to take Green Section down to investigate. Accordingly, Crook, Flying Officer Tadeuz Nowierski, a Pole, and Pilot Officer John Curchin investigated, but as Green Section got closer, Crook realised that they were in fact Me 109s. The Spitfires had the elements of both surprise and sun in their favour, Nowierski, Green 2, firing at the rearmost 109. White, then 'very thick black smoke', came from the enemy aircraft which dived away. Green 2 then made after another Me 109 on his right, attacking from astern. After just one two-second burst white and black smoke also emitted from that aircraft. As Nowierski broke left, he saw the German pilot bale out, but his parachute failed to deploy sufficiently as a cord had fouled half-way up the canopy; *Unteroffizier* Alois Dollinger of 5/JG 2 subsequently fell dead at Grimstone, his Me 109 exploding on the Dorset Downs at One-Hundred-Acre Field, Spriggs Farm, Sydling St Nicholas.

As the Me 109s broke up, Crook went after one which took 'the most violent evasive tactics' for nearly two minutes. The 109 dived, zoomed and turned madly all over the sky but was unable to shake off the Spitfire, its pilot desperately trying to line up a shot:

> After a dive even faster than before, he zoomed up almost vertically for 2,000 feet, going straight into the sun in an effort to shake me off that way. Almost completely dazzled, I managed nevertheless to follow him up and when he did a stall turn at the top I got another quick burst at him but without any apparent effect. At the top of the zoom I rolled over on to my back, but the recoil of my guns practically stalled me and I hung there for a second upside down and then fell away in a very drunken dive after the 109. He streaked away in front of me, going hard for a layer of cloud. I went down vertically after him, gathering speed like a bullet and doing

> a quick aileron turn to get into line again. Outside the cockpit I could see the earth and clouds and sky all apparently revolving crazily around my head, but they did so in a curiously detached way because I was conscious only of the small racing object in front. He managed to reach the cloud below and I chased after him, missed him with another burst, and then hunted him through this cloud for some miles, dodging in and out, seeing him just for a fleeting instance every now and then. He wasn't very clever about this, and he never changed course in the cloud, and thus, if I lost him, I had only to keep straight on to pick him up again. We tore over Weymouth, going very fast indeed, and passed out to sea. This was his undoing, as he probably thought he had shaken me off and he made the bad mistake of climbing out of the cloud. I climbed up behind, came into very close range, and then absolutely blasted him. He turned over and spun down into the cloud, streaming glycol smoke, which meant that his radiator had been hit. I dived below cloud but could see no trace of him at all, and I think there can be very little doubt that he crashed into the sea as he was badly hit and could not have reached France with a radiator leaking like that.

No. 609 Squadron's Pilot Officer Keith Ogilvie remembered this particular action:

> We arrived in time to engage the He 111s. I did not see any results but I found a He 111 and fired from his rear. The rear gunner returned my fire but then stopped. I began to pull in for a better target when there was an almighty bang behind me which destroyed my radio. A hole in the port wing told me that I had company! I was quick to break off, but never did see my attacker, nor indeed any other aircraft after that time. I made for home and landed gingerly but without incident with a, [*sic*] flat tyre. As I recall we were so short of aircraft that I had to fly my plane to the Spitfire plant for repairs, returning to Middle Wallop with a serviceable example. [The] 30 September 1940, was an exciting day, but all I could claim in both engagements was experience.

By now, the raid was approaching Yeovil, only to find that the covering of cloud had extended inland like a shroud. KG 55's crews were frustrated, therefore, that having fought their way inland again, the target could not be seen. The formation leader, hoping to find a break in the cloud through which the target could be identified, swung around to the south-west, then led the formation in a south-easterly direction. In roughly the right place such a hole appeared, through which could be seen a town of similar size to Yeovil, also straddling a railway line. Kless decided that this was his intended target and ordered the attack to go ahead. As at Filton, the Heinkels changed formation into *Ketten* line astern, so as to concentrate the bombing pattern. KG 55 approached the town travelling from north-east to south-west. At 16.40 hrs, the bombs began falling.

No. 152 Squadron was poised to attack the bombers again, when Squadron Leader Peter Devitt saw

> their bombs falling away from their bellies. On looking down to see what the target was to my horror I saw the old Sherborne School Courts, which I knew so well. I was at that time just about to attack, which I did, but was molested by a pack of Me 109s. After that I could not see much of where the bombs fell, as I was too intent upon what was happening in my immediate vicinity, but I did see a great deal of smoke around my old school's buildings, and so knew that there were some hits and possibly casualties.

Pilot Officer Roger Hall, also of 152 Squadron, remembered that

> We intercepted the raid over what we now know was Sherborne, but at the time, due to the poor weather with lots of cloud, it could have been anywhere.

Flight Lieutenant Frederick Thomas saw 'some fires in Sherborne'.

High up, over 800ft above sea-level, near the Chalk Pit on Pond Farm, 18-year-old Leslie Griffin was thatching a corn rick when, over the hill and from a direction of Cerne Abbas, the German formation appeared, travelling towards Yeovil:

> On spotting me they loosed off a burst of machine-gun fire. I slid off the roof as fast as possible. A few minutes later I returned to my work, watching those planes making their way, by which time the Yeovil barrage balloons had appeared and the Germans turned away. I could see everything. The Germans were en route for Sherborne, suddenly I heard and felt the shock of bombs as they were dropped on what had been, until then, a peaceful market town. A few minutes passed, then a pall of dust rose into the cloudy sky, and the sun shone through.

Clinton Trewlany of the Observer Corps at Yetminster, saw the bombs fall: 'Then the whole sky was filled with dust, and suddenly the sun came out and the dust was gold; it was a lovely sight.'

Sherborne – a picturesque, biscuit-coloured, provincial town of no military significance whatsoever, would remember this as 'Black Monday'. Monica Hutchings never expected anything to happen in the small town of 5,000, there being 'nothing worth bombing'. Furthermore, the town lay on the bombers' route to Bristol, so German aircraft passing overhead were not uncommon, and when the siren sounded the young accounts clerk took little notice. As she made her way to shelter at the Swan Hotel, Hutchings was momentarily petrified by the crash of exploding bombs – she threw herself down on the ground and lay in the centre of the main road. All around her flew masonry, and thick dust gathered in a great cloud. Next to her a man lay dying; he had forgotten the oft repeated instruction to lie flat.

Frank Childe had been accepted as a police constable in Dorset Constabulary in 1933, 'when to be so was considered an honour'. Having served at various stations throughout the county as a single man, he had moved into married quarters on Sherborne's Lenthay housing estate in 1938.

PC58 Childe remembered,

> During those times [throughout the air raid] a policeman was on duty for 24-hours a day and was expected to be available for each alert. On this day, when the alert sounded, I was off-duty and immediately dressed for the occasion and made for my designated post, which was at the Lenthay Post Office, about three doors away. There I met Ted Lemon, the Postman, who was collecting the mail, a resident of Nether Compton. We stood there outside the Post Office chatting and thinking 'Oh, just another raid that would pass over heading elsewhere', when we were soon abused of this idea by the menacing roar of an extraordinary number of aircraft engines, the air vibrating from the concentrated noise. I looked westwards into the sky and saw what appeared to be a double handful of peas thrown towards the earth and breaking through the clouds. Ted and I dashed into the Post Office and threw ourselves on the floor. The time was 16.40 hrs. All hell broke loose. It felt as though the whole world was a bouncing ball. For myself, it felt as though nothing could survive such an onslaught. Suddenly, dead silence, which after the bombs was uncanny on the hearing. Ted and I got up, both surprised that we were still alive. He took me by the hand and said 'Thank you for saving my life', and after that moment we were lifelong friends.

Ten-year-old Gerald Pitman was a pupil at the Abbey Junior School in Horsecastles:

When the siren went I ran as hard as I could along Trendle Street, up the steps in front of the Digby Memorial where a group of people were talking, and up Cheap Street. When I reached the Eldridge Pope & Co premises at the top of Cheap Street I could see my Grandmother at the door of our house and shop which was on the corner of Higher Cheap Street by the Milborne Port bus-stop. She called out to me to hurry, and I was soon inside the shop. Inside the little shop were two ladies waiting for my father, who ran a taxi, to drive them out into the country. They had just arrived from London to escape the raids.

I showed my grandmother a lead soldier that I had either swapped or been given that afternoon and it was then that the noise of bombs became obvious. We hurried for shelter under the stairs which had been shorn up as a shelter. The front door seemed as though it was being continually thumped. The people from, the bus queue had taken shelter on our stairs. The bird's cage, which was hanging in the window with 'Joey' in it, went up and down. One of the ladies from London fainted but by that time, the bombing had ended.

Gwynne Douglas James was a 16-year-old pupil at Sherborne School – of which Squadron Leader Peter Devitt, fighting in his Spitfire high above the town, was coincidentally an 'Old Boy':

I was down at School when the siren went during English. We sighed – with relief or disappointment, and wandered, I'm afraid to say rather slowly, up to Lyon House. There was not the sound of an aeroplane to be heard, in fact it was just the same as many other raids we had been having and we were rather bored with them.

Another English pupil was an anonymous member of Lyon House who also committed his memory to paper just two days after the raid:

I was having an English lesson in the Lower Library, and, as that veritable hive of historical books is considered safe enough in an air raid, we stayed where we were and did not go to the Cloisters as people in the other classrooms do when the siren sounds.

About a quarter of an hour later we heard the sound of aero engines, rather like the characteristic zoom-zoom of Boche planes. Then a minute or two later we heard a distant whistle and 'crump', then some more ominous bangs nearer, so we all crawled under the massive oak tables and waited in suspense. Nearer and nearer came the explosions, the lights went out, thud

> followed thud in a hideous deafening roar, the big library above seemed as if it would fall down on us at any moment. Glass split and cracked. Then gradually it got further and further away and stopped altogether. We crawled out from under the tables, rather dazed, and looked out of the windows. The whole air was filled with like a thick fog.

Charles Burgess:

> Surely I cannot die at fourteen? Far too young. Gradually the detonations came nearer and nearer. Suddenly a terrific explosion rocked the Cloisters. The pressure on my eardrums was enormous. A piece of shrapnel whined over my head. That is my most vivid impression, that piece of shrapnel. A cloud of brown dust rolled over the lying figures. Then someone laughed and before I knew where I was, I was laughing too. We all laughed when Scott appeared with his face caked with dust. I think he must have escaped death by a hair's breadth.

Anonymous: 'They were the longest 86 seconds I have ever experienced and I wish to state that I hope never to experience them again.'

John Meredith Williams (14): 'A silver Spitfire banked low over the Abbey and restored a great deal of my spirit.'

Denzil Kingston Freeth (16):

> God, don't let me be buried under debris. I don't mind dying but don't let me lie there cold, bleeding, wounded, unable to move; perhaps buried alive. Why have I got to die? Please God don't let me die. Glass crashing around. My fingers in my ears. Oh God – and the noise dies away in the distance.

Geoffrey Leonard Baker (16):

> When the siren went, we being an industrious maths set, went on with our work. A few minutes later we heard bombs being dropped about a mile away and leathered that some place was getting a rather sticky time, not guessing for a moment that it would be our turn soon. At the first sound of a bomb, work stopped and we all listened. Mr Randolph, who was taking us, told us to put our heads down under the desks while he, on the other hand, went outside to see if he could spot any planes, not yet having seen a German plane himself. As the bombs came nearer and everything started to shake, Mr Randolph wasn't so keen on looking for planes and came in with us pretty quickly!

> The noise was terrific, nothing but whistles, bumps, explosions and the roar of aeroplane engines in the background. The door shook like anything so that in the first lull Mr Randolph went and sat with his back to it. When the second lot of bombs started falling everyone's head darted under the desks again, and we lay there thinking that our last day had come, because it was then that the bombs in the Courts were dropped. I could see out of the window and when those dropped I saw a great pile of earth and stones thrown high into the air, and at the same time glass fell out of the windows.

The boys of Sherborne's Foster's School were also ushered out of class when the siren went and up floated the Yeovil balloon barrage. Harold Osement was amongst them, and remembered,

> The western sky had the look of dull, mild oatmeal and it was from there that the drama unfolded. From somewhere out there, beyond the horizon of dark roofs and chimneys of The Avenue, out there in the oatmeal haze, came what sounded like heavy wagons crumping across hard, rough ground. Still nobody talked. The sound effects out there demanded to be heard in their own awful way. Into the muzzy off-yellow sky came what looked like strings of black sausages, and falling from them were flights of cloves. 'Get Down!', the French master shouted. A great hiss scythed up through the sky, but then nothing more seemed likely to happen so we came up. I looked at a band of jagged, blackish metal at the edge of the trench. 'Don't touch it', the French master shouted, 'It's still hot!'. It looked like the mane of a little sea-horse, and as I admired our trophy with almost affectionate contemplation, I noticed that the grass nearest to it was faintly steaming. Over to the left, in front of the school buildings, a two-storey house burned, flaming away in a business-like way as if it enjoyed doing what it had to, and the northeast wind bent the flames in long streams and continually brightened its red centre.

In Sherborne's shopping area, Mrs Minterne had taken cover within the building firm premises owned by her husband, opposite Parson's Butchers in Half Moon Street. Suddenly there was a loud bang as a bomb exploded nearby, and a lump of shrapnel 'as big as a dustbin lid' came hurtling through the shop's plate glass window. At the time Minterne's was being decorated, and the blast knocked all the paint over which splattered everywhere 'like a rainbow'.

The ground even tremored in Yeovil, 6 miles due west. There, 11-year-old Norman Collard had taken shelter in Eastland Road, and remembered that 'the building shook all the time'.

At Houndstone Camp, a Royal Artillery depot on the western edge of Yeovil and some 7 miles from Sherborne, Private Martin, a cook in the officers' mess, clearly heard the bombs and saw the cloud of golden dust rising into the sky from Sherborne's direction. Fourteen-year-old John Gaunt was standing on the roof of his parents' home at Charles Dairy, Yeovil, and after the siren went saw columns of smoke lifting over Babylon Hill. Suddenly the boy saw a parachute, and a fighter aircraft tumble out of the sky and crash near Yeovil Junction railway station.

Fred Denham was a member of Yeovil's St John Ambulance Brigade, and when the siren sounded made haste to the Police Station to be deployed. Overheard he saw

> Fifty bombers plus fighters which turned over Yeovil and bombed Sherborne. As I arrived at the Station, the Superintendent was running out to his car, strapping on a revolver. 'Quick, man!', he said, 'Come with me, we'll capture him', and looking up I saw a parachutist descending in a direction of Yeovil Junction. Off we went and found that a Hurricane had crashed at Newton House, to the south-east of Yeovil, and we later found the pilot taking tea in a cottage at East Coker.

John Hall was cycling up Grove Avenue in Yeovil, when he saw the

> Hurricane attacking a great formation of enemy aircraft. There was no other sound, just the machine-guns of that lone fighter rattling away until it was hit and disappeared over towards Sherborne. It was undoubtedly an act of great courage.

At 10.30 hrs that morning, the Robinsons had emerged from Yeovil Registry Office, a newly married couple, to an air raid warning, of which, 'As there had been so many', they took no notice. During the afternoon, the couple, Mr Robinson being a regular soldier in the Royal Artillery, were having a cup of tea when the alert sounded again. However, on that occasion they did take shelter as the bombers could be heard flying overhead. AA guns were firing, and as the newlyweds ran to their garden's surface shelter, Sybil Robinson saw a parachute drifting down. Next the loud thuds of bombs dropping on Sherborne could be heard.

Schoolboy Michael Trevett:

> I saw a Hurricane attack the wave of German aircraft, it was destroyed and dived to earth in flames. Its pilot baled out and parachuted to safety.

Certainly 87 Squadron's Sergeant Herbert Walton had pursued the enemy inland and was himself shot down whilst attacking the raiders over Sherborne. Fortunately, he baled out and his parachute was seen by many boys of Sherborne School, amongst them John Ching:

> They've got one down, I think its a Jerry! Then a cheer, such as I've never heard before rent the air, or I should say the dust. This encouraged me, and I felt happier.

Walton's Hurricane impacted at Burdon's Nurseries, Osborne Road, Sherborne, the pilot admitted to Sherborne Hospital slightly wounded. Peter Lane, another pupil at Sherborne School, saw

> a parachute drifting down in Thornford direction. We cheered thinking it was a German, but later discovered it to have been a British pilot.

Whether Lane saw Walton, or the parachutist who landed at East Coker (in roughly the same direction as Thornford, i.e. to the south-west of Sherborne), it cannot be said, as neither the pilot or aircraft concerned in the latter instance have been identified, although there is no doubting that a Hurricane did indeed crash at Newton House in Yeovil, at this time.

The bombs extended along the length of Sherborne in a distinct triple line from Bedmill Copse to Crackmore. Around fifty bombs fell on the town centre itself. The bombs crashed down on Lenthay, through Horsecastles, Richmond Road, Acreman Street, Sherborne School Garden, Abbey Road, the School Courts, Half Moon Street, Cheap Street, Newland Road and North Road. At Sydney Villa in The Avenue, and at a bungalow and garages in Tinney's Lane, two large fires burned. Several roads were blocked, but the main A30 was clear. Gas and water mains were seriously damaged and the electricity supply had also failed. UXBs lay in the main road at Cheap Street, in a garden at Back Abbey, in St Swithin's Road, in a garden off The Avenue, and in a lawn at the back of Monks Barn, Newlands. Southern Railway reported the up and down lines damaged between Yeovil Junction and Sherborne, and all traffic stopped. There was also a direct hit to the cemetery where coffins were blown out of the ground. Incredibly, however, Sherborne Abbey, in the town centre and overlooking the scene of destruction, was undamaged.

In Cheap Street there was the Post Office, at which was located the telephone exchange. The telephone system was maintained throughout the raid due to the bravery and devotion to duty of the telephonist supervisor, Miss Maude Steel, a local girl, who remained at her post despite the devastation around her. By her action, and that of the temporary telephonist who remained with Maude Steele, the emergency and ARP services were kept in constant touch with their headquarters until local landlines were put out of action. Even then, when a bomb exploded within the Post Office's precincts, Maude Steele proceeded from the refuge room to the telephone exchange in the hope that she could be of assistance. She was magnificent in the face of real danger, and by her action contributed greatly to the effective working of the ARP and other services. She had remained at the telephone exchange until the position became impossible, but, even then, she was reluctant to leave. For such selfless acts of courage, Maude Steel later received the George Medal, which had only been instituted six days previously.

As the Heinkels' bomb doors closed and the raiders set course for France, the attack over, the stunned populace of Sherborne took stock.

The boys of Sherborne School have left us with a rich record of their feelings after the bombing.

Anthony Harbottle:

> After the four bombs fell in the Courts we were dumbfounded. One or two gingerly stood up and peered out of the window. One of the masters then informed us that no-one had been hurt.
>
> We were then summoned to the Cloisters. Whilst walking across the Courts untold damage could be witnessed. Pieces of leaden window-frames were hanging despondently, as if suspended in mid-air, all twisted and shattered. Cruel scars were to be seen on the stone walls, craters twenty feet and more in diameter were gaping at us as we walked across the Courts that fateful afternoon. There was truly change and decay in all that we saw around, though the destruction wrought might have been a hundred times worse.
>
> When we arrived in the Cloisters many were talking and laughing cheerfully, none the worse for the providential escape from death. Suddenly there was a hush, the Headmaster was speaking to us. In an unemotional voice he told us to go back to our Houses and 'Work, work, work!' Several had lost valuable possessions, but all were thankful to have been spared.
>
> On the way back, several Spitfires could be seen and heard circling round. Going up the hill I saw a workman with a gory bandage round his head, making his way to hospital but looking as cheerful as ever.
>
> Since there was neither gas, electricity, nor water, the 'Raiders Passed' was never sounded, and thus it was we found ourselves eating a ham roll for tea, and two large kettles boiling on the coke fire. Later on, after much

gossip, we vainly tried to do our Hall by candlelight, during which time we despatched brief postcards to our parents to confirm our escape.

Frank Nicholls:

> I went to see if I could be of any assistance to the neighbours. I was greeted in the yard by Mrs Palmer and her maid, shouting that there was a dead man in her garden. I handed her over to Mr Ross and ran down through the garden to Thorn's house to see if he was hurt. I climbed over a heap of debris, caused, I discovered later, by a time-bomb, and found both he and his wife uninjured, though busy having hysterics. I promised to come down and help him soon, and ran off up the road, negotiated a bomb crater in the road, a dead gardener, messy but not sickening, telegraph and power wires. The stench of explosives was everywhere, an aircraft did a victory roll over the school, and a man, one of ours, I saw coming down by parachute.

John Maxwell Ward:

> A fatal casualty in Mr Palmer's garden. I went there and found Jimmy Lintern in the garden approximately five yards from a crater. Thence I ran down to the First Aid Post and told them that there was no hope for the fellow and returned to poor Jimmy whose heart and eyes I inspected with the obvious negative result. Then Hamerseley appeared with a sheet to cover the unfortunate fellow. Later on a stretcher party arrived and simultaneously an ambulance, but having seen their patient remarked that it would be a waste of time to do anything, and so left poor Jimmy to get colder and stiffen A warden came up soon afterwards and later on an old van from a gar age. The Warden and the other two then asked me if I could find some sacking – I ran off and as I was passing through the House, Wilson asked me whether I had 'cleared out' my study – not quite understanding quite what on earth he was on about I replied 'No'. To which he roared in response 'Well go and do it then, and brace up!' Thinking that other things were more important, I hurried on without paying any attention to him.
>
> We four, the Warden, two others and myself then lifted the corpse on to the van and the latter moved off. I then moved off in search of Thorne, who was weeping in the back parlour, and tried to console him. Little did I know that I was standing directly over a 550lb unexploded bomb!

Anthony Harbottle described the scene that night:

> We had an early bed. Just before settling in our attention was riveted on a burning house, not far distant. The rafters could clearly be seen against the red glow.
>
> During the night we were called up no less than three times by police whistles. At about 2 o'clock there was a violent explosion – one of the time bombs dropped during the raid had gone off. This was followed a few minutes later by another, and the sound of falling masonry. Neither bomb did serious damage. The suspense while waiting for the explosion was ghastly. No more exploded, however, and the rest of the night was spent in comparative peace and calm.

For other pupils sleep did not come so easily.

John Maxwell Ward: 'When night came with more contemplation I felt physically sick and very unhappy.'

Donald Moffat Wilson:

> My impressions of the bombing are these, cold fear as the bombs whistled down, immediate reaction of excitement and laughter, cheerfulness till nightfall which brought with it exhaustion and nervousness; and for the next few days cheerfulness but finding it very difficult to concentrate.

The boys had all come through their ordeal. According to young Frank Nicholls, they could 'Take it and take it again and again if necessary to beat the dastardly Hun.'

Monica Hutchings, shocked at having discovered her friend, Miss Gartell, dead, waited for a kettle to boil on a fire made from the timber of bombed buildings.

Hampered by the UXBs, Mr Edward J. Freeman, the district air raid precautions controller, and his men, assisted by an ARP detachment and a rescue party from Yeovil, soon commenced restoring the town's essential services and helping the injured. The dead ultimately numbered eighteen, including a youngster from London who, ironically, had been evacuated to escape the bombing there only the day before. Thirty-two people were injured and detained in hospital. Of the 1,700 properties in the town, 31 were demolished and 776 damaged. In true wartime spirit, a fund for the relief of victims was opened immediately, started by a lady resident with the generous gift of £200. Blankets were brought into the town by the Red Cross Society, and offers of assistance came from as far afield as Sherborn, Massachusetts. Surrounding villages sent tarpaulins for gaping roofs, and oil stoves to combat the lack of power, and candles and bedding and food; many of them threw open their doors to the bombed townspeople until their homes were restored.

PC58 Frank Childe remembered the aftermath,

After Ted Lemon and I had picked ourselves up, I ran the short distance home to check that my wife was alright. She was in a shelter that I had made in our garden against such an occasion. She had survived, so I ran back to my post and duties. I was obliged to pick my way back over tangled telephone and electricity cables. Work went on throughout the area and we found that all public services, water, electricity and telephones were completely cut off. It was a case of 'make do and mend'.

I found myself in the Lenthay council housing estate at a premises which had sustained a direct hit. The complete roof had been blown off and came down again on the demolished house. Neighbours told us that the house had contained a mother and three children. We had no proper tools or equipment but started making a way through the roof and rubble. The mother was located by her fingers showing beneath the door of the under stairs cupboard. It was whilst we were working our way through the debris of this house with domestic tools that we were encouraged by the arrival of a small ARP squad from Yeovil, complete with more suitable tools and a doctor who crawled through the tunnel we had made and gave the trapped woman an injection.

At this point I must give credit to the licensee of the 'Traveller's Rest' in Horsecastles, for his gallant gesture, in spite of the law and regulations, of keeping his Pub open until midnight providing refreshments FREE to all those persons helping in the rescue operation. All public services, of course, were out of action.

The path of the enemy planes was from Yeovil towards Templecombe, leaving a path of death and destruction in their wake. It was not until the following Any, however, that we learned the true extent of damage and casualties. A friend of mine, Harry Ireland, had a saddlery business in Half Moon Street, next door to the 'Phillips' drapery shop. His premises was demolished by a direct hit and poor Harry was later found, still in his chair, beneath the debris in the cellar.

Percy Coaker, a well-known local character, ran a furniture store in Cheap Street, opposite the Methodist Church. His premises were extensively damaged, but a large notice, typical of the spirit of the time, appeared on his shop: 'WE HAVE BEEN BOMBED, BUGGERED & BEWILDERED, BUT BUSINESS IS AS USUAL!'

Mr Harold Pitman, a taxi-cab owner of Cheap Street, was driving from Chetnole to Sherborne when he saw a parachute descending. This would

> have been the gallant pilot of a fighter plane who attacked the Germans but was himself shot down. This occurred immediately before the bombs fell.
>
> 'n spite of the fact that particularly all the roads in the centre of Sherborne were blocked with debris and essential services completely disrupted, the local services and authorities did a wonderful job in getting everything going again in the shortest time possible.

Having bombed Sherborne in error, KG 55 now had to fight its way back to France.

At 16.30 hrs that afternoon, Squadron Leader John Sample, Red 1, had led twelve Hurricanes of 504 Squadron off from Filton with orders to patrol base at Angels 20. Red 1 was then vectored 205° for ten minutes and told to increase height to 25,000ft and patrol Yeovil. There, the squadron saw two close formations of Heinkels,

> numbering twenty and thirty aircraft respectively, flying north at 17,000 feet. The enemy aircraft were roughly twenty miles East of our Squadron, each formation was a rough vic composed of smaller vies of three aircraft. [ORB]

As the Hurricanes manoeuvred into position for an attack, the enemy turned slowly to the right and flew on a south-westerly course. Shortly after that, Sherborne was bombed, but due to the range involved the Hurricane pilots could not see this. As the squadron now approached, the Germans turned south onto a course that would ultimately take them out over Weymouth.

When 87 Squadron was scrambled from Exeter at 16.50 hrs, Pilot Officer Ronald 'Bee' Beamont, Pilot Officer Harry Mitchell, a Canadian, and Sergeant Ivor Badger, had been left behind as their Hurricanes were being re-fuelled. Beamont remembered,

> After take-off (I was leading), the R/T told us to 'Buster Portland Angels 20, very many bandits heading South'. Over Dorchester we briefly saw some Me 110s diving fast towards the coast but we lost them in cloud. It was frustrating.

An even more frustrated 87 Squadron pilot was Flying Officer Derek Ward, a New Zealander, who had dashed back to the airfield from the local cinema upon hearing the siren. Off too late, he failed to contact the enemy at all.

After 609 Squadron's first charge at the enemy, Pilot Officer Noël le Chevalier Agazarian, the squadron's weaver, had lost the other Spitfires and was thereafter unable to locate them. Instead, he decided to intercept the Heinkels during their return flight, alone. Inland of Warmwell 'Aga' attacked the rearmost bombers from abeam. Breaking away, however, he realised that his glycol tank had been hit. After one final attack, Agazarian left the He 111 streaming black smoke from its starboard engine and apparently on fire. The bomber was not losing height, but, losing coolant fast, Agazarian had no choice but to land quickly at Warmwell. In his combat report, he later noted,

> The Heinkels, between fifty and sixty of them, bombed in 'V' formation and as they turned South to go home changed into a thick solid echelon port. The return fire was terrific, highly concentrated.

At 16.10 hrs, Squadron Leader Duncan MacDonald had scrambled from the 11 Group sector station at Tangmere with his 213 Squadron Hurricanes behind him. The squadron was initially vectored to intercept a 200+ raid which had crossed the Kent coast just two minutes previously. However, Sergeant Geoffrey Stevens clearly remembered an unexpected turn of events:

> Quite abruptly and without warning we were ordered to turn 180° and told 'Buster' [author's note: proceed at full boost and with all haste]. R/T talk between our 'Bearskin Leader' and Ground Control elicited the information that it was a 60+ raid. We soon saw the enemy, first as dots which gradually developed into a mixture of He 111s and Me 110s, and some Me 109s which were, as usual, above us. We were at about the same height as the bombers and 110s.

No. 213 Squadron intercepted the withdrawing enemy at 17.00 hrs over Portland. Stevens continued,

> I initially went for one of the latter, but he evaded by executing a spiral dive. I did not follow as I wished to retain height, but then saw a formation of three He 111s below me, so I dived on them, selecting the left-hand aircraft as my target. I got a fair amount of stick from all three gunners and opened with quite a long burst. However, I was travelling too fast and broke away left and downwards. 1 pulled back into a steep, almost vertical climb at full throttle, intending to come around again for another go, feeling quite sure that I had silenced the gunner in the aircraft I had fired at. At this point, near the top of the climb, the belly of an Me 110 slid into view going from right to left. I opened up and continued climbing. I saw strikes all along the underside, but I had reached the point of stall and at that moment ran out of ammunition. I fell out of the skies, as the saying goes,

> and as there was no point in returning to the fray I let the aircraft dive. This was very nearly my undoing, as I had built up too much speed and had great difficulty in getting out of the dive. The airscrew over-revved and sprayed oil all over the windscreen, but thankfully I made it by about 100 feet. Later, the airframe fitter told me that several wooden slats which ran underside and aft of the cockpit had been stoved in by the pressure of my pull out.

For no loss, Squadron Leader Duncan MacDonald and Flying Officer Raymond Kellow each claimed a Me 110 destroyed. Sub-Lieutenant Dennis Jeram, a FAA volunteer pilot seconded to Fighter Command, claimed a further 110 as a probable, whilst Sergeant Geoffrey Stevens and Sergeant Hector Barrow each claimed one damaged. Pilot Officer Harold Atkinson claimed an Me 109 destroyed.

Just south of Portland, 504 Squadron eventually caught the enemy formation over the sea, just after 213 Squadron, and Squadron Leader John 'Johnny' Sample DFC, Red 1, led his Hurricanes into a quarter astern attack in sections on the rearmost German bombers. Tucked in behind Squadron Leader John Sample was Flying Officer Michael Royce, Red 2. He noticed no effect from his first attack but then spotted two stragglers, firing several bursts at one of these. During this attack his Hurricane also became covered in oil from the enemy aircraft, but as he broke away he 'noticed that both engines were smoking badly with the airscrews just ticking over. The aircraft was losing height gradually.' Noting his own rapidly decreasing oil pressure, however, Royce then broke off and returned to Filton, landing at 17.30 hrs.

Following Sample's Red Section was Flight Lieutenant Tony Rook, Yellow 1, who attacked the port rear section of Heinkels; the starboard engine of one 'gave off lots of smoke and on my second attack, stopped'. By the time Rook had broken away, this machine had left the formation and was flying very slowly on one engine, and even that was emitting black smoke. Yellow 1 then got into a spin, but by the time he recovered 'there was nothing in sight'.

Flight Lieutenant William Royce, Blue Leader, carried out a quarter astern attack on the Heinkels in company with Red 1, and his younger brother, Flying Officer Michael Royce. Blue Leader continued firing until he was

> dead astern, black smoke appeared from the port engine and oil covered my machine. I was then hit in the wing and front fuselage, so broke away. Whilst doing so I saw an He 111 fly above the formation, stall and spin down. Before entering cloud its port wing broke off and the aircraft burst into flames as it hit the sea.

Undoubtedly the latter Heinkel was one of those also attacked by Sergeant Herbert Jones, Green 2:

> We went into attack from astern and I picked the aircraft on the starboard side of the rear formation. I closed in to 250 yards and, put a 5-second burst into the starboard engine causing pieces to fly off and black smoke to pour out of the enemy aircraft. It then broke away from the enemy formation upwards and across the top and eventually went into a spin. The starboard wing fell off and it crashed into the sea and burst into flames. I then noticed another enemy aircraft which had dropped out of the formation and was making for clouds. I closed to 250 yards and put a 5 second burst into the fuselage and engines. Pieces flew off and my windscreen became smothered in oil. I broke away at about 25 yards, there was no return fire. I went round and made a further astern attack of a 4 second burst. Both engines appeared to have stopped and the undercarriage dropped down as the enemy aircraft disappeared into the clouds. Green 1, Pilot Officer White, was watching this encounter, dived down through the clouds and saw the Heinkel crash into the sea. There was no sign of anyone getting out. I was then attacked by 7 Me 109s which came out of the sun, so I did a steep turn and sought refuge in the clouds.

By the time 504 Squadron broke off its attack, Sample's Hurricanes were very near the French coast. Flying Officer John Reginald Hardacre, though, was missing. Shot down over the Channel, his body later washed ashore on the Isle of Wight and buried at All Saints' Church in Fawley. Sergeant Basil 'Mike' Bush of 504 Squadron remembered that 'When pilots did not return, we were told not to dwell on it, their names were simply not mentioned again.'

Three other 504 Squadron Hurricanes would not reach Filton: Pilot Officer Murray Frisby forced-landed his damaged aircraft near Whitcombe Church, east of Dorchester and Sergeant William Banks forced-landed his shot-up fighter in the Yeovil area. Bush had quite an adventure, however:

> After the interception I was unable to obtain radio contact with Filton. As it was getting dusk and I was lost somewhere South of Bristol I was fearful of getting caught in balloon cables, so decided to land in a field. I picked what I thought to be a long landing run in a particular field which I had spotted, but on the approach I came in low over a hedge and landed, only to discover that it was in a much shorter field than the one I had selected, and ahead I saw a brick wall. Having landed I could do nothing but jam on my brakes and switch off the engine. The action of applying

> the brakes hard resulted in tipping my Hurricane up on its nose. It then flipped over on to its back and I was left hanging by my harness upside down and several feet from the ground. Thankfully I was soon released by men of the Observer Corps from nearby Priddy village.

Fortune too was the fact that Bush's Hurricane did not catch fire.

So ended the last great daylight air battle of summer 1940, on which the Luftwaffe had flown 173 bomber and 1,015 fighter sorties – figures never again to be equalled or exceeded in the ongoing battle over Britain.

On 30 September 1940, the Luftwaffe lost a total of forty-six aircraft destroyed, another twelve damaged, and two more written off in a flying accident. Of these, twenty-four were Me 109s, eleven pilots of which were killed and thirteen captured. Indeed, the 109s had paid a high price for defending the bombers, and for *Major* Adolf Galland's JG 26 it was one of the unit's worst days throughout the entire sixteen-week battle, losing four pilots but filing only seven victory claims. In sum, the *Jagdwaffe* had received a sound beating.

That afternoon, KG 55 had lost four He 111s, all shot down over the sea, all but four crewmen perishing. Amongst those rescued by the *Seenotdienst*, albeit after thirty-six uncomfortable hours afloat in a dinghy, was *Major* Dr Ernst Kühl, the *Geschwader* operations officer who had planned much of the raid. The 1/(F)123 Ju 88 attacked by Pilot Officer John Cock also crashed into the sea, that crew also being killed, and 5/JG 2 had lost *Unteroffizier* Alois Dollinger, killed at Grimstone, and *Gefreiter* Fritz Schumacher, who was missing, shot down over the Channel. Yet again, though, the selection of Westland Aircraft as the target of such a daylight great effort represented another failure of Luftwaffe intelligence, considering that the factory was only producing Lysanders and the new, and ultimately unsuccessful, twin-engined and cannon-armed Whirlwind fighter bomber. Like the albeit successful raid on Filton, even had this attack succeeded, it would have had no effect on the flow of replacement Spitfires and Hurricanes.

Fighter Command lost a total of thirteen Spitfires and Hurricanes destroyed, twenty-three more damaged, with five pilots killed and eight wounded. Again, the scales had tipped in the defenders' favour during a day of intense fighting on a broad front, from Rochester in the east and Portland to the west, and as far inland as London and Yeovil. Six separate raids had been launched, three simultaneously – none of which achieved anything of military significance. By night, the German bombers returned, however, targeting Central London and Merseyside – but the battle in the dark is a different story.

On the same day, 109 Coastal Command aircraft flew the usual round of patrols, reconnaissance and offensive sorties; 19 convoys were escorted. At dawn four 59 Squadron Blenheims successfully attacked Lorient concurrently with 42 Squadron mining the Weser and Jade estuaries. One of 53 Squadron's Blenheims crashed into the sea off Sheerness, target Rotterdam, its crew killed, as was a Hudson crew after their aircraft crashed on taking-off from RAF Aldergrove. Lack of cloud cover over north-west France led to 2 Group scrubbing reconnaissance of the Channel ports, and a sweep of the North Sea proved uneventful for a flight of Blenheims. By night, though, Bomber Command mounted a 'maximum effort'.

German ports and shipping were to be the main focus of this substantial attack, along with the RLM in Berlin, and IG Farben's Leuna works, the second largest chemical operation in Germany and one of the biggest synthetic oil producing plants. The Ruhr's vitally important marshalling yards were also to be hit, and more mines laid in the Elbe; over 100 aircraft were involved. Thirty-four Blenheims went 'barge bashing' at Boulogne, Calais, Dunkirk and Ostend, and seventeen of the forty-two Hampdens, Wellingtons and Whitleys sent to the RLM reported having successfully bombed their target – but the six Whitley crews concerned described flak over the target as 'severe'. Leuna was hit by twelve Wellingtons, and nine more attacked targets in the Ruhr, known as 'Happy Valley' to Bomber Command's crews. Hampdens also attacked shipping at Antwerp and carried out the Elbe mining; a lone Whitley hit shipping at Le Havre. Inevitably considering the number of aircraft involved, there were casualties arising.

RAF Wattisham's Blenheim-equipped 107 Squadron:

> Nine aircraft, captained by Squadron Leader Hull, Squadron Leader Harte, Sergeant Ralston, Sergeant [Jack Edwin] Merrett, Pilot Officer Culling, Pilot Officer Bywater, Pilot Officer Smith, Sergeant Dunn and Sergeant Williams were detailed to take-off in the early evening to attack concentrations of barges at Calais and Dunkerque [Dunkirk]. Squadron Leader Harte and Sergeant Ralston successfully attacked Dunkerque. Bomb bursts were not observed and little opposition was experienced. Three enemy fighters were seen patrolling the target area but no contact was made. One aircraft, Sergeant Merrett, unfortunately crashed when taking-off. The aeroplane caught fire and the bombs exploded. [ORB]

Loaded with just four 250lb bombs, Merrett's Blenheim had attained 150ft when the starboard engine failed. The aircraft slewed to port, crashing in flames near the control tower. Wing Commander Laurence Sinclair of 110 Squadron was in the officers' mess and rushed out to help. Before he reached the burning wreck, two bombs exploded, blowing open the fuselage, in which, through the flames, Sinclair saw a prone airman. Dashing into the blaze, the wing commander dragged the air gunner to safety, and helped by the SMO, loaded the injured man into an ambulance. Unfortunately, the man died, as did the pilot and navigator, but for his complete 'disregard for his own safety', Sinclair was awarded the George Cross. Later knighted and retiring from the service as an air-vice marshal, Sinclair's abiding memory of that fateful night was not of his own gallantry, but of shame at the behaviour of those who, he felt, should have stayed to help but did not; Air Vice-Marshal Sir Laurence Sinclair DSO GC died in 2002, aged 93.

Returning from Berlin, a 50 Squadron Hampden crashed on landing near Bircham Newton, but the crew were unhurt. RAF Marham's 38 Squadron lost a Wellington on the Leipzig run, and Marham's 115 Squadron lost two. No. 10 Squadron, based at Leeming, lost two Whitleys, one of which ditched in the Irish Sea, somewhat lost, on the return flight, the crew of which being rescued, but the other was shot down over Badbergen by *Oberleutnant* Werner Streib of 2(N)/JG 1; two of the crew were killed, two captured. Streib also claimed Wellingtons destroyed that night over Bersenbrück and Menslage, becoming the first *Nachtjäger* to achieve three victories in a single night (he would survive the war with sixty-eight aerial victories, all but one after dark). *Oberleutnant* Heinrich Greise of I/NJ 1 – who would not survive the war – also accounted for a Wellington destroyed over Löningen.

Daily Home Intelligence Report:

> The army are still fretting against inaction and are inclined to feel that all the praise and glory are going to the RAF. The air raid near Belfast seems to have been welcomed by the troops as a diversion which made them feel less out of it.
>
> It is reported that land mines have been dropped in the district (Willesden) by parachute, and cases have been known of people thinking they were parachutists and rushing towards them with very dire results. It is felt that some immediate announcement should be made to prevent this sort of thing happening.
>
> Confidence still strong … Refugees are lowering morale by their lurid stories of bombing London, but the situation is not at all serious.

Reflections

The period of 18 September 1940–30 September 1940, beyond doubt, saw the Luftwaffe's daylight offensive against Britain substantially defeated.

The period under review saw much reduced daylight bombing by the Germans, the three main raids being those on 25 September 1940 against the BAC at Filton, the following day's attack on Supermarine at Woolston, and the raid directed at Westland Aircraft on 30 September 1940, which devasted Sherborne by mistake. All three raids were mounted by KG 55, the history of which states:

> September 1940 was the hardest month of action for everyone involved in the Battle of Britain, friend and foe alike. KG 55 alone lost twenty aircraft and fifteen crews, not to mention those wounded. Time and time again *Geschwader* personnel from various roles had to – and wanted to – step in as gunners … *Oberleutnant* Miller often flew along, bypassing a preventative order by choosing a military rank – he was the III *Gruppe*'s senior physician. So too did the *Geschwader* Meteorological Officer, Friedrich Wobst, all these comrades helping relieve the burden on the aircrews, who are exhausted.
>
> In the thirty days of September 1940, the Luftwaffe lost irreplaceable experience: four *Geschwader Kommodore*, thirteen *Gruppenkommandeur*, and twenty-eight *Staffelkapitän*.

These were serious losses – which were unsustainable in terms of aircrew or aircraft – and by 30 September 1940 the *Kampfgeschwadern* had been reduced to 52 per cent in aircraft strength and aircrew numbers were only 68 per cent.

On 27 September 1940, on the ill-fated Yate raid, *Erprobungsgruppe* 210 lost 40 per cent of its strength and its third *Gruppenkommandeur* of the Battle of Britain, *Hauptmann* Martin Lutz, who had just received the *Ritterkreuz* for his part in the destruction of Supermarine; this previously dangerous fighter-bomber unit would not participate in any further significant activity of England. Indeed, the same day also saw exceptionally heavy losses to *Luftflotte* 2's *Zerstörer* force, effectively neutralising the Me 110 as a day fighter – a bitter pill for *Reichsmarschall* Hermann Göring, having placed so much faith in the twin-engined heavy fighter. This was especially galling for the Luftwaffe chief considering how well the earlier phases of the Battle of Britain, fought over shipping and coastal targets, had begun for his 110s.

The Me 109 force was at a disadvantage owing to the single-engined fighter's limited range and restricted freedom of action given the need to escort slower and more vulnerable bombers. The 109 force was also significantly weakened. By 28 September 1940, for example, JG 53 only had 93 aircraft, only 72 of which were serviceable – just 60 per cent of the *Geschwader*'s authorised strength of 124 Me 109s. This shortage of operational Me 109s was compounded by Göring's insistence that one *Staffel* in every *Gruppe* would become fighter bombers. The German aircraft factories were simply unable to keep pace with the demand for replacement machines – in September 1940, for example, Germany produced 218 single-engined fighters; Britain, on the other hand, whose aircraft industry was under attack and had suffered the virtual destruction of Supermarine on 26 September 1940, manufacturer 467 – only 29 less Spitfires and Hurricanes than in July 1940.

Inadequate provision for the supply of replacement aircraft meant, in simple terms, the level of superiority required to defeat such an opponent as Fighter Command was impossible to achieve. This was partly because such an intense and drawn-out aerial campaign was unprecedented and, therefore, the number of replacement machines now required, and the production facilities required, had not previously been considered. Quite simply, the Luftwaffe lacked the means, in every respect, to destroy the British aircraft industry – in fact, British production figures confirm that the greater the attacks and danger of invasion, the workers' output actually increased. Suffice it to say that on 1 October 1940, the Germans had 275 operational Me 109s – compared to the RAF's 732 serviceable single-engined fighters recorded on 28 September 1940.

In terms of pilots, by 30 September 1940, taking JG 53 as an example, the *Geschwader* had suffered twenty-four killed or missing, eighteen more were POWs and six had been wounded. In sum, at the start of the battle, in July 1940, JG 53's establishment was 113 pilots, of which 48, 40 per cent, were now out of action. The *Jagdwaffe* had now reached the point whereby it was unable to replace casualties with experienced pilots, these places being filled by increasingly young and inexperienced officer candidates and junior NCOs fresh from flying training schools. Indeed, 30 September 1940 was one of the worst ever days for the highly successful JG 26: four pilots lost offset against only seven combat claims (and those were inflated as only two can be confirmed).

German flying training programmes lacked urgency, and the majority of pilots trained and available were bomber pilots who could not be swiftly re-trained as fighter pilots. Conversely, RAF Training Command was now working at full stretch, prioritising producing fighter pilots, given the current need – and replacement pilots, although lacking in combat experience, were made available – not least through the influx of free Poles and Czechs, whose English had sufficiently improved for there to be two Polish and one Czech squadron operational, in addition to pilots from those and free men of other occupied nations to be embedded throughout Fighter Command's squadrons. Of course, RAF pilots enjoyed one advantage over the Luftwaffe, in that if they survived being shot down over Britain, they would soon fight again – whereas Luftwaffe airmen brought down over England faced long years in a prison camp.

It is interesting to review the days during the battle to date on which the numbers of RAF fighter pilots killed reached double figures.

8 August 1940:	fifteen pilots
11 August 1940:	twenty-five pilots
12 August 1940:	ten pilots
15 August 1940:	thirteen pilots
18 August 1940:	ten pilots
7 September 1940:	thirteen pilots
11 September 1940:	eleven pilots
15 September 1940:	eleven pilots
27 September 1940:	nineteen pilots

Traditionally, thanks to the British historian Dr Alfred Price writing in 1979, 18 August 1940 will forevermore be popularly known as 'The Hardest Day', because both sides lost more aircraft than on any other day in the Battle of Britain:

> [There were] 100 aircraft put out of action, 69 of them wrecked or damaged beyond repair. Fighter Command had 73 fighters put out of action, 39 of them wrecked or damaged beyond repair.

From Fighter Command's perspective, however, it was replacement pilots, at that time, which was the issue, not aircraft. That being so, surely 11 August 1940 (see Volume 2, *Battle of Britain: The Breaking Storm, 10 July 1940 – 12 August 1940*) was 'The Worst Day', and 27 September 1940 – the events of which are included in this book – a close second.

Despite deficiencies in manpower and aircraft, there were occasions between 18 September 1940 and 30 September 1940 when the Me 109 pilots demonstrated how lethal they could still be when left free to roam, with the immeasurable advantages of height, sun and surprise. A primary case in point is 27 September 1940, when in the Battles over southern England, twenty-six RAF fighters were destroyed, with nineteen pilots killed – a day considered by Churchill to be the Battle of Britain's third greatest day. The defending fighters, of course, had the advantage of early warning from RDF, but often that was short, squadrons having insufficient time to reach 20,000ft or more in good time to intercept the enemy on equal terms. 'Spotters' were being used, single Spitfires at high altitude, watching the enemy forming up and able to report back more accurately than radar regarding the size and composition of assembling and approaching raids, but even this could not fundamentally alter the situation. What is enormously significant, however, is that when the Battle of Britain began, Air Vice-Marshal Keith Park responded using small formations of sections, flights or lone squadrons – but as the battle progressed and enemy formations both increased in size and penetrated deeper, providing greater opportunities to intercept, he had no qualms about scrambling squadrons in pairs or threes, as wings, to operate together, meeting the enemy in strength. Considering the row that broke in October 1940 over the 12 Group wing, the long-accepted narrative that Park only ever met the Germans in small formations is yet another myth of the Battle of Britain. Indeed, this will be explored in greater detail in Volume 7, *Battle of Britain: The Final Curtain, 1 October 1940–31 October 1940.*

Another thing Air Vice-Marshal Keith Park did was use Spitfire squadrons in pairs, at high altitude, the Spitfire having a far superior performance to the Hurricane at those great heights the Me 109s intruded at. This provided a high-altitude umbrella, allowing the Hurricanes to operate lower down and tackle the bombers, which generally approached between 15,000 and 19,000ft. It was a perfect arrangement – and without the Spitfire's high-altitude performance, things could have turned out very differently, because the Me 109s would always have had the height advantage, and lots of it. Indeed, *Generalfeldmarschall* Albert Kesselring wrote that 'Only the Spitfires really bothered us', although, as Group Captain Peter Townsend charged, 'The Luftwaffe seemed to be suffering from "Spitfire Snobbery".' There was certainly more kudos attached to shooting down a Spitfire, as evidenced by *Leutnant* Heinz Knocke of I/JG 52:

> The Supermarine Spitfire, because of its manoeuvrability and technical performance, has given the German formations plenty of trouble. '*Achtung* [attention] Spitfire!'. German pilots have learned to pay particular attention when they hear this warning in their earphones. We consider shooting down a Spitfire to be an outstanding achievement, which is most certainly is.

The results of German daylight bombing during the period covered by this book were generally poor, mainly owing to cloud coverage and, on certain occasions, heavy fighter opposition. Only on two occasions was truly significant damage caused to aircraft factories, namely by KG 55's attack on Filton on 25 September 1940, and the following day's successful raid on Supermarine at Woolston. Only the latter raid, however, had any real impact, and virtually none in respect of fighter production. What that raid did do, however, was see Lord Beaverbrook shut the vulnerable Woolston site down and disperse Spitfire production hither and thither. Great though the damage had been to the BAC at Filton, given that the site concerned bomber production, the only effect it had on Fighter Command was temporarily stalling deliveries of the new Beaufighter. The other raids, aimed at Parnall and Westland Aircraft, even if successful, which they were not, would similarly have had no effect on the production of Spitfires and Hurricanes, given that neither site was manufacturing fighters – which brings us, yet again, to that perennial problem of poor Luftwaffe intelligence. This not only led to questionable target selection and, therefore, wasted effort and resources, but also over estimations of the damage inflicted upon Fighter Command equally misinformed strategy.

During this phase, the Germans continued attacking on a broad front, often from Rochester to Portland, and launching simultaneous attacks on the 10 and 11 Group areas in an attempt to overwhelm the defences. Again, this ignored von Clausewitz, who made clear that concentrated effort on a single point was the key to victory. Instead of doing just that and using one huge force to obliterate a specific target, Luftwaffe resources were too thinly spread, and target selection was inconsistent and confused. Moreover, the dwindling bomber force was attacking both night and day – and the night bomber force was already substantial, in itself weakening the daytime effort, with anything between 150–300 bombers operating over Britain at night, mainly attacking London and Liverpool.

With diminishing resources and unsustainable losses, the German bombers, excepting the fast and heavily armed Ju 88, were now pulled out of the day battle to attack Britain under the much safer cloak of darkness. Arguably, then, the Germans had lost the daylight battle by 30 September 1940. Going forward, the last month of day-fighting, October 1940, would feature high-flying fighter sweeps, fighter-bomber attacks, and small numbers of heavily escorted Ju 88s occasionally sallying forth along with lone Ju 88s flying nuisance attacks when weather permitted. Again, such plan as there was by day continued targeting the British aircraft industry – but whatever lay ahead, with winter fast approaching and with it the air fighting season's conclusion, the effect was unlikely to impede British aircraft production. That being so, and considering the postponement of Operation *Seelöwe*, the crisis had passed.

An important thing about this particular book is that with most of the aircraft factories concentrated in the West Country, it has been a neglected phase of the Battle of Britain compared to those concerning attacks on airfields and London. The courage of the factory workers involved, under fire, facing the prospect of attack on a daily basis, however, must not be overlooked, or the fact that the Battle of Britain did not just take place over London and the south-east. Now, we have a robust and comprehensive record and narrative of this phase – which is long overdue.

On 30 September 1940, the bombing of Sherborne had been a tragic accident, caused by cloud concealing the intended target of Westland Aircraft at nearby Yeovil and confusing the enemy formation leader. Surprisingly, the Germans publicly accepted that a mistake had been made. Opening with the familiar phrase 'Germany calling, Germany calling', 'Lord Haw Haw', the traitor William Joyce, actually broadcast an apology to Sherborne – whilst ominously predicting that Yeovil's turn was still to come. As we will see in Volume 7, *Battle of Britain: The Final Curtain, 1 October 1940–31 October 1940*, he was right…

Appendix

German Bomber Tactics and Formations

The basic battle formation around which the entire *Kampfgeschwader* was built was the *Kette* of three aircraft flying in an arrowhead formation, similar to the RAF vic. In daylight, each *Gruppe* disposed its aircraft in three principal variations (see figs. 1–3). These formations were used for both cruising and attacking and could be fluidly changed in the air. For example, during the raids on the BAC at Filton (25 September 1940) and Supermarine at Southampton (26 September 1940), *Major* Friedrich Kless put KG 55 into *Ketten* line astern, to concentrate the fall of bombs (see fig. 4). When more than one *Gruppe* was flying together, both usually flew this formation, with one *Gruppe* 500ft above the leading *Gruppe* with between a quarter and up to 3 miles separating them. On occasions, the raiders operated in shallow vics, giving the impression of abreast formations in three waves (fig. 2). All formations, whether in line astern or abreast, were usually flown stepped up.

German bomber formations generally operated between 10,000–20,000ft, the preferred operational height being 13,000–17,000ft. RAF intelligence noted,

> It has been observed that the various units forming the main formation fly very close together and often succeed in maintaining their cohesion when attacked.

Such close formations ensured mutual fire support – and as evidenced in this book, that combined crossfire could be lethal. RAF intelligence also noted that evasive tactics included:

i. Seeking the nearest available cloud cover.
ii. Descending to ground or sea-level at high speed, making a jinking low-level escape at full throttle.
iii. Using dive brakes, when fitted, to enable execution of a steep dive, combined with turns, thus causing attacking fighters to overshoot.
iv. Simulating damage by emitting smoke from an apparatus fitted either in the tail or behind the engine nacelles.

GERMAN BOMBER FORMATIONS (*not to scale*)

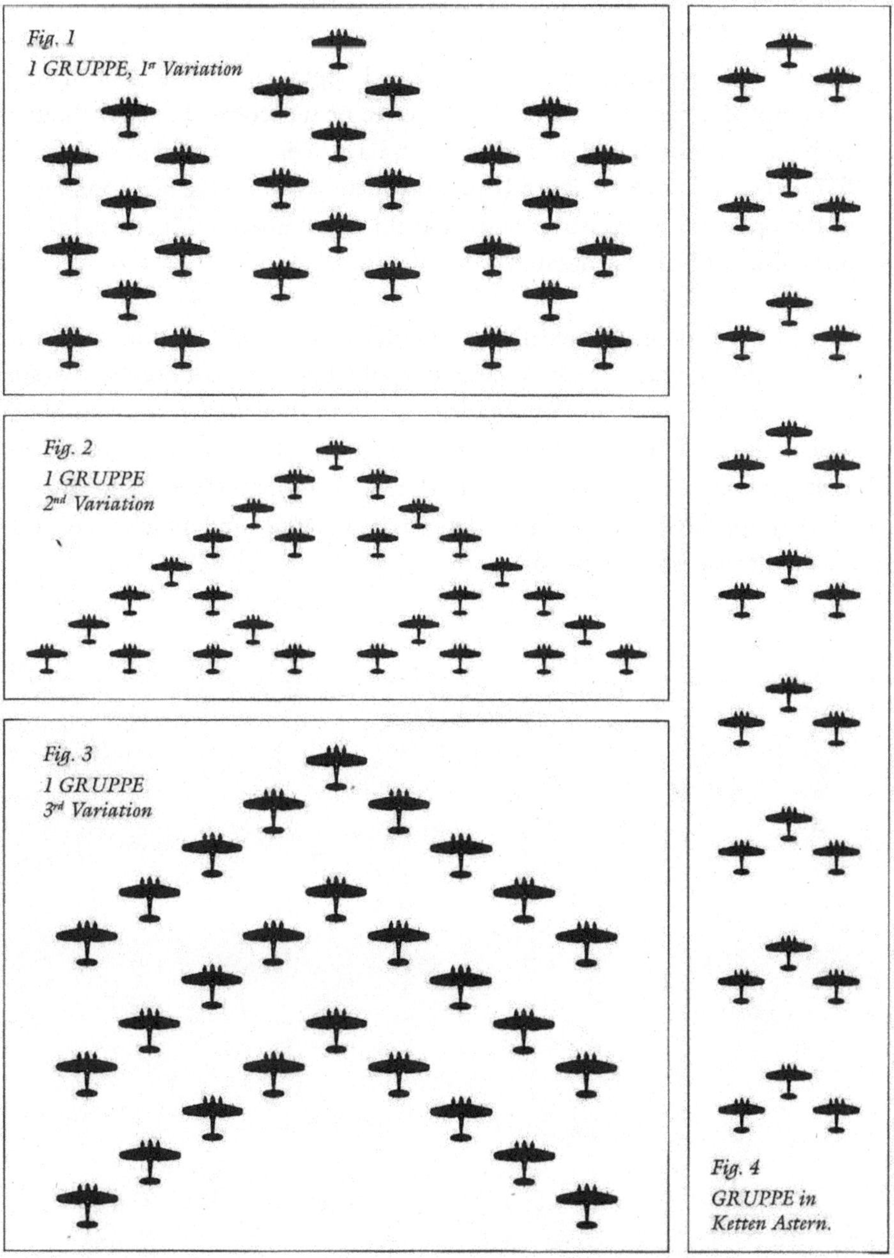

Mass formations often separated into sub-formations on crossing the English coastline, or shortly afterwards, and small groups of aircraft sometimes flew independently towards the same objective.

According to RAF intelligence, it was often just one group that would penetrate to their target

> with any degree of determination … the subsequent behavior [*sic*] of the remaining groups has given the impression that their role has been to confuse our defence and divert our fighters from the main intention. These subsidiary formations have either dropped bombs on what has been an unidentifiable target short of the objective or turned for home without taking any offensive action. These tactics have been successful in that our fighter control has experienced difficulty in anticipating the development of the operation in its early stages and this has sometimes increased the difficulties of bringing about a successful interception.

The reader will doubtless recall and identify various raids recounted in this narrative and to which these comments apply. The German bombers would also frequently fly a confusing 'dog leg' course to their target, an example of this being KG 55s run to Filton via Portland, west of Yeovil, only turning for their Bristol target over Weston-super-Mare – the formation's intention having previously appeared to be to cross the Bristol Channel and attack Cardiff. It was a clever ruse – and worked.

Acknowledgements

This unique series of books has arisen from over forty years of research and study of the subject, throughout which time I led a privileged relationship with survivors, and the relatives of casualties – too many to thank individually, but all have my appreciation.

In relation to this special project, I must thank Charles Hewitt, Martin Mace and Matthew Potts of Pen & Sword, and the production and marketing teams, who are always a pleasure to work with and collectively do a first-class job. Martin, of course, deserves a special mention for his sterling work on my behalf at The National Archives, and for being a very good friend and kindred spirit, always helpful and sharing my passion for making history both accessible and inclusive.

Suffice it to say, it has been an absolute privilege to produce this work for the Battle of Britain Memorial Trust and National Memorial to The Few, and I must thank our Chairman, Richard Hunting CBE, Honorary Secretary, Group Captain Patrick Tootal OBE DL RAF, Trustee Wing Commander Andrew Simpson RAFVR(T), Major (Ret'd) Jules Gomez, Site Manager, National Memorial to The Few, and both Malcolm Triggs and Becca Collier-Cook for their help in promoting the work. I would also acknowledge kind assistance from Edward McManus of the Battle of Britain London Monument.

All the pilots, other survivors and eyewitnesses mentioned in this book are all now sadly deceased – but all still have my gratitude for so kindly supporting my work many years ago and helping reconstruct the dramatic past.

As always, my old friend Andy Long was ever helpful; pioneering researchers and historians Allan White and Ken Wakefield helped me over thirty years ago when researching the raids on West Country aircraft factories, as did Chris Goss, the late Dr Alfred Price, and the late Fred Ballam of Westland Aircraft. Sherborne School kindly provided forty written accounts of the 30 September 1940 raid, written by shocked pupils immediately afterwards; others who helped were the Museum of South Somerset, the ROC Museum, Dorset County Record Office, Somerset County Record Office, the National Meteorological Library and Archive, and the Bundesarchiv. This time around, Amy Seadon, Head of Collections, Learning and Interpretation at Aerospace Bristol was particularly helpful in respect of the raid on 25 September 1940, and I am equally grateful to The Reverend Elizabeth L.A. Gregory, Rector of St Peter's Church, Filton, for permission to quote the civilian first-hand accounts of the raid collated and published by the church and local history society. Dave Key, who runs the 'Supermariners' website dedicated to those who worked for the famous aircraft manufacturer, kindly showed me around the former factory site and Peartree Green at Woolston, where the shelter was hit on 24 September 1940, a moving experience indeed, and also generously provided first-hand accounts of the various relevant raids. Kate Hedges-Gower came up trumps at eleventh hour with unique information from the log book and notes of her august ancestor, Pilot Officer Alan Hedges of 257 Squadron.

Finally, I must reserve a special thanks to my wife, Sue. This particular eight-volume project is an unprecedent investigation into the Battle of Britain, from many angles, and the process is intense. The forbearance of my family, especially Sue, and friends, therefore, is essential, and I am also grateful for the interest and support reflected by my Facebook and other social followings.

Bibliography

The National Archives

The National Archives at Kew is the main repository for primary source documents; the following documents were consulted during the course of research for this book.

Operations Record Books

AIR27/2018: 'A' Flight, 1 Photographic Reconnaissance Unit
AIR27/2015: 'B' Flight, 1 Photographic Reconnaissance Unit
AIR27/589: 1 Squadron
AIR27/528: 1 (RCAF) Squadron (Listed as 401 Squadron by TNA)
AIR27/32: 3 Squadron
AIR27/164: 12 Squadron
AIR27/202: 15 Squadron
AIR27/252: 19 Squadron
AIR27/287: 23 Squadron
AIR27: 305: 25 Squadron
AIR27/317: 26 Squadron
AIR27/341: 29 Squadron
AIR27/360: 32 Squadron
AIR27/441: 43 Squadron
AIR27/447: 44 Squadron
AIR27/460: 46 Squadron
AIR27/554: 50 Squadron
AIR27/503: 53 Squadron
AIR27/511: 54 Squadron
AIR27/528: 56 Squadron
AIR27/554: 59 Squadron
AIR27/598: 66 Squadron
AIR27/624: 72 Squadron
AIR27/629: 73 Squadron
AIR27/640: 74 Squadron
AIR27/655: 77 Squadron
AIR27/664: 79 Squadron
AIR27/681: 82 Squadron
AIR27/712: 87 Squadron
AIR27/776: 97 Squadron
AIR27/801: 101 Squadron
AIR27/807: 102 Squadron
AIR27/813: 103 Squadron
AIR27/826: 105 Squadron
AIR27/841: 107 Squadron
AIR27/857: 110 Squadron
AIR27/866: 111 Squadron
AIR27/882: 114 Squadron
AIR27/969: 141 Squadron
AIR27/984: 145 Squadron
AIR27/1008: 150 Squadron
AIR27/1025: 152 Squadron
AIR27/1298: 210 Squadron
AIR27/1315: 213 Squadron
AIR27/1340: 217 Squadron
AIR27/1360: 219 Squadron
AIR27/1365: 220 Squadron
AIR27/1371: 222 Squadron
AIR27/1385: 224 Squadron
AIR27/1428: 232 Squadron
AIR27/1442: 235 Squadron
AIR27/1445: 236 Squadron
AIR27/1453: 238 Squadron
AIR27/1471: 242 (Canadian) Squadron
AIR27/1495: 248 Squadron
AIR27/1498: 249 Squadron
AIR27/1511: 253 Squadron
AIR27/1526: 257 Squadron
AIR27/1553: 264 Squadron
AIR27/1558: 266 Squadron
AIR27/1661: 302 (Polish) Squadron
AIR27/1663: 303 (Polish) Squadron
AIR27/1680: 310 (Czech) Squadron
AIR27/1941: 500 Squadron
AIR27/1949: 501 Squadron

AIR27/1964: 504 Squadron
AIR27/2059: 600 Squadron
AIR27/2068: 601 Squadron
AIR27/2028: 604 Squadron
AIR27/2088: 605 Squadron
AIR27/2093: 607 Squadron
AIR27/2102: 609 Squadron
AIR27/2106: 610 Squadron
AIR27/2112: 612 Squadron
AIR27/2123: 615 Squadron
AIR27/2126: 616 Squadron
AIR27/2263: 928 Squadron

Pilots' Combat Reports
AIR50/1: 1 Squadron
AIR50/4: 3 Squadron
AIR50/9: 17 Squadron
AIR50/10: 19 Squadron
AIR50/16: 32 Squadron
AIR50/18: 41 Squadron
AIR50/19: 43 Squadron
AIR50/20: 46 Squadron
AIR50/21: 54 Squadron
AIR50/22: 56 Squadron
AIR50/24: 64 Squadron
AIR50/25: 65 Squadron
AIR50/26: 66 Squadron
AIR50/31: 73 Squadron
AIR50/32: 74 Squadron
AIR50/33: 79 Squadron
AIR50/36: 85 Squadron
AIR50/37: 87 Squadron
AIR50/40: 92 Squadron
AIR50/43: 111 Squadron
AIR50/62: 145 Squadron
AIR50/63: 151 Squadron
AIR50/64: 152 Squadron
AIR50/83: 213 Squadron
AIR50/84: 219 Squadron
AIR50/85: 222 Squadron
AIR50/88: 232 Squadron
AIR50/89: 234 Squadron
AIR50/91: 238 Squadron
AIR50/92: 242 (Canadian) Squadron
AIR50/96: 249 Squadron
AIR50/100: 257 Squadron
AIR50/104: 264 Squadron
AIR50/105: 266 Squadron
AIR50/116: 302 (Polish) Squadron
AIR50/177: 303 (Polish) Squadron
AIR50/122: 310 (Czech) Squadron
AIR50/163: 504 Squadron
AIR50/165: 601 Squadron
AIR50/166: 602 Squadron
AIR50/167: 603 Squadron
AIR50/171: 609 Squadron
AIR50/173: 611 Squadron
AIR50/172: 610 Squadron
AIR50/175: 615 Squadron
AIR50/176: 616 Squadron
AIR50/473: 7 OTU

Casualty Files
AIR81/3504: Pilot Officer E. Burgoyne
AIR81/3461: Pilot Officer P.C. Cardell
AIR81/3395: Pilot Officer A.L. Hedges
AIR81/3460: Pilot Officer R.G. Miller
AIR81/3356: Pilot Officer H.L. Whitbread

Miscellaneous Documents
AIR22/296: Personnel: Casualties, Strength and Establishment of the RAF
AIR16/300: German Bomber Tactics
CAB66/12/38: Loss of Time Due to Air Raid Warnings

RAF Station Operations Record Books
AIR28/64: RAF Biggin Hill
AIR28/178: RAF Croydon

AIR28/345: RAF Hawkinge
AIR28/384: RAF Hornchurch
AIR28/512: RAF Manston
AIR28/526: RAF Martlesham Heath
AIR28/419: RAF Kenley
AIR28/509: RAF Lympne
AIR28/601: RAF Northolt
AIR28/815: RAF Tangmere
AIR28/907: RAF West Malling
AIR28/603: RAF North Weald

Ministry of Home Security Daily Intelligence Reports
HO203/4: 24/06/40–29/09/40
HO203/5: 29/09/40–31/12/40

Pilots' Flying Log Books (ranks as at time consulted)
Air Vice-Marshal Sir Keith Park (courtesy RNZAF Museum)
Squadron Leader D.R.S. Bader, 242 (Canadian) Squadron (courtesy RAF Museum)
Squadron Leader R.G. Kellett, 303 (Polish) Squadron
Squadron Leader H.C. Burton, 66 and 616 Squadrons
Squadron Leader B.J.E. Lane DFC, 19 Squadron (AIR4/58)
Flight Lieutenant G.C. Matheson, 222 Squadron
Flight Lieutenant E. Thomas, 222 Squadron
Flight Lieutenant F.M. Thomas, 56 Squadron
Pilot Officer D. Crowley-Milling, 242 (Canadian) Squadron
Pilot Officer H.S.L. Dundas, 616 Squadron
Pilot Officer D.M. Crook DFC, 609 Squadron (AIR4/21)
Pilot Officer A.L. Hedges, 257 Squadron
Pilot Officer F.W. Higginson DFM, 56 Squadron
Pilot Officer R.L. Jones, 19 and 64 Squadrons
Pilot Officer A.G. Osmand, 213 Squadron
Pilot Officer A.F. Vokes, 19 Squadron
Flight Sergeant G.C. Unwin DFM, 19 Squadron
Sergeant B.J. Jennings, 19 Squadron

German Documents
OKW Directives for Invasion of the UK, Operation *Seelöwe*, Summer and Autumn 1940, Bundesarchiv
Luftflotte 2 and 3 records, available via Digital History Archive (see website detailed below)
German fighter combat claims can be found in the OKL records of the Chef für Ausz. und Dizsiplin Luftwaffe-Personalamt L.P.(A)V OKLs (available via various online sources)
German loss records can be found in the Oberfehlsaber der Luftwaffe Genst. Gen. Qu/6 Abteilung/40.g. Kdos.I.C., records, preserved by the Imperial War Museum

Miscellaneous Sources
Interview of Air Chief Marshal Sir Keith Park: BBC Archive/British Library 01 January 1961 https://www.bbc.co.uk/archive/battleofbritain/11422.shtml

Unpublished Sources

Correspondence, papers and interviews, Dilip Sarkar Archive

Original and uncensored manuscript of *Spitfire Pilot*, Flight Lieutenant D.M. Crook DFC

The memories and thoughts of the late The Reverend J.H.K. Dagger, Battle of Britain Padre: RAF Exeter 1940–41 (courtesy of his son Christopher Dagger)

Unpublished memoir of Group Captain R.G. Kellett

Unpublished notes of Pilot Officer A.L. Hedges

Published Sources

Ackroyd, P., *London: The Biography*, Chatto & Windus, London, 2000

Adams, P., *Hurricane Squadron: 87 Squadron at War 1939-1941*, Air Research Publications, New Malden, 1988

Aders, G. and Held, W., *Chronik:* Jagdgeschwader *51 'Mölders'*, Motor Buch Verlag, Stuttgart, 2009

Addison, P. and Crang, J.A. (eds.), *Listening to Britain: Home Intelligence Reports on Britain's Finest Hour – May to September 1940*, Vintage Books, London, 2011

Addison, P. and Crang, J.A. (eds.), *The Burning Blue: A New History of the Battle of Britain*, Pimlico, London, 2000

Alexander, K., *Australia's Few and the Battle of Britain*, Pen & Sword Books, Barnsley, 2015

Allen, Wing Commander H.R., *Fighter Squadron: A Memoir 1940–42*, Granada, London, 1982

Anonymous, *The Battle of Britain: August–October 1940*, Ministry of Information on behalf of the Air Ministry, London, 1941

Anonymous, *The Battle of Britain*, Air Ministry Pamphlet 156, Issued by the Department of the Air Member for Training, August 1943

Anonymous, (Ministry of Information), *Roof Over Britain: The Official Story of the AA Defences 1939–1942*, HMSO, London, 1943

Anonymous, *Air/Sea Rescue: The Second World War 1939–1945*, Royal Air Force, Air Publication 3232, Air Ministry (AHB), London, 1952

Anonymous, *The Rise & Fall of the German Air Force 1939–45*, Air Ministry Pamphlet 248, Public Record Office, London, 2001

Ashworth, C., *RAF Coastal Command: 1936–1969*, PSL, Sparkford, 1992

Bekker, C., *Hitler's Naval War*, Corgi, London, 1976

Bekker, C., *The Luftwaffe War Diaries*, Corgi Books, London, 1972

Bialer, U., *The Shadow of the Bomber: The Fear of Air Attack and British Politics 1932–39*, Royal Historical Society, London, 1980

Bishop, E., *The Battle of Britain*, George Allen & Unwin Limited, London, 1960

Bowyer, M.J.F., *2 Group RAF: A Complete History, 1936–1945*, Faber & Faber, London, 1974

Calder, A., *The People's War: Britain 1939–45*, Pimlico, London, 2008

Caldwell, D., *JG 26: Top Guns of the Luftwaffe*, Orion Books, New York, 1991

Caldwell, D., *The JG 26 War Diary: Volume One, 1939–42*, Grub Street, London, 1996

Campion, G., *The Good Fight: Battle of Britain Propaganda and The Few*, Palgrave-Macmillan, London, 2010

Cannadine, D. (ed.), *The Speeches of Winston Churchill*, Penguin, London, 1990

Churchill, W.S., *The Second World War – Volume II: Their Finest Hour*, Cassell & Co., London, 1949

Clapson, M., *Britain in the Twentieth Century*, Routledge, Abingdon, 2009

Collier, B., *The Defence of the United Kingdom*, HMSO, London, 1957

Cox, J.S., 'RAF & Luftwaffe Intelligence Compared' in Handel, M.I. (ed.), *Intelligence & Military Operations*, Frank Cass, Abingdon, 1990

Cox, S. and Probert, H. (eds.), *The Battle Re-Thought: A Symposium on the Battle of Britain*, Airlife, Shrewsbury, 1991

Dean, Sir M., *The Royal Air Force and Two World Wars*, Cassell, London, 1979

Deere, Air Commodore A.C., *Nine Lives*, Hodder Paperback Limited, London, 1959

Deighton, L., *Fighter: The True Story of the Battle of Britain*, Triad/Panther Books, St Albans, 1979

Dierich, W., Chronik: Kampfgeschwader 55 'Greif', Motorbuch Verlag, Stuttgart, 2012

Dierich, W., Kampfgeschwader *'Edelweiss': The History of a German Bomber Unit, 1939–45*, Purnell Book Services Limited, London, 1975

Devon, S., *'Glorious': The Life-Story of Stanley Devon, Twice 'British News Photographer of the Year'*, George G. Harrap & Co. Limited, London, 1957

Dimbleby, J., *The Battle of the Atlantic: How the Allies Won the War*, Penguin Books, London, 2016

Donnelly, L., *The Other Few: The Contribution Made* by *Bomber and Coastal Aircrew to the Winning of the Battle of Britain*, Red Kite, Walton-on-Thames, 2004

Donnelly, M., *Britain in the Second World War*, Routledge, London, 1999

Dowding, Air Chief Marshal Lord H.C.T., *Dispatch: The Battle of Britain*, *London Gazette*, London, 1946

Ellan, Squadron Leader B.J., *Spitfire! The Experiences of a Fighter Pilot*, John Murray, London, 1942

Filton Parish Church, *Remembering Filton: The Air Raid Targeting the Bristol Aeroplane Company (BAC) Factory at Filton, 25th September 1940*, Filton Parish Church with Filton Community History, Filton, 2010

Fleming, P., *Invasion 1940*, Rupert Hart-Davis, London, 1957

Flint, P., *RAF Kenley: The Story of the Royal Air Force Station 1917–1974*, Terence Dalton, Limited, Lavenham, 1985

Forbes, A. and Allen, H.R. (eds.), *Ten Fighter Boys*, Collins, London, 1942

Foreman, J., *RAF Fighter Command Victory Claims of World War Two: Volume One*, Air Research Publications, Red Kite, Walton-on-Thames, 2003

Forrester, L., *Fly for Your Life: The Story of R.R. Stanford Tuck DSO, DFC and Two Bars*, The Companion Book Club, London, 1956

Galland, A., *The First and the Last: Germany's Fighter Force in the Second World War*, Fontana, London, 1954

Gleave, Group Captain T.P. (writing as 'RAF Casualty'), *I Had a Row With a German*, MacMillan & Co., London, 1941

Gleed, Wing Commander I.R., *Arise to Conquer*, Victor Gollanz Limited, London, 1942

Green, W., *Aircraft of the Battle of Britain*, MacDonald & Co. (Publishers) Limited and Pan Books Limited, London, 1969

Hallam, I.N., *One of The Few: Ian Lewis McGregor Hallam*, privately published, 2020

Handel, M.I. (ed.), *Intelligence and Military Operations*, Frank Cass, Abingdon, 1990

Honeysett, J., *Death in the Afternoon: The Bombing of Vickers-Supermarine Works, Southampton, September 15th, 24th and 26th 1940*, privately published, Southampton, 2000

Hough, R. and Richards, D., *The Battle of Britain: The Jubilee History*,
Hodder & Stoughton Limited, London, 1990

Humphreys, R., *Dover at War 1939–1945*, Alan Sutton, Stroud, 1993

James, T.C.G., *The Battle of Britain*, Frank Cass, London, 1990

Jenkins, R., *Churchill*, MacMillan, London, 2001

Johnson, Air Vice-Marshal J.E., *Wing Leader*, Chatto & Windus Limited, London, 1956

Johnstone, Air Vice-Marshal A.V.R., *Spitfire into War*, William Kimber & Co. Limited, London, 1986
Jones, Wing Commander I., *Tiger Squadron*, Award Books, New York, 1966
Kesselring, Field-Marshal A., *The Memoirs of Field-Marshal Kesselring*, Greenhill Books, London, 1997
Kershaw, I., *Hitler: 1936–1945, Nemesis*, Penguin Books, London, 2001
King, R., *303 Squadron: Battle of Britain Diary*, Red Kite, Walton-on-Thames, 2010
Kingcome, Group Captain B.F., *A Willingness to Die: Memories from Fighter Command*, Tempus Publishing, Stroud, 1996
Legg, R., *Battle of Britain Dorset*, Dorset Publishing Company, Wincanton, 1995
Lisiewicz, Squadron Leader M. (ed.), *Destiny Can Wait: The Polish Air Force in the Second World War*, William Heinemann Limited, London, 1949
MacDonell, Air Commodore A.R.D. (MacDonell L. and MacKay A., eds.), *From Dogfight to Diplomacy: A Spitfire Pilot's Log 1932–1958*, Pen & Sword Books Limited, Barnsley, 2005
Mason, F.K., *Battle Over Britain*, Aston Publications, Bourne End, 1990
Middlebrook, M. and Everitt, C., *The Bomber Command War Diaries: An Operational Reference Book 1939–1945,* Midland Counties Publications, Hinckley, 1996 (republished by Pen & Sword Books Limited, Barnsley, 2014)
Morgan, E. and Shacklady, E., *Spitfire: The History*, Key Publishing, Stamford, 1987
Moyes, P.J.R., *Bomber Squadrons of the RAF and Their Aircraft*, MacDonald, London, 1964
Muggeridge, M. (ed.), *Ciano's Diary 1939–1943*, William Heinemann Limited, London, 1947
Nash, P., *Beachy Head! Angels 20: The Battle of Britain around Eastbourne Over the Summer of 1940*, privately published, Eastbourne, 2008
Orange, V., *Dowding of Fighter Command: Victor of the Battle of Britain*, Grub Street, London, 2008
Orange, V., *Park: The Biography of Air Chief Marshal Sir Keith Park*, Grub Street, London, 2001
Overy, R., *Goering: The Iron Man*, Bloomsbury Revelations, London, 2021
Overy, R., *The Air War 1939–1945*, first edition, Europa Publications Limited, London, 1980
Overy, R., *The Battle of Britain*, Penguin, London, 2004
Penny, J., *Bristol at War*, The Derby Books Publishing Company, Derby, 2010
Pilsen, I., *More Memories of Bitterne: Patchwork of People and Places We Loved,* Bitterne Local History Society, Southampton, 1984
Pope, R., *War & Society in Britain 1899-1948*, Longman, Harlow, 1991
Price, A., *Battle of Britain Day: 15 September 1940*, Sidgwick & Jackson, London, 1990
Prien, J., Jagdgeschwader *53: A History of the 'Pik As' Geschwader*, March 1937–May 1942, Schiffer Publishing Ltd, Sedona, Arizona, USA, 1997
Priestley, J.B., *Postscripts*, William Heinemann Limited, London, 1940
Quill, J.K., *Spitfire*, Arrow Books, London 1985
Ramsay, W. (ed.), *The Battle of Britain: Then & Now, Mk V Edition*, Battle of Britain Prints International Limited, London, 1986
Ramsay, W. (ed.), *The Blitz Then & Now, Volume I*, Battle of Britain Prints International Limited, London, 1989
Rayner, G.H., *One Hurricane: One Raid*, Airlife Publishing Limited, Shrewsbury, 1990
Richards, D., *RAF Bomber Command in the Second World War: The Hardest Victory*, Penguin, London, 2001
RAFHS, *Air Intelligence: A Symposium*, RAFHS, London, 1997
Rootes, A., *Front Line County: Kent at War, 1939–45*, Robert Hale Limited, London, 1980
Roskill, Captain S.W., *The War at Sea 1939–45: Volume 1*, HMSO, London, 1954

Rohwer, J. and Hummelchen, G., *Chronology of the War at Sea*, Ian Allan Limited, London, 1972

Russell, B., *Which Way to Peace?*, M. Joseph Limited, London, 1936

Russell, C.R., *Spitfire Odyssey: My Life at Supermarines 1936–1957*, Kingfisher Railway Productions, Southampton, SO2 4BE

Sarkar, D., *Battle of Britain 1940: The Finest Hour's Human Cost*, Pen & Sword Books Limited, Barnsley, 2020

Sarkar, D., *Forgotten Heroes of the Battle of Britain*, Pen & Sword Books Limited, Barnsley, 2022

Sarkar, D., *Letters from The Few: Unique Memories from the Battle of Britain*, Pen & Sword Books Limited, Barnsley, 2020

Sarkar, D., *Missing in Action: Resting in Peace?*, Ramrod Publications, Worcester, 1998

Sarkar, D., *'Sailor' Malan: Freedom Fighter: The Inspirational Story of a Spitfire Ace*, Pen & Sword Books Limited, Barnsley, 2021

Sarkar, D., *The Final Few*, Amberley Publishing, Stroud, 2015

Sawyer, Group Captain T., *Only Owls and Bloody Fools Fly at Night*, Crecy Publishing, Manchester, 2000

Schenk, P., *Operation Sealion: The Invasion of England*, Greenhill Books, Barnsley, 2019

Shirer, W.L., *The Rise and Fall of the Third* Reich, Simon & Schuster, New York, 1960

Shores, C. and Williams, C., *Aces High: A Tribute to the Most Notable Fighter Pilots of the British & Commonwealth Forces in WWII*, Grub Street, London, 1994

Smith, M., The RAF, Addison, P. and Crang, J.A. (eds.), *The Burning Blue: A New History of the Battle of Britain*, Pimlico, London, 2000

Spurdle, B., *The Blue Arena*, William Kimber & Co, London, 1986

Steinhilper, U. and Osborne, P., *Spitfire on my Tail: A View from the Other Side*, Independent Books, Bromley, 1989

Taylor, A.J.P., *English History 1914–1945*, Oxford University Press, Oxford, 1965

Titmuss, Professor R.M., *Problems of Social Policy*, HMSO, London, 1950

Toliver, Colonel R.F. and Constable, T.J., *Fighter Aces of the Luftwaffe*, Schiffer Publishing Ltd, Atglen, PA, 1996

Townsend, Group Captain P., *Duel of Eagles: The Classic Account of the Battle of Britain*, Weidenfeld & Nicolson, London, 1990

Townsend, Group Captain P., *Time & Chance: An Autobiography*, Collins, London, 1978

Trevor-Roper, H.R. (ed.), *Hitler's War Directives 1939–45*, Pan Books, London, 1966

Vasco, J.J., *Bombsights Over England: The History of* Erprobungsgruppe *210 Luftwaffe Fighter-Bomber Unit in the Battle of Britain*, JAC Publications, Norwich, 1990

Vasco, J.J. and Cornwell, P.D., *Zerstörer: The Messerschmitt 110 and its Units in 1940*, JAC Publications, Norwich, 1995

von Below, N. (translated by Brooks, G.), *At Hitler's Side: The Memoirs of Hitler's Luftwaffe* Adjutant *1937–1945*, Greenhill Books, London, 2001

von Clausewitz, C., *Principles of War*, Dover Publications Inc, New York, 2003

Wakefield, K., *Luftwaffe Encore*, William Kimber & Co. Limited, London, 1979

Wakefield, K., *The First Pathfinders: The Operational History of* Kampfgruppe *100, 1939 –1941*, Crécy Books, Somerton, 1992

Wallington, N., *Firemen at War: The Work of London's Fire-Fighters in the Second World War*, David & Charles, London, 1981

Warner, G., *RAF Biggin Hill: The Immortal Story of One of the Battle of Britain's Most Famous Fighter Stations*, Putnam & Co. Limited, London, 1969

Wellum, Squadron Leader G.H.A., *First Light*, Penguin, London, 2003

Wicks, B., *Waiting for the All Clear: True Stories from Survivors of The Blitz*, Bloomsbury, London, 1990
Willis, J., *Churchill's Few: The Battle of Britain Remembered*, Guild Publishing, London, 1985
Wheatley, R., *Operation Sealion*, Oxford University Press, Oxford, 1958
Wright, R., *Dowding and the Battle of Britain*, Corgi, London, 1970
Ziegler, F.H., *The Story of 609 Squadron: Under the White Rose*, MacDonald, London, 1971
Ziegler, P., *London at War 1939–1945*, Pimlico, London, 1995

Magazines
Der Adler

Newspapers
New York Post

Websites
Battle of Britain London Monument:https://www.bbm.org.uk
Battle of Britain Memorial Trust: https://www.battleofbritainmemorial.org
Battle of Britain: The People's Project: https://www.battleofbritainthepeoplesproject.com
Brooklands Museum: https://www.brooklandsmuseum.com
Commonwealth War Graves Commission: https://www.cwgc.org
Dilip Sarkar: https://www.dilipsarkarauthor.com
Digital History Archive: http://www.digitalhistoryarchive.com
Kenley Revival Project: https://www.kenleyrevival.org
The National Archives: https://www.nationalarchives.gov.uk
The Supermariners: https://www.supermariners.wordpress.com

Films
Battle of Britain, directed by Guy Hamilton, Spitfire Productions, 1969

Television
First Light, directed by Matthew Whiteman, Lion Television, 2010
The World at War, directed by David Elstein, ITV, 1973

Books by Dilip Sarkar

Spitfire Squadron: No 19 Squadron at War, 1939–41
The Invisible Thread: A Spitfire's Tale
Through Peril to the Stars: RAF Fighter Pilots Who Failed to Return, 1939–45
Angriff Westland: Three Battle of Britain Air Raids Through the Looking Glass
A Few of the Many: Air War 1939–45 – A Kaleidoscope of Memories
Bader's Tangmere Spitfires: The Untold Story, 1941
Bader's Duxford Fighters: The Big Wing Controversy
Missing in Action: Resting in Peace?
Guards VC: Blitzkrieg 1940
Battle of Britain: The Photographic Kaleidoscope, Volumes I–IV
Fighter Pilot: The Photographic Kaleidoscope
Group Captain Sir Douglas Bader: An Inspiration in Photographs
Johnnie Johnson: Spitfire Top Gun, Part I
Johnnie Johnson: Spitfire Top Gun, Part II
Battle of Britain: Last Look Back
Spitfire! Courage & Sacrifice
Spitfire Voices: Heroes Remember
The Battle of Powick Bridge: Ambush a Fore-thought
Duxford 1940: A Battle of Britain Base at War
The Few: The Battle of Britain in the Words of the Pilots
Spitfire Manual 1940
The Sinking of HMS Royal Oak in the Words of the Survivors (re-print of Hearts of Oak)
The Last of the Few: Eighteen Battle of Britain Pilots Tell their Extraordinary Stories
Hearts of Oak: The Human Tragedy of HMS Royal Oak
Spitfire Voices: Life as a Spitfire Pilot in the Words of the Veterans
How the Spitfire Won the Battle of Britain
Spitfire Ace of Aces: The True Wartime Story of Johnnie Johnson
Douglas Bader
Fighter Ace: The Extraordinary Life of Douglas Bader, Battle of Britain Hero (re-print of above)
Spitfire: The Photographic Biography
Hurricane Manual 1940
River Pike
The Final Few: The Last Surviving Pilots of the Battle of Britain Tell Their Stories
Arnhem 1944: The Human Tragedy of the Bridge Too Far
Spitfire! The Full Story of a Unique Battle of Britain Fighter Squadron
Battle of Britain 1940: The Finest Hour's Human Cost
Letters from The Few: Unique Memories of the Battle of Britain
Johnnie Johnson's 1942 Diary: The War Diary of the Spitfire Ace of Aces
Johnnie Johnson's Great Adventure: The Spitfire Ace of Ace's Last Look Back

'Sailor Malan' – Freedom Fighter: The Inspirational Story of a Spitfire Ace
Spitfire Ace of Aces – The Album: The Photographs of Johnnie Johnson
The Real Spitfire Pilot, being the previously unpublished original manuscript of *Spitfire Pilot* by Flight Lieutenant David Crook, with introduction, commentary and photographs by Dilip Sarkar
Bader's Big Wing Controversy: Duxford 1940
Bader's Spitfire Wing: Tangmere 1941
Spitfire Down: Fighter Boys Who Failed to Return
Forgotten Heroes of The Battle of Britain
Faces of The Few
Spitfire Faces
Arise to Conquer: The Real Hurricane Pilot by Wing Commander Ian Gleed, introduction, commentary and photographs by Dilip Sarkar
Free French Spitfire Hero: The Diaries of and Search for René Mouchotte (with Jan Leeming)
I Had a Row with a German by Group Captain Tom Gleave, introduction by Dilip Sarkar
Battle of Britain: The Finest Hour in Cinema
Battle of Britain: The Movie (contributor to and publisher of the now late Robert Rudhall's original edition (2000), and editor and substantial contributor to 2022 revised edition)
Faces of HMS Royal Oak: The 'Mighty Oak' Disaster at Scapa Flow
Battle of Britain, Volume 1: The Gathering Storm – Prelude to the Spitfire Summer of 1940
Battle of Britain, Volume 2: The Breaking Storm – 10 July 1940–12 August 1940
Battle of Britain, Volume 3: Attack of the Eagles – 13 August 1940–18 August 1940
Battle of Britain, Volume 4: Airfields Under Attack – 19 August 1940–6 September 1940
Battle of Britain, Volume 5: Target London – 7 September 1940–17 September 1940
Battle of Britain, Volume 6: Daylight Defeat – 18 September 1940–30 September 1940

Index